"*BodyDreaming* brings together the analytic legacy [...] develop ments in the fields of Body Oriented Psych[...]herapy. It shows that we remain, elusively, disconnected from our dreams (and inner images), until we can embody them through interoceptive awareness. This transformative process, catalyzed through connection to the Living, Sensing, Knowing Body, bridges the dream world to here-and-now experience. In this way, we nourish the deep Self, the true Self and our connection to inner aliveness and vitality. I believe that this book contributes to a rich dialogue between analytic and experiential therapies; a dialogue that will certainly enhance both."
— **Peter A. Levine**, author of *Waking the Tiger, Healing Trauma*
and *In an Unspoken Voice: How the Body Releases
Trauma and Restores Goodness*

"In this highly readable book, Marian Dunlea shows us the seamless constant unconscious conversation between the body and the mind. Every thought we think is companioned by a physical response. 'When you do not know what matters most to you that, then, can become the matter with you.' It is essential to understand that trauma becomes an emotional pattern and/or a symptom that can unconsciously govern your life perspective and your self-esteem. The talking cure alone does not free the body from the emotional responses that it carries. The body cannot and does not lie.

Dunlea offers both the practitioner and the participant the vital keys to unlocking this deeply healing truth."
— **Paula M. Reeves**, PhD, psychotherapist and author of *Women's Intuition:
Unlocking the Wisdom of the Body* and *Heart Sense: Unlocking
Your Highest Purpose and Deepest Desires*

"We live at a time when body and psyche are both in a traumatized state; where we are not in a relationship with nature, soul or body but dissociated from all three. The great imperative of our time is reconnection and moving to a more developed, evolved and individuated state of consciousness. Profoundly steeped in Jung's approach to the psyche as well as other methodologies (particularly the work of Marion Woodman, Donald Kalsched, Peter Levine, and Allan Schore), this inspiring book shows us how great a transformation can be wrought through the medium of BodyDreaming. Marian Dunlea approaches the client with the utmost reverence, gentleness and awareness of the fragility of psychic processes and their connection to neural pathways and nervous system responses.

Dunlea shows us how, through reconnection with our heart and the dawning of insight, we can become illumined, healed and restored to wholeness."
— **Anne Baring**, PhD, author of *The Dream of the Cosmos:
A Quest for the Soul*

"*BodyDreaming*, Marian Dunlea's new and unique approach, arrives as a breath of fresh air. It provides us not only with a new way to think about our work theoretically, but with new practical ways of perceiving and attending to how our patients actually experience our interventions in the body. It represents a creative synthesis of new findings in the fields of affective neuroscience, attachment theory, infant observation, and body-sensitive approaches to therapy, as they apply to somatically informed psychotherapeutic work with trauma, dissociation, and dreams.

Marian Dunlea's *BodyDreaming* provides a way of getting 'underneath' the seemingly intractable defenses and resistances that our traumatized patients present to us, without our having to forsake the mytho-poetic imagination and its symbolic riches found in dreams, active imagination and the other products of the unconscious.

The extensive verbatim write-ups of actual clinical vignettes in the text demonstrate Marian's exquisite attunement to the felt experience reported by her clients. For all of us seeking a more relevant and effective way of working, these verbatim accounts are illuminating to read. Doing so has already improved my practice as an analyst."

– Donald E. Kalsched, PhD, Santa Fe, New Mexico

BodyDreaming in the Treatment of Developmental Trauma

Marian Dunlea's *BodyDreaming in the Treatment of Developmental Trauma: An Embodied Therapeutic Approach* provides a theoretical and practical guide for working with early developmental trauma. This interdisciplinary approach explores the interconnection of body, mind and psyche, offering a masterful tool for restoring balance and healing developmental trauma.

BodyDreaming is a somatically focused therapeutic method, drawing on the findings of neuroscience, analytical psychology, attachment theory and trauma therapy. In Part I, Dunlea defines BodyDreaming and its origins, placing it in the context of a dysregulated contemporary world. Part II explains how the brain works in relation to the BodyDreaming approach: providing an accessible outline of neuroscientific theory, structures and neuroanatomy in attunement, affect regulation, attachment patterns, transference and countertransference, and the resolution of trauma throughout the body. In Part III, through detailed transcripts from sessions with clients, Dunlea demonstrates the positive impact of BodyDreaming on attachment patterns and developmental trauma. This somatic approach complements and enhances psychobiological, developmental and psychoanalytic interventions. BodyDreaming restores balance to a dysregulated psyche and nervous system that activates our innate capacity for healing, changing our default response of "fight, flight or freeze" and creating new neural pathways. Dunlea's emphasis on attunement to build a restorative relationship with the sensing body creates a core sense of self, providing a secure base for healing developmental trauma.

Innovative and practical, and with a foreword by Donald E. Kalsched, *BodyDreaming in the Treatment of Developmental Trauma: An Embodied Therapeutic Approach* will be essential reading for psychotherapists, analytical psychologists and therapists with a Jungian background, arts therapists, dance and movement therapists, and body workers interested in learning how to work with both body and psyche in their practices.

Marian Dunlea is a Jungian analyst and head of training in BodySoul Europe, part of the Marion Woodman Foundation. She is a Somatic Experiencing Trauma therapist based in the west of Ireland and is the creator of BodyDreaming.

BodyDreaming in the Treatment of Developmental Trauma

An Embodied Therapeutic Approach

Marian Dunlea

 Routledge
Taylor & Francis Group

LONDON AND NEW YORK

First published 2019
by Routledge
2 Park Square, Milton Park, Abingdon, Oxon OX14 4RN

and by Routledge
52 Vanderbilt Avenue, New York, NY 10017

Routledge is an imprint of the Taylor & Francis Group, an informa business

British Library Cataloguing-in-Publication Data
A catalogue record for this book is available from the British Library

Library of Congress Cataloging-in-Publication Data
Names: Dunlea, Marian, author.
Title: Bodydreaming in the treatment of developmental trauma : an
    embodied therapeutic approach / Marian Dunlea.
Description: Milton Park, Abingdon, Oxon ; New York, NY : Routledge,
    2019. | Includes bibliographical references and index.
Identifiers: LCCN 2018060674 (print) | LCCN 2019003557 (ebook) |
    ISBN 9780429398827 (Master eBook) | ISBN 9780429677274 (Adobe
    Reader) | ISBN 9780429677250 (Mobipocket) | ISBN 9780429677267
    (ePub) | ISBN 9780367025939 (hardback) | ISBN 9780367025946
    (pbk.) | ISBN 9780429398827 (ebk)
Subjects: LCSH: Neuropsychology. | Dreams—Therapeutic use.
Classification: LCC QP360 (ebook) | LCC QP360 .D86 2019 (print) |
    DDC 612.8/233—dc23
LC record available at https://lccn.loc.gov/2018060674

ISBN: 978-0-367-02593-9 (hbk)
ISBN: 978-0-367-02594-6 (pbk)
ISBN: 978-0-429-39882-7 (ebk)

Typeset in Times New Roman
by Swales & Willis Ltd, Exeter, Devon, UK

To my parents Kay and Michael and the line of women
I come from and those that come after me ... Hanorah
McCarthy Cogan, my maternal grandmother, May O'Keefe
Dunlea, my paternal grandmother, my mother Kathleen
Cogan, and my three daughters Mary-Anna, Claire and
Ruth Kearney.

To artist and friend Dorothy Cross for producing the
image of the black pearl for the cover. "It must be
something beautiful," she said. And it is.

Contents

Acknowledgements

"It takes a village" and in my case it has taken the love, faith and practical support of a global tribe to encourage, inspire and sustain me in writing this book.

My first thanks go to all my clients and to the workshop participants, who unwittingly were engaged in the "smithy of my soul", the co-creation and emergence of the BodyDreaming approach to healing. In particular, I am indebted to those people who so generously agreed to their material being transcribed and included in the book. Their work has been seminal in the development of BodyDreaming.

To my editor-in-chief Ann Yeoman, who worked tirelessly, creatively and with dedication way beyond the call of duty to bring form and structure to each idea. And to my colleague and editor Sheila McCarry, whose support and faith in BodyDreaming fostered the emerging writer during my Zurich days. To Harriet Castor, who brought her editing skills to bear as the book came into its last phase and to Maggie O'Neill, who was my midwife in chief, regulating and encouraging me in the delivery room.

To my inspired teachers Marion Woodman, Mary Hamilton and Ann Skinner, co-founders of BodySoul Rhythms, whose brilliance, creativity and love awakened me to the intimate, creative and healing relationship of my particular BodySoul. I am forever grateful to them as midwives for the visceral discovery of that inner marriage.

To Paula Reeves, a foundational pillar in BodySoul Rythms, wise crone, master story teller, creative mentor and friend whose collaboration in presenting workshops in Ireland provided the community with a depth of engagement which became a springboard for my work to take root.

To Candace Loubert, dancer and choreographer, friend and inspiring workshop collaborator who encouraged me to teach dreams from a place of embodied experience—grounded in the breath, bone and tissue of my nature and the natural world around us. Her unique approach to "the body" brought a highly distinctive flavour to our collaboration and out of this temenos BodyDreaming developed.

To my dear friends, colleagues and fellow teachers, who inspired me to learn to "speak a new language" whilst creating my version of a somatic integrative practice.

In particular, my dance of three partners, Wendy Willmot, whose love brings such safety that she gets the best out of me, whose heartfelt accompaniment at my first BodySoul Intensive remained steadfast over the years and helped to provide the crucial temenos for writing this book in Zurich. To our mutual colleague and friend Virginia Holmquist; wise sage and inspiratrice always ready with her humorous twist on the challenges of life.

To my longstanding co-facilitating teachers, Wendy Bratherton, Sue Congram, Patricia del Losa, Sheila Langston, Pauline Sayhi, Wendy Willmot, and Lia Zografou, whose curiosity, creativity, and faith supported the emerging voice of BodyDreaming. My thanks also to BodySoul teachers Susan Adams, Fran Burns, Mary Condren, Berni Divilly, Marych O'Sullivan Sanford, Janice Rous, Olivia Russell, Christina Shewell, Tina Stromstead, Meg Wilbur, and Heba Zaphiriou-Zarifi who co-facilitated programmes with me.

To the sustaining presence of my dear friends who "housed and fed" me, providing body and soul nurturance—Karen Bohn and Dimitrus Panagiotidis, Danilo and Bruna Calza, Cristina Calza, Adrienne Candy, Dorothy Cross, Nellie Curtin, Simon Dawson, Berni Divilly and Sharon Murphy, Jill Gairdener, Hanne and Rowan Gillespie, Mimi Tatlow-Golden and Jem Golden, Anne Hayes, Joan and Louis Heyse-Moore, Maureen Keady, Mary Kelly, Barbara Kohnstamm, Deirdre Linehan, Ted McNamara, Martin Melyler and Archie Simpson, Maggie Mulpeter, Jean and Eoin O'Flynn, Mary O'Sullivan and Clare Sawtel, Camilla Powell, Louise Rowan, Inger Safestad, Helen Sands, Marych O'Sullivan-Sanford and Frank Sanford, Peter and Felicia Schaerer, Pat Toibin, Eli and Tony Trimis, Jot Wojakowski, and Dr. Jiai Wang.

To my colleagues and mentors whose encouragement and presence was decisive throughout the process: Anne Baring, Grazia Calza, Carole Cunningham, Joan Davis, Brigitte Egger, Jim Fitzerald, Berns Galloway, John Hill, Lisa Holland, Bjoern Jacobsen, Don Kalsched, Claudine Koch, Rita McCarthy, Margarete Merkle, Cedrus Monte, Kathryn Morrison, Christina Mulvey, Mairin Ni Nuallain, Toni O'Brien Johnson, Madeleine O'Callaghan, Therese O'Driscoll, Kusum Prabhu, Ursula Regis Muller, Maja Reinau, Ewa and Chris Roberston, Lida Ruiter, Andreas Schweizer, Ursula Shields-Huemer, Daniela Sieff, Murray Stein, Ursula Stussi, Robin van Loben Sels, Keren Vishny, Marcus West, and Aileen Young.

To those who help to administer and keep the wheels turning for BodyDreaming: Fionnuala Bates, Angela Browne, Musa Christo Englebrecht, Marie d'Hubert, Aisling Gynn, Brenda Harris, Louise Holland, Ana Kirby, Benedicte Lampe, Eimear McNamara, Antoinette O'Callaghan, Fiona Rooney Fitzpatrick, Maroon Tabel, and Abigail Whyte.

To my siblings: my sister Hilary McNamara—whose unfailing support I shall never be able to thank enough. Hilary, as well as my brothers Eric, Kieran, Michael, Colm, and Brendan Dunlea, took the main share of caring for my mother. To my three daughters, Mary-Anna, Claire and Ruth Kearney and my three grandsons, Elliot, Alex and Finn, in whose love and humour I am carried.

To the four-legged ones who kept me company in body and spirit.

To those dear friends who died before this oeuvre was complete and whose presence accompanies me: John Harrington, Candace Loubert, Una Maguire, Pat McManus, Gabby Riand, and most recently my beloved pioneering and visionary mentor Marion Woodman.

Foreword

By Donald E. Kalsched, PhD

Recent discoveries in the fields of affective neuroscience, attachment theory, infant observation and body-sensitive approaches to therapy have revolutionized our understanding of trauma and its treatment, and led to a major paradigm shift within the field of psychoanalysis and analytical psychology. My friend and colleague, Marian Dunlea, a Jungian analyst with an extensive background in psychotherapy, has been an active and passionate student of these new developments, seeking, over the past 30 years, for new and creative ways to apply them in the conventional setting of analytic psychotherapy. *BodyDreaming* is the culmination of these inter-disciplinary pursuits. It represents a unique and creative synthesis of the new findings as they apply to somatically informed psychotherapeutic work with trauma, dissociation, and dreams. It provides those of us who have been practising a more "interpretive" psychoanalysis with a way of getting "underneath" the seemingly intractable defenses and resistances that our traumatized patients present to us. And it provides this service without our having to forsake the mytho-poetic imagination and its symbolic riches found in dreams, active imagination and the other products of the unconscious that have proved so useful to those of us who practise Jungian analysis.

The author's thesis, both simple and profound, is that early trauma and its neuro-biological activation of primitive circuits in the emotional brain and body can injure the autonomic nervous system's normal regulatory rhythm of expansion and contraction, sending the patient into either hyperarousal (fight or flight), hypoarousal (collapse/freeze) and eventually immobilization, shutdown and dissociation. When this happens the patient usually moves "up into the head" to try and restore coherence and regulation, but the resulting defensive narratives and "explanations" almost always make things worse. These defensive narratives turn into trance states which can be ferocious and intractable. Patients may live major portions of their lives in such hyper- or hypoaroused states of stress, dissociation, and dysregulation. Moreover, such self-states, the author points out, can also happen *in the session* while traumatic memories or trauma-linked dreams are being processed. The resulting activation can quickly take the patient out of a "window of tolerance", rendering talk-therapy ineffective and potentially re-traumatizing the patient.

In this situation the BodyDreaming therapist, who knows how to recognize and attune to the subtle state-changes involved in the regulation/dysregulation cycle, works with the slow, measured steps of attuning to body-sensation, to affect in the body, and to the calming, orienting responses of the social engagement system (including the transference) to help restore greater coherence and homeostatic balance. For example, the therapist meticulously tracks the felt sense of experiences in the here and now, uncovering buried emotions and releasing blocked energy on the one hand, but also utilizing items in the immediate surroundings as "resources" for regulation—such as the smell of a rose, the texture of a fabric, a favourite recording of music etc., increasing one's capacity to stay present when activated. This slow process of "pendulation" and "titration" between the hyperaroused states of trauma and the calm states of embodied safety and regulation keeps the activation of the sympathetic system within a window of tolerance so that the patient begins to feel safe again in his body. Once this happens, the normal process of therapeutic exploration can continue. Overall the process helps to align sympathetic and parasympathetic parts of the autonomic nervous system—right and left hemispheres of the brain—and higher (cortical) and lower (brain stem) centers, effectively opening new neural pathways and increasing the flow of energy throughout the system. The result is an increase in the patient's sense of aliveness and the secure sense of an animated core self.

For those of us who have been struggling for years with the question "why isn't conventional therapy more effective with our dissociated patients?" this book arrives as a breath of fresh air. It provides us not only with a new way to think about our work *theoretically*, but with new practical ways of perceiving and attending to how our patients actually experience our interventions *in the body*. In this way it gives us tools with which to get "underneath" our usual "top down" verbal/interpretive interventions with patients, including our usual "symbolic" ways of working with dreams in terms of associations, amplifications, and "meanings".

The author's 30-year odyssey through the many fields of discovery related to the body (an odyssey I have observed with curiosity and interest over the years), is a story worth telling. Having been a student of Jung for many years, and while training in psycho-synthesis, she became acquainted with Jungian analyst Marion Woodman's work (now called "BodySoul Rhythms") and Woodman's conviction that the body had its own "cellular wisdom" operating underneath the conscious mind's trauma-based thoughts, beliefs, and convictions about the self. Woodman's work also acquainted her with the negative "scripts" (shadow-material) and the trance-like powers present in the "somatic unconscious" where the body is left holding the rejected, wounded aspects of the soul. Facilitating group work with other Woodman students gave her an experience of how to access and work with these exiled contents through mask-work, active imagination, voice-work and dreams.

Through her work with Woodman, the author also became acquainted with my own early work on the *Inner World of Trauma* (Routledge 1996) and the fact that, owing to a self-attacking defensive system of internal working models or "scripts" laid down in early childhood (what I call the Self-Care System), the traumatized psyche is self-traumatizing. These internal working models provide a lens on reality that is riddled with fear and terror, requiring vigilance, and repeatedly sensing danger and assault. In their original form, they help the child to predict danger and thus aid survival, but they become a major problem later because they distort reality and re-activate an addictive hyperarousal cycle by plunging the patient again and again back into a "trauma vortex". No matter how well intentioned or empathically sensitive our interventions are with trauma-survivors in psychotherapy, the relational field can easily be "hijacked" by this defensive system which fights for a life of its own in the psyche. Several detailed case-reports in the following pages sensitively describe these moments of "hijacking" and how they lead to re-activation of the client's sympathetic nervous system. They also describe how the author works with her patients moment to moment in the here-and-now dyadic interactions, focusing on energetic resonance in the body, to help the patient dis-identify from the narrative of these defenses and return to homeostatic balance. This is done, first through a familiarization with the defenses and their narratives of fear— a mapping of the "system", including a certain amount of psycho-education—then through a careful monitoring of the patient's level of autonomic nervous system activation in moment-by-moment tracking of their feelings in the body. None of us knew how to do this in the early years of trauma therapy.

As the author pursued her growing conviction that the body needs to be included in psychotherapy, she was led further into the work of Candace Loubert, and Eugene Gendlin, called *Focusing*, which emphasizes attention to the "felt sense" experience in the body and demonstrates how tracking sensation in the body and noticing how it moves, informs us about how image and thought actually emerge from somatic impulse—in other words, how the body operates "underneath" the cognitive/symbolic level on which interpretive psychoanalysis has conventionally operated. Citing important research by Ruth Lanius (pp. 182–183) the author reminds us that traumatized individuals are often deficient in sensory self-awareness or a basic sense of self. BodyDreaming, she has found, helps to rehabilitate this basic orienting instinct by attempting to get below emotion to explore the physical sensation of experience. In this way, perceiving or sensing the body ("interoception") can actually offset emotional flooding and be a counterbalance to emotional dysregulation.

Continuing her journey, the author discovered Allan Schore's early demonstration of how the early infant–caregiver relationship (Bowlby's attachment theory) helps form the neural pathways that shape the right hemisphere of the brain. This reading further inspired her to find out how early secure-attachment patterns can be re-created in the transference relationship and within the patient's psyche/body interface. In a novel application of Bowlby's notion of the child's "secure base" in the mother, she suggests that on an intra-psychic level, the "secure base" needs to be the body itself! The body becomes the mother. BodyDreaming, she suggests, offers an effective way to develop a "learned secure" attachment to the body—fostering a sense of "coming home" to oneself and promoting a conscious alignment with the imagination and its symbolic unfolding as it opens in dreams, creativity and play.

In addition, Schore's focus on affect-in-the-body and on the co-regulation of affect in the mother–infant dyad, helped secure the role of affect and affect-regulation in the author's emerging body-based model. Hearkening back to her work with Marion Woodman she affirms a central conviction of her new theory—that *emotion is the carrier of consciousness* (p. 257). Her work, under the aegis of "BodyDreaming" seeks to aid her patients in becoming more affectively competent and emotionally literate by growing their capacity to experience, and witness, strong affect *in the body*. And she does this in an extremely sensitive way, by lending herself and her own body-awareness to the co-regulation of affect in her work with patients. The extensive verbatim write-ups of actual clinical vignettes in the text demonstrate her exquisite attunement to the felt experience reported by her clients. And through these vignettes, we can learn how to track the regulation/dysregulation cycle moment to moment—even as we try to process a dream, a traumatic memory, or a current life-experience. For all of us seeking a more relevant and effective way of working, these verbatim accounts are illuminating to read. Doing so has already improved my practice as an analyst.

A further major contribution to the author's understanding came through her training in the work of Peter Levine, called "Somatic Experiencing". Training in Levine's trauma theory shifted her clinical work dramatically as she realized that trauma is not in the event itself (or the recovery of its memory) but is embedded in the nervous system's (and hence the body's) *response* to the event. Hence therapy must include the felt sense of the body, its sensate and affective states, if efforts to heal trauma are to be effective. Levine's sensitivity to the issue of "pendulation"—moving back and forth between a calming "resource" on the one hand and exploration of traumatic memory on the other—became of central importance in her emerging technique. And connected with her training in Levine's model, the work of Steven Hoskinson on affect-regulation (called "Organic Intelligence") helped in her understanding of how to use resources in the environment in order to regulate the activated ANS in her patients, as these patients may have been "triggered" in the transference.

Finally, there is one additional investigator (among the many others whose work is referenced in the text) whose neurological research the author returns to again and again in the text of BodyDreaming—and that is Steven Porges and his "Polyvagal Theory". Summarized in Chapter 1 of her book (a not-to-be-missed chapter titled "How the Brain Works") Porges contributes a basic understanding of the defences that are organized on the neuro-hormonal level, thus determining the trauma response. This understanding is fundamental to the author's way of working as described in BodyDreaming.

Porges's theory is based on a "default hierarchy" in which "higher" and "newer" brain-body circuits default to older, more primitive ones, under the impact of trauma. Porges suggests that regulated, calm bodily states where the autonomic nervous system is balanced, are mediated by the "newest" (evolutionarily speaking) circuits in the body/brain interface, i.e., those of the ventral vagus nerve. Among the behavioral systems overseen by the ventral vagus is the "social engagement system", often used to promote calm states, to self-soothe and to engage with others. Marian Dunlea points out that the BodyDreaming therapist makes extensive use of the social engagement system as she works within the relationship to restore a sense of safety and autonomic regulation in the therapy session. To this end she shows various ways to utilize the resources in the immediate environment of the patient to promote this.

However her case examples also show what happens when the "window of tolerance" is exceeded and the social engagement system is "overridden" by "older" circuits and ultimately by the dorsal vagus, leading from fight/flight responses to immobilization, shutdown and dissociation. In this case, an effort is made to restore the "newer" circuits of the social engagement system in order to restore autonomic regulation and end the trauma cycle.

Porges's default-hierarchy system is important to the author and has also become important to me. This is because it gives a physiological basis for the triggering of those defences that Marian Dunlea works with so skillfully on the level of the body, and that I have been working with for years on the basis of the inner world of imagination and the powerful self-destructive affects that trigger the trauma response in the inner world of the traumatized individual. These tyrannical self-attacking energies which have an archaic and typical (hence archetypal) form frequently appear as demonic presences in what I call the Self-Care System of the dissociating psyche. It is apparent to me that they "live" at the most primitive level of Porges's default hierarchy, i.e., the level of the immobilization response.

What is interesting is that when this level of trauma is triggered in the body by the amygdala's response on the level of the brain stem and emotional brain—and perhaps triggered repeatedly over a lifetime—it seems to *recruit* narratives, convictions, and internal working models from higher cortical centers in the brain and imprints these as fundamental convictions and belief systems in a person's self-representation and self-identity. This seems to be the origin of the notorious shame response and negative convictions about the self—the person's intractable conviction of unworthiness and "badness". These wounded self-perceptions seem to inhere in a part of the system that frequently presents itself in dreams as a lost, exiled, or orphaned child. And the judgements against this "child" are usually invested in part-self representations that are highly judgemental, violent and seem to "hate" this child's vulnerability and the way its needs are endangering the "system". It is these persecutory voices that close the imagination, jam the circuits, and keep the defensive system in control. In addition, they feed back into the trauma cycle and keep the body dysregulated.

Marian Dunlea certainly knows about these Self-Care narratives, and instead of working with them as affective "parts" of the self as I do, she attempts to work "underneath" these thought-forms and affect images—directly with the constricting effect they have in freezing or shutting down the body's natural rhythms, trying not to engage their "narratives" directly. Instead, she draws the patient's attention to the sensation being experienced in the body or to the feeling that accompanies a self-attack as it registers in body sensation. In this way the author feels she can have more immediate impact on the embodied feelings and sensations the patient is experiencing in the activated state, potentially restoring regulation and deepening the patient's sense of safety in the moment.

In either of our respective ways of working, it seems to me, the author and I are striving towards a similar goal, i.e., to release from captivity in the defensive system, those negative shadow-elements of the affectively wounded childhood psyche—affects that have been caught and trapped within a dissociative "system" built partly by the *body*'s hyper-vigilance and constriction, and partly by the *psyche*'s hyper-vigilance and constriction. By whatever avenue we reach it, the lost and dissociated (orphaned) affect must be found, experienced in the body, and re-integrated into the narrative memory of the patient. This is the home-coming for which the patient is searching—the return of the lost soul—its *indwelling* and *personalization*, to use the language of D.W. Winnicott.

It took many years for Marian Dunlea to integrate the disparate contributions of body-sensitive modalities into her psychoanalytic practice, and her splendid new book is the result.

In a statement that fittingly celebrates her new synthesis, the author says:

> Here at last I had a means to address the body in a one-on-one therapy session, to listen to the body's deep impulses, intuitions and resonances without having the client do *floor work* and move around in the room to access the body. Through tracking felt sense experience, the client and I could access *internal* physical sensation, mapping feeling in the body, and opening both client and therapist to the embodied imaginal as a result.
>
> (p. 23)

By "opening to the imaginal" I think the author means opening the "flow" of unconscious material including all the facets of whole experience, affect and sensation in the body—image, thought and concept in the mind—all of which are crucial elements in the richness of symbolic living.

One of the very interesting facets of her presentation is the way she is able to demonstrate that important dreams often follow in direct response to BodyDreaming sessions. One patient who was otherwise oppressed by constricting negative judgments and shame, dreamed of buildings and containers filled with golden light—directing her attention, in effect, to the neglected and despised matter of her embodied life, and demonstrating to the author that the body is alive with psyche. In BodyDreaming, she suggests, we cultivate the idea "that our matter and all matter is alive, and that by developing a more regulated secure base within our own matter, we may discover ourselves to be in a participatory relationship with the matter around us" (p. 231).

This latter thought has an interesting "mystical" dimension and the author is not afraid to suggest that as we become aware of the "living body"—our instinctual nature—we are brought into greater alignment with the universal process through which the Spirit becomes flesh, and incarnates in the world.

These moments, the author says, are like those moments of "alignment" at the great megalithic cairn of Newgrange on the Boyne river in her native Ireland, where each year at the Winter Solstice, as it has for 5,000 years, a shaft of light penetrates the dark inner chamber and illuminates the mysterious matter it contains. Like at Newgrange, when this alignment occurs in a patient between psyche and soma, spirit and matter, body and dream, something "new" is born and the patient experiences herself in the presence of a great mystery. This, the author suggests, is an experience of the numinous and no-one who has had such an experience will ever forget it.

> For the individual, such an experience is one of *embodiment* and amounts to a creation story of spirit becoming flesh. A new insight is born that affects *body and psyche*; it resonates in the cells of the body; it makes the dreamer momentarily aware of being part of something much bigger than the ego, a life force that ... "resides in the depths of our soul—in every cell of our matter—in the caves and caverns of our heart" (Reeves, 2003, p. 65).

(p. 9)

Credits and Permissions

Part I

Setting the Scene

A Note to the Reader
How This Book Works

The first section, *Introducing BodyDreaming* presents the poignant image of the ancient Cairn at Newgrange, Ireland, at the time of the Winter Solstice—an image that serves as an overarching metaphor capturing the essence of BodyDreaming. The section goes on to outline BodyDreaming theory and practice. Then, in *Why This Book Now: The Origins of BodyDreaming*, I trace the story of my background and the various psychotherapeutic modalities in which I trained and which inform my development of BodyDreaming. This is followed by an *Invitation to the Reader* to engage as experientially as possible with the BodyDreaming processes described in the excerpts from case studies and group sessions that form the main body of the text. Practical guidance on how to engage with the text in this way is also provided.

Chapter 1, *How the Brain Works*, explains the essential terminology and key concepts used throughout the text. It describes the way the brain functions and how the brain is currently understood to affect and be affected by body and psyche. This chapter provides an overview of recent developments in neuroscientific research and addresses ways in which neurophysiological theory impacts, informs, and supports therapeutic practice; it also introduces key theories of scientists, thinkers, practitioners and analysts whose research has a direct bearing on the development of BodyDreaming work.

Each of the following chapters takes as its focus essential elements in BodyDreaming therapeutic practice, the goal of which is to establish greater coherence in our dysregulated systems. By uncovering buried emotions and releasing blocked energy, BodyDreaming enables us consciously to align with the body-mind and psyche's innate capacity for affect regulation and homeostasis. To this end, key concepts outlined in Chapter 1 are revisited, and detailed examples from BodyDreaming sessions are used to illustrate the relevance of therapeutic, psychological, and neuroscientific theories. My observations and interventions are included in parentheses, as are explanations of the client's behaviour and responses. At key points in each excerpted session, case material is punctuated with theoretical asides and explanations of what might be occurring physiologically, in the brain, from the perspectives of neuroscience, developmental theory, and Jungian psychology.

The *Bibliography* provides a comprehensive list of texts I have found essential to my research and will, I hope, serve as a stimulus to further reading.

*

INTRODUCING BODYDREAMING

> *The dream is a little hidden door in the innermost and most secret recesses of the soul, opening into that cosmic night ... All consciousness separates; but in dreams we put on the likeness of that more universal, truer, more eternal man dwelling in the darkness of primordial night. There he is still the whole, and the whole is in him, indistinguishable from nature and bare of all egohood.*

(Jung, 1933/4)[1]

*

Newgrange, or *Bru na Boinne* as it is known in early Irish texts, translates as *the mansion or abode by the Boyne*, and was believed to be the home of Dagda, the sun god. It is a megalithic cairn,[2] a vast, stone, chambered mound that is about 280 feet in diameter and 44 feet high; it is approximately 5,000 years old. It is situated in the Boyne valley, which has the largest number of megalithic tombs in Europe. One enters the cairn through a passageway, which leads to a central chamber with a stunning 19-foot-high corbelled ceiling. There are three recesses, each containing massive stone basins, one to the left, one to the right, and one at the back of the central chamber. Many of the stones that form the cairn are decorated, both along the passageway leading to the chamber and in the central chamber itself.

The mound is built in such a way that on the morning of the Winter Solstice (21 December), and for a few days before and after, a shaft of light from the rising sun penetrates an aperture above the lintel of the entrance. This roof box provides a link between the inside of the cairn and the outside world. As the cairn is built on a slope, sunlight shining through the entrance cannot reach all the way into the chamber. The size and position of the rectangular shape of the roof box allow the shaft of sunlight to inch its way slowly up the length of the passage over a period of 10 minutes, at which point it reaches the central chamber to illuminate the innermost space. For the rest of the year the interior of the cairn lies in darkness. We can only speculate as to the significance of such precise engineering. Baring and Cashford propose that "[t]he ritual enacted must have been one of the sun fertilizing the 'body' of the earth and so awakening her after her winter sleep to the renewed cycle of life" (1993, p. 98).

The alignment of sunlight with the passageway leading to the womb-like inner chamber serves as a tangible testament to the belief system of the peoples who constructed the Newgrange cairn. Home to the all-powerful god Dagda, the cairn is the place where, it is said, he lay with the goddess Boinn—a manifestation of the river Boyne—and conceived their son Angus, whose name is translated as *the real vigour* (Jones, 2007, p. 202). Baring and Cashford suggest that the communal lives of the people of this time "may have been aligned in some way with the cyclic drama taking place in the sky" (1993, p. 97). Undoubtedly their religious beliefs must have inspired the sacred geometry of Bru na Boinne. Its construction suggests a deep sense of the spiritual significance of the cyclic drama of the seasons, celebrating the return of the sun at the darkest point of the year and promising the death of winter, as symbolized by the physical alignment of outer light and inner darkness, a marriage of sky and earth, solar masculine and chthonic feminine energies. On a practical level, the lengthening of the daylight hours as the sun moved into the Northern hemisphere meant the earth once again became warm, fecund, fertile, and ready for planting, ensuring the continuance of life in body, in matter.[3]

The Gnostics believed that in the process of creation, Sophia, the divine wisdom and feminine aspect of God, descended into earth, into matter. During the course of her descent "she became lost and imprisoned in matter, thus becoming the hidden God which is in need of release and redemption" (Edinger, 1972, p. 102). At Newgrange, on the Winter Solstice, the sun's rays penetrate matter and illuminate the darkness. I understand this image as a metaphor for the awakening of the feminine principle[4] in matter. The earth awaits the sun's penetration (the masculine principle), and the resultant conjoining or *coniunctio* of sun and earth, spirit and matter carries with it promise of regeneration. Marion Woodman, Jungian analyst, writes that "our whole world runs on the Inner Marriage—on that day-and-night principle where there's obviously a time of opening and receiving (the feminine), and where there's an alternate time of thrusting and permeating (the masculine). The two energies work together. They are complementary" (in conversation with Ryley, 1998, p. 76). The annual occurrence at Bru na Boinne serves well as a fundamental orienting image of psychological alignment, or the ego's conscious alignment with the organizing principle of the psyche which Jung calls the Self—that is, alignment within and without, the conjunction or *marriage* of light and matter initiating regeneration and possibility. I will use it as such throughout the text.

Thousands of years after the construction of the site at Newgrange, the alchemists of the Medieval and Renaissance periods actively explored the relationship between matter and spirit, darkness and light. They "discover[ed] that in the very darkness of nature a light is hidden, a little spark without which the darkness would not be darkness" (Jung, 1942, par. 197). The alchemists, in many ways the forerunners of modern scientists, understood the complementarity of light and dark, and the essential unity of all things. Paracelsus, for one, believed that:

> Not separation of the natures but the union of the natures was the goal of alchemy. ... Nature not only contains a process of transformation—it is itself transformation. It strives not for isolation but for union, for the wedding feast followed by death and rebirth.
>
> (Jung, 1942, par. 198)

At Newgrange, the transformation and "union of the natures" of which Paracelsus speaks is represented, for me, by the shaft of sunlight that penetrates the stone passageway into the inner chamber, symbolic of the transformative and generative powers of Nature. However, the roots of the alchemists' investigations were pagan, and the alchemical tradition of the Middle Ages in Europe ran counter to the mainstream tradition of Christianity which turned pagan deities into demons, separated light from dark, spirit from matter, soul—or psyche—from the body, and so, according to Jung, "alienated man from his own nature" (*ibid.*). Like the alchemists of the Middle Ages, Jung argues that humankind's "true" nature is not only physical but psychic, in other words, it comprises both matter *and* spirit.

What occurs at Newgrange at the Winter Solstice serves well as a poignant metaphor for BodyDreaming work. The passageway at Newgrange is precisely oriented toward the sunrise in order that the sun's rays pierce the darkness of the inner chamber spiral. In the practice of BodyDreaming, when the client's system is activated, the therapist invites her to orient outward, allowing the senses to be drawn wherever they want to go, allowing the eyes to settle on an object that draws her attention in a positive way.[5] This engages the client's curiosity and has the effect not only of bringing her into the 'here and now' but also, as Hoskinson suggests, short-circuiting the habitual response to threat, the repetitive pattern of paying attention to danger; it has the calming effect of regulating the nervous system.[6] For example, in BodyDreaming work the client often begins by simply speaking a dream. She may already be activated—heart racing, anxious, with shortness of breath and clammy hands—as the act of speaking the dream may have made her apprehensive in anticipation of all that is as yet unknown about its content. The activation in the nervous system is short-circuited when she allows her eyes to focus on what attracts them. This calms the system and simultaneously engages both the Social Engagement System[7] and the right hemisphere of the brain. As soon as a dream is spoken, left-hemisphere consciousness grabs hold of it, trying to control, analyze, categorize, and fix the dream images in time and space. If, however, we shift our attention and orient to the outside, we are, by that action, inviting the right hemisphere's relational, curious nature to connect us to our surroundings. This change in orientation from inner to outer awareness is facilitated by the Social Engagement System which comprises the muscles of the face and head, i.e., the eyes, ears, jaw, throat and neck, and has a direct calming impact on the heart rate, pulse rate and breathing, enabling us to recalibrate the nervous system to a state of homeostasis.[8] No longer activated, we are more receptive and better able to open to whatever new thing is presented in the dream as well as to any associated feelings in the body.

By orienting to our surroundings we begin to experience a participatory relationship with the world psyche or soul. Exploration of the relationship between inner sensation and outer experience grounds us simultaneously in the here and now of the body and in the material world around us. David Abram, influenced by the philosophy of French phenomenologist Merleau-Ponty, speaks to the connection he makes with a particular object that has engaged his senses, in this case, a bowl:

Each time that I return to gaze at the outward surface of the bowl, my eyes and my mood have shifted, however slightly; informed by my previous encounters with the bowl, my senses now more attuned to its substance, I continually discover new and unexpected aspects. ... [T]he bowl awaits the further exploration of my eyes and my hands ... invites the further participation of my senses.

(Abram, 1997, pp. 51–52)

As I listen to a client's dream, I may ask the dreamer, "What do you notice happening in your body in response to speaking the dream?" The dreamer may recognize that the body is responding in a particular way, resonating with the dream; for example, there may be physical sensations in the gut, throat or chest, and emotions may be triggered. Because the dream introduces an unexpected and potentially unsettling image, the significance of which the conscious personality is unaware, it often causes an activation of the system. In acknowledgement of the client's psychic and often physical distress, I invite the dreamer to orient outward by suggesting, "Take your eyes for a walk in the room. Let them go where they want to go. What is drawing their attention? Allow yourself to take a moment to be curious." And, once the dreamer's eyes have settled on an object, "What are you noticing about that object?", we register together what engages the eyes. The choice of object is always a mystery, and may feel like a synchronicity, as the found object invariably turns out to be one that acts as an appropriate counterpoint to the dream or to the presenting symptom or issue. As Jung reminds us in *The Red Book*, "Nothing happens in which you are not entangled in a secret manner; for everything has ordered itself around you and plays your innermost" (2009, p. 260). The "secret manner" in which we are part of a greater order playing out our innermost selves is implicit in BodyDreaming, and during the course of this book will become more and more clear.

In the BodyDreaming process, therapist and client engage in a conversation about the object that is now the centre of the client's attention. Each soon becomes aware that the process of orienting outward has enabled a shift, or *regulation*, as the client's nervous system begins to calm itself in response to the dialogue taking place between client and therapist, and between the client's inner and outer experience. Focusing away from activation occurring on the inner plane often makes possible a de-activation of arousal in the Autonomic Nervous System, noticeably through a decrease in the heart rate and a slowing of the rhythm of the breath.[9] While dream content may affect and cause activation in the body, inviting the client to focus on a found object in the outer environment also has its effect on the body. As Jung and the alchemists before him claim, body and psyche are not distinct entities, inner and outer are connected: mind/spirit affects body/matter and *vice versa*. The *matter* of the found object has an impact on the *matter* of the body. When I talk to the client about the object that has engaged her attention, I allow the conversation to go where it will. However, I am aware that my bias as listener is focused on the positive responses that I notice in my client, for example, any positive language she is using and any changes in her body, specifically changes in skin tone, breathing, facial muscles (e.g., smiling). I listen for and cultivate all positive responses through mirroring. I gently guide the dreamer to build a felt sense connection with whatever has drawn her attention. For example, I may ask, "Do you notice anything happening in your body while we are speaking about it (the found object)? Do you notice where in your body you feel you are resonating with it? What do you notice happening? Where do you feel that in your body?" Together we may observe the effects of the process of deactivation: slower heart rate, deeper breathing, reduction of tension held in the muscles and tissues. As we chat[10] about the object, we engage the right hemisphere of the brain, which enables greater capacity for openness, curiosity, associative thinking, making links, making whole. It sees things in context, in relationship to other things (McGilchrist, 2009, p. 27).[11]

Activation of the right hemisphere through orienting to the outside expands our horizon and broadens our field of perception, enabling us to experience what is immediately before us, what is *present*. The right hemisphere "alone can bring us something other than what we already know" (*ibid.*, p. 40). In contrast, the "left hemisphere deals with what it knows, and therefore prioritizes the expected—its process is predictive. It positively prefers what it knows" (*ibid.*). Consequently, when we orient toward a positive resource, away from the dream image, body symptom, or therapeutic issue, we engage the right hemisphere which has an immediate effect on our capacity to receive new information and make new connections "more capable of a 'frame shift,' ... [and] ... 'flexibility of thought'" (*ibid.*). In terms of the metaphor of Newgrange, we might say that, as we engage with the found object through the focus of the right hemisphere of the brain, the nervous system is regulated and we find we can open ourselves to the unknown, inner chamber of the dream or symptom, "illuminating bone, breath and blood" (Candace Loubert in unpublished writings).[12] In this way we sidestep the left hemisphere's fixed mode of apprehension with its tendency for narrow, focused, abstract attention and categorization. Facilitated by the right hemisphere, the dreamer is more able to be receptive to the dream, circumambulating the dream imagery, playing with the inherent energies of the images and with possibilities of meaning. The dreamer finds herself able to dream the dream onward instead of trying to fix its meaning once and for all, as the entomologist would once have pinned a specimen of a rare butterfly. Just as at Newgrange, where the aperture is oriented toward the Winter Solstice sunrise and allows the light to enter the passageway leading to the inner chamber, so BodyDreaming orients body and psyche in an alignment that enables the system to receive the life-giving energy carried by the dream and resonating in the body. Alignment, with the play possible between outer and inner, matter and psyche, fosters in us a sense of wholeness, and embodiment, generating a dance that is key to the practice of BodyDreaming.

When therapist and client look again at the dream, each may begin to notice a correlation between the dream imagery and the outside object with which the client has engaged. I am reminded of Jung's idea of the compensatory function of the dream. Jung argues that the dream often compensates a one-sided conscious position and I have found repeatedly that the outer found object compensates the inner dream image. The choice of found object, though seemingly random, turns out, in fact, to be purposive—not from the perspective of consciousness but from that of the unconscious. Qualities attributed to the outer object by the dreamer are very often the opposite or precisely complementary qualities to those of the dream image or the complex to which the dream image points: outer image provides a counterpoint to dream image. Both dream image and outer object may be understood as products of the unconscious psyche—the energy of the life force, *Chi*, or the Self in Jungian terms. They serve as expressions of the Self's—the total organism's—innate drive towards wholeness. In BodyDreaming we align to this innate drive for wholeness which regulates body and psyche and places us in profound connection with physical matter—our own and that of the world around us.

The moment of discovery, when the dreamer recognizes the just-so-ness of the supposedly randomly found object, is often pivotal in BodyDreaming practice. I understand the dreamer's choice of found object as synchronistic, essential to the on-going process of the dream work: the dream continues dreaming itself through the body and in relation to its immediate environment. Realization of the complementarity of inner and outer images initiates a dialogue between inner and outer, and sometimes the dreamer may experience herself in the presence of mystery. She may speak of a felt sense of something not present earlier, something that might have become apparent through any of the four functions of the conscious personality identified by Jung: sensation, intuition, feeling or thinking. Such a moment may be accompanied by a feeling of awe and curiosity because of the *numinous* quality of the experience.[13] We might say that the dreamer has experienced an embodied sense of the conjoining (*coniunctio*) of psyche and soma, spirit and matter. In terms of our metaphor of Newgrange, such an experience would correspond to the moment when the light of the solstice sunrise reaches the very depths of the winter darkness in the cairn to illuminate the stone carving of the triple spiral in the inner chamber.[14]

For the individual, such an experience is one of *embodiment* and amounts to a creation story of spirit becoming flesh. A new insight is born that affects *body and psyche*; it resonates in the cells of the body; it makes the dreamer momentarily aware of being part of something much bigger than the ego, a life force that Paula Reeves refers to as:

> a non-tangible vibrational lifeforce ... far more internal than external. It resides in the depths of our soul—in every cell of our matter—in the caves and caverns of our heart. This life force which Asians call *chi*, physicists call electromagnetic energy, and the religious call spirit, is always knocking on the door of our consciousness.
>
> (Reeves, 2003, p. 65)

The whole process can bring us into alignment with ourselves *in the world*—an experience of *Be-ing in the world* (Merleau-Ponty) in a way that leaves us with a sense that we are no longer at odds with ourselves or our surroundings but connected and participating in what the alchemists refer to as the *unitary world* or *unus mundus*. David Abram, drawing on Merleau-Ponty's work, suggests that:

> [P]articipation is a defining attribute of perception itself. ... Phenomenologically ... we mean that perception always involves at its most intimate level, the experience of an active interplay, or coupling, between the perceiving body and that which it perceives.
>
> (Abram, 1997, p. 57)

In BodyDreaming, when we engage our right hemisphere (the relational hemisphere), along with our felt sense perception of what is ultimately a found, not ego-chosen, *object*, we often experience a "reciprocal encounter" (*ibid.*, p. 56). The found object becomes a dynamic presence, drawing us into relation with ourselves and the world. Such an experience of felt sense attunement engages us in a dual awareness, the capacity both to be in tune with our inner experience and in relationship with what surrounds us in the present moment. Thomas Berry, cultural historian and ecotheologian, reminds us of the *inseparability* of subject and object:

> This is not a 'knowing' subject simply 'knowing' an object that's out there in space. It's a question of a rapport between two subjects in intimate communion with one another. ... What we perceive cannot be separate from us. We need to shift perspective from the sense of a universe as a collection of separate objects, and into the perception of it as a communion of subjects.
>
> (In conversation with Ryley, 1998, p. 242)

What results is a grounded, embodied connection to ourselves and, simultaneously, our consciousness expands to include that which engages our attention. BodyDreaming practice has the potential to open us to an expansion of consciousness, an experience not only of self-regulation but also of *Self*-regulation, if we use the term *Self* in the sense that Jung meant when he spoke of the Self as "the principle and archetype of orientation and meaning. Therein lies its healing function" (1995, p. 224).

*

In the early 2000s, I co-facilitated workshops with colleagues Paula Reeves, the late Candace Loubert (1947–2011) and Wendy Willmot. Paula Reeves— psychotherapist, author and teacher—held the seat of the elder and led our exploration into myth, dream, mindful mirroring and contemplative movement. Candace Loubert—dancer, educator, co-founder and artistic director of LAMDI (Les Ateliers de Danse Moderne de Montréal), a Montréal-based professional dance academy—engaged our felt sense awareness, teaching us to build trust in the body to enable energy to flow with ease and be expressed, at an appropriate pace, in painting or clay. Wendy Willmot—Jungian analyst and environmentalist—held the role of container, offering a loving, witnessing presence. Marion Woodman, an important figure to us all—Reeves, Loubert, Willmot and myself—emphasizes, with co-author Elinor Dickson, the importance of the person who serves as consciously embodied container:

> What is going on in the heart and mind of the perceiver will be picked up in the body of the perceived. ... The level of consciousness of one person holding the concentration for the group can change an entire room.
>
> (Woodman and Dickson, 1996, p. 197)

As a team we were interested in the connection between the inner landscape of the psyche and the geography of some of the megalithic sites in Ireland. During the workshops, we brought successive groups to visit a particular site, exploring both physically and psychically the larger container it afforded. We spent some time at the site, listening to its history and legends, walking the contours of the land. We used felt sense awareness to discover our own particular *bodily* resonance with the environment as we each connected with particular stones, laid out in a particular pattern on a particular piece of land dominated by a particular tree or ancient well. It often felt as though the veil between worlds was thin: inner and outer experience, present time and ancient time commingled as if the present moment reached beyond temporal time and space. The psyche, *held* in the larger landscape of megalithic architecture and myth, informed our experience in a profound way. Many participants acknowledged feeling a deep transformation: in attuning with the ancient stone, one woman felt her soul mirrored and held; she felt received and embraced in both body and soul.

One participant described her experience as follows:

> The image of standing stones gives a sense that what we are doing here in this lifetime is part of something larger than the individual's struggle, but the individual's struggle does matter ... in the sense that the standing stones are complete as they stand side by side, each stone sharing in the formation of the circle.
>
> (Reinau, 2016, p. 86)

Another participant wrote:

> Body meets body of stone,
> each meeting the other's
> standing,
> the matter of flesh and the matter of stone ...
> the membrane between
> alive
> pulsating to a universal cord.

The experience of standing in the stone circle in her sensing body had rooted this participant in the collective story of our human nature (Abram, 2011), deepening her sense of trust in being part of, participating in, and belonging to the natural world. Her body-knowing sensed a reciprocity between self and Other; her body-feeling sensed her body's fluids pulsating alongside the living body of stone, and so recognized (from the latin—*recognoscere*—'know again') her place, as poet Mary Oliver describes "in the family of things".[15]

Yet another participant, who had undergone cancer surgery prior to the workshop, felt drawn to lie on the ancient threshold stone, perhaps as an offering to a god or laying her body willingly on the surgeon's table. This particular stone stands in situ where it was found and is the threshold stone to a passage grave, a womb/tomb some 5,000 years old. The stone is impressive in size and elaborately carved with megalithic patterns inscribing generational stories but also, in this instance, reflecting the pattern of the surgeon's incision on the body of the participant. The participant felt an impulse to spread her body across the stone, body against body, matter against matter. In that moment, she felt her body and soul held and received by the vastness and depth of the ancient stone in a spontaneous ritual which helped to restore her to a sense of wholeness.

*

WHY THIS BOOK NOW: THE ORIGINS OF BODYDREAMING

*[T]he difference we make between the psyche and the body is artificial.
... In reality, there is nothing but a living body. That is the fact; and psyche is as much a living body as body is living psyche: it is just the same.*
(Jung, 1989, p. 396)[16]

*

Contemporary culture, worldwide, finds itself caught in a process of accelerated change that seems on the point of spinning out of control. Almost every time we watch the news we are reminded that our planet is in crisis: it is threatened by climate change; more species are becoming extinct; people are losing their homes to earthquake, hurricane, drought, flood and war. There are over sixty million refugees and displaced persons, many living in war zones and refugee camps. Others experience themselves as disconnected, uprooted, alienated from and by political systems, with little sense of community, purpose or meaning.

Let us imagine for a moment that, in the evolution of our species, we have been traumatized—repeatedly. Certainly there is enough evidence for this if we consider the wars, colonization, natural catastrophes, religious persecution, and oppressive regimes that have held and still hold many parts of the world hostage, with on-going transgenerational trauma as a consequence. Hans Selye, author of the classic study *The Stress of Life*, writes:

> Stress is essentially reflected by the rate of all the wear and tear caused by life.... [M]any common diseases are largely due to errors in our adaptive responses to stress, rather than to direct damage by germs, poisons, or life experience.[17]
>
> (Selye, 1978, pp. xvi–xvii)

We might argue that the legacy of daily stresses, combined with our response to global trauma, has caused our Autonomic Nervous Systems to become overwhelmed and permanently set in a state of hyperarousal/over-heating, or hypoarousal/shutting-down. A state of heightened arousal causes us to respond to repeated stress, crisis or trauma by a *fight/flight* or *collapse/freeze* response according to our individual neural wiring and the wiring of our parents and fore-bears. These mechanisms constitute the body's default adaptation to the stresses and strains of existence. If we suppose that our nervous systems have become calibrated to a heightened state of hyper- or hypoarousal, our response to life may arguably no longer be *in measure* but dangerously out of alignment with the natural order or natural law of measure which allows the nervous system to reset itself and achieve homeostasis. Unlike the animal in its natural habitat that lives and survives not through excess but in relation to need,[18] human beings often act in a dysregulated manner, pushed beyond their respective *windows of tolerance*[19] by an Autonomic Nervous System set on overload and unable to self-regulate.

The organic process of self-regulation is fundamental to the survival of human life on the planet. Nature is adaptive and strives continually to return the organism from a state of chaos and dissonance to one of greater cohesion and flow. Our contemporary world, with its culture of globalization, may well be out of sync with our intrinsic capacity for self-healing and self-regulation, leaving our nervous systems more often than not in a state of dysregulation. However, if we can *learn* how to reset our Autonomic Nervous Systems we may find that our stressed and traumatized systems are able to realign with the inherent organic capacity for self-regulation.[20] Jung argued repeatedly that the body and psyche are two aspects of one and the same thing: "The separation of psychology from the basic assumptions of biology is purely artificial, because the human psyche lives in indissoluble union with the body" (1937, par. 232). He pointed out that each is self-regulatory—always attempting to return the system to a state of homeostasis. Walter Bradford Cannon, 1932, first coined the phrase *homeostasis* referring to the physiological processes which maintain steady states in the body including:

> [t]he brain and nerves, the heart, the lungs, the kidneys and spleen, all work-ing cooperatively. ... The word does not imply something set and immobile, a stagnation. It means a condition—a condition which may vary, but which is relatively constant.
>
> (Cannon, 1932, p. 24)

Neuroscientist Antonio Damasio argues for the connection between our emotions, cognitions and physiology. He points out that "emotions are part and parcel of the regulatory process we call homeostasis. It is senseless to discuss ... [emotions] ... without understanding that aspect of living organisms and *vice versa*" (Damasio, 2000, p. 40). Realignment of the nervous system requires establishing homeostasis in our systems through building a conscious relationship with the inherent self-regulatory aspect of our psychical and physical selves.

Jung reminds us that any global change in consciousness, attitude and values can only occur in and through the individual, and must begin with the individual:

> As any change must begin somewhere, it is the single individual who will experience it and carry it through. The change must indeed begin with an individual; it might be any one of us. Nobody can afford to look round and to wait for somebody else to do what he is loath to do himself. But since nobody seems to know what to do, it might be worthwhile for each of us to ask himself whether by any chance his or her unconscious may know something that will help us.
>
> (Jung, 1964, p. 101)

For significant change to occur in our relationships, in our world, we each need first to recognize and then take responsibility for the default patterns of response of our own Autonomic Nervous Systems. While this may sound like an impossible task, we might begin by asking how we, as individuals, engage with the world. Are our nervous systems hard-wired with a sense of safety sufficient to allow us to be curious, open to novelty, and to connect with strangers and strangeness, all of which depend on a deeply embedded sense of security? Or are we battling with daily pressures in a constant state of overwhelm, thrown by the unexpected, resistant to change, fearful of conflict and anger, be it our own or that of another?

We might discover that our nervous system's default mode is predominantly a *fight* or *flight* response to perceived threat or danger. Alternatively, our system's default mode might be that of *freeze* or *collapse*. When we perceive ourselves to be under threat or our survival to be at stake, the Autonomic Nervous System mobilizes an essential survival response. When the danger has passed, the natural rhythm of the system reasserts itself and homeostasis is once again attained. However, we might come to realize that our system is set in a one-sided position, and our response to the world in general is dominated by either hyperarousal—or the opposite—hypoarousal. For many reasons, the nervous system does not always register that the perceived danger is passed. And we seldom allow enough time or bring sufficient awareness to the process of re-establishing homeostasis in our systems after they have been activated.

Our responses to perceived danger or trauma are encoded in our nervous systems from the very beginning and are conditioned by the early attachment relationship between infant and primary caregiver. In adult life, we may find that the nervous system is still responding, or firing, in a way that indicates it is stuck in response patterns encoded in infancy. The energy that is blocked as a result of outmoded patterns of response forms, or constellates as, psychological *complexes*. When activated, these complexes trap us in a one-sided position, distort our conscious perceptions and responses, and throw us out of alignment with our system's inherent organic rhythm. It is, then, imperative that therapists work with developmental trauma focusing on complexes and attachment patterns that are entrained in the neural wiring, to bring about the rehabilitation of the Autonomic Nervous System.

Complexes

Emotion evokes a strong response in the body (Damasio, 2000, p. 40). Any strong reaction is in itself an indication that a complex has been constellated, that is, activated. "[I]t seems that only after the body has reacted can the conscious mind become aware of the reaction and recognize the constellation, if at all" (Krieger, 2014, p. 18). Jung conducted the Word Association Test at the Burghölzli psychiatric hospital in Zürich between 1900 and 1909, observing and measuring patients' responses to a list of stimulus words and recording any reactions triggered in the body. This work established a correlation between the *feeling tone* or *emotion* activated by the stimulus word and the sympathetic nervous system's response to that activation.[21] Jung's experiments revealed to him "the interconnectedness of mind and body. … [W]hen an unconscious complex was activated in a subject, the intense feeling tone at its centre produced a perseverating and cumulative effect on *both* body and psyche" (Greene, 2005, p. 199). In his 1934 essay, "A Review of the Complex Theory", Jung uses the term *feeling-toned complex* to describe the disruption of consciousness experienced by the patient in response to certain stimulus words: "Every constellation of a complex postulates a disturbed state of consciousness" (1934, par. 200). The current use of PET scans and fMRI[22] imaging clearly shows that a brain-mind-body response is triggered in emotion-laden situations which activate the ingrained patterns of neural reactions we commonly call *complexes*. Jung claims that "the *via regia* to the unconscious ... is not the dream, as he (Freud) thought, but the complex, which is the architect of dreams and of symptoms" (*ibid.*, par. 210). The discoveries Jung made through extensive use and study of the Word Association tests teach us all, as individuals and therapists, to heed the body if we are to understand both the psyche's and the Autonomic Nervous System's response to a stimulus, since the two "are essentially connected through reciprocal action" (1928, par. 33).

In the 1930s, Jung indicates the psychotherapeutic focus required when he claims that "no individuation [conscious development of the full potential of the personality] can take place without [the body] ... It is the spirit of this particular body, and it is this particular body that makes this thing particular" (1988, p. 64). Jung reiterates the importance of the body:

> The body is the guarantee of consciousness, and consciousness is the instrument by which meaning is created. There would be no meaning if there were no consciousness, and since there is no consciousness without the body, there can be no meaning without the body.
>
> (Jung, 1988, p. 350)

Somatic Unconscious

I am privileged to have had Marion Woodman, Jungian analyst and author, as my teacher and mentor over a considerable number of years. From Woodman's writings and the workshops she offered in London, UK in the early 1990s I first learnt about the *living body* and to appreciate the importance of *experiencing* the living body in relation to healing the psyche-soma, body-soul split. Woodman, writing in the 1980s, argues that *shadow* material (negative affect) is often, though not necessarily, created as a result of developmental trauma and the relationship with our primary caregiver, in particular. It lies deep in the body and that it is only through active engagement *with* the body that we can begin to bring it to consciousness and redeem the body from its shadow position. She teaches that when an individual cannot accept herself fully and fails to root herself in the world, in the *matter* of her particular body, the body is left holding the rejected, wounded aspects of the soul:

> The shadow is in the body, too far from consciousness even to appear in dreams, and there is no ... conscious[ness] enough to make the link between body and psyche. Then *Mater* (mother) concretizes into *matter* and holds together with flesh what should be held together with love.
>
> (Woodman, 1982, p. 86)

Woodman describes the rejected, wounded aspects of the personality that become dissociated, split off from consciousness, and fall into the body, as forming the *somatic unconscious*. It is my belief that if we learn to regulate the Autonomic Nervous System we gain greater access to the messages and signals emanating from the *somatic unconscious*, whether in the form of an image, gesture, movement, dream, symptom or the quality of one's breathing. But first we have to learn to reset our neural wiring so we are not continually firing, or responding, from a place of stress, trauma or an activated complex. In so doing, we expand our *window of tolerance*: we increase our capacity to tolerate powerful emotions and create a more holding and safe environment in our bodies and psyches which makes us less susceptible to the triggering of old, negative complexes, and more receptive to self-regulating positive impulses and dream images that contain the seeds of new life.

Neuroscience shows us that the early relationship between infant and caregiver shapes the infant's brain and neural patterning. The repeated pattern of *attunements* and *misattunements* between infant and primary caregiver contributes to the formation of positive and negative complexes respectively. However, the plasticity of the brain ensures that the patterning of the neural wiring is adaptable and can shift when exposed to an enhanced positive environment. Learning to reset the Autonomic Nervous System increases our capacity for self-regulation and enables the creation of lasting changes in our neural wiring, especially the development of new neural pathways concerned with compassion and empathy. To this end, BodyDreaming engages an approach to psyche/soma that awakens us to the default responses of our particular body's nervous system, opens our hearts and minds, and refines our capacity for inner and outer attunement. BodyDreaming is grounded in a view of humanity that prizes the individual's inherent capacity for healing and self-regulation through the attunement of body, mind and soul within a particular and immediate environment.

*

The foundation of BodyDreaming is traceable to a number of professional, body-focused, somatic approaches to psychotherapy that I have studied throughout my career, namely BodySoul Rhythms, Focusing, Authentic Movement, and trauma therapies Somatic Experiencing and Organic Intelligence. My engagement with somatic therapies began with BodySoul Rhythms work, founded by Marion Woodman, Mary Hamilton and Ann Skinner. BodySoul Rhythms forms the ground on which BodyDreaming has been developed. I was first drawn to Marion Woodman's writings while in training to become a Psychosynthesis psychotherapist in London in the 1980s. The Psychosynthesis training opened a gateway to an innovative, imaginative and creative approach to therapy, that I deeply resonated with.[23] The theory included an integrative map of body, mind and spirit. However, at that time the training did not embrace a practical somatic approach to therapy.

L'Arche Community

Prior to my training in Psychosynthesis and my introduction to Marion Woodman through her writings, I lived and worked from 1977–78, and from 1982–83, with people suffering from mental disabilities in the L'Arche community[24] just north of Paris. My time at L'Arche proved to be formative and convinced me that the healing component of any relationship, therapeutic or otherwise, is contingent upon the quality of *presence* that we bring to our interactions with another person. In the words of Jean Vanier, teacher, philosopher and founder of L'Arche communities internationally, "You can only discover you are precious if someone sees you as precious."[25]

Vanier draws on the image of the infant lying in his mother's arms, touching his mother's cheek, to illustrate the connection of the loving presence between mother and child: "You are the most beautiful child in the world. Life begins with that knowledge that 'you are beloved'."[26] The pair are held in mutual tenderness: In reality many people have not lived that experience when they first come to L'Arche. Vanier emphasizes the key role of being present in relationship. Presence brings about the discovery of a mutual recognition—"I am giving you something, you are giving me something". We each, giver and receiver, discover that we are precious through our presence to each other. We could substitute attunement for presence and affirm that when we attune to one another we come into mutual recognition and, perhaps, "arrive where we started / and know the place for the first time".[27]

Many of the individuals with whom I lived and worked in L'Arche communities had been placed, or abandoned, in unsuitable institutions at an early age. Angelique was one such person who had lived since infancy in an institution for Insane Adult Women. Angelique developed attachment behaviours within the community of older women with whom she lived, one minute mimicking their rage, punitive attacks and abandonment, the next becoming the innocent child with an enormous capacity for fun and humour, engendering love in those around her. The swings between these extremes identified Angelique's attachment pattern as *disorganized disoriented* (see Chapters 5 and 6).

I met Angelique when she was in her thirties and had been at L'Arche for approximately six years. I quickly became aware that it had taken many years of daily commitment on the part of her carers to help Angelique find emotional stability and to establish greater equilibrium in her system. When Angelique had arrived, in her twenties, from the institution to L'Arche she had been assigned two carers and placed in a "community house" that she would later come to recognize as home. However, it took many years before Angelique was able to trust rather than destroy positive experiences, and tolerate good feelings while withstanding the disappointments and abandonment that, with frequent changes of staff, were inevitable in such a community. I was privileged to witness how the container of Angelique's relationship with her two special carers held through countless attacks and extreme emotional swings. Throughout these years Angelique's carers brought particular focus to the daily rituals of personal hygiene, meals, bedtime, etc. Van der Kolk, quoting Damasio, reminds us how careful attention to basic needs provides the basis for future healing:

> [A]ll of the brain structures that register background feelings are located near areas that control basic housekeeping functions such as breathing, appetite, elimination, and the sleep-wake cycle. … This is because the consequences of having emotion and attention are entirely related to the fundamental business of managing life within the organism.
>
> (van der Kolk, 2014, p. 94)

The L'Arche community provided Angelique with the opportunity to regress to her infant self, since what Damasio calls the *housekeeping cycles*, i.e., eating, dressing and bathing, were taken care of by her carers. Damasio refers to the areas of the brain concerned with "housekeeping" as the "'proto-self,' because they create the 'wordless knowledge' that underlies our conscious sense of self" (van der Kolk, 2014, p. 94). In Angelique's case, her "proto-self" was mediated through *attunement* in body-to-body, non-verbal communication with her carers, which, in turn, helped her develop a bodily experience of herself—a *conscious sense of herself.*[28] The quality of attunement on a daily basis enabled a rewiring of Angelique's attachment pattern and she slowly became more settled within herself and trusting of her environment. Most remarkable was the gradual diminishment of Angelique's rageful, aggressive outbursts during periods of obvious overwhelm and fragmentation. Once renowned for her ferocity and violent eruptions, over time she grew less reactive, less volatile, and her witty sense of humour began to be a catalyst for change among those around her. She could say something that would transform the room into peals of laughter. During these years she had a doll, to whom she became attached and looked after with a similar quality of attention to that which she had received from her carers, demonstrating and exercising her capacity for love, repair and agency. Stern writes:

> Attunement feels more like an unbroken process ... it must be able to work with virtually all behavior. ... Attunements can be made with the inner quality of feeling of how an infant reaches for a toy, holds a block, kicks a foot, listens to a sound. Tracking and attuning with vital affects permits one human being to 'be with' another in the sense of sharing likely inner experiences on an almost continuous basis. This is exactly our experience of feeling-connectedness, of being in attunement with another. It feels like an unbroken line.
>
> (Stern, 1985, p. 157)

Over time she developed a remarkable sensitivity to those more vulnerable than herself. Just as she had received love and attention, over the years, Angelique became more loving and actively caring of others, especially those with greater disabilities than herself. She experienced reciprocity in the giving and receiving of love, which strengthened her sense of meaning and self-agency as she participated as an engaged member of the community. Angelique had developed a sense of a secure base within herself on which she could rely.[29] Her carers had also grown exponentially through their relationship with Angelique and their lives were forever transformed, taking up leadership positions among the international community of L'Arche.

I felt both challenged and privileged to witness the relationship forged between Angelique and her carers. The experience taught me how, at a non-verbal level, presence and loving attunement serve as the transformative elements throughout the healing process, otherwise, as cited above, the body "holds together with flesh what should be held with love" (Woodman, 1982, p. 86).

BUILDING A MORE EMBODIED THERAPEUTIC APPROACH

BodySoul Rhythms

When I completed my psychoanalytic psychotherapy training, I was left hungry for a more archetypal approach to therapy, one that included the body. In the 1990s,

I undertook a training to become a Jungian analyst, at the same time travelling to North America to participate in BodySoul Rhythms workshops offered by Marion Woodman and her colleagues, Ann Skinner and Mary Hamilton.[30] While recognizing the dream as a portal to the unconscious, Woodman preferenced the role of the body: "The body is the unconscious in its most immediate and continuous form, the dream is also the unconscious, though as a body of images it lacks both the immediacy and continuity of the physical body" (1985, p. 79). BodySoul Rhythms workshops, which I attended over many years, became seminal for me, helping me to build a relationship to my own body while releasing psychic energy that had been blocked, trapped in symptom and complex. The workshops deepened my understanding of the archetypal dimension of complexes and psychic dynamics in general. BodySoul Rhythms grounded me in the here-and-now of my bodily experience and enabled me, through safe and playful body- and voice-work, to release blocked energy, recognize habitual patterns of response and behaviour, and embrace new energy arising from my dreams, body and mask work. Over several years, the workshops brought me into life in a way I had never before realized and enabled me to experience a sense of embodied soul that I knew had been missing from other training programmes. Subsequently, I became a BodySoul Rhythms facilitator and have been teaching the work since the late 1990s.

BodySoul Rhythms uses movement, relaxation, breath work, voice and art to bring to consciousness the shadow material held unconsciously in the body and that presents in our dreams; most importantly, it encourages creative expression.[31] Embodied active imagination is also used to engage with images from dreams and myths, as well as those arising from physical symptoms and the body. BodySoul Rhythms work requires the building of a loving, conscious container in the body that is strong enough to hold the energy and images that emerge.[32] Where traditional psychoanalysis and psychoanalytical psychology value the transference relationship as the primary container, BodySoul Rhythms sees a loving relationship with the body itself as equally vital. Mary Hamilton reminds us:

> The challenge is to open flesh to the awareness that it is a dance beautiful with light. Human awareness, encoded in ego reality, cannot feel its flesh-robe as open space, it feels dense and dark. ... The closed circuit of ego has not awakened to its flesh body.
>
> (Hamilton, 2009, p. 221)

The presence of other participants in the BodySoul Rhythms groups supports and strengthens one's connection with the loving container of the body, the flesh. The dynamic role of witnesses who accept and mirror the participants' process encourages and supports each participant to move into an embodied, authentic relationship with herself. In the early 1990s, BodySoul Rhythms relied on experience, practice and intuition to steer the course of the work. However, with the rapid developments in neuroscience in the 1990s, containing, witnessing and mirroring—key practices essential to healing in BodySoul Rhythms programmes—have been afforded scientific validation.

Allan Schore

In 2005 I was writing a thesis entitled "Psyche and Soma—an Interconnected Field". It concerned the importance of including the body in the practice of psychoanalysis. I struggled with, and was at a loss to know, how to write about this question in a psychoanalytic academic paper from a clinical point of view until I was introduced to Allan Schore's work and his publications on affect regulation. Schore's gift lies in his ability to synthesize new discoveries in neuroscience and apply them to psychoanalytic practice. By this time, I had undergone a Psychosynthesis psychotherapy training, a psychoanalytic psychotherapy training, a training in Jungian analytical psychology, and BodySoul Rhythms leadership training. Schore, with his extensive research into neurobiology and psychobiology, provided me with the bridge for which I was looking. Neuroscience, utilizing PET scans and fMRI imaging, demonstrates clearly that (1) body-mind comprises one unit, and (2) the early primary relationships help to form the neural pathways that shape the personality. It gave me great satisfaction to include Allan Schore's work in my thesis, validating, as it did, the psyche-soma link and the work of BodySoul Rhythms, and confirming that if we continue to marginalize the body in our psychoanalytic practice we do so at our peril. This idea became central to the development of BodyDreaming.

Schore's presentation of neuroscientific research on infant development and attachment theory included images, footage and studies of mother/infant interactions, and Edward Tronick's Still Face experiment. It focused on the effects on early development of attunement and misattunement, disruption and repair. Schore's work confirmed my passion for infant observation and its relevance to what I have found to lie at the core of the healing relationship: attunement and affect regulation. It rekindled my interest and research into early infant development and its role in encoding the neural networking (the pathways linking body and mind) of baby and mother. Schore argues that attachment theory is "fundamentally a regulatory theory" (2003, p. 37):

> [T]he attachment object acts as an external psychobiological regulator of the "experience dependent" growth of the infant's nervous system, and ... these attachment experiences are imprinted into the neurobiological structures that are maturing during the brain growth spurt of the first two years of life, and therefore have far-reaching and long-enduring effects.
>
> (Schore, 2003, p. 37)

I became keen to explore possible links between the psychology and neuroscience of a client's early relationship and that with the therapist, in other words, the therapist–client relationship explored in terms of the neuroscience of early development. I was also interested to learn what light neuroscience might throw on the question of what we need to focus on in order to heal a problematic early relationship and rewire an early traumatized system. To address these issues I had first to find ways to incorporate the body as a living entity into my clinical practice.

Focusing

In the early 2000s, I began teaching BodySoul workshops in collaboration with Candace Loubert, dancer and movement and somatics educator. Candace's work reflected her firm belief that image begins with impulse in a somatic movement— in other words, it originates in a movement that springs from a *current of change* in the tissues. "I think of the pattern of the tissues (because the nervous system works in patterns) which send up whisperings of form and impulse through dreams, movement and image" (Loubert, unpublished writings). Candace introduced me to the process of tracking the sensation field in the body, and to *Focusing*, the work of American philosopher and psychologist Eugene Gendlin, which empha-sizes attention to *felt sense* experience in the body. Gendlin developed Focusing from research he undertook with Carl Rogers, investigating "why doesn't therapy succeed more often?" (Gendlin, 1981, p. 3). He believes that therapy is most suc-cessful for the client who is able to access an inner or embodied sense within the therapeutic frame (Bacon, 2007). Gendlin is influenced by Merleau-Ponty's idea of our "being-in-the-world" as essentially our being in a *participatory* relationship with the world—our immediate environment and everything in it. In particular, Gendlin champions Merleau-Ponty's notion of perception:

> Merleau-Ponty rescued the body from being considered merely as one *sensed* thing among other sensed things (as it still is in physiology). For him the body, sensing from inside, is an internal-external orienting centre of percep-tion, not just perceived, but perceiving.
>
> (Gendlin, 1992, p. 5)

Gendlin takes Merleau-Ponty's concept of the *living body* and argues:

> It is not the case that you have only your perception of me, that our percep-tions of each other are between us. Rather, we affect each other, bodily and situationally, whether we sense or see it or not. My warmth or hostility will affect your ongoing bodily being whether you perceive it or not. You may find it there, if you sense how your body has the situation.
>
> (*ibid.*, p. 6)

Gendlin highlights the body as a *self-sensing body*—a bodily sensing, a bodily thinking, a bodily knowing. We know, feel, sense we are in the world through body sensing and when we focus on this perspective we enlarge our experience of being in the world. "We sense our bodies not as elaborated perceptions but as the body sense of our situations, the interactional whole-body by which we orient and know what we are doing" (*ibid.*, p. 8).

The work of tracking sensation in the body and noticing how it moves and informs image and thought gave me the therapeutic tool that I had been looking for in my clinical practice, opening a path for me to incorporate the body into psychotherapy. Prior to this, my experience had been limited to teaching body-soul work in a workshop context, exploring dreams, body and voice *on the floor*. Here at last I had a means to address the body in a one-on-one therapy session, to listen to the body's deep impulses, intuitions and resonances without having the client do *floor work* and move around in the room to access the body. Through tracking felt sense experience, the client and I could access *internal* physical sensation, mapping feeling in the body, and opening both client and therapist to the embodied imaginal as a result. Working in this way slows the pace and affords the body the time it needs to register what is emerging from the somatic unconscious, allowing "the new impulse to come forward from the deep well of bone, breath and blood" (Loubert, unpublished writings).

When I began to practise Focusing—felt sense awareness—in my work I witnessed a growing capacity for attunement, both to myself and to my client. When using felt sense awareness, we bring attention to the body's experience by asking questions such as "What do you notice is happening in your body?" Such focused and carefully paced attention supports the client's inherent capacity for self-regulation and orientation. Awareness of the felt sense of what is occurring in one's body, while calming the nervous system, regulates affect, and also grounds the client, bringing him or her into the here-and-now, the present moment of immediate bodily awareness.

Somatic Experiencing

My clinical work shifted dramatically when, in the early 2000s, I trained in Somatic Experiencing, Peter Levine's groundbreaking approach to working with trauma.[33] According to Levine, "[t]rauma is not in the event, trauma is in the nervous system" (1997, p. 3) and it can therefore never be fully healed "until we also address the essential role played by the body". Somatic Experiencing teaches the importance of finding a *resource*, a positive image—memory, place, person, animal, object—to act as ballast for the trauma. When the nervous system is in *overwhelm*, a positive resource is evoked through the felt sense experience or "awareness of physical body sensations" (Levine, 2010, pp. 9–10) which has the effect of regulating autonomic arousal, unblocking energy and supporting the body to discharge excess emotion, regulating autonomic arousal, and facilitating the resolution of chronic or traumatic stress. This is accomplished through "the completion of thwarted, biologically based, self-protective and defensive responses" (Payne, Levine and Crane-Godreau, 2015, p. 1). Levine argues that traditional psychotherapeutic approaches to trauma are rarely adequate and in some cases perpetuate the trauma through the repeated recall of events, maintaining the client in a continual state of overwhelm. Somatic Experiencing teaches the therapist to develop the skills to align the nervous system with the body's "innate drive for perseverance and triumph" (Levine, 2015, p. xvi). Levine's work of releasing trauma in the body focused my attention on the vital role of the nervous system in the process of self-regulation.

Organic Intelligence

More recently, in 2012, I was introduced to **Organic Intelligence**, Steven Hoskinson's unique approach to working with trauma. Organic Intelligence builds on Levine's Somatic Experiencing, which Hoskinson has taught internationally for many years. It teaches how "healing happens from the nervous system up" and maps the psychic states and behaviour patterns that accompany particular nervous system responses. Aligning the client with the system's innate capacity to reorganize itself, Organic Intelligence uses positive reinforcement and interventions to support the organism's integrative biology and re-establish stability and greater coherence.[34] Hoskinson has developed a proprioceptive technique that he refers to as *orienting* in order to re-stimulate the intrinsic capacity for healing in the human organism (see Chapter 2). By incorporating the theory and practice of both Somatic Experiencing and Organic Intelligence in the development of BodyDreaming, I was able to acquire and utilize in my clinical work a deeper appreciation of the body's inherent capacity for self-regulation, and a greater sense of attunement with the nervous systems of both myself and my clients.

*

AN INVITATION TO THE READER TO ENGAGE EXPERIENTIALLY WITH THE TEXT

When I am working with a client or workshop participant, I stay present to the process by tracking my body's responses as I listen to my client's experience. The process is one of mutual regulation: I cannot engage with my client and offer regulation unless I myself am regulated and have a grounded sense of my body in the here-and-now of where we are situated. I need to be present in myself in the space where we are meeting before I can engage in a regulating, attuned witnessing of another. The capacity to witness is essential to the process of regulation.

I would like to invite you, as reader, to assume the role of witness. The role of witness is a dynamic role. If you elect to engage with the text in this way, you will need to stay present to what is happening in your body at a felt sense level. This means making relationship with your body as witness to the work presented in the text and tracking the way you are affected by what is happening for the clients. You will need to pay close attention to sensations, emotions, thoughts and images, tracking moments when you experience both hyper- and hypoarousal, and moments when you experience a sense of integration, flow and coherence.

I encourage you to join with the client in orienting outward—allowing your eyes to be drawn by something that attracts them, or you may wish to recall an image or memory and engage with it as a positive resource at those moments in the text when I invite my client to do the same. The cardinal rule is that we orient toward pleasure, enjoyment.[35] I invite you to follow your internal processes—noticing body sensations, emotions, images, dreams, impulses, to gesture, sigh, make sounds, stretch—that may present themselves to consciousness in response to the client's work. My hope is that, as you follow the sessions with the clients in an active, co-participatory manner, you will have an embodied learning experience of how I use specific interventions such as attunement, mirroring, orienting, tracking sensation, timing, pacing. Your active witnessing will serve as a mirror to guide your process of self-awareness and self-regulation. The material is alive, the text is alive, and just as we know that the perceiver affects what is perceived, you, as active reader, can stay alive to your own dynamic process through inner attunement and remain attuned to the "spontaneous life of our sensing bodies" (Abram, 1997, p. 56). My wish is that you have a reading experience in which meaning comes to you through the cellular resonance in your bodysoul as you respond to and digest the material. I am hoping that the content, or *matter* of the text, will prove effective and that you, as reader, will find yourself affected.

If you find your empathy stirred and your emotions engaged, you will have succeeded in embodying the role of witness. In terms of neuroscientific theory, this will mean that your witnessing of the BodyDreaming process of each person presented in the following chapters has brought your *mirror neurons* into play (i.e., the neurons responsible for activating feelings of empathy and compassion). If you are able to witness the clients' experiences in a dynamic way, and stay present to how you resonate with what is happening, you may find that you begin a conversation with your own body and psyche that starts to move and change patterned, learned responses, your habitual way of being and moving in the world. I hope that your experience of being an active witness will develop your capacity for self-regulation, encouraging you to reimagine your own life's story and relationships as you find you are no longer reacting (predominantly) from an activated nervous system. You may feel more consciously connected to the life force deep in the materiality of your own body, resonating with the material body around you, all of which affords you greater ease and flow and pleasure in your engagement with the world.

Here is how we might proceed:

I invite you to do an awareness exercise, bringing your attention to your body and the changes that are happening in your body as I guide you to orient yourself in the space that surrounds you.

When working with a client, I first introduce her to the space in which we will work, and I now invite you, too, to take a minute to look around your own room. Allow your senses to take a walk, to wander freely and notice what they find, what draws their attention. Pause for a moment and allow time to become curious about what attracts your attention—what found object captivates you? It could be that your eyes have noticed something familiar: the painting on the wall. You may be struck by the way the sun lights up an object in the room ... the movement of the wind outside in the clouds or the branches ... or it may be that you are drawn to the smell of cut grass ... or to the textures and fabrics of your surroundings, the sensation of a particular fabric on your skin.... Allow yourself to be curious about what it is you are noticing in the moment. Take time to engage with it. You may be aware of some small changes happening in you as your body responds to its engagement with the found object—for example, you may notice a change in your breathing, your heart rate, your pulse rate. You may have been racing ahead as you read and perhaps now you notice a slowing down. You may wish to change position in your chair, or feel the need to yawn or stretch. Continue, slowly, to shift your awareness back and forth between the two positions, the two perceptions—outer and inner—tracking your responses—sensations, emotions, images, thoughts—as you do so.

If you engage in such an exercise, you will find yourself more consciously connected to your body and simultaneously to your physical surroundings. Through orienting toward something pleasurable and bringing your awareness to that object, your nervous system will regulate itself. This action alone has a calming effect and enables you to witness and be more receptive to and empathic towards the clients' material. You will find yourself more present, more actively engaged with yourself, and simultaneously with the clients' processes. Learning to observe and track changes in your body as it resonates with what you are attending to, and developing your capacity for regulation of your nervous system, form the seed bed of the work of BodyDreaming. Developing your ability to observe changes in yourself, in the physical matter of your body, will enable you to observe changes in others. In this way you develop your capacity for attunement[36]—both to yourself (internal attunement) and to others or the environment (external attunement). What begins as an exercise will, I hope, with the experience of reading the text, grow into a fascinating and 'easeful' exploration. With repetition the practice develops into a capacity for an enhanced emotional connection with one's own matter and the materiality of what is immediate—other human beings and the living environment of which we are all a part.

I hope that this exercise will have whetted your appetite to engage actively with the material presented in the following chapters. When we adopt a practice such as BodyDreaming, we increase our capacity to relate to ourselves and to adjust our individual nervous system's responses, which support our relationships with one another and our connection to the physical world in which we all participate. We begin to build a felt sense awareness of being at home in our bodies, of belonging to and participating in the wider world, and living in alignment with the rhythms and self-regulating principles that are increasingly being understood to govern both our selves and our universe.

*

THE BLACK PEARL

The image on the cover of the book is a black Baroque pearl.[37] The pearl is formed underwater when a piece of sand or organic matter finds its way into the oyster shell. The sand acts as an irritant and a coating of calcium carbonate, called 'nacre', builds up around it, layer upon layer, until the irritant eventually becomes the pearl. The image of "the pearl ... self-made in the fleshy oyster" serves as a fitting metaphor for the practice of BodyDreaming (Ronnberg and Martin, 2010, p. 784). The work consists of titrating the 'irritants'—the complexes, attachment patterns, and traumas held in our somatic unconscious, our dreambody, our flesh and bones until the pearl of great price reveals itself.

> Look at
> beauty's gift to us—
> her power is so great she enlivens
> the earth, the sky, our
> soul.
> (Mirabai, "A Hundred Objects
> Close By", translated by
> Daniel Ladinsky)[38]

*

Notes

1 C.G. Jung, "The Meaning of Psychology for Modern Man", Vol X (Jung, 2000, par. 304).
2 Cairn literally means a pile of stones. It is used loosely as a generic term for structures such as passage tombs or dolmens (Brennan, 1994, p. 10).
3 Although we may suppose that peoples living over 5,000 years ago would be living in an intuitive but largely unconscious relationship to nature (*participation mystique*), it is useful to remember what Jung writes of the symbolism of the sun in his seminars on Nietzsche's *Zarathustra.*

> [T]he sun surely is the symbol of the center of consciousness, it is the principle of consciousness because it is light. When you understand a thing, you say: 'I see' – and in order to see you need light. The essence of understanding, of cognition, has always been symbolized by the all-seeing of the sun ... that moves over the earth and sees everything in its light.
>
> (Jung, 1988, p. 16)

4 I would say that the feminine principle (not female—we are not associating this with gender, but with the feminine energy in men and women), can be associated with certain words: process, presence, being here now, paradox, resonating, receiving, surrendering, listening.

> (Woodman in conversation with Ryley, 1998, p. 72)

5 Steven Hoskinson in conversation with Serge Prengel, May 2016: "'Let the eyes go where they want to go' ... implies that maybe the eyes may *want* to go some place that *I* may not think of" (Prengel, 2016, p. 5).
6 [T]he attention into the external environment, gives a feedback response into my system that gives me a response into the here and now. But also there is something [else] really important in that it short-circuits the repetitive patterns of threat response.

> (Hoskinson in conversation with Prengel, 2016, p. 4)

7   The Social Engagement System is an integrated system with both a somatomo-
        tor component regulating the striated muscles of the face and a visceromotor
        component regulating the heart via a myelinated vagus. The system is capable of
        dampening activation of the sympathetic nervous system ...

                                                                    (Porges, 2009, p. 41)

8   [These] psychological-physiological interactions are dependent on the dynamic
        bidirectional communication between peripheral organs and the central nervous
        system connecting the brain with these organs.... [T]he neural circuits, provid-
        ing a bidirectional communication between brain and heart, can trigger either a
        rapid increase in heart rate to support protective fight/flight behaviours, or a rapid
        decrease in heart rate to support social interactions.

                                                                    (Porges, 2009, p. 27)

9   The Autonomic Nervous System (ANS) is a part of the peripheral nervous system. It
    regulates internal organ functions, such as heart rate, respiration, digestion rate and pupil
    dilation. The ANS is usually conceptualized as consisting of two branches: the **sympa-
    thetic** and the **parasympathetic**. The sympathetic nervous system, acts as the body's
    accelerator, especially during emergencies (the *fight* or *flight* response). The parasympa-
    thetic system, which acts as its brake, is calming (*rest* and *digest*). The balance between
    the two systems is usually said to determine ANS functioning.
10 I use the term "chat" to denote a light conversation in which I suggest no definite direc-
    tion. I encourage the client to free associate, let the associations happen without the
    compulsion to focus and follow a particular line of thought. Hoskinson, in conversation
    with Serge Prengel, refers to this kind of intervention as a "free association conversa-
    tion" and explains that "the psyche and the biology gets to speak on its own terms" (it
    is not therapist-led) (Hoskinson in conversation with Prengel, 2016, p. 4).
11 See Chapters 1 and 2 for a fuller description of the different hemispheres of the brain.
12 In 2004, Loubert produced a film co-written with Cristina Lella and directed by Tzu-
    Hui Chan, entitled *Body Focused Creative Resources*.
13 Jung describes the *numen* as "the influence of an invisible presence that causes a pecu-
    liar alteration of consciousness" (1938, par. 6).
14 The physical structure of Newgrange mirrors the womb and birth canal, connecting the
    mysteries—the cycle of birth, death and rebirth represented in the triple spiral—with
    the Winter Solstice and symbolizing the impregnation of the fecund earth by solar
    energy, a *coniunctio* of matter and spirit—a creation story.
15 Mary Oliver's "Wild Geese" (Oliver, 1992).
16 C.G. Jung, Lecture V, 20 February 1935 (Jung, 1988, 1989, p. 396).
17 "Many nervous and emotional disturbances, high blood pressure, gastric and duodenal
    ulcers, and certain types of sexual, allergic, cardiovascular, and renal derangements
    appear to be essentially diseases of adaptation" (Selye, 1978, pp. xvi–xvii).
18 Notes from a lecture by Jungian Analyst Brigitte Egger at the International School of
    Analytical Psychology (ISAP), Zurich, 2012.
19 See Chapter 1, p. 43 and n. 9. One's *window of tolerance* describes one's capacity to
    tolerate intense emotions without going into either hyper- or hypoarousal (overheating
    or shutting down).

20   Under normal conditions people react to a threat with a temporary increase in
        their stress hormones. As soon as the threat is over, the hormones dissipate and the
        body returns to normal. The stress hormones of traumatized people, in contrast,
        take much longer to return to baseline and spike quickly and disproportionately in
        response to mildly stressful stimuli.

                                                                  (van der Kolk, 2014, p. 46)

21 "The sympathetic nervous system, originating in the spinal column, controls not only the sweat glands and heart rate, but also the blood pressure, pupil dilation, breathing, and digestion" (Krieger, 2014, p. 18, citing Zillmeret).

22 fMRI = Functional Magnetic Resonance Imaging; the fMRI registers blood flow to functioning areas of the brain, that is, it monitors brain activity. PET = Positron Emission Tomography; the PET scan shows how body tissue looks and how it is working.

23 The Institute of Psychosynthesis, London; and the Revision Centre for Integrative Psychosynthesis, London.

24 L'Arche communities are an organization of worldwide communities where people with and without intellectual disabilities share life together in community (www.larche.org).

25 Vanier (n.d.).

26 Ibid.

27 T.S. Eliot (1943, pp. 241–242).

28 "The self as agent arises out of the infant's perceptions of his presumed intentionality in the mind of the caregiver ... and out of his interpersonal experience, particularly object relationships" (Fonagy cited in Knox, 2011, p. 51).

29   The parent's capacity to mentalize acts is a powerful relational stimulus for the child's developmental trajectory of self-agency, from bodily action to thought and feeling. Fonagy *et al.* (2002) highlighted the relational basis for this process, suggesting that the parent's attuned reactions reflect back to the infant his own behaviour but in a different, more explicit format—the use of facial expression, tone of voice, and simple language—which facilitate the infant's own re-encoding of his behavioural experience into implicit and then explicit knowledge. A developmental and emergent view of the self proposes that we become fully human, aware of ourselves and others as psychological and emotional beings and capable of empathy and identification with each other, only when others consistently relate to us as fully human from the earliest moments of infancy.

(Knox, 2011, p. 52)

30 Marion Woodman, MA, PhD (Hon), author and Jungian analyst, teacher of English Literature, international lecturer; Mary Hamilton, M.Ed., a graduate of the National Ballet School of Canada, taught dance, drama and choreography at the University of Western Ontario, Canada; Ann Skinner, Head of Voice (Emerita) at Canada's Stratford Shakespeare Festival and the National Theatre School of Canada.

31   Through body and voice work designed to help the body open safely (a practice facilitated by highly skilled practitioners), together with the use of play and theatre techniques, participants "can [be encouraged] ... to play with the imagery, allowing it to take whatever form it happens to come up with, the energy locked in the shadow will emerge, bringing with it the buried creative fire."

(Woodman, 1990, pp. 100–101)

32 "In whatever ways the process of bringing the body to consciousness develops, a strong container in which the energies can transform, physically and psychically, is essential" (Woodman and Dickson, 1996, p. 196).

33 "Somatic Experiencing helps to create physiological, sensate and affective states that transform those of fear and helplessness. It does this by accessing various instinctual reactions through one's *awareness of physical body sensations*" (Levine, 2010, pp. 9–10).

Body sensation can serve as a guide to reflect where we are experiencing trauma, and to lead to our instinctual resources. These resources give us the power to protect ourselves ... and once we learn how to access them we can create our own shields to reflect and heal our trauma.

(Levine, 2010, p. 66)

34 Steven Hoskinson, founder of Organic Intelligence (www.organicintelligence.org).
35 Gustav Theodor Fechner (1802–1887), German philosopher, physicist and experimental psychologist, published "Some Ideas on the History of Creation and Development of Organisms" in 1873, the first known paper to address what is now called the principle of the tendency toward stability and self-organizing systems. Fechner was led to postulate the principle of Pleasure/Unpleasure. Freud was greatly influenced by Fechner in developing the ideas presented in "The Pleasure Principle". He attended many of Fechner's lectures and incorporated many of his ideas into his own psychoanalytical thinking (Heidelberger, 2004). However, Leri writes:

> There is a significant difference between Freud's and Fechner's 'pleasure principle.' In Freud's theory of drives organisms have physiological needs that when unmet create anxiety and a negative state of tension. When a need is satisfied the drive tension is reduced, giving pleasure as the organism returns to a state of homeostasis. The origin of the notion that it's healthy to release 'bottled up' feelings started with Freud. For Fechner pleasure was the concomitant result of the re-establishment of equilibrium (the more so if it can be established on a higher order). Freud: Pleasure = release of tension; Fechner: Pleasure = coming into dynamic equilibrium. We see in Fechner's version a resonance with Feldenkrais' rejection of 'pent up' energies that must be released. Fechner would assent to the pleasure found in becoming 'harmoniously balanced.' For Feldenkrais there's additional joy to be had in knowing how to find balance.

(Leri, 2014)

36 "When we attune to others we allow our own internal state to shift, to come to resonate with the inner world of another" (Siegel, 2010, p. 27).
37 Baroque is the term used to describe irregular and non-symmetrically shaped pearls that have been formed in freshwater mussels or saltwater oysters.
38 Ladinsky, 2002, p. 245.

References

Abram, D. (1997) *The Spell of the Sensuous*, New York: Vintage Books.
Abram, D. (2011) *Becoming Animal*, New York: Vintage Books.
Bacon, J. (2007) "Active Imagination and Focusing in Movement-based Performance and Psychotherapy," *Body Movement and Dance Psychotherapy*, March 2007, 2(1): 17–28.
Baring, A. and Cashford, J. (1993) *The Myth of the Goddess: Evolution of an Image*, London: Arkana; Penguin Books.
Brennan, J.H. (1994) *A Guide to Megalithic Ireland*, London: The Aquarian Press.
Cannon, W.B. (1932) *The Wisdom of the Body: How the Human Body Reacts to Disturbance and Danger and Maintains the Stability Essential to Life*, New York: W.W. Norton & Co.
Damasio, A. (2000) *The Feeling of What Happens: Body, Emotion and the Making of Consciousness*, London: Vintage.
Edinger, E.F. (1972) *Ego and Archetype: Individuation and the Religious Function of the Psyche*, Boston, MA: Shambhala.
Eliot, T.S. (1943) "Little Gidding," in *Four Quartets*, New York: Harcourt, Brace, and Company, pp. 241–242.
Gendlin, E. (1981) *Focusing*, New York: Bantam Books.

Gendlin, E. (1992) "The Primacy of the Body not the Primacy of Perception: How the Body Knows the Situation and Philosophy," excerpt from *Man and World*, 25(3–4): 341–353. Accessed 29 August 2018 at: www.focusing.org/pdf/primacy_excerpt.pdf

Greene, A.U. (2005) "Listening to the Body for the Sake of the Soul," *Spring, A Journal of Archetype and Culture*, Body & Soul: Honouring Marion Woodman, 72: 189–204.

Hamilton, M. (2009) *The Dragon Fly Principal: An Exploration of the Body's Function in Unfolding Spirituality*, London; Ontario: Colenso Island Press.

Heidelberger, M. (2004) *Nature from Within: Gustav Theodor Fechner and his Psychophysical Worldview*, trans. Cynthia Klohr, Pittsburgh, PA: University of Pittsburgh Press.

Jones, C. (2007) *Temples of Stone: Exploring the Megalithic Monuments of Ireland*, Cork: Collins Press.

Jung, C.G. (1928) *On Psychic Energy*, Collected Works 8, Princeton, NJ: Princeton University Press.

Jung, C.G. (1934) *A Review of the Complex Theory*, Collected Works 8, Princeton, NJ: Princeton University Press.

Jung, C.G. (1937) *Psychological Factors Determining Human Behaviour*, Collected Works 8, Princeton, NJ: Princeton University Press.

Jung, C.G. (1938) *Psychology and Religion*, Collected Works 11, Princeton, NJ: Princeton University Press.

Jung, C.G. (1942) *Paracelsus as a Spiritual Phenomenon*, Collected Works 13, Princeton, NJ: Princeton University Press.

Jung, C.G. (1964) *Man and his Symbols*. Conceived and edited by Carl G. Jung, New York: Doubleday.

Jung, C.G. (1988, 1989) *Nietzsche's Zarathustra: Notes of the Seminar Given in 1934–1939*, James L. Jarrett (ed.), in two volumes, Bollingen Series XCIX, Princeton, NJ: Princeton University Press, 1988; London & New York: Routledge: 1989.

Jung, C.G. (1995) *Memories, Dreams, Reflections*. A. Jaffé (ed.), trans. R. Winston and C. Winston, London: Fontana.

Jung, C.G. (2000) *Collected Works of C.G. Jung*, Sir Herbert Read, Michael Fordham, Gerhard Adler (eds) and William McGuire (executive editor), Bollingen Series XX, Princeton, NJ: Princeton University Press; London & New York: Routledge.

Jung, C.G. (2009) *The Red Book: Liber Novus*, S. Shamdasani (ed.), trans. M. Kyburz, J. Peck, and S. Shamdasani, New York: W.W. Norton.

Knox, J. (2011) *Self-Agency in Psychotherapy: Attachment, Autonomy and Intimacy*, London: W.W. Norton and Co.

Krieger, N. (2014) *Bridges to Consciousness: Complexes and Complexity*, London: Routledge.

Ladinsky, D. (2002) *Love Poems from God: Twelve Sacred Voices from the East and West*, New York: Penguin Compass.

Leri, D. (2014) "The Risk of Serious Inquiry – Part Three: Fechner Makes a Difference." SEMIOPHYSICS. Accessed 26 August 2018 at: http://semiophysics.com/SemioPhysics_Articles_risk_3.html.

Levine, P. (1997) *Waking the Tiger: Healing Trauma - The Innate Capacity to Transform Overwhelming Experiences*, Berkeley, CA: North Atlantic Books.

Levine, P. (2010) *In an Unspoken Voice: How the Body Releases Trauma and Restores Goodness*, Berkeley, CA: North Atlantic Books.

Levine, P. (2015) *Trauma and Memory: Brain and Body in a Search for the Living Past: A Practical Guide for Understanding and Living with Personal Trauma*, Berkeley, CA: North Atlantic Books.

McGilchrist, I. (2009) *The Master and his Emissary: The Divided Brain and the Making of the Western World*, New Haven, CT and London: Yale University Press.

Merleau-Ponty, M. ([1945] 1962) *Phenomenology of Perception*, Paris: Gallimard; London: Routledge.

Oliver, M. (1992) *New and Selected Poems*, Boston, MA: Beacon Press.

Payne, P., Levine, P.A., and Crane-Godreau, M.A. (2015) "Somatic Experiencing: Using Interoception and Proprioception as Core Elements of Trauma Therapy," *Frontiers in Psychology*, 6: 1–18. Accessed 30 August 2018 at: www.frontiersin.org/article/10.3389/fpsyg.2015.00093

Porges, S.W. (2009) "Reciprocol Influences Between Body and Brain in the Perception and Expression of Affect: A Polyvagal Perspective," in *The Healing Power of Emotion: Affective Neuroscience, Development and Clinical Practice*, D. Fosha, D. Siegel, and M. Soloman (eds.), London and New York: W.W. Norton & Co., pp. 27–54.

Prengel, S. (2016) In conversation with Steven Hoskinson. Relational Implicit, https://relationalimplicit.com/somatic-perspectives/ Accessed 31 August 2018 at: https://relationalimplicit.com/zug/transcripts/Hoskinson-2016-05.pdf, pp.1–10.

Reeves, P. (2003) *Heart Sense: Unlocking your Highest Purpose and Deepest Desires*, Boston, MA: Conari Press.

Reinau, M. (2016) *Love Matters for Psychic Transformation: A Study of Embodied Psychic Transformation in the Context of BodySoul Rhythms*, Sheridan, WY: Fisher King Press.

Ronnberg, A., Martin, K. and Archive for Research in Archetypal Symbolism (2010) *The Book of Symbols: Reflections on Archetypal Images*, Köln: Taschen.

Ryley, N. (1998) *The Forsaken Garden, Four Conversations on the Deep Meaning of Environmental Illness*, Wheaton, IL: Quest Books.

Schore, A.N. (2003) *Affect Dysregulation and Disorders of the Self*, London and New York: W.W. Norton & Co.

Selye, Hans ([1956] 1978) *The Stress of Life*, New York: The McGraw-Hill Companies, Inc.

Siegel, D.J. (2010) *Mindsight: Transform your Brain with the New Science of Kindness*, London: One World Publications.

Stern, D.N. (1985) *The Interpersonal World of the Infant: A View from Psychoanalysis and Developmental Psychology*, London: Karnac.

van der Kolk, B. (2014) *The Body Keeps the Score: Mind, Brain and Body in the Transformation of Trauma*, St Ives, UK: Penguin Random House.

Vanier, J. (n.d.) "Love and Belonging (50 Years at L'Arche with Jean Vanier)". Moses Znaimer & Richard Nielson (Producers). YouTube. Accessed 2 February 2019 at: www.youtube.com/watch?v=vDnfdHQu-rg. Last updated 4 Feb. 2015.

Woodman, M. (1982) *Addiction to Perfection: The Still Unravished Bride*, Toronto: Inner City Books.

Woodman, M. (1985) *The Pregnant Virgin: A Process of Psychological Transformation*, Toronto: Inner City Books.

Woodman, M. (1990) *The Ravaged Bridegroom: Masculinity in Women*, Toronto: Inner City Books.

Woodman, M. and Dickson, E. (1996) *Dancing in the Flames: The Dark Goddess in the Transformation of Consciousness*, Dublin: Gill & MacMillan.

Part II

Neuroscientific Background

Chapter 1

How the Brain Works

A Brief Outline and Discussion of the Neuroscientific Theory That Informs BodyDreaming

My aim in this chapter is to give a very brief overview of how the brain works and an outline of recent developments in neuroscientific theory that have a bearing on BodyDreaming practice. I will explain key terms. However, all terms and concepts touched on in this overview will be reintroduced and elaborated in the chapters that follow. I hope to introduce the terminology of neuroscience sufficiently clearly to enable you to engage with the matter of my book from the beginning, while each chapter will expand and deepen your understanding of particular aspects of neuroscientific research. I also hope this overview and the theoretical introductions to each chapter will enable you to appreciate scientific theory as both *operative* and *embodied*. On the one hand, the theory allows us to understand the neurological and physiological processes operative in an individual that underpin emotions, complexes, and behaviour; on the other, the understanding of neurophysiological processes that theory provides supports the development of therapeutic strategies, responses and techniques designed to release and transform energy trapped in complexes, behavioural patterns, and body symptoms. In subsequent chapters, I will utilize annotated excerpts from BodyDreaming sessions to illustrate the physiological and emotional impact that can result from the *conscious reorientation* of a client's attention to the *regulation* and *homeostasis* of a previously over-activated, distressed system.

Neuroscience opens a window onto the workings of the brain. Since the early 1990s, new technology using fMRIs and PET scans provides us with images that identify which part of the brain 'lights up' in response to particular stimuli. Scans also allow us to determine how the brain processes information by identifying which parts of the brain respond to different situations. This advance in technology has contributed to the transformation of our understanding of trauma and its effects, prompting the DSM V (The Diagnostic Manual of the American Psychiatric Association, edition V) to refine its classification of PTSD (post-traumatic stress disorder) and trauma.[1] In recent years, psychoanalysts and psychiatrists have widened their use of the term *trauma* to include *early relational trauma*. Marcus West points out:

Whilst experience of physical, sexual, or verbal abuse may be clearly traumatic, equally a parent's prolonged unavailability, inconsistency, emotional
bullying or neglect of the child will lead to substantial relational trauma …
This gives rise to powerful defensive responses to the trauma, … the development and incorporation of internal working models which allow the child
to attempt to predict, and therefore have some degree of control over, their
environment.

(West, 2016, p. 27)

These *working models* are embedded in the nervous system and neural pathways
of the child. An understanding of trauma and its imprint on the nervous system, as
well as attachment theory, constitutes the core of BodyDreaming work. But first,
we need to understand the basic structure of the brain and for that I refer back
to the 1960s and a simple map of the *Triune Brain* developed by the American
physician and neuroscientist, Paul D. MacLean. MacLean identified three evolutionary components of the brain corresponding to our development from reptilian
to mammalian creature and then to *homo sapiens*.

It is estimated that the **reptilian brain** (the *basal ganglia*), the component of
the brain that is the most primitive, evolved in reptiles approximately 300 million
years ago. The reptilian brain, or **brain stem**, connects to the spinal cord and is
essential to the life of all land-based vertebrates as it controls the cardiovascular
and respiratory systems, the heart and lungs. The *carry-over* or still operative
effect of the reptilian brain on human behaviour today is evident in the automatic,
instinctual, compulsive quality of many human responses to stimuli.

The **paleo-mammalian** or **midbrain**, also known as the **limbic brain**, sits on
top of the **reptilian brain**. It consists of a number of subcortical components,

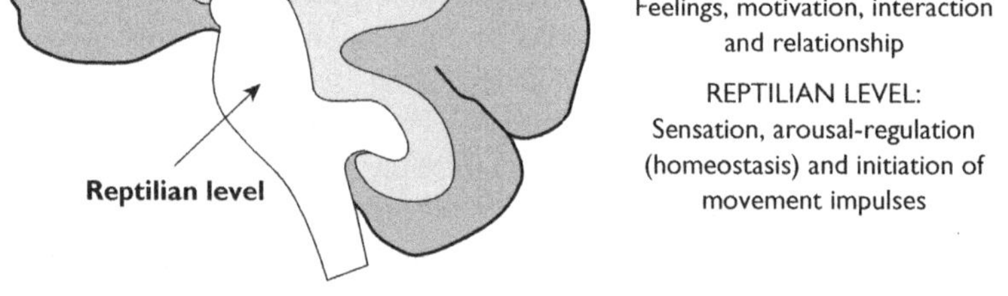

The Paul MacLean Triune Brain Model

Primate level

Limbic, mammalian level

Reptilian level

PRIMATE LEVEL:
Thinking, conscious memory,
symbols, planning and inhibition
of impulses

LIMBIC, MAMMALIAN LEVEL:
Feelings, motivation, interaction
and relationship

REPTILIAN LEVEL:
Sensation, arousal-regulation
(homeostasis) and initiation of
movement impulses

Figure 1.1 The Paul MacLean Triune Brain Model[2]

including the hippocampus, hypothalamus, thalamus, pituitary gland and amygdala, all of which comprise the limbic system. The mid- or limbic brain "is the seat of emotions, monitors danger, [is] the judge of what is pleasurable or scary, the arbiter of what is or is not important for survival purposes" (van der Kolk, 2014, p. 56). With the development of this complex but still primitive part of the cerebral cortex, three forms of behaviour emerged that distinguish mammals from reptiles and herald the beginnings of conscious awareness: (1) maternal care and mother-infant proximity; (2) the capacity for audio communication to maintain mother-infant contact; and (3) play, which promotes affiliation between individuals and group cohesion, as well as the skills and behaviours essential to survival as an adult.

Together the **reptilian** and **limbic** parts of the brain form the **subcortical** *emotional* **brain** and its main function is to ensure survival. If it detects danger it triggers the production of hormones and "[t]he resulting visceral sensations (ranging from mild queasiness to the grip of panic in your chest) will interfere with whatever your mind is currently focused on and get you moving—physically and mentally—in a different direction" (*ibid.*, p. 57).

The **neo-mammalian brain** or **neocortex** is shared by all mammals but is much thicker in humans and is often referred to as the **human brain**. The neocortex is largely made up of four lobes: the occipital lobe, the parietal lobe, the temporal lobe and the large frontal lobe. Each lobe is situated in both the left and right hemispheres of the brain and linked by the corpus callosum, which serves as a bridge between them and helps the brain integrate and consolidate information. The neocortex is the seat of sophisticated perceptual processes, cognition, and behaviours considered to be conscious, rational and voluntary, as opposed to instinctual, automatic and involuntary. We associate the evolution of the human brain with the development of the dominant left hemisphere, which is largely responsible for language, conceptual and rational thinking, and logic. It is only in the second year of life that the frontal lobes begin to develop rapidly. The frontal lobes are "jointly implicated in all 'higher-order' consciousness, the exercise of choices, the assessment of consequences, and the achievement of innovative solutions" (Stevens, 2003, p. 307). They underlie our creativity, culture and the communal and spiritual practices that shape our lives. However, it is of critical importance to recognize that the **frontal lobes** "are, nevertheless, richly connected to the mammalian and reptilian portions of our brains" (*ibid.*, p. 307).[3]

The brain is the response organ that ensures the survival of the species. In the human being, the three sections of the **triune brain** interact, and Daniel Siegel uses the image of a fist to describe the relationship and function of the three parts of the triune brain.[4] If one holds one's hand open and upright one can see the thumb as the main trigger in the brain. This main trigger is known as the **amygdala** and its main function is to signal danger. If we then fold the thumb into the centre of the palm, we are situating the **amygdala** in the centre of the **mid-brain** or **limbic system**, often referred to as the **emotional brain**.

The amygdala, triggered in response to perceived danger, sounds the alarm and activates the older part of the brain, the reptilian brain, home of the instincts; the reptilian brain, in turn, prompts a reflex action: *fight, flight* or *freeze*. Siegel illustrates the neocortex or newer part of the brain by closing the fist to show the knuckles and the fingers—they correspond to the front of the brain. In simple terms, the neocortex may be understood as the CEO or executive capability of the brain. It has the capacity to override the amygdala's response to perceived danger, to discriminate and assess information and modify the autonomic response[5] triggered by the amygdala. The neocortex provides a self-regulatory function. An example is that I go for a walk; there is a coiled rope on the ground, which may alert my system to jump as if the rope were a snake, even though I might not be consciously aware of the rope (i.e., the amygdala is triggered unconsciously and activates an autonomic response, to jump aside). I then look and realize that it isn't a snake but a coiled rope (i.e., the neocortex evaluates the situation and regulates my system to respond appropriately).

An understanding of the **triune brain** enables us to realize that in every interaction with the environment there is a response in the brain. Any response in the brain activates the **Autonomic Nervous System** and manifests in the body's reaction to the brain's interpretation of events—i.e., if it reads 'safety', the system regulates and returns to homeostasis; if it detects 'danger', then it is in *fight, flight* or *freeze* response until the danger passes, at which point it returns to a state of homeostasis. The **autonomic nervous system**, or **ANS**, functions as a system of rhythmic opposites: *expansion—contraction, activation—deactivation*. It is divided into the **sympathetic** and the **parasympathetic** nervous systems. A simple metaphor is perhaps helpful in understanding how the sympathetic and parasympathetic nervous systems function: I am in my car—I have my foot on the accelerator—I increase my speed, which in terms of the body would equate to an *increase* in cardiac output; in other words, the sympathetic nervous system causes an *expansion, activation* or increase in cardiac output. I then take my foot off the accelerator and put it on the brake—my

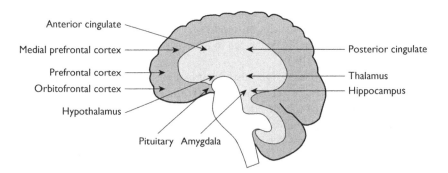

Figure 1.2 Brain Map

speed decreases. This would correspond to a *decrease* in cardiac output and a *contraction* or *deactivation* of energy, effected by the parasympathetic nervous system. The sympathetic and parasympathetic nervous systems comprise the neural circuits that link the brain to the principal organs of the body and are governed by triggers in the amygdala. In general terms, an *inhalation* of breath is an activation, expansion or increase in energy; a *deactivation*, decrease or contraction of energy would be the corresponding *exhalation*. This rhythm—activation/deactivation, expansion/contraction—describes the continuous rhythm of our bodies and of our experience of being alive. However, though continuous, this rhythm is not always regulated, especially when the system is under stress or responding to a perceived threat. When the amygdala receives the message that the environment is not safe, it fires neurons that are directly connected to the **hypothalamus** and the **brain stem**, "recruiting the distress hormone system and the autonomic nervous system to orchestrate a whole-body response" (van der Kolk, 2014, p. 60). "The **hypothalamus-pituitary-adrenal (HPA) axis** manages the interaction between the nervous system and the endocrine systems."[6]

> [The HPA] consists of a complex set of interactions among the *hypothalamus* (responsible for linking the nervous system to the pituitary), the *pituitary gland* (which secretes nine hormones that regulate homeostasis), and the *adrenal glands* (small, conical organs on top of the kidneys that release stress hormones). The HPA axis is critical to regulation: it helps regulate body temperature, digestion, the immune system, tissue function, growth and development, mood, sexuality, and energy usage.
>
> (Heller and LaPierre, 2012, pp. 108–109)

Heller and LaPierre emphasize the importance of understanding the function of the HPA when it comes to trauma, as the wide range of the HPA's functions "affect almost every organ and tissue of the body, including the brain" (*ibid.*). Consequently, the HPA is implicated in neurobiological processes that affect a number of disorders, including post-traumatic stress disorder and other psychiatric and psychological disorders that result from trauma.

Bessel van der Kolk gives a detailed account of how we process information from both the environment and our body states, received through the senses: sight, sound, touch, taste, smell and kinaesthetic awareness. He describes the pathways in the brain that operate as information is received through the senses:

> [Firstly, the information] converges on the **thalamus**, where it is processed and then passed on to the **amygdala** to interpret its emotional significance. This occurs with lightning speed. If a threat is detected the amygdala sends messages to the hypothalamus to secrete stress hormones [cortisol and adrenaline] to defend against the threat.
>
> (van der Kolk, 2014, p. 61)

These chemicals increase heart rate, blood pressure, and speed of breath, preparing the body for *fight* or *flight*. Van der Kolk reminds us that Joseph Le Doux calls this the "low road":

> The second neural pathway, the high road, runs from the **thalamus**, via the **hippocampus** and **anterior cingulate**, to the **prefrontal cortex**, the rational brain, for a conscious and much more refined interpretation. This takes several milliseconds longer ... The prefrontal cortex is wired directly to the limbic brain and can regulate the emotional brain's response, correcting or modulating it. However, PTSD people often lose control over automatic emergency responses ... if the amygdala's message to the frontal cortex is too strong, or the higher areas of the brain too weak.
>
> (van der Kolk, 2014, p. 61)

Van der Kolk refers to the **medial prefrontal cortex (MPFC)** which regulates the emotional brain's response as the "watchtower" because it is "located directly above our eyes ... offering a view of the scene from on high. [It] enables people to observe what's going on, predict what will happen if they take a certain action, and make a conscious decision" (*ibid.*, p. 62). The medial prefrontal cortex "down-regulate[s] the activity of the fear-generating limbic amygdala ... [and releases the self-soothing] ... GABA, gamma-aminobutyric acid ... the 'cortical override' that enables awareness to modulate subcortical fear states" (Siegel, 2010a, pp. 229–230).

We now know that the brain is a self-organizing system and that neural circuits of the brain are wired individually in response to the environmental and social conditions of each life from conception to death. We also know that neural pathways are established in direct correlation to the pattern of attachment behaviour that develops between the mother and infant in the mother–infant dyad, as particular circuits will be activated in the infant's brain according to the quality and valence of mother–infant interaction. The infant's nervous system is set in tandem with the bio-rhythms of the mother's nervous system. The essential task of the first year of life is the creation of a secure attachment bond between the infant and his mother. Allan Schore, in his pioneering work on developmental neuropsychoanalysis, stresses that:

> [s]ecure attachment depends upon the mother's sensitive psychobiological attunement to the infant's dynamically shifting internal states of arousal. Through visual-facial, auditory-prosodic, and tactile-gestural communication, caregiver and infant learn the rhythmic structure of the other and modify their behaviour to fit that structure.
>
> (Schore, 2009, p. 116)

Mother–infant communication is largely non-conscious, right hemisphere to right hemisphere. "The mother appraises the non-verbal expressions of the infant's arousal and affective states, regulates them and communicates them back to the infant" (*ibid.*, p. 117).

The more frequently a neural circuit fires, the more established it becomes and the more easily it will be activated in the future. In other words, according to Hebb's Law, which states that *cells that fire together, wire together*, "when a circuit fires repeatedly, it can become a default setting—the response most likely to occur" (van der Kolk, 2014, p. 56). It is therefore imperative to understand the structure and functioning of the brain in order to appreciate how the early relational *holding* environment into which we are each born impacts the development of the brain and our capacity for emotional security. Schore refers to the mother/caregiver as the emotional regulator in the first year of life:

> [I]n moments of interactive repair, the 'good-enough' caregiver who induces a stress response in her infant through a *mis*attunement, reinvokes in a timely fashion a *re*attunement [emphasis added], a regulation of the infant's negative state. Maternal sensitivity thus acts as an external organiser of the infant's biobehavioural regulation.
>
> (Schore, 2002, p. 13)

The womb provides the initial holding environment in which the autonomic nervous system of the baby is already developing patterns of responsiveness to inner and outer stimuli. In turn, the environment of the baby in the womb is affected both by the mother's own nervous system and the physical environment in which she lives, be that a state of sufficiency and well-being, famine, war, abuse or a stressful working life. The condition of the mother's nervous system will directly impact the autonomic nervous system of the baby in the womb: a positive mothering or holding environment will regulate the autonomic nervous system of the baby in a correspondingly positive way. The converse, of course, is also true: the negative impact of an unsafe, dysregulated *in utero* environment will be encoded in the baby's nervous system. If the post-natal environment continues to be unsafe, the infant will later respond to negative and threatening experiences with whichever default defence strategy is available to him—*fight, flight* or *freeze*—according to the early patterning of his **autonomic nervous system** and **HPA**. The idea that an infant's physiology will reflect the attachment pattern of the early infant–mother relationship is supported by Peter Fonagy's argument that the brain is a "social organ" (cited in Reinau, 2016, p. 208). Reinau quotes Fonagy as saying, "We know that a poorly handled baby develops a more reactive stress response and different biochemical patterns than a well-handled baby", and refers to Fonagy's extensive research into early attachment which shows that "the quality of the baby's early relationship shapes the developing brain and body (neuronal pathways regulating the muscular tension, heart rate, homeostatic balance etc. in the body)" (*ibid.*).

Heller and LaPierre (2012) stress the long-term impact of very early trauma and the dysregulation that results during the early stages of development. Early (including *in utero*) coping strategies become 'wired' into the regulatory system of the new-born:

> This is particularly important to take into account in the case of early trauma where coping strategies have not developed beyond those used by the helpless child. ... In cases of developmental trauma, as neglect and abuse intensify, and as streams of stress hormones signal ongoing danger, the dysregulation of the HPA axis spirals, ... [causing] a tragic dysregulating effect ... [and also depriving] ... the body of the all-important wash of opioids[7] that supports bonding and the feeling that all is well.
>
> (Heller and LaPierre, 2012, p. 109)

An understanding of the *modus operandi* of the autonomic nervous system and HPA axis is fundamental in therapeutic work with early attachment patterns and will be further elaborated in Chapters 4 and 5.

Traditionally we think of the brain as having two sides or hemispheres: the **right hemisphere** and the **left hemisphere**. Neuroscience helps us to understand why it makes more sense to think not in terms of two hemispheres but in terms of *two brains*, each developing on a particular timeline and having its own particular role to play (Schore in conversation with Sieff, 2015, p. 114). The right brain develops first and is responsible for processing every experience during the first eighteen months of the infant's development. Information is received by the amygdala in the right hemisphere, which responds *autonomically*, that is, below the level of consciousness. The information is then transferred to the **right hemisphere's anterior cingulate**[8] and from there connects to the **right hemisphere's orbitofrontal cortex**. Schore reminds us that these regions do not, however, come 'on line' at the same time:

> The amygdala begins a critical period of growth during the last trimester of pregnancy, so it is essentially functioning at birth. The right amygdala is the brain's alarm centre, mediating the fight and flight responses. It is also the first port of call for mediating both the non-verbal facial expression of others, and our own non-verbal bodily states.
>
> (Schore in Sieff, 2015, p. 114)

At the earliest stages of development (pre-natal to eighteen months), the **right brain** operates in a primitive way—information from the external environment is imprinted with a positive or a negative charge depending on whether the situation is registered as nurturing or threatening. The consequent responses are instantaneous and manifest as reflexes.

When the infant is approximately two months old, the **right anterior cingulate** begins to operate, allowing for more complex processing of social emotional information; the right anterior cingulate is responsible for the development of attachment behaviour. At around 10 months, the **right orbitofrontal cortex** begins to develop its capacity to process and make sense of information. It modulates the amygdala's initial response by communicating to the amygdala through the connecting pathways in the **limbic area** and **brain stem**, and consequently plays a critical role in affect regulation. The development and maturation of increasingly complex self-regulatory structures, Schore argues, is a "product of early dynamic object relational environmental interactions" (1994, p. 34). The right orbitofrontal cortex, in the simplest terms, links outer and inner: it links visual, auditory, tactile and olfactory information received from the outer environment with the inner (visceroendocrine or 'gut feeling') environment. It is, therefore, intimately connected with the limbic brain and is consequently often referred to as the highest level of the limbic/emotional brain.

> The right orbitofrontal cortex gives rise to conscious emotions and is capable of much finer-grained (albeit slower) information processing than the earlier developing parts of the brain. It is also the area of the brain that enables us to maintain a sense of continuity and to create an integrated and stable sense of who we are, which in turn forms the platform for self-reflection.
>
> (Schore in Sieff, 2015, p. 115)

By the time the infant is two years old, the orbitofrontal cortex establishes strong bi-directional connections with the limbic system, monitoring, refining and regulating responses and making them more appropriate to the circumstances. The development of a healthy orbitofrontal cortex is, therefore, key to building a *window of tolerance* (Siegel, 1999)—that is, the infant's capacity to tolerate intense emotions without going into either hyper- or hypoarousal (i.e., over-heating or shutting down); intense emotions may be positive, such as excitement, happiness and joy, or negative, such as rage, fear, terror, disgust, shame and despair.[9] The orbitofrontal cortex also determines how flexibly and adaptively we respond to our environment, our interpersonal world; it reads the subjective states of others through subtle facial expressions, as well as other forms of non-verbal communication, and auditory cues such as tone of voice.

> An infant between 3 and 6 months will use sight to gauge his mother's emotional response, then when eye contact is established, both mother and infant implicitly know that the feedback loop between them is closed. The mother's face reflects her infant's reality and aliveness back to him and he learns to be with whatever it is that he is feeling.
>
> (Schore in Sieff, 2015, p. 117)

In the interactive play between mother and infant the mother is helping the infant to expand his *window of tolerance* for intense emotional experiences. Sometimes there is a misattunement and the emotional intensity is too much for the infant. Then the mother needs to turn her gaze from the infant and allow him times of disengagement to recover, taking her cue from him when to re-engage. Inevitably there will be moments of misattunement, when she misreads his signals. The rupture that takes place between them, she can repair by re-regulating his upset. Tronick and other attachment researchers show that "when infants and caregivers are in sync on an emotional level, they are also in sync physically. Babies cannot regulate their own emotional states, much less the changes in heart rate, hormone levels, and the nervous system activity that accompany emotions" (van der Kolk, 2014, p. 112). When a child's emotion is regulated by his attuned caregiver, this is reflected in his physiology—steady heartbeat and breathing, and a low level of stress hormones. In the course of the day there are many disruptions which are reflected in changes in physiology. Equilibrium is restored when the physiology settles again to homeostasis. Tronick's Still Face experiment[10] demonstrates the changes that can occur when the infant is confronted with a disruption of expectations and the subsequent repair work. In their description of Tronick's experiment, Beebe and Lachmann (2002) shift the focus from the infant's sole dependency for regulation on the caregiver, arguing instead for an integration of self- and interactive regulation: "The infant operates in a dyadic system to which both partners actively contribute" (*ibid.*, p. 164). They highlight the organism's own self-regulatory capacities (*ibid.*, p. 160). This is important in the practice of BodyDreaming as we attune to the organism's inherent capacity for regulation and engage in an interactive regulatory process.

Schore states that occasions "of interactive repair that modulate negative emotions are the fundamental building blocks of attachment and its associated emotions" (in Fosha, Siegel and Solomon, 2009, p. 117). He points out that the mother facilitates the growth of connections between the **orbitofrontal cortex** and the **limbic**, **mid brain** and **brain stem subcortical structures** that neurobiologically mediate self-regulatory functions (Schore, 1994, p. 33). Before the orbitofrontal cortex is active (after approximately 10 months) and while it is developing, the role of the higher structures is played by the mother: she is "the child's auxiliary cortex" (*ibid.*, p. 30). Once developed, the **orbitofrontal** lobe is "especially enlarged in the right hemisphere" as the work of growing the connection between the **orbitofrontal cortex** and the **hypothalamus**, for the purpose of regulation of affect, is done through the right hemisphere, the side of the brain that is largely responsible for our emotional life" (*ibid.*, p. 35). The **orbitofrontal cortex** more than any other site in the higher cortex controls the autonomic nervous system because it is in direct communication with the **hypothalamus**, which elicits hormonal changes and "is involved in a number of essential functions … [which include] … a generalized arousal reaction, homeostatic regulation, drive modulation, modulation of ascending excitatory influences, and the suppression of heart rate, behaviour, and aggression" (*ibid.*, p. 41).[11] Thus Schore notes, "the orbitofrontal region [of the cortex] is uniquely involved in social and emotional behaviours, in the regulation of body and motivational states, and in the adjustment or correction of emotional responses. [Consequently] … it is critically involved in attachment processes" (*ibid.*, p. 42). It is also the part of the brain that enables us to maintain a sense of continuity and to create an integrated and stable sense of who we are (Schore in Sieff, 2015, p. 115). In his view, the role of regulation is so important that Schore came to see "attachment theory as primarily a theory of emotional and bodily regulation" (*ibid.*, p. 116). The **frontal lobes** in the **right hemisphere** of the brain are also the seat of empathy and compassion—our ability to feel into another's reality and to read their subjective states through an appraisal of subtle facial expressions and other non-verbal communications (*ibid.*, p. 114). The capacity for empathy is developed through self- and inter-regulation. The infant's otherwise chaotic emotional states are regulated through recognition of the mother's (or other's) feelings and this, in turn, promotes attachment, closeness and affection. Indeed, Schore defines attachment as "the interactive regulation of biological syncronicity between organisms" (2003a, p. 39).

The body, like all known systems in our universe, is a self-regulating system. Both the infant's brain and the mother's brain release oxytocin to promote bonding and pleasure that is life-enhancing for both. Oxytocin, the bonding agent of attachment behaviour, is first released in the mother and infant during labour, which strengthens their sense of smell and consequently their ability to recognize one another.[12] It continues to be passed to the infant through the mother's milk and is also produced in the baby in response to sensory stimuli emanating from the mother—her tone of voice and smiling face, her smell, and skin-on-skin touch, etc. This process promotes the building of trust and social bonding between mother and baby. Regular and consistent contact with the nurturing, attuned mother maintains high levels of oxytocin in the infant and acts as a regulator to reduce levels of stress hormones (e.g., cortisol) in the system.[13]

The production of endorphins in the infant's brain is triggered by positive interactions with the attuned mother or caregiver. Hebb's law applies again here: what fires together, wires together—so the infant learns to associate positive social interactions with feeling good. When the mother/caregiver is attuned to the infant, the infant's brain produces high levels of dopamine, serotonin and noradrenalin/norepinephrine, as it is sometimes referred to:

> When the level of these molecules is sufficient, an infant's growing brain builds more receptors for them, whereas when levels are very low, fewer receptors are created. This difference in the number of receptors is retained in adulthood, and a deficit can increase the risk of psychiatric disorders such as depression or PTSD.
>
> (Schore in Sieff, 2015, p. 118)

The infant is born with the potential to grow nerve cell connections—synapses. Synapses will only fire—and make connections between nerve cells—when they are stimulated. Synapses activated by the environment—in positive interactions between an attuned mother and infant—become established; those that are not atrophy and die. The nature of the early relationship consequently has a growth-enhancing or growth-inhibiting effect on the right brain of the infant and leaves a lasting imprint. The negative impact of trauma, neglect, or insecure attachment behaviour on the part of the mother may affect later stages of brain growth and "prohibit the development of a healthy self-regulation emotional system" (*ibid.*, p. 119). When infants are permanently stressed and the levels of cortisol are chronically high in the system permanent damage to the self-regulatory system of the infant may result. The infant may grow into an adult, "not able to recover quickly from stressful events" (Gerhardt, 2011, p. 87),[14] and too much cortisol at an age when the important connections are being made and pathways established in the frontal cortex of the infant can affect the structure of the brain. "Children who are traumatised early on often have reduced brain volumes in a number of areas, especially the pre-frontal cortex—literally they have smaller brains" (*ibid.*, p. 87).

Memory

There are two kinds of memory: **explicit memory** that is conscious, and **implicit memory** that is relatively unconscious. Both kinds of memory serve separate functions and are mediated by distinct neuro-anatomical brain structures (Levine, 2015, p. 16). Up until the age of approximately 18 months, memory is stored in the **right hemisphere**, and is referred to as **implicit or implicit-only memory**.[15] This is because (1) the **right brain** functions as the encoder and storehouse of non-verbal, body- or sensation-focused perceptions, and (2) because the area of the brain which enables directed, focused attention and is responsible for the encoding of **explicit memory** (the **hippocampus**) has not yet developed. **Implicit memory** describes the way in which the infant stores sensations, smells, tastes, and sounds—the warmth of the milk, his mother's smile, hunger pangs in the belly, the fear of loud noises. Siegel explains how implicit memory primes the infant to expect a particular response—he hears a sound and knows he will soon be fed or that his mother is approaching. This means that memories of early relational or attachment trauma (0 to 18 months) will be held in the right hemisphere as implicit memories. Implicit memories are not subject to recall[16] and, if activated by later events, an implicit memory will remain inaccessible to cognition; the cause of its activation will therefore remain unexplained, lying as it does beyond the reach of the left brain's verbal understanding and analysis, and its capacity to locate the memory in the episodic frame of one's life-story.

> **Implicit memory** stores information that is out of our conscious awareness and verbal experience. Consequently, even though it constantly influences our current functioning, it does not feel like memory to us. It feels more like who we are. Stored in implicit memory are the memory of shapes and forms; the bodily memory of motor skills, habits, and routines; and the memory of our emotional and relational responses.
>
> (Heller and LaPierre, 2012, p. 112)[17]

This means that early trauma is held in **body memory**. An infant can experience an emotional reaction, an activation of the nervous system, the repetition of a behaviour pattern or physical pain but there is no actual event "tagged" to these sensations. **Body memories** create *beliefs*, which Siegel refers to as 'implicit mental models' and Jung might call complexes: "implicit memory can influence our present without our awareness that something from the past is affecting us" (Siegel, 2010b, p. 149).

Although it is assumed "we have extremely limited memory of early preverbal events … 'hidden' memory traces do exist (in the form of procedural memories) as early as the second trimester *in utero* and clearly around the period of birth" (Levine, 2015, p. 94). Levine elaborates further on implicit memories:

> [They] cannot be called up deliberately or accessed as 'dreamy' reminiscences. Instead, they arise as a collage of sensations, emotions, movements and behaviours. Implicit memories appear and disappear surreptitiously, usually far outside the bounds of our conscious awareness. They are primarily organized around emotions and/or skills, or 'procedures'—things that the body does automatically (sometimes called 'action patterns').
>
> (Levine, 2015, p. 21)

Levine reminds us that memories are experienced in the body as physical sensations and distinguishes between *emotional memory* and *procedural memory*. *Emotional memories* are generally triggered by situations in the present in which the emotions and emotional intensity are similar to those of past *procedural memories*, i.e., survival-based actions.

Procedural memory involves movement patterns and is made up of the impulses, movements, and internal body sensations that guide our actions, skills, attractions and repulsions (Levine, 2015, p. 25). "These action programmes include 1) learned motor skills, 2) valences of approach/avoidance, and 3) survival reactions" (*ibid.*, p. 37). Levine points out that procedural memory is critical to therapeutic practice:

> [I]nstinctual survival reactions are the deepest, most compelling and, in times of great stress, generally override the other implicit and explicit memory subtypes... .Indeed, persistent maladaptive procedural and emotional memories form the core mechanism that underlies all traumas, as well as many problematic social and relationship issues.
>
> (Levine, 2015, pp. 37–38)

Peter Levine[18] stresses the importance of accessing the incomplete gesture or failed response of the procedural memory formed at the time of the trauma and creating an opportunity for the *completion* of the earlier failed gesture. This work is key to BodyDreaming and involves the release of energy in order to create new episodic memory which enhances motivation and enables the client to move forward with greater confidence and a sense of inner strength. Once the therapist has "accessed the truncated form of the procedural memory" by recognizing the incomplete gesture or failed response in a movement or sound, she can encourage further sensate exploration of the truncated defensive action as the gesture finds its original intended completion (Levine, 2015, p. 63). This enables the re-establishment of the core regulatory system, greater homeostasis in the nervous system, and a state of relaxed alertness. The traumatic procedural memories, with their maladaptive (incomplete) form, are now repatterned into healthy agency. Working to heal trauma by resolving previously unresolved (i.e., thwarted) procedural memories restores vital self-protective impulses, here and now orientation, coherence, and a confident sense (and expression) of flow (*ibid.*, p. 146). It promotes the emergence of new (updated) emotional and episodic memory.

Childhood patterns of attachment behaviour—secure and insecure—are encoded as procedural memories of approach or avoidance in later, *present time* relationships. Approach or avoidance, attraction or repulsion, are fundamental organismic response tendencies which include the motor acts of stiffening, retracting, and contracting in response to repulsion; and expanding, extending, and reaching in response to attraction. "These movement patterns, of approach and avoidance, form the motivational rudders in our lives" (Levine, 2015, p. 26). They operate below our conscious awareness much of the time, being triggered by procedural memories. Something about that person attracts me; I find I am curious to know more about him. I later realize that something in the way in which he dresses and moves reminds me of someone I cared about in the long distant past. My nervous system is put at ease when prompted by the implicit memory. Alternatively, I may find that I retreat into a constricted, defensive body posture on meeting someone new, only to discover that I was caught in an old complex, revisiting a fear of being bullied, an implicit memory determining my actions and responses.

Explicit memory, however, "depends on the ability to focus attention and integrate elements of an experience into factual or autobiographical representations" (Siegel, 2010b, p. 153). In other words, while *implicit* **(perceptual) memories** are *activated* by a stimulus but not subject to recall, one may start to recall *explicit* **memories** from around the age of two years when the **hippocampus** comes 'on line'. As the hippocampus develops, we begin to create both factual and episodic memories. Because the hippocampus lies in the limbic area of both hemispheres, it affects the right brain and the left brain:

> In the left hemisphere it builds our factual and linguistic knowledge; in the right it organizes the building blocks of our life story according to time and topic. ... We can think of the hippocampus as a master puzzle piece assembler, which draws together the separate pieces of images and sensations of implicit memory into the assembled 'pictures' of factual and autobiographical memory.
>
> (Siegel, 2010b, p. 154)

Siegel discusses how recent research shows that the **hippocampus** shuts off in response to heightened states of emotion, inducing high levels of stress.

"The fight-flight-freeze response floods the body with the hormone cortisol which has been shown to block hippocampal function" (2010b, p. 157). When the hippocampus is disengaged in this way explicit memory is blocked and a simultaneous increase in the amygdala's release of adrenalin intensifies the encoding of implicit memories.[19] Because the human system releases high levels of memory-blocking stress hormones when its survival is at stake, Siegel argues that a blocked hippocampal function may explain many post-traumatic stress disorder (PTSD) symptoms, namely, the eruption "of implicitly encoded traumatic memory fragments ... into our lives years after the event with terrifying power" (*ibid.*, p. 159). And so, Levine reminds us that "conscious explicit memory is only the proverbial tip of the iceberg. It barely hints at the submerged strata of *primal implicit experience* that moves and motivates us in ways that the conscious mind can only begin to imagine" (2015, p. xxii).

Levine insists that the therapist develop a working model of "how trauma becomes inscribed as memory imprints in the body, brain, and mind, as well as in the psyche and soul, ... [otherwise] the healer is sure to lose his way in the labyrinth of cause and effect" (2015, p. xxi). The body and brain and psyche need to be considered as one interconnecting field, and Levine exhorts therapists "to address the sensation body and brain mechanism" that are impacted by trauma. BodyDreaming, while its focus is not necessarily on trauma, takes Levine's recommendation as a given, affirming that we must always and continually register body sensation and the nervous system's response in the here and now of every interaction.

*

Below is a brief explanation of some of the key neuroscientific terms that you will encounter in the following chapters, together with examples of how theoretical knowledge helps the therapist develop effective and particular strategies for intervention when working with trauma clients.

Mirror Neurons—"the brain-to-brain links that give us our capacity for empathy"[20]

The role of **mirror neurons** has been discovered to be central to the development of the infant's capacity for relationship and to psycho-social well-being throughout life, as early developmental processes greatly influence later mental health. Mirror neurons get their name from the way in which they act like mirrors in our brains. They register an action I see being carried out by someone else and my brain responds as if I, too, have performed that action. Not only does the brain mirror an action or *motion* but also the *e-motion* that accompanies the action. We can actually *feel* the emotion that lies behind an action or gesture. In other words, our brains *mirror* and we take in the *whole* action: the facial expression, the tone of voice, the emotion, the gesture and, most importantly, the *intention*[21] behind the gesture. If a mother, for instance, gives a smile to a baby, this will elicit a smile from the baby in return, and a feeling of well-being. Mother and baby share the action and the emotion involved. There is reciprocity. The synapses in the baby's brain fire and, when the mother receives the baby's smile, the synapses in her brain fire in return. Such *mutuality* grows each brain: the brain's capacity is enlarged, and our ability to tolerate new behaviours and emotions increases. When an experience of mutuality is pleasurable, it increases the production of endorphins, which whets the appetite for more such experiences. This neural mechanism is fundamental to the development of intersubjectivity:

> [P]ersonal, body-related experiential knowledge enables our *intentional attunement* [emphasis added] with others, which in turn constitutes a shared ... 'we-centric' space ... [that] ... allows us to ... understand the actions performed by others, and the emotions and sensations they experience.
>
> (Gallese, 2006, p. 53)

For example, the language through which a mother and her new baby communicate consists of "signals produced by the autonomic, involuntary nervous system" in both mother and infant (Basch, 1976, cited in Schore, 2003b, p. 157); mother and baby connect to each other right hemisphere to right hemisphere, allowing *affective information* and early experiences of *tactile and spatial perception* to be encoded directly in the *non-verbal memory* of the baby's right brain. In the *symbiotic* pleasurable state of cradling one's baby and of the baby's being cradled, the homeostatic systems of both adult and infant are linked—the *internal* state of the mother is attuned to the *internal* state of the infant and *vice versa*. It is, then, through the function of the mirror neurons that we learn how to empathize and to attune to our own and another's inner feelings:

> Mirror neurons link what we see from others with what we feel and what we do. ... [O]ur body serves as a kind of antenna enabling us to pick up the sometimes subtle signals from others, shift our bodily state, and then sense these changes in our own body to ... imagine what another person might be feeling.
>
> (Siegel, 2012, p. 11–3)

The role that mirror neurons play in the development of self-understanding and in our capacity for healthy, empathic social interaction highlights the critical importance of a positive connection in the early attachment relationship. Siegel points out that "mirror neurons learn from experience, so they interpret the predicted data from initial data in unique ways based on prior experience" (*ibid.*, p. 42). In the case of unresolved trauma, actions will be interpreted through the lens of vigilance for danger and assault. "Past experiences create patterns of plateaus through which we filter ongoing sensory input to bias our perception" (*ibid.*).

The Polyvagal System

The ventral vagal system links the muscles of the heart and respiratory system directly with the muscles of the social engagement system—the head, neck, shoulders, and face including eyes, ears, jaw, and the vocalization centre of the larynx and pharynx. This means that, if we perceive the environment to be safe, we can use the social engagement system to soothe, and calm the heart and breathing. If we perceive danger, these muscles become ready for action—cry for help, tension in shoulders and arms, the eyes are startled.

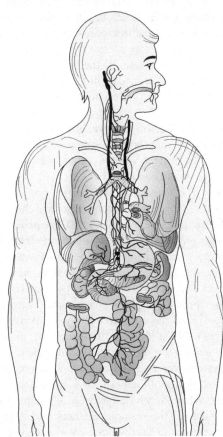

The dorsal vagus is the slowest system to respond to danger and is the last defence when all else fails. It causes immobilization of the system and affects muscles in the intestines and bowel. It slows down the intake of oxygen to the body, affecting many organs and bringing a state of hypoarousal, collapse and freeze. It leads to a sense of numbness, dissociation, separation from oneself.

Figure 1.3 The Vagus Nerve with its Two Branches: Ventral and Dorsal

Polyvagal Theory

Stephen Porges, who developed the **polyvagal theory of emotion** when he was director of the Brain Body Center at the University of Illinois, Department of Psychiatry, provides a thumbnail sketch of his theory in the following words, the implications of which we will explore in the next few pages:[22]

> The first [part of the theory] is the link between the nerves of the face and the nerves that regulate the heart and the lungs. The second is the phylogenetic hierarchy that describes the evolutionary sequence from a primitive unmyelinated[23] vagus related to conservation of metabolic resources, to a sympathetic-adrenal system involved in mobilization strategies, to a myelinated vagus related to

modulating calm bodily states and social engagement behaviours. The hierarchy emphasizes that the newer "circuits" inhibit the older ones.[24] We use the newest circuit to promote calm states, to self-soothe and to engage. When this doesn't work, we use the sympathetic-adrenal system to mobilize for fight and flight behaviours. And when that doesn't work, we use a very old vagal system, the freeze or shutdown system. So the theory states that our physiological responses are hierarchically organized in the way we react to challenge, and the hierarchy of reactions follows the sequence in which the systems evolved.[25]

The **vagus**, known as the **10th cranial nerve**, is the major nerve of the **parasympathetic nervous system**. It may best be imagined as a tube that carries nerve energy from the base of the brain to various parts of the body: the gastrointestinal tract, respiratory tract, heart and abdominal viscera. The **vagus nerve** is known as "the wanderer" because of its many tributaries in the body that connect with particular organs and muscles. It is rooted near the **pons** at the base of the skull and responds to threats by alerting one of its **two distinct prongs or branches**. The two branches of the vagus nerve comprise the newer **ventral vagus**, which affects the heart and respiratory tract and links to the cranial nerves that control facial expression and vocalization; and the older **dorsal vagus**, which affects muscles in the intestines and bowel. Porges proposes that the two branches of the vagus nerve relate to different behavioural strategies—one to social interactions and safe environment (ventral vagus), and the other to adaptive responses to life-threatening situations (dorsal vagus). When threat is first perceived, the **sympathetic nervous system** is alerted and affects the **ventral vagal system** which comprises the **social engagement system**. We use this system to communicate directly with others. It incorporates the muscles of the head, neck, shoulders, eyes, ears and jaws, together with the arms. When the whole system is in a state of arousal, these muscles become ready for action (for example, the neck and shoulder muscles tense, the fists clench, the jaw drops, a startled look enters the eyes). Porges makes the important observation that "the linkage between the nerves that regulate the face and the nerves that regulate the heart and lungs implies that we can use the facial muscles to calm us down. Think about it: when we're stressed or anxious, we use our facial muscles, which include the ears. We eat or drink, we listen to music, and we talk to people to calm down" (Porges in interview with Dykema, 2006).

The **social engagement system** is able to facilitate "rapid engagement and disengagement with the environment and in social situations by regulating the heart without mobilizing the sympathetic nervous system" (Ogden, Minton and Pain, 2006, p. 30). For example, we may talk rapidly one minute and listen intently the next, fine-tuning our facial, vocal and middle ear muscles accordingly (*ibid.*). However, the social engagement system can only *work* when the nervous system perceives the environment to be safe (for example, in an environment which the nervous system has registered unsafe or dangerous one would be unable to behave in a socially engaged manner and might become nervous, agitated, socially *disen*gaged and consequently unable to listen or converse).

An important contribution of polyvagal theory is the recognition of how many psychiatric and psychological disorders which cause feelings of panic, anxiety, and social unease are at base *physiological*; they are triggered by very specific neural circuits and cannot be helped—for example, an individual who becomes nervous and fidgety because the neurophysiology perceives the environment as dangerous cannot *help* his behaviour—and we must not forget that the amygdala may respond to a situation as threatening because an implicit memory has been activated. Polyvagal theory has enhanced our understanding of autonomic nervous system responses and highlighted the need for mental health professionals to employ interventions that will alleviate symptoms of hyper- or hypoarousal and ensure the efficacy of the practitioner's engagement with the client (for example, the adoption of appropriate facial expressions and vocal intonation; the capacity to remain present and connected, attuned to the client in the here and now). In the following chapters you will notice that, when I work with clients, I place particular importance on key social engagement cues such as eye contact, intonation, prosody, pacing, mirroring, movements of the head and neck. When the BodyDreaming therapist orients first herself, then the client, she enlists the social engagement system, which has the effect of stabilizing the system, decreasing or increasing the heart rate, allowing both therapist and client to down-regulate, while inhibiting *primitive* defensive reactions. In this way, the social engagement system "fosters more tranquil, flexibly adaptive overall states" which help the therapist keep levels of arousal and activation within the client's *window of tolerance* (Porges cited in Odgen, Minton and Pain, 2006, p. 30).

Peter Levine explains Porges' polyvagal theory in terms of three "basic neural energy subsystems ... [that] underpin the overall state of the nervous system and correlative behaviors and emotions" (2010, p. 97): the most primitive (the **dorsal parasympathetic** branch of the **vagal nerve**) causes *immobilization* of the system in response to danger; the second (the **sympathetic system**) *mobilizes* the system; and the third (the **social engagement system**) *regulates* "the so-called mammalian or 'smart' vagus nerve, which is neuroanatomically linked to the cranial nerves that mediate facial expression and vocalization ... [animating] ... [t]he unconsciously mediated muscles in throat, face, middle ear, heart and lungs, which together communicate our emotions, both to others and to ourselves" (*ibid.*, p. 98). Levine emphasizes the importance of using the social engagement system as a powerful tool in therapeutic intervention in cases of dysregulation, both hyper- and hypoarousal (*ibid.*, p. 105), to encourage a healthy parasympathetic down regulation. He suggests that, despite attempts (and too often the success) of the ventral vagal and dorsal vagal arousal systems to override the social engagement system, "the power of human contact to help change another's internal physiological state (through face-to-face engagement and appropriate touch) should not be underestimated" (*ibid.*, p. 107). When, in threatening circumstances, the social engagement system is overridden by the ventral vagus system, mobilizing the *fight or flight* response of the **sympathetic nervous system**, the therapist is likely to see in the client emergency reactions:

These 'emergency reactions' (Cannon, 1932) mobilize energy in anticipation of the vigorous activity needed to meet the threat and [which] include both energy-mobilizing and energy-consuming processes: accelerated, deeper respiration in response to the need for more oxygen; increased blood flow to the muscles (Frijda, 1986); decreased blood flow to the cortex; increased vigilance toward the environment; and the suppression of all physical systems not essential for defence.

(Ogden, Minton and Pain, 2006, p. 31)

The client is catapulted outside his or her *window of tolerance* into a state of hyperarousal which maximizes the chance of survival (Levine, 1997). Hyperarousal enhances action and its target in the body is the limbs (Levine, 2010, p. 98). Consequently, when a client is in *sympathetic hyperarousal*, "the therapist can observe a tightening of the muscles in the front of the neck ..., a stiffened posture, a general jumpiness, darting eyes, an increase in heart rate ..., dilation (widening) of the pupils, choppy, rapid breathing and coldness in the hands ..." (*ibid.*, p. 105). When the danger has passed, the hyperarousal may gradually recede to within the *window of tolerance*. If, however, the **ventral vagal** *fight or flight* system has been unsuccessful in assuring safety, the **dorsal** branch of the **vagus nerve** becomes the next line of defence. The **dorsal vagus** (the *un*myelinated vagus), also originating in the brain stem, is the slowest system to respond and is the last defence when all else fails. It slows down the intake of oxygen to the body, bringing the organism into a state of hypoarousal, that is, into a state of *freeze, collapse, immobilization* and *dissociation*.[26] This directly affects the internal organs of the body. "Many functions of the body begin to slow down, leading to a relative decrease in heart rate and respiration and accompanied by a sense of 'numbness,' 'shutting down within the mind,' and separation from the sense of self" (Siegel cited in Ogden, Minton, and Pain, 2006, p. 31). Levine points out that "a person going into shutdown often collapses (as though slumping in the diaphragm) and has fixed or spaced-out eyes, markedly reduced breathing, an abrupt slowing and feebleness of heart rate, and a constriction of the pupils" (Levine, 2010, p. 105). Ogden, however, reminds us that there "seem to be at least three types of immobility defences: (1) the sympathetically mediated freeze response (alert immobility), (2) the parasympathetically mediated feigned death response (floppy immobility), and (3) submissive behaviour" (Ogden, Minton, and Pain, 2006, pp. 93–98; Ogden, 2009, p. 208).

While Porges' **polyvagal theory of emotion** points out that the "hierarchy of reactions follows the sequence in which the systems evolved", Levine speaks of a similar progression that happens in reverse when healing begins. Clients trapped in a *freeze* or shutdown response first need to move out of a state of **immobilization**.[27] Levine recommends that the therapist reaches shutdown clients by first helping them to mobilize their energy:

to become aware of their physiological paralysis and shutdown in a way that normalizes it, and to shift toward (sympathetic) mobilization. The next step is to gently guide a client through the sudden defensive/self-protective activation that underlies the sympathetic state and back to equilibrium, to the here-and-now and a reengagement in life.

(Levine, 2010, p. 106)

The sudden escalation of energy that can accompany coming out of *freeze* and into sympathetic arousal can be overwhelming and the client needs to learn to tolerate such a state of activation. This is accomplished by the therapist's helping the client to slow down, explore the felt sense, the body sense of the experience, get to know the emotions that are triggered in the state of activation, recognize feelings *precisely* "name them to tame them"[28] and eventually discharge any excess energy still active in the sympathetic system. The **social engagement system**, according to Levine, only comes back on line at this point: "An individual who has been able to move out of immobility, and then through sympathetic arousal, begins to experience a restorative and deepening calm. … [A]n urge, even a hunger, for face-to-face contact emerges" (Levine, 2010, p. 106). Consequently, in BodyDreaming sessions, the therapist working with an understanding of the neurophysiological theory outlined above consciously and deliberately enlists the *social engagement*

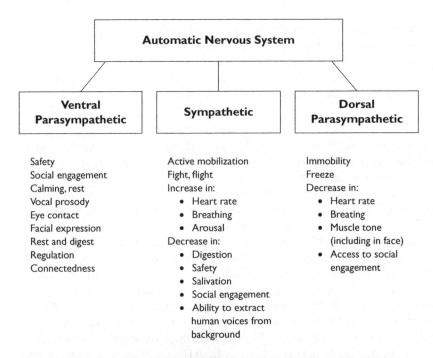

Figure 1.4 Summary of the Actions of Each of the Three Branches of the ANS in Accordance with the Polyvagal Model.

Source: *Nurturing Resilience: Helping Clients Move Forward from Developmental Trauma – An Integrative Somatic Approach*, by Kathy L. Kain and Stephen J. Terrell. Reprinted by permission of North Atlantic Books.

system as a key strategy to free the client's system from the vice grip of activation. This she does, as you will see illustrated in the following chapters, by orienting the client outward, by mirroring, and through the use of pace, prosody and *free-association conversation* (see below, Chapter 5).

Neuroception

Neuroception is the term Stephen Porges uses for those neural circuits that function as a detection system by reading the environment to determine whether specific situations and people are safe, dangerous, or life threatening (2009, pp. 27–54).

We receive information from the environment through neural transmitters and nerve ends: the **Lamina I** and the **vagal nerve** take in information and direct the flow of energy through the spine and **vagal** subsystems to the **brain stem**. Neuroception may flag a particular person as threatening because of something about his or her voice that triggers a past **sense-implicit memory**. It explains why a baby might coo at a caregiver but cry at the sight of another familiar adult or recoil from the hug of a stranger. As Siegel explains:

> Neuroceptive evaluation involves prefrontal, limbic, and brainstem processes and is shaped by ongoing appraisal of the significance of an event and the reference to historical events of a similar type. … [We] filter input from the world in a particular way and then make a specific action or interpretation [according to past experience of what is] more likely to occur.
>
> (Siegel, 2010a, pp. 21–22)

Porges argues that faulty neuroception lies "at the root of several psychiatric disorders, including autism, schizophrenia, anxiety disorders, depression, and Reactive Attachment Disorder" (2004, pp. 19–24). If, however, we perceive the environment to be safe, our social engagement system inhibits the more primitive limbic and brain stem structures that are responsible for activation of a *fight* or *flight* response to perceived danger. Likewise, the social engagement system of the caregiver may be utilized to regulate the neuroceptive evaluation of the baby: the mother can calm the baby and reduce its level of activation by the tone of her voice, soothing the baby's anxiety by affirming, "Everything is alright. That big noise is the sound of the oil delivery truck." Siegel's observation that "[p]erceived danger removes us—shuts down our options, and limits presence" emphasizes how the essential first step for the therapist is to know her "own tendencies of neuroceptive evaluation" (2010a, p. 22) so that she may remain present to the client; the second step returns us to the heart of BodyDreaming practice, as it involves the development of therapeutic interventions that teach the client "inner ways of sensing the world" in order that he or she may remain "present with mindfulness" (*ibid.*, p. 23) to himself/herself and to others.

Hoskinson utilizes our capacity for **neuroception** as a resource in the practice he calls **orienting**: allowing our attention to be drawn toward something in our surroundings that attracts it.[29] By orienting to the external environment, and creating positive experiences, our defensive strategies of fight, flight or freeze are not required and the vagal brake is applied. We are brought into our immediate response to the 'here and now' and away from the tendency to be pulled into the internal sensations, emotions, images of the trauma vortex. The social engagement system comes on line, which "inhibits the more primitive limbic and brain stem structures that control flight and fight" (Levine, 2010, p. 99).

Perception

We develop **perceptions** of ourselves and the world when we connect our feelings and physical sensations to our conscious awareness. Perception provides the brain with a comprehensive map of the body which enables us to construct a sense of ourselves and develops our ability to interact with and be effective in the world. The three basic forms of **perception** are as follows:

Interoception concerns our sense of the body's *internal stimuli* experienced, for example, as pain, temperature, itch, touch, activation of the nervous system, heartbeat, pulse, sweaty hands, tingling (Siegel, 2010a, p. 39). Our perception of the state of the *interior* of our bodies is received via signals passed from the vagus nerve, the heart and lungs, the gut, the muscles and facial expressions, through the spinal cord to the **brain stem** and the **hypothalamus** in the **limbic region of the brain**. This "bodily data shapes our state of reactivity or receptivity via the brainstem mechanisms and alters our hormonal milieu via the hypothalamus" (*ibid.*, p. 39). The **posterior insula** moves the information upward through the **insula**, an area of the cortex that registers bodily states but does not yet relate them to consciousness until it reaches the **anterior insula** in the **ventrolateral prefrontal cortex**, a fundamental part of the middle prefrontal area. "It is the anterior insula that is invariably activated when people have awareness of the internal state of their body—the important process of our sixth sense, called *interoception*" (*ibid.*, p. 40). The information is then conveyed at great speed to the **anterior cingulate**, also part of the middle prefrontal area, whose role involves the self-organizational processes. Siegel makes the important observation, central to the therapeutic practice of BodyDreaming, that "awareness of the body's state influences how we organize our lives. Knowing your body strengthens your mind" (*ibid.*). He attributes to interoception the capacity for empathy: "as we are open to receiving information pertaining to our bodily state (interoception), we can become conscious of the other's feelings through what we are feeling in ourselves" (Siegel in conversation with Sieff, 2015, p. 150). And van der Kolk (2014) argues that *agency* has its roots in interoception:

> Agency starts with ... interoception, our awareness of our subtle sensory, body-based feelings: the greater that awareness, the greater the potential to control our lives. ... If you have a comfortable connection with your inner

sensations—if you can trust them to give you accurate information—you will feel in charge of your body, your feelings, and your self.

(van der Kolk, 2014, pp. 95–96)

Exteroception describes the body's sense of the external world, received through the sensory nerves of the five senses. There are two aspects to this process: "the physical act of sensing and the individual's perception of the sensory input" (Ogden, Minton, and Pain, 2006, p. 17).

Proprioception concerns the body's sense of its location in space; it is provided by "special sensory receptors in the joints that signal the position of all the parts of the body in relation to gravity" (Levine, 2010, p. 299). Under the broader heading of **proprioception**, Levine also includes **kinaesthesia**, the sense of the degree of tension in the muscles, and **visceral sensation**, which arises through receptors in the gut—the enteric nervous system (*ibid.*).

The most intimate sense we have of ourselves is through proprioception, kinaesthesia and visceral sensation. … Without the visceral sense we literally are without the vital feelings that let us know we are alive; it's our guts that allow us to perceive our deepest needs and longings.

(Levine, 2010, pp. 299–300)

In his preface to *The Phenomenology of Perception*, Merleau-Ponty writes that phenomenology concerns the study of essences (in this work, the essence of perception); it seeks to understand the human being and the world from the starting point of their *facticity*, and is a philosophy "for which the world is always 'already there' before reflection begins—as an inalienable presence; and all its efforts are concentrated upon re-achieving a direct and primitive contact with the world" (1962, p. vii). David Abram, in *The Spell of the Sensuous*, emphasizes Merleau-Ponty's contention that *participation* is a defining attribute of *perception*:

By asserting that perception … is inherently participatory, we mean that perception always involves, at its most intimate level, the experience of an active interplay, or coupling, between the perceiving body and that which it … perceives.

(Abram, 1997, p. 57)

Abram describes perception as an experience of *reciprocity* or "on-going interchange between my body and the entities that surround it … a sort of silent conversation that I carry on with things … that unfolds far below my verbal awareness" (*ibid.*, pp. 52–53). He argues:

[t]o the sensing body *all* phenomena are animate, actively soliciting the participation of our senses, or else withdrawing from our focus and repelling our

involvement. ... Each thing, each phenomenon, has the power to reach us and to influence us.

(Abram, 1997, p. 81)

These ideas are also central to the work of Bonnie Bainbridge Cohen (founder of Body Mind Centering) who writes, in *Sensing, Feeling and Action: The Experiential Anatomy of Body Mind Centering*: "Perception is about how we relate to what we are sensing. Perception is about relationship—to ourselves, others, the Earth, and the Universe" (1993, p. 114). She reminds us that nerves myelinate in order of their importance and points out how *perception as relationship to what we are sensing* begins *in utero*, affecting the pre-natal development of the nervous system: "The vestibular nerves begin to myelinate *in utero* by registering the movement of the foetus and its environment (mother). ... [T]hey perform the first essential function for survival" (*ibid.*). In BodyDreaming, we set the scene to enable greater homeostasis in the system and then wait for the organism's self-regulating healing impulse (often in the form of a gesture or image) to point the way forward. An impulse for new life is commonly felt as an impulse to movement—an *inner* sensation resulting in an outward image resonating in the sensing, moving body.

Eugene Gendlin, who developed **Focusing** and explored *felt sense experience* in his work (see below), argues that

Merleau-Ponty rescued the body from being considered merely as one *sensed* thing among other sensed things (as it still is in physiology). For him the body, sensing from inside, is an internal-external orienting center of perception, not just perceived, but perceiving. ... [T]he body is not just an orienting center *of perceiving*, not only a center *of motions*, a [*sic*] but also of *acting and speaking in situations*. ... We sense our bodies not as elaborated perceptions but as the body sense of our situations, the interactional whole-body by which we orient and know that we are doing that.

(Gendlin, 1992, pp. 5–8)

Gendlin postulates that *body sense* provides us with a vast amount of environmental information whether we are conscious of it or not, and that it can "move [us] in new ways" (1992, p. 6). He invites us to consider *body sense knowing, body sense thinking, body sense acting* as modes of perception that serve as a means to expand consciousness and open us to the great unconscious or, in Jung's terms, "the collective unconscious that represents a deeper stratum of the psyche"(Jung, 1943, par. 944).[30] Gendlin argues that "[t]he body senses the *whole* situation, and it urges, it implicitly shapes our next action. It senses itself living-in its whole context—the situation ... [it] can think beyond anything ever formulated before ... it senses on the edge of human thinking" (1992, pp. 2–7).

In the practice of BodyDreaming, both client and therapist may have the experience of being brought to the *edge of our thinking* through the sensing body. Sometimes the body takes us where the rational mind cannot and we experience a *body sense consciousness* that expands to include the sensing world around us. I am reminded of Jung's assertion: "[A]t bottom, the psyche is simply 'world'" (1949, par. 291).

Felt Sense

The term **felt sense** was coined by Eugene Gendlin to describe a particular way of experiencing the world:

> A *felt sense* is not a mental experience but a physical one. *Physical.* A bodily awareness of a situation or person or event. An internal aura that encompasses everything you feel and know about the given subject at a given time—encompasses it and communicates it to you all at once rather than detail by detail.
>
> (Gendlin, 1981, p. 32)

To be aware of the felt sense, the embodied, somatic sense of an experience, serves as a defence when dealing with trauma and protects us from over-activation, overwhelm and dissociation. It keeps us in the present moment as we pay attention to how our body is responding to a particular event, person or situation, by slowing down the autonomic nervous system, cultivating "awareness of sensations (e.g., tingling, buzzing, heaviness, temperature changes) and micro-movements (e.g., trembling and minuscule changes in muscular tension) as they fluctuate in texture, quality, and intensity" (Ogden, Minton, and Pain, 2006, p. 253). This is why Levine likens the felt sense experience to the shield which Perseus uses to defend himself in his confrontation with Medusa. Instead of being *turned to stone*, overwhelmed by the archetypal force of Medusa's power (in other words, the immobilizing power of trauma), Perseus is able to remain present and conscious, defeating Medusa by confronting her *in*directly, through her image reflected in his shield. Our internal body sensations, or felt sense,

> serve as a portal through which we find the symptoms, or reflections of trauma. In directing our attention to these internal body sensations, rather than attacking the trauma head-on, we can unbind and free the energies that have been held in check.
>
> (Levine, 1997, pp. 65–66)

In this way, we are less likely to be *turned into stone*, or thrown into a dissociative *freeze* by the reactivation of past trauma.

The felt sense experience encompasses our awareness of our internal physical, emotional, and mental states—in other words, the *inner* field—at the same time as it encompasses our response to the *outer* field, current situation, or environment. For example, in the therapeutic setting the client is aware of being witnessed by the therapist at the same time as she reports her felt sense of a past experience. The therapist's active listening, engaged presence, mirroring words and gestures serve to amplify, strengthen, and, most importantly, *validate* the felt sense of the client's experience which keeps her present in the here-and-now, safe in her body and in the healing container of the therapeutic *temenos*.[31] Felt sense process strengthens the ability to separate emotions, thoughts and beliefs from underlying sensations, increasing the capacity to tolerate overwhelming states such as terror, rage and helplessness.

Heller and LaPierre speak of the felt sense as the coming together of:

> (1) the body's direct sensory and emotional responses to internal and external events, (2) the mind's attention to and synthesis of the information gathered by the senses, and (3) the level of congruence between these channels of experience and their integration to form the awareness of a particular state of being, a situation, or a problem.
>
> (Heller and LaPierre, 2012, p. 270)

Focus on the felt sense may slowly bring awareness to formerly inexplicable and intangible sensations and shades of memory, making present and manageable in the context of the present the ghostly reflections of past trauma. It engages both hemispheres of the brain in the search for language (metaphor) to match a sensation, a process which gives rise to a tension that, Gendlin suggests, is essentially creative, enabling a shift of energy both in the body and in the emotional (limbic) and cognitive (neocortex) areas of the brain. Heller and LaPierre describe felt sense as an integration of body, mind and psyche:

> On the somatic level, to access the felt sense is to retrieve the knowledge and wisdom implicit in bodily experience. On the level of the mind, it is a process of developing a capacity for sustained, focused attention that supports relaxed, non-judgemental awareness so that internal processes, both psychological and physiological, can be truly heard and tended to.
>
> (Heller and LaPierre, 2012, p. 270)

An inherent characteristic of felt sense is its power to change, that is, to integrate and regulate; this characteristic prompts a healing process. According to Levine,

> The felt sense helps people feel more natural – more grounded, more at home in their bodies. It can enhance our sense of balance and coordination. It improves memory and provides us deeper access to the subtle instinctual impulses that guide the healing of trauma. It increases creativity. It is from the felt sense that we experience well-being, peace, and connectedness. It is how we experience the "self."
>
> (1997, p. 72)

Learning to pay attention to the felt sense experience consequently increases our capacity for self-regulation and for calming arousal, as it strengthens the integrative and meaning-making circuits of the brain, and helps build a resilient sense of self-hood grounded in a newly realized, embodied connection to body, mind and soul.

Attunement

Siegel describes **attunement** as "the act of focusing on another person (or ourselves) to bring into our awareness the internal state of the other in inter-personal attunement (or the self, in intrapersonal attunement)" (2010a, p. 54). Ideally, the mother/primary caregiver who is accurately **attuned** to the needs of the infant responds appropriately to the infant's need for stimulation as well as for disengagement. The attuned caregiver is able to *repair* any regulatory rup-tures or misattunements that might occur either in the inner world of the infant or in the relationship between infant and caregiver. If the caregiver's capacity for attunement and reattunement is consistent and accurate, the quality of the attachment relationship between caregiver and infant will be positive, laying the ground for successful interpersonal relationships in the future. Positive or successful attunement necessitates and supports an open attitude to the inner world—that of ourselves and that of others. If we are attuned to another, an interpersonal resonance is created that allows each person to feel heard, seen, and felt by the other: two subjective inner worlds become joined and each person experiences a sense of *we*, often referred to as ***intersubjectivity***. When an experience of intersubjectivity is one of respect and care, we speak of **inter-personal attunement**; a positive interpersonal attunement between mother/caregiver and infant supports the development, in the infant, of an embodied sense of secure attachment to himself which, in turn, provides the basis for positive interpersonal relationships with others and the world in the future. Positive interpersonal attunement enables compassion.

Siegel explains the neurophysiology of **attunement** in the following words:

> With attunement, we focus on signals from others and embed this flow of energy and information from their internal state deeply into our nervous sys-tem. The key issue is that the antennae of how we perceive are not limited to the five senses we use to see the physical world. ... Instead, taking in the inner world of another person is a process that drives information downward, beneath our cortex, beneath initial awareness, and its outcome is embedded subcortically ... The signals we perceive from our own body, brainstem, and limbic zones, these subcortical areas, are the access we have to 'know' anoth-er's world. If the ... mirror neurons are our receiver, then our subcortical areas are the amplifier.
>
> (Siegel, 2010a, p. 38)

Sometimes information about another person is picked up unintentionally, at other times because we focus attention on the other person's signals and read their body language to get a sense of 'where they are coming from'. Siegel makes the point, which I think is critical for BodyDreaming work, that "if we fail to be open to our own subcortical communication from inside ourselves we'll miss out on being aware of the outcome of attunement" (*ibid.*, p. 39). To remain *open* in the clinical setting entails, in Siegel's view, the willingness "to say 'I don't know' and 'tell me more'" (*ibid.*, p. 43). Consequently, awareness (through interoception) of one's own internal states and inner 'blocks' that may inhibit one's capacity to remain open is essential if one is to attune to another. Should the therapist have a narrow *window of tolerance*, be triggered by something or tend to be reactive rather than receptive, attunement cannot happen and resonance with the client will not occur. As you will see in the following chapters, BodyDreaming offers us the possibility of regulating our responses and becoming increasingly conscious of what shuts off, or can open up, our "resonance circuitry", as Siegel calls the subcortical shifts that underpin attunement (2012, pp. 23–25).

To attune to *ourselves*, we need to take time to reflect on our inner experience. "[T]his creates an internal resonance in which our observing circuitry aligns with our experiencing self and we have an open, mindful *state* of *awareness* … a deep sense of internal *integration*" (Siegel, 2012, pp. 23–1 to 23–2). Internal attunement enables and reinforces interpersonal attunement, and *vice versa*; it also has an impact on our neurophysiology and a healing effect on the nervous system:

> The more we focus our attention toward bodily sensations within our subjective experience in awareness, the more we activate the physical correlate of insula activation and subsequent growth … and the more interoception and insula activation, the more capacity we'll have for attuning to others and being empathic toward their experience.
>
> (Siegel, 2010a, p. 46)

When we focus our attention, there occurs an increase in specific neural firing patterns (*ibid.*); when we intentionally engage our capacity for interoception, connecting inner feelings, states and sensations with our conscious awareness, homeostasis and integration of the nervous system occur. The flow of energy, or *feedback*, between different levels of the brain, subcortical and cortical, when we attune to ourselves or another, is bidirectional. Consequently, our ability to maintain awareness of the felt sense or embodied experience (see below) activated as a result of a *positive* attunement exerts a correspondingly positive influence on emotional and cognitive processing, and *vice versa*. "To open ourselves to compassionate connection with others, we … actively cultivate a compassionate attunement to ourselves" (*ibid.*). To know others in any depth necessitates and, at the same time, facilitates, our knowing ourselves as deeply as possible.

Pendulation

In BodyDreaming, the therapist accesses the self-regulatory capacity of the body to facilitate a return to a natural homeostasis when dealing with activation in the system caused by implicit or explicit trauma. We touch into the arousal and then direct the client's attention back toward a regulating resource, a shift that brings with it a palpable sense of soothing and settling. We use felt sense awareness of sensations and interoception to track experience. The continuous backward and forward movement between the two positions—arousal and resource—begins to find its own rhythm, the innate rhythm of the client's particular organism, which may be dysregulated due to trauma. The nervous system starts to reset, building confidence in the knowledge that the movement is constant between the two opposites—we are not confined to only one end of the spectrum. Homeostasis implies a movement, a dance, not rigidity. "Levine calls this process **pendulation**. In this way patients are helped to gradually expand their window of tolerance" (van der Kolk, 2014, p. 218).

Levine uses the term pendulation to describe:

> [t]he body's natural restorative rhythm of contraction and expansion. ... [It] is the primal rhythm expressed as movement from constriction to expansion— and back to contraction, but gradually opening to more expansion. It is an involuntary, internal rocking back and forth between these two polarities. It softens the edge of difficult sensations such as fear and pain. The importance of the human ability to move through 'bad' and difficult sensations, opening to those of expansion and 'goodness,' cannot be overstated: it is pivotal for the healing of trauma ... it is vital for the client to know this rhythm ... no matter how bad you feel in the contraction phase, expansion will inevitably follow. ... This vital awareness lets people learn that whatever they are feeling will change.
>
> (Levine, 2010, p. 79–80)

Titration

Levine uses the term **titration** to convey the approach to renegotiating trauma as a gradual, step-by-step process" (2010, p. 82). Titration is a word borrowed from chemistry, according to Heller and LaPierre:

> When the contents of two vessels—one holding acid, one a base—are poured together, all at once, into a third vessel, an explosion will result. However, if the two solutions are combined drop by drop, the discharge will be very small and gradually the two substances will neutralize each other. This analogy communicates the importance of working with highly charged emotional material one small, manageable step at a time. This measured approach helps avoid catharsis— the explosion—and facilitates the integration of the highly charged affect.
>
> (Heller and LaPierre, 2012, p. 230)

Levine advocates that therapists working with trauma must "neutralize" the sensations of "intense energy" and "primal rage" (2010, p. 83). He claims that at the time of the trauma a healing vortex is created to balance the force of the trauma vortex and the work of oscillating between these two opposing energies brings out the renegotiation of trauma:

> By moving between these vortices, we release the tightly bound energies at their cores—as if they were being unwound. We move toward their centres and their energies are released; the vortices break up, dissolve, and are integrated back into the mainstream. This is renegotiation.
>
> (Levine, 1997, p. 199)

> In slowing down the process, we are titrating. In consciously encouraging clients to shift attention back to the body and away from the narrative, we are pendulating. **Pendulation** is used simultaneously with **titration** to support the nervous system's capacity to integrate highly charged affects in a way that brings increasing self-regulation.
>
> (Heller and LaPierre, 2012, p. 232)

Fechner—Just Noticeable Difference

When, in BodyDreaming work, we practice *titration* to regulate highly charged emotional material, we focus on bringing about greater homeostasis in the system, moving between the opposites of activation–deactivation, stability–instability. In the process, a *Just Noticeable Difference* makes *all* the difference. Fechner[32] highlights the pleasure one experiences when one's system is harmoniously balanced. Consequently, a *Just Noticeable Difference* comes to serve as a motivation for change, accompanied as it is by a sense of pleasure. In today's terms, we might refer to a greater ease, flow and coherence in the system, which we notice and on which we focus our awareness. Awareness of the *Just Noticeable Difference* and its positive effect on the system helps achieve a state of relative stability in the moment and create new neural pathways.

Top-down and Bottom-up Processing

Top-down and *bottom-up* processing describes the two ways in which we can work to reduce stress and hyperarousal in the system. When we work *top-down*, we work "via modulating messages from the medial prefrontal cortex" (van der Kolk, 2014, p. 62), that is, we use a more cognitive approach, often serving as *auxiliary cortex*[33] for the client; this approach supports the limbic system to soothe the nervous system and calm high arousal. When we work *bottom-up*, we do the opposite, using a body-focused approach. Ogden, Minton, and Pain remind us that these two approaches "represent two directions of information flow, and their interplay holds significant implications for the occurrence and treatment of trauma" (2006,

p. 23). BodyDreaming therapists need to be finely attuned to the body and to work at the body's pace. The appropriate use of a *top-down* or *bottom-up* approach, or sometimes a carefully monitored alternation between the two, will depend upon the individual needs of each client. While a *top-down approach* often helps a client to understand and distance herself from past trauma, the therapist needs to be fully aware that a *bottom-up approach* may trigger a trauma response in the client who continues to feel radically unsafe inside her own body.

*

Notes

1   [W]hilst in 1980, in DSM III, PTSD was diagnosed as for an anxiety disorder, by 2013, in DSM IV, it was recognized in its own right as a trauma and stress-related disorder. In fact, DSM V represents a marked shift in the acknowledgement of the significance of trauma underlying many psychiatric syndromes.

(West, 2016, p. 40)

2   From Levine, 2010, reprinted by permission of the publisher.

3   Stevens reminds us: Jung anticipated by many years MacLean's hypothesis that the brain bears functional regions of ancient phylogeny in the midbrain and brain stem, and he made the surprising suggestion that animals in dreams represent activity in these regions, the 'lower' the animal on the phylogenetic scale the more primitive the region represented: 'with the snake the psychic rapport that can be established with practically all warm-blooded animals comes to an end ... [T]he Gnostics identified the serpent with the spinal cord and the medulla. These are synonymous with the reflex functions.'

(Stevens, 2003, p. 312)

4   This demonstration may be viewed on YouTube (Siegel, n.d.).
5   *Autonomic* describes something happening below the level of consciousness, something of which I am not aware that 'happens' to me before I am able to respond consciously.

6   Hans Selye, MD, PhD, first described the stress response in the 1950s. ... [He] developed the theory that stress is a major cause of disease because of the long-term hormonal changes stress causes in the body ... When there has been trauma, stress levels are chronically high and the body loses its capacity to adapt or recover, leading to adrenal fatigue and exhaustion ... Selye also found that the effects of stress depend not only on the magnitude and duration of the stressor, but also on the strategies individuals adopt to cope with it. ... This is particularly important to take into account in cases of early developmental trauma, where coping strategies often have not developed beyond those used by a helpless child.

(Heller and LaPierre, 2012, p. 108)

7   Opioids are naturally produced by the body. They are opiate-like substances that "modulate our reactions to painful stimuli ... and are involved in mood control". (Dubuc, n.d.).
8   The *anterior cingulate* [region of the brain] is also considered limbic and has a direct role in governing *attention*, registering bodily states, influencing *emotion*

regulation and participating in *social cognition* ... The limbic [area also serves] to appraise the *meaning* of incoming perceptions of events. This evaluative process shapes how we feel, determining if something is important and worth paying *attention* to—and so this limbic *appraisal* shapes how we orient our attention to something and then further direct attention.

(Siegel, 2012, pp. 13–2 to 13–3)

9   Ogden, Minton and Pain (2006) employ Daniel Siegel's use of the image of a *window of tolerance* to describe the cycles of activation and deactivation particular to each individual. Some individuals may live in a state of constant vigilance even though the perceived danger, trauma or adverse physical circumstance causing their systems to become *activated* or *aroused* may be in the past or may not seem to be critical. One person's system may be prone to *chaos* and so becomes *stuck* in a hyperaroused state while another's, prone to rigidity, may be caught in a state of hypoarousal, or *immobility*. The state of deactivation, or *freeze*, is phylogenetically older than the state of activation; it served as a survival strategy, an example of which is the possum that plays dead when threatened by a predator in anticipation that the predator will become bored or rest from the chase, enabling the possum to escape. The two extremes, hyper- and hypoarousal (over-heating and shutting down or *freeze*) are at either end of a continuum and an individual's *window of tolerance* operates between them. They represent the default position when an individual's nervous system feels under threat; one person's default position may be *fight* or *flight* while that of another might be *freeze* (pp. 26–29).

10 Beebe and Lachmann (2002) describe Tronick's Still Face experiment as follows:

> Tronick (1989) offers experimental evidence that the nature of interactive regulation is associated with the adaptiveness of the self-regulation. Infants were subjected to the stress of the 'still-face' experiment, where the mother remained oriented and looking but became completely immobile and unresponsive. In those dyads where interactive regulation was going well, the infant's self-regulation capacity, as measured in the still face situation, was more adaptive and vice versa. In the still-face experiment, those infants continued to signal their mother rather than turn to self-comforting, withdrawal, or disorganized scanning.
>
> (Beebe and Lachmann, 2002, p. 159)

11 Both **sympathetic** and **parasympathetic** responses are triggered in the **limbic orbital cortex** but in different sites.

12   Yet a lifetime opportunity for bonding and love is not lost if this initial window is missed. Beyond birth, mother continues to produce elevated levels of oxytocin as a consequence of nursing and holding her infant, and the levels are based on the amount of such contact. This hormonal condition provides a sense of calm and well being. Oxytocin levels are higher in mothers who exclusively breastfeed than in those who use supplementary bottles. Under the early influence of oxytocin, nerve junctions in certain areas of mother's brain actually undergo reorganization, thereby making her maternal behaviors 'hard-wired.'

(Palmer, 2013)

13   Multiple psychology studies have demonstrated that, depending on the practices of the parents, the resulting high or low level of oxytocin will control the permanent organization of the stress-handling portion of the baby's brain—promoting lasting "securely attached" or "insecure" characteristics in the adolescent and adult.

(Palmer, 2013)

14   Another aspect of too much cortisol early on is that it can have a knock-on effect on other biochemical systems – such as the soothing system which is based on the neurotransmitter serotonin. When this system is not in good shape, the baby can grow up with problems in staying calm under stress, and become prone to impulsive outbursts and aggression. Low serotonin levels are part of the picture of mood and anxiety disorders, sleep disturbance and aggression on into adulthood.

(Gerhardt, 2011, p. 86)

15 Implicit memory occurs throughout an individual's lifetime; however, in the first 18 months of life there is *only* the registering of perceptual memory at an implicit level.

16 Siegel explains how implicit memory is something "quite different from the idea of 'unconscious memory,' which implies something buried, inaccessible, or 'repressed' and kept from everyday awareness. A reactivated implicit memory is fully conscious. It just lacks the sensation of recall" (2010b, pp. 151–152).

17   Because implicit memory is non-conceptual and non-linguistic, it is difficult to investigate its content with verbal methods. Techniques that use a bottom-up approach and make room for empathic resonance are better suited to explore experiences encoded in implicit memory... Most authors who address issues of somatization agree that they are rooted in failure of infant-caregiver attunement and that these failures are imprinted in implicit memory.

(Heller and LaPierre, 2012, p. 112)

18 Peter Levine is founder of Somatic Experiencing—a somatic approach to working with trauma, which is one of the core practices in a BodyDreaming approach. See introductory chapter, 'A Note to the Reader', this volume, p. 23.

19 "High levels of adrenaline act to sear into implicit memory traces of the original traumatic experience—the feeling of terror, the perceptual details, the behavioural reactions characteristic of fight-flight-freeze, and any bodily sensations of pain that were suffered" (Siegel, 2010b, p. 157).

20 van der Kolk, 2014, p. 111.

21   Mirror neurons map out intentional states in others and they also prepare us to imitate intentional acts... We take in what we see expressed in the often *nonverbal* signals of others. ... When we see someone with tears on his face, our own *resonance* with those tears brings a heavy feeling in our chest and perhaps tears to our own face. Sensing these shifts in our own bodily state are [*sic*] used by the middle prefrontal area [of the brain] to ascertain first 'how am I feeling in my body' and then 'what do I feel *emotionally*?'

(Siegel, 2012, p. 19–23)

22 Stephen Porges explains Polyvagal Theory in his interview with PsychAlive.org (Porges, n.d.).

23 *Myelination* is a term in anatomy that is defined as the process of forming a *myelin sheath* around a nerve to allow nerve impulses to move more quickly. ("Myelination", Your Dictionary, accessed 26 August 2018: at http://www.yourdictionary.com/myelination.)

24 It is important to note that the way in which Porges describes this *default hierarchy* applies to the healthy organism. Hughlings Jackson, who first described the concept of *default hierarchies* on which Porges bases his **polyvagal theory**, "observed that when the brain is injured or stressed, it reverts to a less refined, evolutionarily more primitive level of functioning" (cited in Levine, 2010, p. 101). In cases of stress, trauma, abuse,

etc., the older circuits are triggered and override the newer. Hughlings Jackson was a preeminent neurologist of the late 19th century; his concept of default hierarchies remains a fundamental principle of neurology.

> The more primitive the operative system, the more power it has to take over the overall function of the organism. It does this by inhibiting the more recent and more refined neurological subsystems, effectively preventing them from functioning ... [Thus, when an old or very early trauma is reactivated] ... [t]he sympathetic nervous system ... blocks the social engagement system, but not as completely as does the immobilization system (the most primitive of the three defenses).
>
> (Levine, 2010, p. 101)

25 Dykema, 2006.
26 [w]hen mobilizing defences prove ineffective or maladaptive, such as in instances when the fight response might provoke more violence from the perpetrator or when the perpetrator and attachment figure are one and the same, passive avoidance or immobilization behaviours are the only remaining survival strategies.

(P. Ogden, in Fosha *et al.*, 2009, p. 208)

27 "Although ... immobilization can assure survival, it can lead to bradycardia, apnea, and cardiac arrhythmias, and can actually be lethal for mammals if it is maintained over a prolonged period" (Odgen, Minton and Pain, 2006, p. 31). Immobilization is meant to function acutely and only for brief periods. However, Levine adds in a footnote to his discussion of immobilization that it can also be evoked by intense and unremitting stress (2010, p. 105). This point is raised by Steven Hoskinson in his understanding of the autonomic nervous system and the tendency for chronic stress to incapacitate the natural cycle of the ventral vagal parasympathetic system's down beat, or deactivation. Instead, there is a total lack of *down* moments and relaxation which impacts incrementally on the over-stimulated system until finally falling into a dorsal vagal immobility *freeze* or collapse. Personal notes taken during a Somatic Experiencing Trauma Training, (2013–2016), in Northern Ireland, facilitated by Somatic Experiencing Trauma Institute.
28 Siegel in conversation with Sieff: "Studies at UCLA have shown that simply naming a feeling diminishes activity in the amygdala and soothes us ... [T]here is a profound difference between saying, '*I am sad*' and '*I feel sad*'. '*I am sad*' conflates who we are with what we feel. '*I feel sad*' acknowledges our feelings, but implicitly acknowledges that we are more than our feelings and that our feelings will pass. Knowing this allows us to create an internal sanctuary from which we can experience what arises in each moment, rather than rushing to escape" (in Sieff, 2015, p. 154).
29 Steven Hoskinson in conversation with Serge Prengel (Prengel, 2016).
30 "Modern psychology knows that the personal unconscious is only the top layer, resting on a foundation of a wholly different nature which we call the collective unconscious" (Jung, 1943, par. 944).
31 *Temenos* is a Greek word meaning 'sacred precinct', and is used in analytical psychology to convey the safe, 'sacred precinct' of the analytical container.
32 See introductory chapter, "A Note to the Reader", this volume, n. 35.
33 Janet (1926) summed up the role of therapist as "auxiliary cortex": "Education thus consists of the production and repetition of a new action performed in the presence of a competent witness, who supervises it, corrects it, and has it repeated until the action becomes, not merely correct, but automatic (p. 736)" (cited in Ogden, Minton and Pain 2006, p. 232).

References

Abram, D. (1997) *The Spell of the Sensuous*, New York: Vintage Books.

Bainbridge Cohen, B. (1993) *Sensing, Feeling, and Action: The Experiential Anatomy of Body-Mind Centering*, Northampton, MA: Contact Editions. Excerpts published in Hanlon Johnson, D. (1995), *Bone, Breath, and Gesture: Practices of Embodiment*, Berkeley, CA: North Atlantic Books.

Beebe, B. and Lachmann, F. (2002) *Infant Research and Adult Treatment: Co-constructing Interactions*, Hillsdale, NJ: The Analytic Press.

Cannon, W.B. (1932) *The Wisdom of the Body: How the Human Body Reacts to Disturbance and Danger and Maintains the Stability Essential to Life*, New York: W.W. Norton & Co.

Dubuc, B. (n.d.) "How Drugs Affect Neurotransmitters". The Brain from Top to Bottom. Accessed 22 August 2018 at: http://thebrain.mcgill.ca/flash/i/i_03/i_03_m/i_03_m_par/i_03_m_par_heroine.html.

Dykema, R. (2006). "How Your Nervous System Sabotages Your Ability to Relate: An Interview with Stephen Porges About His Polyvagal Theory". NexusPub. March/April 2006. Accessed 29 August 2018 at: https://acusticusneurinom.dk/wp-content/uploads/2015/10/polyvagal_interview_porges.pdf. Pp. 1–11.

Fosha, D., Siegel, D., and Soloman, M., eds. (2009) *The Healing Power of Emotion: Affective Neuroscience, Development and Clinical Practice*, New York: W.W. Norton & Co.

Gallese, V. (2006) "Mirror Neurons and Intentional Attunement: A Commentary on David Olds," *Journal of the American Psychoanalytic Association*, February 2006, 54(1): 47–57.

Gendlin, E. (1981) *Focusing*, New York: Bantam Books.

Gendlin, E. (1992) "The Primacy of the Body not the Primacy of Perception: How the Body Knows the Situation and Philosophy," excerpt from *Man and World*, 25(3–4): 341–353. Accessed 29 August 2018 at: www.focusing.org/pdf/primacy_excerpt.pdf.

Gerhardt, S. (2011) "Why Love Matters: How Affection Shapes a Baby's Brain," *Improving the Quality of Childhood in the European Union – Volume II*, The European Council for Steiner Waldorf Education, pp. 80–97. This article is based on a verbal presentation given to the Quality of Childhood Group in the European Parliament in December 2009. Accessed 29 August 2018 at: www.ecswe.net/wp-content/uploads/2011/01/QOC2-Chapter3-Why-Love-Matters-How-Affection-Shapes-a-Babys-Brain-by-Sue-Gerhardt.pdf.

Heller, L. and LaPierre, A. (2012) *Healing Developmental Trauma: How Early Trauma Affects Self-Regulation, Self-Image, and the Capacity for Relationship*, Berkeley, CA: North Atlantic Books.

Jung, C.G. (1934) *A Review of the Complex Theory*, Collected Works 8, Princeton, NJ: Princeton University Press.

Jung. C.G. (1943) *The Psychology of Eastern Meditation*, Collected Works 11, Princeton, NJ: Princeton University Press.

Jung, C.G. (1949) *The Psychology of the Child Archetype*, Collected Works 9/1, Princeton: NJ, Princeton University Press.

Levine, P. (1997) *Waking the Tiger: Healing Trauma - The Innate Capacity to Transform Overwhelming Experiences*, Berkeley, CA: North Atlantic Books.

Levine, P. (2010) *In an Unspoken Voice: How the Body Releases Trauma and Restores Goodness*, Berkeley, CA: North Atlantic Books.

Levine, P. (2015) *Trauma and Memory: Brain and Body in a Search for the Living Past: A Practical Guide for Understanding and Living with Personal Trauma*, Berkeley, CA: North Atlantic Books.

Merleau-Ponty, M. ([1945] 1962) *Phenomenology of Perception*, Paris: Gallimard; London: Routledge.

"Myelination," Your Dictionary, Accessed 26 August 2018 at: www.yourdictionary.com/myelination.

Ogden, P. (2009) "Emotion, Mindfulness and Movement: Expanding the Regulatory Boundaries of the Window of Tolerance," in *The Healing Power of Emotion: Perspectives from Affective Neuroscience and Clinical Practice*, D. Fosha, D. Siegel, and M. Solomon (eds.), New York: W.W. Norton, pp. 204–231.

Ogden, P., Minton, K. and Pain, C. (2006) *Trauma and the Body: A Sensorimotor Approach to Psychotherapy*, London and New York: W.W. Norton & Co.

Palmer, L. (2013) "Bonding Matters ... The Chemistry of Attachment – Baby Reference." 6 August 2013. Reprinted from the Attachment Parenting International News, Vol. 5, No. 2, 2002. Accessed 26 August 2018 at: http://babyreference.com/bonding-matters-the-chemistry-of-attachment/.

Porges, S.W. (2004) "Neuroception: A Subconscious System for Detecting Threats and Safety," *Zero to Three*, 24(5): 19–24. Accessed 27 August 2018 at: https://eric.ed.gov/?id=EJ938225.

Porges, S.W. (2009) "Reciprocol Influences Between Body and Brain in the Perception and Expression of Affect: A Polyvagal Perspective," in *The Healing Power of Emotion: Affective Neuroscience, Development and Clinical Practice*, D. Fosha, D. Siegel, and M. Soloman (eds.), London and New York: W.W. Norton & Co., pp. 27–54.

Porges, S. (n.d.) "Dr. Stephen Porges: What Is the Polyvagal Theory." YouTube. Accessed 27 August 2018 at: www.youtube.com/watch?v=ec3AUMDjtKQ. Last updated 23 April, 2018.

Prengel, S. (2016) In conversation with Steven Hoskinson. Relational Implicit, https://relationalimplicit.com/somatic-perspectives/. Accessed 31 August 2018 at: https://relationalimplicit.com/zug/transcripts/Hoskinson-2016-05.pdf. Pp. 1–10.

Reinau, M. (2016) *Love Matters for Psychic Transformation: A Study of Embodied Psychic Transformation in the Context of BodySoul Rhythms*, Sheridan, WY: Fisher King Press.

Schore, A.N. (1994) *Affect Dysregulation and the Origin of the Self: The Neurobiology of Emotional Development*, Mahwah, NJ: Lawrence Erlbaum Associates.

Schore, A.N. (2002) "Dysregulation of the Right Brain: A Fundamental Mechanism of Traumatic Attachment and the Psychopathogenesis of Postraumatic Stress Disorder," *Australian and New Zealand Journal of Psychiatry*, 36(1): 9–30.

Schore, A.N. (2003a) *Affect Regulation and the Repair of the Self*, London and New York: W.W. Norton & Co.

Schore, A.N. (2003b) *Affect Dysregulation and Disorders of the Self*, London and New York: W.W. Norton & Co.

Schore, A.N. (2009) "Right Brain Affect Regulation: An Essential Mechanism of Development, Trauma, Dissociation, and Psychotherapy" in *The Healing Power of Emotion: Affective Neuroscience, Development and Clinical Practice*, D. Fosha, D. Siegel and M. Soloman, (eds.), New York: W.W. Norton & Co., pp. 112–144.

Sieff, D.F. (2015) *Understanding and Healing Emotional Trauma: Conversations with Pioneering Clinicians and Researchers*, Hove, UK and New York: Routledge.

Siegel, D.J. (1999) *The Developing Mind*, New York: Guilford Press.

Siegel, D.J (2010a) *The Mindful Therapist: A Clinician's Guide to Mindsight and Neural Integration*, New York: W.W. Norton & Co.

Siegel, D.J. (2010b) *Mindsight: Transform your Brain with the New Science of Kindness*, London: One World Publications.

Siegel D.J. (2012) *Pocket Guide to Interpersonal Neurobiology: An Integrative Handbook of the Mind*, New York: W.W Norton & Co.

Siegel, D.J. (n.d.) "Dr Daniel Siegel Presenting a Hand Model of the Brain." YouTube. Accessed 27 August 2018 at: www.youtube.com/watch?v=gm9ClJ74Oxw. Last updated 29 Feb. 2012.

Stevens, A. ([1982] 2003) *Archetype Revisited: An Updated Natural History of the Self*, Toronto: Inner City Books.

van der Kolk, B. (2014) *The Body Keeps the Score: Mind, Brain and Body in the Transformation of Trauma*, St Ives, UK: Penguin Random House.

West, M. (2016) *Into the Darkest Places: Early Relational Trauma and Borderline States of Mind*, London: Karnac.

Part III

BodyDreaming in Clinical Practice

Chapter 2

Orienting, Regulating, Resourcing
"I may be able to find some peace here"

This chapter explores how and when the BodyDreaming therapist enables *affect regulation* by re-orienting the client away from the cause of activation in order to re-establish flow and homeostasis in the system. It also addresses what happens in the body when the nervous system has been activated by a stimulus, an anticipatory state has been triggered, and arousal increased. Any sustained heightened state of arousal or activation results in imbalance and compromises the natural rhythm of the system. A *re-orientation* is required to ensure that both client and therapist are grounded in the body, in the moment, and in a state of receptivity and openness sufficient to engage in the work. When a condition of *flow* has been established in the system, physical, mental, and imaginative levels are positively affected, enabling new material to be integrated and accorded meaning. James Hillman reminds us that "[t]he essence of psyche is the principle of motion" (1975, p. 125), and there is considerable evidence to show that the brain, mind, and body function as a network of systems, each affecting the others, with information travelling between them.

Neuroscientist Candace Pert, whom we may thank for her discovery of *neuropeptides* and the fact that their *receptors* are distributed throughout the body, laid the foundation for our understanding of the human organism as a *flow of information* within its various networks. She stresses the interconnectedness of all systems in the organism:

> I like to speculate that the mind is the flow of information as it moves among the cells, organs, and systems of the body. ... [I]t can be unconscious ... [for example] at the autonomic, or involuntary, levels of our physiology. The mind as we experience it is immaterial, yet it has a physical substrate, which is both the body and the brain. It may also be said to have a nonmaterial ... substrate ... [namely] the flow of that information. The mind, then, is that which holds the network together, often acting below our consciousness, linking and coordinating the major systems and their organs and cells. ... We might refer to the whole system as the psychosomatic information network, linking *psyche*, which comprises all that is of an ostensibly nonmaterial

nature, such as mind, emotion, and soul, to *soma*, which is the material world of molecules, cells and organs.

(Pert, 1997, p. 185)

Certainly, when flow and communication persist between all systems in the organism, there is less likelihood that the client—or therapist—will become stuck in a state of hyper- or hypoarousal. When the organism's natural network of communication is working, *top-down* as well as *bottom-up* information is available, which means that "there are extensive interconnections among all parts of the brain and among all levels of information processing" (Ogden, Minton, and Pain, 2006, p. 25), the brain's left and right hemispheres are connecting, and the integrative and meaning-making circuits are open. In such a condition, we can focus our attention on the body and notice the felt sense resonance of our experience, how it feels in the body. This has the effect of reinforcing the mind/body connection and enabling a more embodied receptivity to the psyche's messages.

The rest of this chapter is organized as follows: there is a detailed discussion of activation and deactivation of the autonomic nervous system, an elaboration of the topic touched on in Chapter 1. Then there is an example of how, as therapist, I prepare myself for a BodyDreaming session by regulating my own system before I engage with my client. I invite you, as reader, to take a moment to self-regulate in a similar way so that you may be more present in the here and now in your sensing body and more fully *witness* the engagements between myself and my clients that follow. These are excerpts from key sessions with three different clients, and the excerpts are designed to demonstrate how a BodyDreaming therapist works. Before the excerpts, I will also provide a discussion of the role and function of the right and left hemispheres of the brain in the processes with which we are concerned in this chapter: ***orienting***, ***regulating*** and ***resourcing***.

*

Activation and Deactivation of the Autonomic Nervous System

As outlined in "How the Brain Works" (see Chapter 1), the autonomic nervous system has two branches, the sympathetic nervous system (SNS) and the parasympathetic nervous system (PNS). These two branches operate in a natural rhythmic relation to each other. The sympathetic nervous system supplies the organism's first line of defence, boosting energy with a "quicker and stronger heartbeat, increased blood supply to the muscles, dilation of bronchi and increases in breathing rate, dilation of the pupils, increased sweating and speeding up of mental activity" (Schore, 2003, p. 244). It stimulates the sweat glands' production of glucose and cortisol which help the body respond to stimuli perceived as a threat (that is, in *fight*, *flight* or *freeze* mode).

The parasympathetic nervous system functions more slowly than the sympa-thetic nervous system. It "has a higher threshold of activation and thus initiates its operations after the sympathetic" nervous system (*ibid.*). The parasympa-thetic nervous system enables deactivation and recuperation of the organism following increased exertion generated by the sympathetic nervous system. It allows the heart rate to slow, and the muscles to relax; it lowers blood pressure and enables papillary constriction; it causes breathing to return to a normal rate, promotes digestion, bowel and bladder activities, and normal functioning of the immune system.

There is a natural rhythm to the functioning of the nervous system, which oscil-lates between the polarities of the sympathetic and parasympathetic systems in an attempt to establish homeostasis. However, we know that trauma and repeated or ongoing stress can activate the autonomic nervous system to the extent that energy becomes polarized, stuck in one mode or another, leaving the organism in either an activated or deactivated state. If such an imbalance is sustained, one may find oneself *fixed* in a habitual one-sided, patterned response to stimuli. Nevertheless, the body has an innate capacity for healing and balance, and, as Schore writes, the autonomic nervous system can naturally return to a state of homeostasis:

> An autonomic mode of reciprocal sympathetic-parasympathetic control is behaviourally expressed in an organism that responds alertly and adap-tively to a personally meaningful (especially social) stressor, yet as soon as the context is appraised as safe, immediately returns to the relaxed state of autonomic balance. In very recent thinking, the ANS is not only sensitive to environmental demands and perceived stresses and threats but will, in a predictable order, also rapidly reorganize to different neural-mediated states.
> (Schore, 2003, p. 245)

The changes in the ANS are regulated by 'higher' limbic structures; in particular, the orbitofrontal cortex acts as a major centre of control over the sympathetic and parasympathetic systems. When the sympathetic and parasympathetic branches of the ANS are working well in a reciprocal manner we say the body's internal state is regulated. In the course of each development, since the early orbitofrontal cortex is not on line at birth and does not begin to develop until the infant is 10 months, the mother/caregiver is the regulator of the infant's ANS, acting as aux-iliary cortex,[1] restoring the system to homeostasis after a disruption of positive or negative affects. In this way regulation becomes encoded in the wiring of the child's nervous system and over time self-regulation begins to take over.

In BodyDreaming, when the therapist works consciously with the body's capacity to self-regulate, she enables the restoration of balance between the sym-pathetic and parasympathetic nervous systems; she regulates the nervous system of her client just as the mother uses her own autonomic nervous system to regulate that of her infant. When a baby has been activated, for whatever reason, his auto-nomic nervous system goes *over threshold* or out of control. He cries and sweats and is unable to regulate himself. Deactivation by the parasympathetic nervous system only happens when the baby is consoled by his carer, otherwise the infant *holds himself* in a state of arousal—a high sympathetic nervous system response. The mother's soothing presence eases the baby's discomfort and re-establishes the natural cycle of activation/deactivation; the heart rate calms and the tummy muscles soften. The infant learns the ability to self-regulate through repeated inter-regulatory experiences between mother and child.[2] In BodyDreaming we use inter-regulatory skills to encourage the practice of deactivation of a height-ened state, calming and *down-regulating* an over-stimulated limbic system; or, if necessary, we may *up-regulate*, that is, animate a state of hypoarousal in order to bring the client out of a condition of *collapse* or *freeze*. In either case, the BodyDreaming therapist works to free energy from a one-sided position and return the client's nervous system to a state of homeostasis to allow an exploration of psychological issues initially presented in bodily symptoms and dream images.

The autonomic nervous system alternates between activation and deactiva-tion, expansion and contraction, in a natural, wave-like rhythm. The particular wave rhythm of each individual moves within the sphere of a *window of toler-ance*, that is, in an *optimal arousal zone*[3] between the two extremes of hyper- and hypoarousal. "Within this window various intensities of emotional and physio-logical arousal can be processed without disrupting the functioning of the system" (Siegel, 1999, p. 252). When the individual experiences excessive arousal, the system exceeds the *window of tolerance* and moves into hyperarousal, a sympa-thetic heightened response triggering a *fight* or *flight* response. Conversely, the system may drop below the window of tolerance into hypoarousal or a parasym-pathetic *freeze*.

Steven Hoskinson's map of the basic rhythmic pattern of the autonomic nerv-ous system when it is in a state of constant arousal differs from that of Ogden, Minton, and Pain (2006). Hoskinson shows that when the system is in a state of chronic activation, for whatever reason, there is often a failure of the parasympa-thetic nervous system to complete the *down* wave of the cycle which would bring the autonomic nervous system back into homeostasis and help it re-establish its own natural rhythm. Failure to achieve full *de*activation means that the level of activation continues to rise and the possibility of completing the cycle (activation/ deactivation) is truncated. Hoskinson argues that the natural rhythm of activation/ deactivation is often supplanted by further activation, producing stress-related addictive chemicals and preventing the parasympathetic *down* wave from occur-ring; in other words, the natural rhythm of activation/deactivation is overridden by a rhythm governed by an addictive response to trauma and hyperarousal. A rise in activation levels may continue until the system crashes and falls into a state of immobility (i.e., the dorsal vagal response).[4]

Hyperactivity is prevalent in Western culture today and may be understood, in the individual, as the failure of the autonomic nervous system to complete the downward wave of the activation/deactivation cycle. The pace of modern Western society seems, at least at present, to be governed by a momentum that in many cases overrides the process of parasympathetic down-regulation and, instead, races to a rhythm driven by chemicals and hormones released by an overactive sympathetic nervous system. This may leave individual organisms in a constant state of arousal with the result that learning and behavioural problems related to hyperactivity are becoming increasingly prevalent. There is also the concern that many are becoming addicted to the *adrenal rush* (with its associated chemicals), whether this manifests in reaching for the next stimulant, engaging in extreme sports, running a business by crisis management, or over-working.

For those who find themselves caught in a dysregulated pattern of behaviour, the prognosis is often an ever-increasing escalation of stress-related symptoms which eventually push an already hyperactive system beyond its *threshold of tolerance* into a state of *freeze, immobility* or total *collapse*. This may manifest in auto-immune illnesses and burn-out, as well as addiction and depression. As long ago as the 1950s, Hans Selye's research on responses to stress linked stress to disease "because of the long-term hormonal changes stress causes in the body when there has been trauma: stress levels are chronically high and the body loses its capacity to adapt or recover, leading to adrenal fatigue and exhaustion" (cited in Heller and LaPierre, 2012, p. 108). Selye argued that the healthy functioning of the hypothalamus-pituitary-adrenal or HPA system is key to the individual's response to stress. As we saw in the last chapter, the HPA system[5] is closely connected to the sympathetic nervous system's response of *fight, flight* or *freeze*; it is responsible for linking the nervous system to both the pituitary glands, which secrete the hormones that regulate homeostasis, and the adrenal glands, which release stress hormones. "Homeostasis is organic stability, or the maintenance of steadiness in every respect" (Selye, 1978, p. 13). The HPA axis is essential to regulation and "is involved in the neurobiology of mood disorders, anxiety disorder, insomnia, post-traumatic stress disorder, borderline personality disorder, attention deficit/hyperactivity disorder (ADHD), major depressive episodes, burn-out, chronic fatigue, fibromyalgia, irritable bowel syndrome, and alcoholism" (Heller and LaPierre, 2012 p. 109). However, when the parasympathetic nervous system fails to complete the *down-regulation* of the activation/deactivation cycle and homeostasis is not re-established, system failure may result, producing many of the syndromes listed above.

The aim of **orienting** in BodyDreaming is often to rehabilitate the parasympathetic nervous system in order to strengthen the organism's capacity to *down-regulate* so that both therapist and client may work in a productive state of homeostasis. When we orient toward something, we use the architecture of the social engagement system (eyes, ears, facial and neck muscles, etc.): we turn our heads towards the object, position ourselves and, with our eyes (i.e., utilizing neuroception, proprioception, and interoception), we engage with the object that has attracted our attention. Jung uses the German word *betrachten* to describe the particular quality of this *active* process of looking:

Looking, psychologically, brings about the activation of the object; it is as if something were emanating from one's spiritual eye that evokes or activates the object of one's vision. The English verb, 'to look at,' does not convey this meaning, but the German *betrachten*, which is an equivalent, means also to make pregnant. ... And if it is pregnant, then something is due to come out of it; it is alive, it produces, it multiplies. That is the case with any fantasy image; one concentrates upon it, and then finds that one has great difficulty in keeping the thing quiet; it gets restless, it shifts, something is added, or it multiplies; one fills it with living power and it becomes pregnant.

(Jung cited in Chodorow, 1997, p. 7)

In light of Jung's observation, we may argue that the object toward which we orient becomes changed and charged by our engagement. It becomes "filled with living power," pregnant with significance, perhaps even numinous, as a result of which our own physiology may be affected, with changes to the heart and pulse rates, to our breathing, our gut and musculature. Reciprocal engagement between perceiver and perceived has the capacity, therefore, to affect the regulation of the perceiver's nervous system. When the engagement is positive, it has the power to re-establish homeostasis and coherence where earlier there was dysregulation; and what is perhaps more important than an analysis of whether such an event may arguably be a product of synchronicity or projection, is that the *charged* object seems to respond to our attention producing *just the right* antidote for the presenting symptom or complex in a way that mirrors the soul's longing, often carrying the necessary salve for the wound in the psyche. Jung's description of this quality of looking and engagement is repeatedly confirmed in BodyDreaming and is foundational to the work.

It almost invariably happens that the client's *chosen object* engages *both* therapist and client in a process of down-regulation, affecting the physiology of both and enabling both to maintain a state of openness and receptivity to feelings, images, dreams and fantasies presented by psyche and soma. Because the movement between activation and deactivation describes the natural, healthy rhythm and functioning of the autonomic nervous system, it is important to recognize that problems arise only when energy becomes *stuck* in one exclusive mode of response: *fight, flight* or *freeze*. Should this happen, the individual finds herself living a half-life with her energy usurped by the maintenance of dysregulatory habits that come to function as the norm. The BodyDreaming therapist works to help the body restore its natural rhythm, re-establish a healthy parasympathetic nervous system response to activation and restore the individual's system to a state of homeostasis. This promotes an empowering experience of *inter*-regulation, which develops in the client a sense of her own capacity for *self*-regulation. Such an experience promotes the client's participation in both the body's and the psyche's innate impulse to wholeness which Jung speaks of as intrinsic to the nature and life of the human being.

How do we do this? How do I regulate myself prior to a BodyDreaming session with a client?

To regulate myself before I open the door to another's experience, I need to be in my own skin—"*être bien dans ma peau*"—in the room where I am to meet my client. I first focus awareness on my present state of body and mind, noticing any activation in my system, paying attention to my sensing body and its resonance with what is going on. Then I become aware of the physical space I will share with a client. I allow my eyes to wander, to look around the room. I notice what it is that meets my gaze. I linger there in conversation with myself about what I am seeing. I describe to myself the colours, the shapes and maybe tell myself a story about what it is I am looking at. I may begin to notice my body's responses, my breathing; my shoulders may have eased, my belly softened. I may feel more connected with myself while simultaneously feeling more connected to an image or the room around me at a felt sense level. To orient in the room in this way helps me to ground myself in my body, "in my particular body," as Jung says.[6] My sensing body's awareness acts as a mirror reflecting myself back to myself: I am here, present, in this body, in this moment. By consciously using the architecture of the social engagement system (my eyes, ears, jaw, movement of my head and neck), I impact the ventral vagus nerve, soothing and calming my heart and lungs. I take a deeper breath. Observing the felt sense resonance in my body (through interoception) helps me anchor my experience and realize that a self-regulatory process has been initiated. My capacity to orient and regulate myself contributes to the creation of an *embodied* field or *temenos* in which I will be more *present* as I engage in the work with my client.

I invite you, the reader, now, to take a moment to try this for yourself, as described in the section *An Invitation to the Reader to Engage Experientially with the Text* (see the introductory chapter, "A Note to the Reader", p. 24). Notice how you are sitting as you read. Do you need to adjust your position to make yourself more comfortable? When you are ready, in your own time, allow your eyes with a soft focus, to "take you for a walk"[7] around your room or outside your window. Allow yourself to notice whatever it is that has drawn your attention. It may be something that catches your eye in a painting, or the soft touch of the fabric against your skin, or a door handle on a piece of furniture, or the sound of the clock ticking. It may be a ray of light in the undergrowth outside, the soft texture of moss on stone, the breeze gently lifting a branch; it may be birdsong, a butterfly hovering above a spring flower. … Notice what it is that engages you. How would you describe the object that attracts your gaze? Before long you will begin to notice a response in your body as you pay attention to the physical details of what you see; you are being affected by the exploration. You may notice your breath change as your energy picks up the energy of what is engaging you. Feel the pleasure it brings. If you don't find pleasure then allow your eyes to wander again. Go with them and see where it is you arrive. Describe what you are drawn to, the shape, colour, position, texture, etc. Is there a particular part of your body that is responding to the image? How would you describe it? Tight? Warm? Slow? Pulsing? Strong? Softening? … The shape of a particular branch may be drawing a line through your body, extending out to your limbs. The trunk of a tree may be rooting you in your legs. The conversation is infinite and may go on and on.

You may already be bored and impatient and want to move on. Notice that energy, too, and how it comes in as a body experience. Where do you feel the impulse to shift focus and move on? Where does it start in your body as a sensation? How does it make you feel? What is the impulse toward? Is this exploration pleasurable? Take your time to come back slowly into your surroundings, opening your eyes if you closed them while focusing on the sensations in your body. Begin to move your head slowly in the direction of one shoulder, then the other, always with soft focus. What are you noticing as you look around now? How do things appear to you? How are you experiencing yourself in your body? How do you feel now? Has there been a change? How does the space around you appear to you now?

You might have noticed an expansion of your awareness through being in conversation with your object or image that has attracted your attention. This *conversation* promotes a condition of dual awareness (i.e., an awareness of the object itself together with an awareness of the felt sense[8] resonance of the interaction you have with the object in your body). Dual awareness allows one to experience the environment as *active matter* or *process*, rather than as an accumulation of *separate objects.*[9] One's self- or inter-regulating *conversation* with the active matter of an outer object or image illustrates that regulation is a connective process; in BodyDreaming work, the connective process between client and object becomes a dynamic and living container in which therapist and client interact. The conversation about the outer object at the beginning of a session becomes the basis of an inclusive *temenos* to support the work. It extends the boundaries of the therapeutic container beyond that of the particular bodies and psyches of client and therapist to include the object chosen and its associations. It enables a sense of connection to the *bigger picture* of self-other-world in an ensouled, embodied way, opening the dyadic process to associative thinking and linking it to the wisdom of body and psyche. The client's surprise discovery of a connection between an object chosen and the inner world announces a participation in, a sense of being part of, something that is vital and meaningful. Siegel describes the circuitry of the nervous system, constructed as it is to respond to everything we observe, in the following words: "If we attune, we come to create *resonance* in which our observing *self* takes on some of the features of that which we are observing" (2012, p. 23). We will see this regulatory process actively demonstrated in the transcripts of BodyDreaming sessions that are presented in this and other chapters.

*

Left and Right Hemispheres and the Process of Orienting

Orienting outward is a way of seeing or apprehending the world, taking in something new that draws us: for this we rely on the right hemisphere of the brain.

As outlined in Chapter 1, "How the Brain Works", the language of the right hemisphere is different from that of the left hemisphere. The right hemisphere, according to McGilchrist

> attends to the peripheral field of vision from which new experiences tend to come; only the right hemisphere can direct attention to what comes to us from the edges of our awareness. ... Anything newly entering our experiential world instantly triggers a release of noradrenaline,[10] mainly in the right hemisphere. ... [I]t alone can bring us something other than what we already know.
>
> (2009, p. 40)

When we orient outwardly it is the right hemisphere that draws our attention away from the dysregulating activation or complex and directs us to what lies on the periphery of consciousness. Chemicals released as a result of the right hemisphere's activity support the process of orientation and exploration by sustaining interest in the object—which means that the object will continue to speak to us, reveal itself to us, acting as the regulating *other* in a developing conversation. "[N]oradrenergic neurons do not fatigue (unlike other neurons) ... but maintain their condition of excitation so that exploratory attention is held open across a greater expanse of both space and time" (*ibid.*, p. 43). Right hemisphere engagement is relational and McGilchrist claims it is this quality that marks the essential difference between the hemispheres. The right hemisphere draws one to what one "is deeply attracted to, and given life by" (*ibid.*, p. 93). This information validates the process of orienting during which we are predominantly in the domain of the right hemisphere. The right hemisphere relates to the chosen object with passionate and generous attention; it does not get bored or impatient but thrives on the associations it makes, and the quality of the relationship that it builds. With its capacity for integration, the right hemisphere is constantly searching for patterns in things. This capacity to make links is noteworthy when orienting because the right hemisphere sees things as wholes and is concerned with the relations between things; it will make a link between the chosen object and the emotional state or inner life of the perceiver. McGilchrist reminds us that the right prefrontal or orbitofrontal cortex is fundamental to emotional understanding and the regulation that we engage here (*ibid.*, p. 59). The right hemisphere has a longer working memory and can retain more information over longer periods than the left hemisphere. Its broader range of attention is an important consideration when we are orienting as the right hemisphere's range of associations is inexhaustible; it is open to whatever may be. If we, as therapists, are able to maintain a right hemisphere focus when we are working to orient a client, the exploration will be engaging, rich and highly regulating for both parties.

The left hemisphere, on the other hand, is the hemisphere of abstraction, "which ... is the process of wresting things from their context" (McGilchrist, 2009, p. 50):

It sees part objects; its world is explicit, ... compartmentalized, fragmented, static, ... essentially lifeless. From this world we feel detached, but in relation to it we are powerful. ... These gifts of the left hemisphere have helped us to achieve nothing less than civilisation itself. ... We need the ability to make fine discriminations, and to use reason appropriately. But these contributions need to be made in the service of something else, that only the right hemisphere can bring. Alone they are destructive ... and may ... [bring] ... us close to forfeiting the civilisation they helped to create.

(McGilchrist, 2009, p. 93)

The right hemisphere has the unique capacity to pay attention to what is *Other*, to "whatever exists apart from ourselves, with which it sees itself in profound relation" (*ibid.*, p. 93). Orienting through the right hemisphere means encouraging openness to what is *other* as interesting, arousing curiosity rather than fear and defensiveness. Curiosity stimulates the sympathetic nervous system, but right hemisphere engagement has the capacity to subvert fear and calm the activated sympathetic system, keeping it within the *window of tolerance* without pushing it over the threshold.

Perhaps the most important attributes of the right hemisphere are its capacity for contextual understanding, for inclusivity, and the ability to see and envision in terms of *wholes* rather than sequential *parts*. Above all, the *modus operandi* of the right hemisphere is metaphorical—its *language* is the language of metaphor. The etymology of the word *metaphor* derives from the Greek *meta*, meaning 'across,' and *pherein*, meaning 'to carry.' When I learnt the etymology of the word, I found myself asking such questions as: What does metaphor *carry across* ... *what* is figuratively *carried across* and from *where* to *where?* The idea of *carrying across* implies a separation or gap that metaphor has the power to bridge. What gap is *bridged* through the use of metaphor and what disparate 'things' might be *associated, linked, joined together* through the power of metaphor? Metaphor joins the discrete language and differentiating focus of the left hemisphere as it works to understand an experience, with the right hemisphere's "concern for the immediacy of experience that is more densely interconnected with and involved in the body, the ground of that experience" (McGilchrist, 2009, p. 118). Metaphor is the right hemisphere's way of linking left hemisphere ideation to the world, to our embodied experience of an object or event: in this way metaphor "embodies thought and places it in a living context" (*ibid.*, p. 118). Paul Kugler, citing Lacan, argues that a linguistic shift from discursive left hemisphere language to the metaphoric language of the right hemisphere indicates a psychic movement from conscious to unconscious, from "an ego emphasis on the signified (meaning) to an unconscious insistence on the signifier (sound-image)" (2002, p. 67). Kugler reminds us that the "ego's habitual linguistic mode tends to linear sequential metonymic reactions. ... For the ego, prosaic metonymy, and for the unconscious, poetic metaphor are the linguistic lines of least resistance" (*ibid.*, p. 68). The correspondence between a linguistic shift (metonymy to metaphor, left hemisphere to right hemisphere processing) and a psychic movement (from an exclusive ego-focus to an inclusive, participatory and experiential mode of perception) is supported by McGilchrist. He notes that metaphor has the power to move us out of a sequential, "narrow beam" focus and return us to the world of experience, rooting us again in the sensing body and, I would add, opening us to the prompt-ings and wisdom of the somatic unconscious. In terms of BodyDreaming practice, orienting a client, inviting a client to let her eyes *roam* the room and to become aware of something that attracts and *speaks to* her, is to initiate a shift away from the "narrow beam" of attention in which she might have become stuck as a result of the activation of a complex or trauma response. The therapist's invitation is in itself freeing and grounding, as it gives the client permission to first allow and then enjoy a spontaneous, immediate, felt sense experience of a *new* object. Almost invariably, a different language accompanies the change of focus, indicat-ing that the client is being opened to the metaphoric, embodied way of seeing of the right hemisphere. Wilkinson cites Levin and Modell's research which shows that "more brain centres light up in response to metaphor than any other form of human communication, thus indicating the formation of new neural pathways arising from and in response to the symbolic" (2006, p. 10). Hence the impor-tance, in BodyDreaming, of orienting and regulating the client through a right hemisphere 'easy', free association style engagement with the metaphoric and symbolic potential implicit in a chosen object, as a gateway to the unconscious.

*

I have chosen the following three excerpts from BodyDreaming sessions because each illustrates a different response on the part of the client to the processes of ori-enting and regulating. This allows me to demonstrate subtle variations in the way in which orienting and regulating *works*, as well as how I respond to the individual needs of my clients.

Maria was a participant in a new group to which I was introducing BodyDreaming work. I led the group in an orienting exercise.[11] In the following vignette, I invite Maria to tell us about her experience as a participant in the exer-cise. Maria shared her explorations with the group:

Maria: *I was very interested in the piece of clay and what it is. I would like to go nearer now and to touch it* (she gets up to explore it more closely). *I thought it was a bear and now I see that it* is *a bear. My name before marriage was* Bear.

MD: *How do you feel when you see the bear now?*

Maria: *It's standing on two legs, it's not on all four. It reminds me of the danc-ing bear or the bear in fairy tales.*

MD: *How do you feel about him standing on two legs?*

Maria: *In a way it's a good feeling. The dancing bear is ambivalent. It could be sad for a bear to be on a chain in the market place. This bear is not that kind of bear. This is a wilderness bear. He stands up to orient, to have an overview.*

MD: *How does that feel in your body, that he stands up to have an overview?*

Maria: *It's a great feeling. And for a child, as soon as he is able to stand up around one year old, it's a great period.*

MD: *How does your body respond to that? What do you notice about your body now? It looks to me as if you are sitting differently. You are more animated in your talking ... you have shifted the position of your feet; your spine looks different.*

Maria: *My spine is more upright; my lungs feel better. I have more breath; there is more freedom around my heart.*

MD: *Lovely ... your spine is more upright and you have more breath in your lungs and more freedom in your heart.* [I mirror her positive experience back to her, which helps to strengthen the new neural connection that is being made.][12]

Maria: *Yes, it feels really good. This gives me strength.* [She sits upright].

MD: *I am noticing your hands ...*

Maria: *Yes ... they are like this* (making fists)—*it feels powerful.*[13]
            [I mirror her tight fists, her spine and head erect.]

MD: *Lovely. That feels like a powerful image.*

Maria: *Yes. I feel strong, connected, empowered.*

[I subsequently learnt that, prior to this session, Maria had been feeling quite anxious about a new role she had accepted in her work. While engaging in orienting toward the object, which she rightly imagined to be a bear, her anxiety shifted. The relational and curious aspect of her right hemisphere's engagement prompted her to embody the posture of the bear—the upright stance and tightly held fists, lending her an attitude of empowerment, strength and connection. It was as if she had an infusion of bear energy, in particular the bear energy to which she was relating and had made a connection at an embodied level. Her family name means Bear, and this points to the depth of the connection to Bear which resonated in her cellular memory. She embodied the metaphor while standing into the image, demonstrating:

> the crucial role body plays in our sense of identity. ... Bodily action, whether carried out or simulated, is the first step in our discovery of our agency—it is through bodily action that we first explore the world around us and find out about the impact it has on us and the impact we have on the world.
>
> (Knox, 2011, p. 41)

You will have noticed how I *mirror* the client's words and gestures. This reinforces the firing of new synapses in the brain in response to the discoveries that Maria makes as she relates to the image of the clay bear. The client opens herself to the new experience and this is enhanced by the therapist's responses in the prosody—the rhythm and tone of voice, the empathy and capacity to mirror which strengthens the neuronal connections that are forming.[14] The positive interaction between client and therapist (led by right hemisphere activity), as they share their enthusiasm over the image of the bear, encourages the release of the chemical *dopamine*, stimulating the firing of new synapses and the growth of new neural pathways. The image has an *effect*.[15] This effect is heightened, firstly by the direct experience of orienting which establishes a felt sense, embodied and relational link between inner and outer worlds—client and object; and secondly, by the interest and encouragement of the therapist. Matter is affected by the way in which we see it and then, in turn, it affects the seer. Our eyes engage what the psyche needs and, from a Jungian point of view, the psyche makes no mistakes: there are no accidents. The object of curiosity almost invariably serves as a compensatory image capable of regulating a one-sided conscious position. In Maria's case, the chosen object—the bear—echoing her own family name, Bear, was the precise compensatory image needed to confirm her strength and capability in taking up the new position at work.

*

Cho was a participant in the same group as Maria. He reports that he was not able to engage with the orienting exercise as it upset him. The experience of orienting to an object is intended to be pleasurable, and draws on the instinctual movement of attraction/repulsion that motivates our actions. If, however, the client chooses an object which stimulates the opposite effect—fear and displeasure—the therapist gently redirects his attention to allow something else to come into view that is more pleasurable.

Cho: *I felt anxious when I looked at the picture hanging on the wall. The image is unclear and it's a mixture of strange colours, light blue, pink, green, and purple. Whoever painted this picture must be anxious. I was uncomfortable with the image. I didn't feel good.*

MD: [It is important that the therapist does not show any activation in response, but holds the tension and uncertainty with ease. If your client has oriented to something that makes him uncomfortable, you invite him simply to find something else in the room that attracts his attention. This process provides an example of how one needs to work at the pace dictated by the client, a pace that allows for change and choice. By taking it 'nice and slow,' we avoid putting pressure on the client's already activated system to find the *right* image. I rely on the principle of self-regulation which is always present and accessible, and which will lead the way if we give it a chance.]
        Is there anything else your eyes are drawn to in the room?

Cho: *Yes. I am comfortable with the carpet.*

MD: *What do you see when you look at the carpet?* (He is looking at a multi-coloured carpet).

Cho: *I see the colours dark brown, black. I notice the texture.*

MD: *The dark brown and black are the two colours that stand out for you, and also the texture.*

Cho: *It's a comfortable feeling to have this carpet on the ground.*

MB: *What words would you use to describe that?*

Cho: *It's an island surrounded by many, many different colours. I may be able to find some peace here.*

MD: *You can imagine finding peace there on the island.* [I mirror Cho's words, reinforcing his positive experience.]

Cho: *It might be because of the perspective I am taking. I am more comfortable when I am looking down than when I am looking up.*

MD: *That's good to notice ... that you are more comfortable looking down. Do you have a sense of how your body feels when you look down? What do you notice, now, as opposed to when you look up?*

Cho: *When I look up I have more tension.*

MD: *You experience some tension, a little bit of activation when you look up?*

Cho: *Yes.*

MD: *And when you look down, what do you notice?*

Cho: *I can feel—well, it's like going to bed, going home.* (He exhales more deeply and appears more relaxed. This indicates to me that his parasympathetic nervous system is coming on board, resulting in a down-regulating, deeper release of energy, or deactivation.)

MD: *How does that make you feel in your body?*

Cho: *I feel relaxed.... I have a soft belly. I can breathe again.* (Nodding his head.)

MD: *Notice how your body feels supported when you allow yourself to take the time to look down: that you have a soft belly and that you can breathe more deeply.*[16]

[When we work at the pace dictated by the client, we are more likely to stumble upon the exact nuance in the image that proves to be regulating for him. We listen to the body's resonance and the words that describe the body's felt sense experience of the image with which Cho feels comfortable, i.e., "*I have a soft belly. I can breathe again.*"]

Again, you will no doubt have noticed that I was concerned to support Cho's own capacity for self-regulation, reminding him of his body's innate wisdom, its "organic intelligence", namely, the need to *look down* in order to regulate his natural rhythm of activation and deactivation. If a client feels *forced* into eye contact, he will not have time to recover from the stimulation of his interaction with the therapist. By listening to Cho I discover what will help to establish his self-regulatory pattern, which, in turn, will expand his window of tolerance, his capacity to feel more, to be more in touch. I am discovering what resources he already uses—his downward gaze. By making this action conscious, by naming it, we strengthen the positive effect—the pleasure—Cho receives in the self-soothing action.[17] We enhance his capacity to self-regulate and "find a little peace". This will allow him to be more present to positive experiences, with less of his attention engaged in needing to defend himself. The practice of orienting brings homeostasis to the nervous system, and psyche's energy can begin to flow more freely. In Chapter 3 I will return to this session with Cho as he presents an important dream.

*

For many years, Helen had been a dynamic and innovative leader in her community. With the sudden, traumatic death of her partner, she experienced anxiety and grief-related issues, including exhaustion and depression. I experienced Helen as depleted, lacking energy and her usual enthusiasm for her work and other creative projects. During the course of our conversation, I noticed that Helen was finishing each exchange with the phrase, "Oh, I don't know."

MD: *I wonder what it feels like when you say "I don't know" at the end of a sentence?*

Helen: *"I don't know." I wipe myself out with that statement. It's like erasing something from the blackboard.* (She gestures vigorously with her arms in a downward sweeping motion.)
        I do this to myself, you know ...

MD: *What is happening in your body as you say that?* [I don't follow Helen's lead—her impulse for narrative at this point, as I want to track her body's energetic resonance to the words, "I don't know."]

Helen: *I don't know ... My knees give way. There's no strength in them.* (Her knees literally bend and her arms hang limply at her sides, indicating a position of helplessness or dorsal vagal collapse. She then overrides the parasympathetic nervous system's response and pulls herself together, standing upright.)
        [I am observing Helen's responses at this threshold moment,[18] noticing how her system flips from one state to the other. In other words, I am monitoring the rhythm of activation and deactivation in her cycle: the dorsal vagal collapse is evident in the weak knees and limp arms but can flip into *fight* mode when she wills herself to stand tall. Helen doesn't complete the cycle and so remains trapped in this dynamic, oscillating between *collapse* and *fight* mode.]

MD: *Let's take a moment to orient. Look around with soft focus and see what draws your attention.*
        (Helen looks at an abstract painting hanging on the wall. The top third of the painting is dark with shades of grey and black, and the bottom two thirds has warmer, brighter colours.)
        What do you see?

Helen: *I see a branch at the top of the painting, with things hanging from it. I am looking at the trunk. In the lower section there is more colour.*

[As Helen describes what she is seeing, the social engagement system activates, with its calming effect on the heart and respiratory organs. I join her in a free-association reflection on the painting, a right hemisphere activity that releases the chemical noradrenaline which supports a positive focus of attention. This will help counteract the collapse of the dorsal vagal freeze and have a calming effect on the ventral system.]

Maybe it's a branch of a larch tree with things hanging from it. The bottom of the painting looks more substantial.

MD: *The bottom looks more substantial.* (I mirror her words, stimulating her body's resonance to the word *substantial.*)

[Helen sighs and a deeper breath follows, indicating the beginning of a parasympathetic nervous system down-beat.]

I notice that you have taken a deeper breath.

Helen: *Yes, I can breathe.*

MD: *What do you notice is happening in your body?*

Helen: *Well, I feel more substantial. Now I can feel the ground.*

[The image and metaphors contained in the painting are speaking directly to her body. Her sensing body is resonating with the image.]

Helen: (She looks back at the image.) *I see the roots.*

MD: *How is that for you, to see the roots?*

Helen: *Well, I can feel the ground in me now. Yes, in my legs and in my feet.*

MD: *You can feel the ground in you now.* (I mirror her words.)

Helen: *Yes, and I can feel my breath.*

[The parasympathetic nervous system, the *down*-wave, is 'on line.']

MD: *And you are feeling your breath now. I notice there is movement happening.*
[I see that her pelvis is beginning to sway from side to side, the area of the dorsal vagus nerve.]

Helen: *Yes, it's like a gentle swaying from side to side.*

[For a minute or so she continues to sway, which allows the parasympathetic response a chance to establish itself. She suddenly raises her voice. When triggered, sensing threat or danger, the amygdala fires instantaneously in *fight or flight* response.]

Helen: *I need to be able to move. Well, I don't want to be stuck in one position, swaying.*

[She says this with vehemence, cutting off the gentle, spontaneous movement in the pelvis as she begins the more deliberate movement of lifting her legs and arms. Her system is re-establishing the known pattern of the sympathetic *fight or flight* response overriding the parasympathetic nervous system's down-regulatory response.]

MD: *You* do *need to be able to move.* [I echo her feeling tone, joining with her to reassure her.] *Let's take a moment to orient again. What do you notice now?*
[All is quiet.]

Well, it seemed to me that your body was making its own statement. Your body knows exactly what it needs—the deeper breath and the lovely, gentle swaying.

[In recalling and describing the movement, I am reminding her body that it knows what movement is needed. I am hoping to realign Helen with the innate wisdom of her body.]

Let's take a moment and look at the image again.

Helen: (She looks at the painting and, after a while, begins to sway again in small movements at first. Little by little the movement grows as she relaxes more into the rhythm, taking her time in the movement, which allows the down-regulation to complete its cycle.)

Yes, I have roots and I can move. It's important. I need to be flexible.

MD: *Yes, you* do *need to be flexible to be able to move* and *you have roots.*

Helen: *I need to be able to move, to know my legs are not inflexible.*

[She repeats what she has just said so I can hear it again and mirror it again; both she and I need to receive this information from her body.]

MD: *It is important for you to know that your legs are not inflexible, to know you have roots and that you are able to move.*

(She nods in approval. We have got the message.)

How are you feeling in yourself now?

Helen: *I feel good. I am not wiped out.* (There is a feeling of *gravitas*, suggestive less of heaviness than a grounded truth: *this is how it is*.)

[This is a moment of coherence, in which things have come together: meaning, emotion, felt sense, and movement, right hemisphere and left hemisphere. Helen is no longer trapped between the two states of *fight* and *freeze*. There is both greater flexibility and greater stability in her system. The movement in the pelvis—swaying from side to side—has rooted her in a rhythmic flow, a reflection of being able to negotiate between two systems of the ANS, the sympathetic and parasympathetic. Pendulation,[19] according to Levine, connects us "to the body's innate wisdom … the body's natural restorative rhythm of contraction and expansion that tells us that whatever is felt is time-limited … that suffering will not last forever" (2010, p. 78). Helen can safely take her place back in life again.]

Commentary

Since the traumatic event of the death of her partner, Helen had been held in a vice-like grip, caught between a dorsal vagal *freeze/collapse* response on the one hand ("I don't know"), and a ventral vagal *fight/flight* response on the other ("I must be able to move"). Any solution could trigger simultaneously both the ventral and dorsal vagal responses[20]—sympathetic and parasympathetic; the *accelerator* and *brake* mechanisms fire concurrently,[21] leaving Helen exhausted and her system in a constant state of vigilance. Initially, I had been struck by the degree of exhaustion her body held. She was feeling "wiped out" since the sudden death of her partner, just as her partner had been "wiped out" and I could see that her system was caught in the interplay between sympathetic *fight/flight* and parasympathetic *freeze/collapse* mode. Perhaps her system, though seeming to crave recuperation and rest, was living with a dread of annihilation: should she slow down to allow her body some repose she, too, would die.

Helen had experienced many years of therapy and understood her symptoms and their origins. At the beginning of the session, she had wanted to tell me more about her response to the tragedy. However, I decided to steer the conversation away from discussion of the trauma. I did not want us to be pulled back into the trauma vortex.[22] We had reached a threshold moment that we needed to navigate together and I deliberately intervened to encourage Helen to orient to a positive image in the room. I wanted to engage the curiosity and open-endedness of the right hemisphere in order to move away from old complexes and behaviour patterns, and from further explanations—all part of the province of the left hemisphere.

Helen chose to orient toward the painting, and very quickly the language became the language of metaphor, aided by my mirroring her descriptive words. Metaphor links body, mind and emotion. The words that Helen used to describe the image— *substantial, rooted, grounded*—awakened her sensing body to the felt sense experience. McGilchrist notes that "the chosen metaphor is both cause and effect of the relationship. Thus, how we think about ourselves and our relationship to the world is already revealed in the metaphors we unconsciously choose to talk about it" (2009, p. 97). Hearing herself speak the words to me and then receiving them back through the mirroring I gave, strengthened the metaphor; Helen's body immediately sensed the image and responded. The tension visibly eased. She shifted position, standing now more upright, her spine straightening from her sacrum, her weight dropping down into her pelvis and legs as her knees softened. The *lower* half of her body mirrored the quality of the *lower* section of the painting: she could feel more substantial, grounded in her body, as if she had *roots*, and her breath dropped deep into her belly. At this threshold moment, Helen is solid in her groundedness and we wait for the autonomic body response, the place where the new impulse will rise out of the deep belly, pelvis, spine, and soft knees. The parasympathetic response both soothes and strengthens her. In time, the impulse for movement stirs first in her sacrum and flows into her lower belly and hips; she begins to sway from side to side. Then, in a moment, she is triggered, the amygdala sensing the relaxation as danger; terrified of collapse, she spins into *fight or flight* mode.

Helen: *I need to be able to move. Well, I don't want to be stuck in one position, swaying ...*

The parasympathetic response brought ease into Helen's body, allowing the spontaneous autonomic movement—the swaying—to come to the surface. However, her body experienced this ease as a threat to the hyper-vigilance in her sympathetic system and the *fight* response and ventral vagus were activated.

Helen shifted position and made deliberate movements with her arms and legs, resuming a more familiar position; the sympathetic system was taking control, overriding the soothing that had occurred.

MD: (I stay calm, and do not mirror Helen's anxiety. I mirror her words in a reassuring tone of voice.)
          You do *need to be able to move.*
          [I experience Helen as though challenged in a life/death situation and by mirroring the gravity of that in the tone of my voice I reassure her. This calms her arousal. Her body quietens. There is a stillness in the room. Helen's parasympathetic system is coming back on course. I take advantage of the calm and speak to her from a *top-down* cognitive position as I recall what I have witnessed, hoping that her mirror neurons will pick up once again the cellular memory of her *swaying.*]
          Well, it seemed to me that your body was making its own statement. Your body knows exactly what it needs—the deeper breath and the lovely, gentle swaying.
          [This is another threshold moment. Helen's window of tolerance has expanded through the repeated practice of titrating arousal, moving from moments of activation to deactivation. In this way we are re-establishing a more healthy rhythm of the sympathetic and parasympathetic systems. I invite her to return to the image—the resource of the painting—to look, sense, perceive once again. Her body responds with further swaying. She witnesses herself as she speaks.]
Helen: *Yes, I have roots and I can move. It's important. I need to be flexible.*

Helen's body is now capable of holding the "tension of opposites"[23]—negative and positive, grief and hope—without being triggered. She can allow herself to be resourced in the fluidity of her movement pattern that is the deep swaying in her pelvis. Jung writes:

> Opposites can be united only in the form of a compromise, or *irrationally*, some new thing arising between them which, although different from both, yet has the power to take up their energies in equal measure as an expression of both and of neither. Such an expression cannot be contrived by reason, it can only be created through living.
>
> (Jung, 1921, par. 169)

Our work together has allowed for a new attitude to be *lived*, embodied, step by step—the sympathetic and the parasympathetic systems are once again in flow and Helen's nervous system has attained a fluid homeostasis. We have reached a defining moment in which a deep integration is happening and new neural pathways are strengthening. There is a profound sense of resolution as Helen affirms: "*I am* not *wiped out.*"

Notes

1 See Chapter 1, p. 44.
2 See Beebe and Lachmann (2002).
3   When hyper-aroused, clients experience too much arousal to process information effectively and are tormented by intrusive images, affects, and body sensations. But when hypo-aroused, clients suffer another kind of torment stemming from a dearth of emotion and ... sensation—a numbing, a sense of deadness or emptiness, passivity, possibly paralysis. ... Falling between the two extremes of hyper- and hypo-arousal, this zone is described as the 'window of tolerance'.

(Ogden, Minton, and Pain, 2006, p. 6)

4 Personal notes taken during a Somatic Experiencing Trauma Training, (2013–2016), in Northern Ireland, facilitated by Somatic Experiencing Trauma Institute.

5   As distress levels build up in a crying baby a hormonal chain reaction is set in motion. It starts deep within the lower brain in a structure called the hypothalamus: the body's general hormone controller. The hypothalamus produces a hormone that triggers the nearby pituitary gland to release another hormone called ACTH. This in turn stimulates the adrenal glands (just above the kidneys) to release the stress hormone called cortisol. Cortisol then washes over the body and brain. This stress response system is known as the HPA.

(Sunderland, 2006, p. 40)

See also Heller and LaPierre, 2012, Chapter 1, p. 39.

6   ... the damnable fact is that you are rooted just here, and you cannot jump out of your skin; you have definite necessities. You cannot get away from the fact of your sex, for instance, or of the color of your eyes, or the health or the sickness of your body, your physical endurance. Those are definite facts which make you an individual, a self that is just yourself and nobody else.

(Jung, 1988, p. 63)

7 Personal notes taken during a Somatic Experiencing Trauma Training, (2013–2016), in Northern Ireland, facilitated by Somatic Experiencing Trauma Institute.
8 Levine comments:

When working with physiology, the first thing to recognize is that the felt sense is closely related to awareness. It's like watching the scenery, or in this case, sensing the scenery. Awareness means experiencing what is present without trying to change or interpret it. ... Sensations are the physical phenomena that contribute to our overall experience. ... Once you become aware of them, internal sensations almost always transform into something else. Any change of this sort is usually moving in the direction of a free-flow of energy and vitality.

(1997, pp. 81–82)

9 Fritjof Capra writes:

[T]he universe is no longer seen as a machine, made up of a multitude of separate objects, but appears as a harmonious indivisible whole; a network of dynamic relationships that include the human observer and his or her unconsciousness in an essential way.

(1982, p. 32)

10 Noradrenaline is often referred to as a *fight* or *flight* chemical, as it is responsible for the body's reaction to stressful situations, producing effects such as increased heart rate, increased blood pressure, widening of pupils, widening of air passages in the lungs and narrowing of blood vessels in non-essential organs. This enables the body to perform well in stressful situations.

11 When we invite our client to look around the room and allow the eyes to be drawn to something, we are engaging what Jaak Panksepp calls The Seeking System, which Margot Sunderland describes as follows:

> The lower brain contains a Seeking System, one of the seven genetically ingrained systems in the brain. When this system is stimulated in other mammals, they explore and investigate their environment with curiosity. In humans, the Seeking System can activate an appetite for life, an energy to explore the new, and an eagerness to seek out whatever the world has to offer. It also stimulates curiosity or intense interest in something and the sustained motivation and directed sense of purpose that help us to achieve our goals. When the Seeking System is working in a well-coordinated way with the frontal lobes, it means you can enjoy the necessary drive to transform the seed of an idea into an amazing reality. ...
> There are many chemicals in the Seeking System but Dopamine is the one that turns things on. It cascades all over the frontal lobes, enabling a person not only to have a great idea but also to have the directed purpose to see it through to completion.
>
> (Sunderland, 2006, pp. 94–95)

This is the system we are engaging when we use the tool of orienting to something new—MD.

12 "Mirror neurons are the antennae that pick up information about the intentions and feelings of others, and they create in us both emotional resonance and behaviour imitation. We engage in mirroring automatically and spontaneously without conscious effort or intention" (Siegel, 2010, p. 225). At this point, my mirror neurons are firing and their resonance helps to forge the new pathways forming in the client—MD.

13 Levine underscores the importance of posture and gesture in the generation of new behaviours, sensations, feelings and meanings (2010, p. 145). You will find more on this in Chapter 3.

14 Hebb's Law, as described by Heller and LaPierre:

> [C]ells that fire together, wire together. If two neurons are electrically active at the same time, they will automatically form a connection.... This activity-dependent wiring together is the basic mechanism of all learning and adaptation. With new learning comes the growth of new neurons and the branching of dendrites that allow the brain to change and expand the established connections among existing neurons. ... By working bottom-up—by specifically slowing down the pacing of the session in order to give attention to sensations and emotional responses as they are experienced in the moment ... [we] ... make room for new learning opportunities that can directly contribute to changing neural connections and building new networks.
>
> (2012, p. 102)

15 Jung uses active imagination, as the way in which he enhances the effect of an image by encouraging the patient to engage with the image through different modalities: drawing, painting, clay, dance.

> [B]usying himself with it (his fantasy) ... increases its effect upon him. Moreover, the concrete shaping of the image enforces a continuous study of it in all its

parts, so that it can develop its effects to the full. ... [S]omething of inestimable importance is won—the beginning of independence, a step towards psychological maturity. The patient can make himself creatively independent through this method. ... For what he paints ... is active within him. ... [I]t is himself in a new and hitherto alien sense, for his ego now appears as the object of that which works within him. ... [H]e strives to catch this interior agent, only to discover in the end that it is eternally unknown and alien, the hidden foundation of psychic life.

(1929, par. 106)

16 'Name it to tame it' describes how "placing a linguistic label on an internal or external process can help calm the mind and stabilize attention so that one can perceive with more clarity into the nature of an experience" (Siegel, 2012, A1-54). This is what I am doing by reflecting back to Cho the changes in his body that he has noticed, mirroring his words.

17   The *nucleus basalis*, part of a region close to the brain stem, has neural projections that secrete the chemical acetylcholine throughout the cortex. Acetylcholine is a neuromodulator, and its presence enables any neurons that are activated at the same time to strengthen their connections to one another.

(Siegel, 2010, p. 133)

18 A *threshold moment* is a moment of activation in which the nervous system is triggered and is about to shift into a habitual pattern of either sympathetic arousal *(fight/flight)* or parasympathetic arousal *(freeze/collapse)*. In BodyDreaming, the threshold moment presents the therapist with the possibility of repatterning a habitual response by regulating the nervous system and returning it to homeostasis by *up-regulating* or *down-regulating* the system according to the individual's response. Repeated interventions to navigate threshold moments can lead incrementally to the establishment of new neural pathways and the rewiring of old complexes.

19 See Chapter 1, p. 63.

20 See Chapter 1, p. 51, Porges' Polyvagal Theory for a detailed account of the three systems: social engagement, ventral and dorsal vagal.

21 In Levine's *Somatic Experiencing*, this is known as Global High Intensity Activation (GHIA).

GHIA is understood ... to refer not only to activation in the autonomic nervous system but also in the central nervous system. ... GHIA affects every system and every cell within these systems: skin and connective tissues, brain chemistry, organ systems, nervous and endocrine systems, and the immune system.

(Heller and LaPierre, 2012, p. 134)

Levine notes that the "bodies of traumatized people portray 'snapshots' of their unsuccessful attempts to defend themselves in the face of threat and injury ... [and that] these failed defences can be rediscovered and revitalized by giving attention to the body and thereby re-establishing a sense of mastery and competence" (cited in Odgen, Minton and Pain, 2006, p. 88).

22 Freud, in his 1914 essay, "Beyond the Pleasure Principle", defines trauma "as a breach in the protective barrier against stimuli leading to feelings of overwhelming helplessness" (quoted in Levine, 1997, p. 197). Levine continues: "Using the analogy of the stream, shock trauma can be visualized as an external force rupturing the protective container (banks) of our experience. This breach then creates a turbulent vortex" (*ibid.*). Hoskinson also points to the *addictive* cycle of trauma that draws us over the threshold

and into its vortex (personal notes taken during a Somatic Experiencing Trauma Training (2013–2016), in Northern Ireland, facilitated by Somatic Experiencing Trauma Institute).
23 "The greater the tension, the greater the potential. Great energy springs from a correspondingly great tension of opposites" (Jung, 1942, par. 154).

References

Beebe, B. and Lachmann, F. (2002) *Infant Research and Adult Treatment: Co-constructing Interactions*, Hillsdale, NJ: The Analytic Press.

Capra, F. (1982) *The Turning Point: Science Society and the Rising Culture*, London: Flamingo.

Chodorow, J., ed. (1997) *Jung on Active Imagination: Encountering Jung*, Princeton, NJ: Princeton University Press.

Heller, L., and LaPierre, A. (2012) *Healing Developmental Trauma: How Early Trauma Affects Self-Regulation, Self-Image, and the Capacity for Relationship*, Berkeley, CA: North Atlantic Books.

Hillman, J. (1975) *Revisioning Psychology*, New York: Harper & Row.

Jung, C.G. (1921) *Schiller's Ideas on the Type Problem*, Collected Works 6, Princeton, NJ: Princeton University Press.

Jung, C.G. (1929/33) *The Aims of Psychotherapy*, Collected Works 16, Princeton, NJ: Princeton University Press.

Jung, C.G. (1942) *Paracelsus as a Spiritual Phenomenon*, Collected Works 13, Princeton, NJ: Princeton University Press.

Jung, C.G. (1988) *Nietzsche's Zarathustra: Notes of the Seminar Given in 1934–1939*, James L. Jarrett (ed.), in two volumes, Bollingen Series XCIX, Princeton, NJ: Princeton University Press (London & New York: Routledge: 1989).

Knox, J. (2011) *Self-Agency in Psychotherapy: Attachment, Autonomy and Intimacy*, London: W.W. Norton and Co.

Kugler, P. (2002) *The Alchemy of Discourse: Image, Sound and Psyche*, Einsiedeln, Switzerland: Daimon Verlag. [Revised edition of the earlier, 1982 edition published by Associated University Presses, Inc.]

Levine, P. (1997) *Waking the Tiger: Healing Trauma - The Innate Capacity to Transform Overwhelming Experiences*, Berkeley, CA: North Atlantic Books.

Levine, P. (2010) *In an Unspoken Voice: How the Body Releases Trauma and Restores Goodness*, Berkeley, CA: North Atlantic Books.

McGilchrist, I. (2009) *The Master and his Emissary: The Divided Brain and the Making of the Western World*, New Haven, CT, and London: Yale University Press.

Ogden, P., Minton, K. and Pain, C. (2006) *Trauma and the Body: A Sensorimotor Approach to Psychotherapy*, London and New York: W.W. Norton & Co.

Pert, C. (1997) *Molecules of Emotion: The Science behind Mind-Body Medicine*, New York: Scribner.

Schore, A.N. (2003) *Affect Dysregulation and Disorders of the Self*, London and New York: W.W. Norton & Co.

Selye, Hans ([1956] 1978) *The Stress of Life*, New York: The McGraw-Hill Companies, Inc.

Siegel, D.J. (1999) *The Developing Mind*, New York: Guilford Press.

Siegel, D.J. (2010) *Mindsight: Transform your Brain with the New Science of Kindness*, London: One World Publications.

Siegel D.J. (2012) *Pocket Guide to Interpersonal Neurobiology: An Integrative Handbook of the Mind*, New York: W.W Norton & Co.

Sunderland, M. (2006) *What Every Parent Needs to Know*, London: Dorling Kindersley.

Wilkinson, M. (2006) *Coming into Mind: The Mind-Brain Relationship: A Jungian Clinical Perspective*, London and New York: Routledge.

Chapter 3

Working the Threshold
"Slowly, slowly, I per cent ..."

Expecting the worst, you look, and instead,
here's the joyful face you've been wanting to see.

Your hand opens and closes and opens and closes.
If it were always a fist or always stretched open,
you would be paralyzed.

Your deepest presence is in every small contracting
                                        and expanding,
the two as beautifully balanced and coordinated
as birdwings.
                        (From Rumi, "Birdwings", translated
                                    by Coleman Barks)[1]

Dream—The Body–Psyche Connection

*Whatever you experience outside of the body, in a dream
for instance, is not experienced unless you take it into the body,
because the body means the here and now.*
                                        (Jung, 1998, p. 1316)[2]

Antonio Damasio, neurologist and neuroscientist, argues that "[l]iving organisms are designed with an ability to react emotionally to different objects and events. The reaction is followed by some pattern of feeling and a variation of pleasure or pain is a necessary component of feeling" (2003, p. 11). Damasio was inspired by the seventeenth-century philosopher Spinoza, and his book, *Looking for Spinoza: Joy, Sorrow, and the Feeling Brain*, uses Spinoza's thinking as the framework for his exploration of the neurobiology of emotion and feeling. Acknowledging Spinoza as a thinker whose work prefigures the findings of modern neuroscience and, to a large extent, psychoanalytic practice, Damasio begins with Spinoza's proposal that "the power of affect is such that the only way we have to overcome a detrimental affect—an irrational passion—is by overpowering it with a stronger positive affect, one triggered by reason" (*ibid.*, pp. 11–12). A central premise of

Spinoza's philosophy is that any attempt to subdue the passions, or intense activation, should be made "by reason-induced-emotion and not by pure reason alone"
(*ibid.*, p. 12). Mind and body were not held to be separate and distinct in Spinoza's
philosophy but, as Jung was to argue almost 250 years later, two different manifestations of the same phenomenon.

Towards the end of his book, Damasio sums up in "Spinoza's Solution" the
philosopher's "answer" to questions of human behaviour, happiness and the quest
for salvation:

> The Spinoza solution ... asks the individual to attempt a break between the
> emotionally competent stimuli that can trigger negative emotions—passions
> such as fear, anger, jealousy, sadness—and the very mechanisms that enact
> emotion. Instead, the individual should substitute emotionally competent
> stimuli capable of triggering positive, nourishing emotions. To facilitate
> this goal, Spinoza recommends the mental rehearsing of negative emotional
> stimuli as a way to build a tolerance for negative emotions and gradually
> acquire a knack for generating positive ones. ... Spinoza's solution hinges
> on the mind's power over the emotional process, which in turn depends on
> a discovery of the causes of negative emotions, and on knowledge of the
> mechanics of emotion. The individual must be aware of the fundamental sep-
> aration between emotionally competent stimuli and the trigger mechanism of
> emotion so that he can substitute emotionally competent stimuli capable of
> producing the most positive feeling states.
>
> (Damasio, 2003, p. 275)

I have cited Damasio's analysis of Spinoza's "solution" at length because the basic
tenets (the inseparability of mind and body; the process of substituting positive
for negative feelings, etc.) describe the underlying assumptions of BodyDreaming
work. BodyDreaming promotes the client's understanding of the mechanism of
trauma and the dynamics of emotion. The therapist works with the client to widen
his or her window of tolerance for negative activation, and looks for opportunities
to enhance the role of the neo-cortex—the rational part of the brain that is integrative, capable of making meaning and generating compassion for self and others.
Neuroscience demonstrates that the chemicals released by the neo-cortex soothe
the limbic or emotional brain and open the system to influence from the cortex and
the highway between the right and left hemispheres.

Spinoza writes: "An affect cannot be restrained or neutralized except by a contrary affect that is stronger than the affect to be restrained" (cited in Damasio,
2003, p. 12). Spinoza's idea that strong emotion can be subdued only by *reason-
induced emotion*, not by reason alone, corresponds to what I understand to be the
use of *resourcing* in the work of Levine and Hoskinson—that is, the aim of orienting the client toward *pleasure* or the choice of a *positive* image (or resource). This
same process I have integrated into BodyDreaming. Reason, the neo-cortex alone,
cannot shift attitude or activation in the system without the collaboration of the

transformative *heat* of emotion. Jung's injunction to "stick with the image" and its resonance, and with the feeling-tone of the activated complex,[3] echoes Spinoza's notion that mind and body, thought and feeling, *together* move the distressed individual towards "salvation" (that is, towards pleasure, a sense of well-being or, in our terms, healing). The opposing attitude needed to compensate and rebalance a one-sided conscious attitude, in Jung's view, arises spontaneously from the psyche-soma in the form of dreams, emotions, images, gestures, movements, symptoms. The *work* then consists of bringing these *gifts* from the unconscious to consciousness, so that they may be integrated into the conscious personality—body–mind–soul—transforming the dominant attitude or subduing an excessive or destructive emotion.

Throughout his life Jung was fascinated by the concept of opposites, the point at which opposites meet or do not meet, the tension between the two. He argued that one needs to *hold* the tension between opposites in order that something entirely new, the new *third*, can manifest. In his essay, *The Transcendent Function* ([1916] 1958), he maintains that a tension of opposites yielding eventually to the production of a previously unknown *third* or new possibility that *transcends* or moves beyond the original opposites constitutes the fundamental dynamic of psychic life. In other words, this dynamic persists at the unconscious level and underlies all psychic development if not always perceived or engaged by the conscious personality. In his description of the *transcendent function* Jung clearly indicates that the tension is that between conscious and unconscious, mind and body, argument and affect:

> The shuttling to and fro of arguments and affects represents the transcendent function of opposites. The confrontation of the two positions generates a tension charged with energy and creates a living, third thing—not a logical stillbirth ... but a movement out of the suspension between opposites, a living birth that leads to a new level of being, a new situation. The transcendent function manifests itself as a quality of conjoined opposites. So long as these are kept apart—naturally for the purpose of avoiding conflict—they do not function and remain inert.
>
> (Jung, [1916] 1958, par. 189)

In BodyDreaming, by bringing the opposites into dynamic flow—sympathetic *and* parasympathetic systems, psyche *and* body—we experience how our biology and psyche interact to produce a new position and possibility: a *living third* presents itself.

In a BodyDreaming session a client may present a dream that can, at first, seem unconnected to the issue with which we are consciously concerned, its possible relevance a puzzle. Yet, in working with the emotion of the dream image and the felt sense resonance of the dream in the body through the process of inner attunement, we may discover that the image parallels (or *images*) our physiology and biological processes, and holds the key to new possibilities.[4]

In the terms of neuroscience, the dream image has the potential to effect changes in the original wiring of the brain and create new synapses given, of course, the therapist's understanding of the body-psyche connection. The dream points to the direction in which energy may flow more freely and creatively—physically, psychically and spiritually.[5] Certainly, Jung considered the dream to be a product of the self-regulatory nature of the psyche, one of its roles being that of compensation. In other words, the dream serves to regulate a one-sided position held by the conscious personality—and, we might add, the body, as an individual's psychic *constitution* or "equation" (to use Jung's term), is inseparable from the way in which he or she is wired neurologically.[6]

If we subscribe to the principle of self-regulation—that is, both the body's and the psyche's inherent capacity for self-regulation (homeostasis), we can see that body, mind and psyche comprise, necessarily, a *dynamic* unity of opposites. In BodyDreaming we acknowledge that the archetypal and instinctual impulse to self-regulation in both body, mind and psyche is fundamental to the process of individuation, the natural process of self-realization through which an individual may attain his or her full potential as a human being,[7] the goal, one may assume, of all therapeutic modalities.

Before working on a dream, or early in the dream work, the BodyDreaming therapist invites the client to orient outward in order to access the social engagement system which calms the heart rate, blood pressure and breathing, and brings a greater sense of safety to the system, returning it from activation to homeostasis. Siegel points out that inner and outer attunement share many of the same neural wiring circuits. We can best attune to what is *other*/outside ourselves when we have established inner attunement, the embodied, felt sense experience of internal resonance in which "our observing circuitry aligns with our experiencing self" (2012, p. 23–1). When we attune to ourselves through interoception we become more open to what it is we are engaged with: "the *circuitry* of our own *nervous system* is such that if we attune, we come to create *resonance* in which our observing *self* takes on some of the features of that which we are observing" (*ibid.*).

When we engage the client in the process of orienting to a resource in an affect-regulatory exploration we invite him or her to witness the process, i.e., "what do you notice is happening?" This practice of reflective questioning supports the client's experience of inner attunement which, in turn, opens the neural pathways of outer attunement, enabling the client to be more receptive to what is *other*, on the outside. In the case of a dream or image that has called our attention, inner attunement supports us to be open to what the dream or image may be offering: the unconscious communications and resonances in the field that pertain between *I* and *other*.

When we listen to a dream, we attune to what is new or *other* from the perspective of the conscious mind. In Chapter 2, we met Cho. In what follows, I reintroduce Cho at the point at which he is feeling anxious because of the frightening content of a dream. You will see that I adopt the role of *auxiliary cortex*[8] at threshold moments of activation by orienting Cho outwards in order to regulate his nervous system. In this way we pendulate between activation and deactivation, keeping the system from getting stuck in a one-sided habitually patterned response of *fight/ flight* or *freeze/collapse*. The pendulating rhythm of the regulatory interventions helps Cho slowly to gain a sense of self-agency so that he is no longer driven by the amygdala into a *fight/flight* or *freeze/collapse* response. The therapist's consistent reminder to the client to orient outward at moments of hyper- or hypoarousal helps to activate the social engagement system which soothes the ventral arousal, calming the heart rate and breath. Van der Kolk argues that "[f]or our physiology to calm down, heal and grow we need a visceral feeling of safety" (2014, p. 79). He reminds us that the two options we have for monitoring stress—*top-down* and *bottom-up* processing—work in the following way: *top-down* "via modulating messages from the medial prefrontal cortex" (*ibid.*, p. 63), and *bottom-up*, through subcortical, more body-focused approaches. As cited in Chapter 1, van der Kolk describes the workings of the Medial Prefrontal Cortex (MPFC)

> ... located directly above our eyes—as the watchtower, offering a view of the scene from on high. ... [It] enables people to observe what's going on, predict what will happen if they take a certain action, and make a conscious choice.
>
> (van der Kolk, 2014, p. 62)

While working with Cho I will draw largely on the medial prefrontal cortex by working *top-down* to increase Cho's sense of safety and bring his system back to homeostasis. The medial prefrontal cortex has the capacity to down-regulate "the fear-generating limbic amygdala" and in the process releases "GABA, gamma-aminobutyric acid ... the 'cortical override' that enables awareness to modulate subcortical fear states" (Siegel, 2010a, p. 230).

Of particular relevance to the BodyDreaming therapist is Ogden, Minton, and Pain's reminder that interplay of *top-down* and *bottom-up* processing, representing as they do the two directions in which information flows in the system, is significant both for the initial occurrence *and* the later treatment of trauma (2006, p. 23).

> When we smile we feel happier and we feel happier when we smile. ... The feedback between layers or levels of the brain is bidirectional; if you activate a lower level, you will be priming an upper level, and if you activate an upper level you will be priming a lower level. In order to treat the effects of trauma on all three levels of processing [i.e., cognitive, emotional and sensorimotor] somatically informed top-down management of symptoms, insight and understanding, and bottom-up processing of the sensations, arousal, movement, and emotions must be thoughtfully balanced.
>
> (Ratey (2002) cited in Ogden, Minton, and Pain, 2006, p. 25)

Top-down regulation supports the limbic system to soothe and settle the nervous system, as it calms high arousal, and this top-down approach may be the preferred option with clients who have suffered trauma, as well as clients who have not yet become accustomed to working *in the body*. It is important that the therapist bear in mind how "[p]eople with traumatized disorder suffer from 'feeling too much' and 'feeling too little'. They often experience inner body sensations as overwhelming and distressing" (Ogden, Minton, and Pain, 2006, p. 16). According to van der Kolk they can feel chronically unsafe inside their bodies:

> The past is alive in the form of gnawing interior discomfort. Their bodies are constantly bombarded by visceral warning signs, and, in an attempt to control these processes, they often become expert at ignoring their gut feelings and in numbing awareness of what is played out inside.
>
> (van der Kolk, 2014, p. 96)

Their bodies may have been the scene of activation, holding explicit memories of trauma, e.g., physical injury, surgery or abuse. They may also be carrying implicit memory held in the tissue and muscular systems that long ago have been shut off—disconnected.[9] Consequently, bringing attention to sensation in the body may initially trigger a trauma response. As therapists, we need to be attuned to the body and let the body guide us in the way we pace our work. Even then, images, sensations, emotions may flood the client and the therapist needs to be skilled in regulating arousal to prevent the client from becoming retraumatized by accessing the past (van der Kolk, 2014, p. 101).

*

The Dream

The following excerpt opens with Cho telling me his dream:

Cho: *I am with a female doctor. She listens to my breathing. She asks me to breathe in and out. I try to breathe in deeply, I try to exhale strongly but I can't. I wake up.*

MD: *How did you feel when you woke up?*

Cho: *Suffocated ...*

MD: *Are you in touch with any of that fear now?*

Cho: *Yes, a little, I'm afraid of the limitation of my strength.*

MD: *That's uncomfortable to be faced with—limitation—especially with something as important as breath.*

   [Cho nods in agreement. I am joining with him both in the emotion and through cognition.[10]]

MD: *Do you feel a tightness anywhere in particular in your body?*

Cho: *Not being able to expand my chest.*

MD: *Can you feel that now?*

Cho: *As soon as I recall the dream.*

MD: *So you are experiencing a tightness in your chest when you recall the dream.*

[I am feeling reassured and can relax now into the work knowing Cho is not about to go into cardiac failure.]

Let's take a moment and orient back to your island on your carpet (see Chapter 2). *Notice it from the perspective of your eyes looking down at it. What happens as you do this?*

[I am beginning the process of titration and pendulation. I invite Cho to return to the positive feelings evoked by the resource—the chosen object—which he had already oriented to.[11]]

Cho: *I am worried. Will I feel better?*

MD: *I hear that you are concerned and just for a moment let's see what happens when you take time to look down on your island as you did earlier.*

[To reassure Cho and calm his sympathetic arousal, I take the position of auxiliary cortex, steering him away from the activation in his body toward the counter image of pleasure in the room. In this way I am hoping to down-regulate him.]

Earlier, when you looked down at the island you said that you had a sense of 'coming home' and you could rest there. Are you able to get in touch with that now?

Cho: *No, not much.*

MD: *At all?*

Cho: *Just a little.*

MD: *OK. Let's explore the 'just a little'. Maybe you could tell us something about the island?*

[I attempt to engage Cho in a free-association conversation[12] to counteract his fear by recalling the counter emotion of the positive resource. I focus on *prosody*, keeping my voice light and easy in the way in which a mother attunes to her infant to regulate and soothe the activation.[13]]

Cho: *There's a small house there.*

MD: *Do you know this house?*

Cho: *No.*

MD: *How do you imagine the house?*

Cho: *With not many people.*

MD: *Is it a retreat house that you can get away to?*

Cho: *Yes, for special holidays.*

MD: *A special place, then? .... Are you feeling in touch with that?* (Silence.) *Do you have any feeling connection with this place?*

Cho: *I'm not sure I'm getting a connection with it.[14]*

[I am wondering about the silence and whether Cho is going into *freeze*.]

MD: *This conversation is not coming easily for us.*

Cho: *I'm trying to get in touch with the image and I am being constantly distracted by the dream.*

MD: *That's a sign to let this conversation go.*

[Cho's social engagement system is failing to galvanize which indicates that he feels under threat. The dream image of being unable to breathe easily feels life-threatening for him. My questions are meeting with long silences. This marks a *threshold moment*—which carries with it the risk of an amygdala response driving Cho into a further state of arousal, forcing him to go *over threshold* and into hypoaroused state of *freeze*, marked by longer and longer silences. I need to intervene to help deactivate him and allow the energy in his system to calm down. I decide to *join* him where he is caught in anxiety, and mirror the dream image that holds the fear.]

MD: *The female doctor is asking you to breathe; you can't inhale or exhale deeply. You are feeling a lot of tension around your chest area.*

[In a firm and gentle voice, I mirror the dream content and the anxiety Cho is experiencing, reassuring him that I am still holding the dream he has shared. The dream is in the 'foreground' for Cho; I am 'joining' him there, which may help him to feel safe, met. Cho nods. We have made contact, arriving at another threshold moment.]

MD: *Let's for a moment invite your eyes to take you for a walk in the room, to see if there is anything that catches your attention. Is there anything you notice?*

Cho: *The light from the candle.*

MD: *What do you notice about the light?*

Cho: *The warming atmosphere. It's a really warm colour.*[15]

[Cho's statement reassures me that his social engagement system has calmed his sympathetic arousal].

MD: *Allow yourself to feel the 'warming' quality. Do you feel it anywhere in your body, this warm atmosphere?*

        (Silence.)

MD: *Is there a resonance in your body with it? Does your body connect with the warm light?*

        (Silence.)

        Even 1% as you look at the warm atmosphere of the candlelight?

Cho: *I am not feeling the resonance in my entire body but only in my face and neck.*

MD: *That's great ... in your face and neck.*

[When the social engagement system is functioning, it utilizes the muscles of the face and neck and there follows a direct parasympathetic calming effect on the cardiac and respiratory systems, as well as on the gut.

[I address the group directly, taking the attention away from Cho, which allows his system more time to settle:

[Cho thought he should be having a whole-body response to the image. My question concerning a 1 per cent resonance allowed him to do a body scan, looking for the tiniest shift or change. We could easily have overlooked these changes occurring in his face and neck, the smallest of which is enough to impact the ventral vagal system, that is, the heart, lungs and gut.[16]

[I turn toward Cho.]

MD: *Let's just bring your attention back to the area in the face and neck that you noticed.*

[I wait while he brings his attention to the places in his body where he has noticed the change, and this increases the intensity of what is happening, allowing the energy of the social engagement system to affect the ventral vagus, ultimately calming it. I notice that Cho has taken a deeper breath, a sign of parasympathetic deactivation.]

MD: *What are you noticing now?*

Cho: *The light looks much lighter.*

MD: *Does that feel good?*

Cho: *I'm not feeling very deeply connected.*

MD: *That's OK. What I am hearing, Cho, is that the light is getting lighter. Your capacity to see the light is getting stronger. We can take more in when we are less activated. Even when we experience only 1 per cent less activation, something more can come in from outside. It confirms for me that there is always reciprocity between our inner state and what we are taking in.*

Cho: *I am feeling more curious.*

MD: *Good.*

[Cho is now curious about and oriented toward the compensatory image of the warm colour and light of the candle, the image he chose to counter-act the high activation of the *freeze* that was occurring. This is producing the deactivation in his overall system.]

MD: *Let's come back to the symptom in your chest. What are you experiencing right now?*

Cho: *I don't feel the tightness much now. At the same time, I am worrying that it will come back again any time.*

MD: [What follows is a 'teaching moment' as Cho is engaged in a course in Jungian psychology and is interested in the process.]

Let's take the first part of your statement, 'I don't feel the tightness much now'. You oriented toward the light, the warmth and glow of the candle and this brought some ease to the muscles in your face and neck. You commented that the light seemed brighter, indicating that your Social Engagement system is on line. I know that we haven't unpacked the dream per se, but we are opening the social engagement system that invariably shuts down when we are fearful or anxious. Now your curiosity is awakened and ready to receive the dream image.

[In Damasio's terms, cited at the opening of this chapter, we have been consciously working to counter-balance the negative emotions with positive "reason-induced emotion"; The social engagement system is then available to calm the activated ventral vagus—affecting heart, breath, pulse rate.

[I change my tone a little, allowing curiosity, openness and a lightness to come into my voice.]

MD: *We don't know what the dream means, what the doctor wants from you when she asks you to breathe. We know you are in a Jungian course and you may be thinking the female doctor is an* anima *figure.*[17] *Perhaps it's psyche saying 'breathe, take a breath'.*

(Silence. Cho is looking downward, a self-soothing gesture he spoke about in Chapter 2.)

MD: *And now, maybe for a moment, look again at the light of the candle. What happens as you look at the light now, Cho?*

Cho: *I fantasize that if she were another woman and not a doctor I would be able to breathe easily.*

MD: *The white coat brings fear?*

Cho: *If she appeared as a beautiful woman I may even breathe well.* (He is smiling. He has more eye contact with me. His whole body relaxes, with greater ease coming into the muscles in his face and shoulders. He is sitting in a more open posture.)

MD: *Do I detect some humour here?*

Cho: *Yes.* (He laughs freely. The group enjoys the humour and relaxes.)

[Cho's laughter is a sign that the *dorsal vagal nerve* is relaxing its grip of fear. Curiosity and humour have stepped into the place of anxiety and *freeze.*][18]

MD: *You don't trust this woman in her white coat.*

[I name the emotion: Cho's lack of trust. Then I orient him outward to avoid his being drawn into the trauma or complex circuit; I work to keep the social engagement system active and both hemispheres connected. This opens the integrative circuit in the frontal cortex and introduces the possibility of meaning-making.]

Let's go back to the candle. How is it to look at the candle now?

Cho: *I don't feel the pressure so much in my chest now. Is it because I talked or is it because I am looking at the candle? I'm not sure what's working but something is shifting.*[19]

MD: *That's good to hear that something is shifting.*

[Once we become aware that something is *shifting*, we bring our focus to it to encourage the connecting of new neural circuits, remembering that it takes some minutes for a circuit to forge a pathway throughout the whole body.]

Cho, the dream presents an image of the issue, symptom or complex: in your dream the woman in the white coat who invites you to breathe seems to have caused you more difficulty in breathing. The dream also contains the key to the problem or enigma it presents; it points you toward the solution—to breathe more deeply. However, to do so you will have to feel safe with the doctor. We have been working with the process of orienting to the positive feelings as you connected with your image, which brought you a sense of safety, opening your tight chest and releasing blocked energy. You noticed that you were able to take in more light from the warm candle and fear gave way to curiosity, enabling you to imagine things differently to the extent of wondering, "what if she were a beautiful woman?"

Cho: *I don't notice a big difference. I feel pressure when you say, "what if she were a beautiful woman?"*

[This question could be the trigger for a new wave of activation. However, I see it as a throw-back to a habitual pattern of response—one last attempt to pull us both into the trauma vortex or complex of the controlling, suffocating female figure. Consequently, I hold steady with a calm voice, appealing to the new position that is establishing itself, allowing time for new synapses that may be firing to become established.]

MD: *My question is building up pressure in you; maybe I have become the woman in the white coat?* (I say this lightly).

Cho: *Yes. That's right.* (He laughs out loud.)

[We all laugh in recognition with him and with some relief. The shared humour has released Cho from the grip of the complex. The speed at which the old complex can be retriggered as a new integrative circuit is being established is very clearly demonstrated here. It is important not to get drawn in. Certainly, we need to acknowledge what is present for the client in the moment but we must also stay attuned to what is trying to establish new ground so that the two positions do not become polarized. We can feel that there is now ease and flow with humour playing in Cho's system.]

MD: *How are you feeling now?*

Cho: *I can breathe. And I am curious to meet her.*[20] (He is smiling and nodding and looking at me directly, eye to eye, his social engagement system on line. He is more relaxed and participating openly with the rest of the small group.)

Commentary

Through the BodyDreaming work, we found a way to hold the tension of the opposites, which enabled a new possibility to come into consciousness, for not only is Cho able to breathe for the doctor in the white coat, he is now curious to meet her. He has taken back the fearful projection of the controlling and suffocating figure. The image now holds the possibility of new energy—the new *third*—which expands the dream, dreaming it forward in a creative way. The BodyDreaming approach enables the energy to flow between the points of activation and deactivation, constriction and ease, repeatedly negotiating thresholds. By continually working with the counterpoint—orienting toward the warm light of the candle—Cho was increasingly able to tolerate the difficult and threatening emotions aroused by the initial dream image: his breath became deeper, indicating the release occurring in the parasympathetic system. Play and humour arise spontaneously and are only possible when the client is feeling "safe and in charge and in command of their participation" (Ogden, Minton, and Pain, 2006, p. 173). The denouement came with the recognition of the transference relationship, Cho's acknowledgement of how I had replaced the woman in the white coat with my activating questions. Humour was the final ingredient that *released* him and he found himself curious to meet the woman now that he could experience her from a different perspective. As Cho presented his dream during a short series of seminars I was offering, there was no time to explore the causes of the negative emotion activated by the disturbing dream image of the female doctor in the white coat. I can only speculate that what transpired subsequently in Cho's analysis and personal explorations might have been a growing relationship to the feminine aspect of himself represented by the image of the doctor, since the image was no longer ensnared in a trauma response. Gendlin speaks of an "expansion of consciousness" that happens when we are attuned to the sensing body (see Chapter 1, pp. 59–60). The slow titrating process of repatterning Cho's nervous system's response, a mixture of top-down and bottom-up processing, enabled him to stay present to the interaction and little by little awakened his curiosity and playfulness. He grew more open with me until he finally engaged spontaneously with his dream image—fantasizing with humour "what if the woman were a beautiful woman?" The BodyDreaming work had moved Cho—indeed expanding his consciousness—from a place of terror to greater coherence—his heart rate more regulated and his body and psyche receptive to the dream image.

*

What follows are excerpts from two sessions with Sam. I am using two back-to-back sessions to demonstrate how BodyDreaming involves an interweaving of body and psyche; sometimes one takes precedence, sometimes the other, but always both are connected, present and instrumental in the individuating process of becoming ourselves and realizing our potential as human beings. Sam had been a participant at a number of seminars on BodyDreaming. The excerpt below is from the first of a short series of one-on-one private sessions before she would relocate. When we met for the session, Sam was in a state of shock, having just received news from her family of a redundancy that would seriously strain financial resources and jeopardize the costly health care of her chronically ill grandchild. The shock was immediately evident in her tightly held body posture. She was sitting in an upright, rigid position in a startled response as though "caught in the glare of the news". Her face was pale, her pupils dilated, her jaw and mouth clenched, and her fingers pressing hard against each other in an open gesture of prayer. As the title to van der Kolk's book (2014) declares "The body keeps the score" (Sam's present reaction to the potentially traumatic events clearly has its origins in the early wiring of the brain and nervous system).

Sam: *The news has shattered them* (the family) *and thrown them into even greater uncertainty.*

MD: [I listen as Sam recounts the story and empathize with her.] *It must feel very shocking to have so much uncertainty at this time in particular, given their circumstances.*

[I mirror her word 'uncertainty', which seems to be a trigger word, a *feeling-toned* word that captures the essence of the shock. My mirroring creates a shared field in which Sam can feel that her distress is acknowledged and realize that I am empathic toward her. There is a resonance between us; I am feeling her concern.

[I next invite Sam to choose a positive resource to orient toward which will serve as a counterpoint to her arousal. She chooses the image of a baby she has seen in a restaurant on the previous day. The baby was initially breast-feeding, and then finished. Sam noticed that the baby's cheeks were red and that it was lying nestled on the shoulder of the mother. The baby's big round eyes were gazing at Sam, taking her in. While she recalls this memory, Sam's face lights up involuntarily, her eyes wide open and sparkling, her face smiling. The image of the baby's open face seems to have prompted Sam's social engagement system to respond with a similar ease. I mirror Sam's facial expression and tone of voice, and join in her excitement at having seen the baby snuggled against his mother, gazing at Sam so intently.]

MD: *What do you notice as you describe this baby lying there, well fed, red-cheeked, and nestled in against its mother's shoulder?*

Sam: *I can feel my chest is all warm. I can feel the heat coming in there.* (She places her hand on her chest and leaves it there for some time.)

MD: *What's that like ... to feel the heat come into your chest?*

Sam: *I can feel my chest opening.* (This prompts a spontaneous movement: her arms open wide and her chest lifts up.) *And I can feel my throat opening.* (She strokes her throat.)

MD: *Your throat is opening ... and your chest is open ... and you are smiling.*

[I mirror the movement of Sam's arms opening wide and her chest lifting. Sam repeats the movement. I invite her to pay attention to the *pre-movement movement*: the place where the impulse for movement begins in her body. She repeats the gesture, slowing it right down. She takes a bigger inhalation and with the exhale her shoulders drop and the tension eases in her body.]

MD: *And now maybe begin to notice the rest of your body ... and what is going on there.*

[As there has been an opening in her chest, I invite Sam to direct her attention to the rest of the body where the energy will then naturally begin to flow.]

Sam: *I can feel my back against the chair. I can feel my spine. I am aware of it. I want to straighten myself in the chair.*

(She realigns herself on the chair and places her feet firmly on the floor.)

MD: *How does it feel to shift position and to have your two feet on the ground?*

Sam: *I feel more connected, grounded.*

[Sam is sitting more erect. I mirror the new position, which allows time for her mirror neurons to take in the gesture and reinforce the new alignment in her spine.]

MD: *Let's go back to what happened this morning with the phone call.*

Sam: *Immediately I can feel my belly is clenched, like a fist, the way it was when it happened.*[21] (She sits quietly observing her inner sensations.)

[The image of the clenched belly describes the activity of the dorsal vagus nerve which directly connects with the gut, the shutting down action of *freeze* or *collapse*, the dorsal vagal response in the face of high arousal.[22] However, I notice that her hands do not involuntarily assume the earlier gesture of tightly pressed fingers, which was one of the indicators of where the trauma was being held. This time, after having worked with the resource, Sam is not quite so caught in the grip of the dorsal freeze. This is an example of how her system is titrating the shock, as we moved from shock to resource and back to shock. We bring attention to the *just enough noticeable difference*[23] that supports an opening in the system. Sam's fingers seem relaxed, palms open, which tells me that she has more capacity to feel emotion now. Literally, she has more space in her system as she is no longer caught in the clenched belly of the dorsal responses.

[At this point Sam's hands begin to move in a spontaneous gesture as if trying to push something away. I mirror the gesture, drawing Sam's attention to the movement.]

MD: *What do you notice with your hands in this position?*

Sam: *I feel heat; they are on fire. I can feel a huge pressure to push away with my hands.*

[Sam is gesturing while she speaks, pushing her hands outward with quite a force. I mirror the gesture.][24]

MD: *Are there words that accompany this movement?*

Sam: *Enough, that's enough. No more. These people have had enough.*

[The emotion is expressed both in Sam's gesture and in her voice, which is sounding clear and strong. I mirror her words back to her with the same intensity and tone.[25] Sam nods her head, lending further conviction to her gesture. I invite her to notice what might be happening in other parts of her body.]

Sam: *I can feel my feet. They are just dangling in the air. They are not touching the ground.*

[Sam changes her position in the chair, takes off her shoes and plants her feet firmly on the floor to have a felt sense of her feet in contact with the ground. She holds her hands steady in the same pushing position. She becomes aware of the energy in the ground pulsing beneath her feet and notices how the 'pulsing' sensation moves into her feet, then into her legs and up through her body. Sam is tracking the felt sense in her body, allowing the energy itself to take the lead, following its trajectory until her whole body is filled with this pulsing energy. I feel her more connected while she articulates the words and pushes with her hands.

These people have had enough.

[I can see that the self-protective defensive response of pushing away needs to be further supported to completion. I am prompted to offer her body some resistance so that she can feel the strength of the impulse to push away, the innate reflex as it motors out through her body.

[Bonnie Bainbridge Cohan, movement educator and founder of *Body-Mind Centering*, points out that "by assuming the reflex is there, you can elicit it".[26] She suggests supporting the reflex that may not be happening, or may be stuck, through touching, stimulation or the use of imagery. I am thinking that we might stimulate the reflex through contact on the skin— by my offering Sam my hands as they mirror hers in this position.

[I invite Sam to stand and raise her hands toward mine as I raise my hands to the same level as hers, initially asking her to hold hers at a distance from mine. I remind Sam of the positive experience in her body. I encourage her to feel into her connection with the ground and track the pulsing energy as it comes through her feet, moving into her legs, pelvis and spine, tracking it right up her spine to the base of the skull and then following it down her arms and into her hands. I invite her to make the choice to touch or not to touch, to push or not to push against my hands. She places her hands against mine and begins to push through her hands. She feels the pressure build through her whole body, until she is really making an effort to push me away. I stand firmly balanced, one foot in front of the other, and hold my ground through my own centre of gravity.[27] I prompt her with her own words ...]

MD: *"Enough, enough."*

[Sam pushes hard against me, staring at me with eyes wide open, emphatically repeating the words.]

Sam: *Enough, enough. These people have had enough.*

[Sam's arms are now fully extended, pushing against my hands, and I hold my position until finally I yield to her strength. She drops her arms with relief and satisfaction. She has accomplished something huge: a developmental sequence—the sympathetic *fight* reflex—that she has now brought to completion, granting her a felt sense of empowerment and opening new neural pathways. I am reminded of Levine's observation:

> The important therapeutic task in the sympathetic/mobilization phase is to ensure the client *contains* these intense arousal sensations without becoming overwhelmed. ... In this way, they are experienced as intense but manageable waves of energy, as well as sensations associated with aggression and self-protection.
>
> (Levine, 2010, p. 106)

[Sam was able to contain the sympathetic arousal—the rising anger in her body—without shutting it down or falling into immobility. Instead, the self-protective defensive *fight* response was enabled to motor through to completion.[28] This achievement gives Sam a sense of strength and agency as she knows she can protect herself and take action if necessary. This is a crucial step in re-educating her system's default response of helplessness and freeze, which most probably originated in developmental trauma.

[We sit down again. There is a growing sense of calm in the room. We sit for some time together in an easy silence.[29]]

MD: *What are you noticing now in your body?*

[Slowly Sam begins to move her hands and fingers in a very particular, stylized gesture. I can see that she is sensing and playing with energy as it moves between her hands, drawing it together and out again in a circular movement, one hand coming downward to meet the other as it moves upwards from below in a rhythmic flow. This free flowing, playful movement is enabling further integration in Sam's system. Levine suggests that such "archetypal movements arise at unique moments when the instinctual is seamlessly wedded with one's conscious awareness—when the primitive brain stem and the highest neocortical functions integrate" (2010, p. 149).]

MD: *What are you noticing as you make the movement?*

Sam: *I feel a warm glow all over my body.*

MD: *Like the baby after the feed?* (A big smile immediately lights up Sam's face.)

Sam: *Oh, that baby! It was so beautiful.* (She lets out a deep and spontaneous exhale, her body clearly relaxing in pleasure. She smiles in recognition of the mirror image that has unfolded and been embodied.)

Commentary

At the start of the session, Sam was sitting in a *freeze*, her body rigid and held tightly. She drew on the image of the smiling, well-fed baby as a resource and that memory enabled her nervous system to re-negotiate the shock of the family's news. The resource opened Sam's social engagement system, i.e., the muscles of the face, throat and head, and her face was open and smiling as she mirrored the image of the baby. This produced a calming of the respiratory circuit of the ventral vagal system—reflected in Sam's opening her arms wide and her chest expanding as she took a deeper breath—and shifting her out of the *freeze* of the dorsal vagal response that held her belly in its grip when we first arrived. Sam was then able to access a healthy sympathetic *fight* response in the spontaneous self-protective, defensive gesture of pushing away with open hands. Her voice, part of the social engagement system, was available to her and strong: "*Enough, that's enough.*" I noticed that the pushing reflex was present but not quite completing, so I invited Sam to push against my hands to give the reflex the opportunity to move through her hands in a grounded way, to complete the gesture. This resulted in a release in Sam's throat and her voice carried greater authority: "*these people have had enough.*" When the sequence of movements had completed itself, we sat down. Like a baby after a satisfying meal, we rested. In its own time, a new impulse arrived: Sam's hands began to dance with each other while she sensed the energy moving between them. Sam was totally present to the movement, her body wrapped in a softness, a mirror image of the baby lying on his mother's shoulder in the after-glow of a feed. Levine speaks of the kind of rhythmic gesture that had followed the completion of the self-protective defence movement of Sam's successfully pushing me back:

> In tracking people's postural shifts, I began to notice subtle hand and arm gestures that were clearly different from voluntary ones. These gestures often appeared at moments of significant therapeutic movement and frequently indicated pleasingly unforeseen resources and shifts toward flow and wholeness.
>
> (Levine, 2010, p. 148)

The energy that Sam released in her pushing had transformed into a spontaneous, healing, integrative gesture in the movement of her hands and fingers (those same fingers that were pressed hard together, holding in the trauma, at the beginning of the session). Sam, like the baby, had enjoyed a good feed; it was time for rest and integration, out of which came a dream.

The Dream

The dream that followed our initial session was the psyche's way of integrating the energy released in the body-work and *dreaming the work forward*. "The psyche is essentially purposive and directed" (Jung, 1912, par. 90), and the dream presents an image of psychic energy that is as yet unconscious but pushing toward consciousness. It often presents a new situation, as yet unlived potential, and points to the direction in which the dreamer's psychic energy is tending. What follows is an excerpt from the following session in which we worked on Sam's dream.

I start by asking Sam to 'check in' with her body. She says she is feeling a bit stiff and cold and that, after she ate a sandwich, her belly developed its usual ache on the left side. Then Sam tells me her dream.

Sam: *There was a dog lying at the back of my house, a brown lab. I went around to the back of the house, and the dog was lying there. The dog is lit from within, he is facing me. There were cats on the perimeter, at the back—no fence but the edge is defined, and they were aware of the dog. They wouldn't hurt me, the dog would protect me. They didn't have the power they might usually have. I was fascinated by them. It was dark. I can barely see them in the shadow, they are walking back and forth as they might do in the zoo. Their movement is so fluid, so beautifully co-ordinated. They are so perfectly built for what they need to do—they are on the hunt—to survive. They wouldn't cross the boundary when the dog was there. I could only see them because of the glow from his body and because they were moving. I know they are there. I love the Big Cats. They*

are majestic to me. Powerful, beautiful. There is a numinous feel to the
whole back yard, a feeling of awe that they are back there.

MD: *How do you feel when you see the dog?*

[I orient Sam to the positive, safe image in the dream—the dog, not toward the powerful numinosity of the Big Cats, which might activate her system at this stage. I am bringing Sam's attention to the regulating image (resource) to help establish homeostasis and a sense of safety, which will access the social engagement system and engender greater curiosity about the dream images.]

Sam: (Smiling, making a gesture to indicate how the dog was lying.) *He's very*
comfortable, lying on its belly, facing the house, not the back garden ...
its head on its paws, which were crossed over ... he was so comfortable in
himself.

MD: *How does it make you feel to see him like that?* [I mirror the position of the
paws to her and also her words.] ... *'so comfortable in himself, lying on its*
belly, its head on its paws.'

(Sam smiles as she adopts the body posture of the dog.)

MD: *Notice your smile and how that feels in your body.... as I look at you I am*
reminded of the baby's appearance as he lay on his mother's shoulder.

Sam: *Oh, yes.* (Her eyes light up a little; she smiles again.)

[The dog in the dream has a similar glow to that of the baby's smile; the glow is coming from inside the dog's body and is casting light on what is lurking in the shadows—the Big Cats that are walking to and fro at the perimeter of the backyard. In other words, to return once more to Damasio's argument presented at the beginning of this chapter, our focus on positive feeling-toned images (baby's smile, glowing dog) enables Sam to manage the activation triggered at seeing the Big Cats at the perimeter of her backyard.

MD: *What are you noticing as you see this dog, lying there ... ?*

Sam: *It's all lit up from inside, the belly is lit up ... like it's orange. The fur is*
brown but the light in the belly under the fur is orange. I don't even like
orange. He seems happy, content, comfortable in himself.

MD: *How does that feel, to see these two resourceful images side by side ... the*
dream image of the dog, happy in himself and the image of the baby lying
contented on his mother's shoulder?

Sam: *I feel more ease ... ease in my shoulders, I can feel them drop down. I feel*
connected again in my body. (Her breath drops deeper. She looks at her feet
...) *They are dangling in the air again. I need to have them on the ground.*

[Sam recalls the felt sense experience of contacting the energy in the ground under her feet in the previous session and now she has that reassurance immediately available as a body memory: her animal body remembers.]

Sam: (Smiling) *I feel solid in myself.* (Her back straightens in a re-alignment.)

[We have taken time to allow the dream image of the dog to re-establish homeostasis and an easy rhythm between the sympathetic and parasympathetic systems. Her curiosity is aroused.]

Sam: *Those are Big Cats, not small, little ones but real CATS.* (Her eyes are wide open. Her shoulders, arms and hands begin to move in small, cat-like gestures.)

MD: [I mirror her movements.] *It appears to me that there is a lot of movement in your shoulders. How does it feel to move in this cat-like way?*

Sam: *I am enjoying it. But I need to be on my feet.* (She stands up and begins to move slowly).

   [Sam begins an *authentic movement* sequence in which we don't form the movement consciously but let the movement happen. We listen to the body and feel into the movement from the inside— "one has to learn to *let it happen* as contrasted to *doing it*" (Mary Starks Whitehouse, founder of Authentic Movement, cited in Chodorow, 1991, p. 25).]

   I feel free.

   [Sam is moving deliberately and slowly like a Big Cat as I see it, in my mind's eye, walking on the plains of the Serengeti. I mirror her actions.]

   My lower body wants to move, too.

   (She expands the movement, engaging her lower body, moving more energetically around the room. Stiff and sore when we started the session, Sam's whole body is now actively joining in the catlike movements.)

   I am trying to get that movement into my hips.

   [I am alerted by the word *trying*, as it tells me that Sam may have an idea of how her hips should be moving; consequently, she may override her body's innate wisdom, which may be presenting as reluctance or pain. I intervene to slow the pace. This is a *threshold moment* in which we want to listen to the body, stay present to the authentic movement and impulse, and not control, direct or perform the movement.]

MD: *Let's just pause and take a moment. How would it be to bring your attention to the hips and notice what is happening there.*

Sam: *I feel like it's not doing what I want to do. It's caught and it's hurting a little, an old ache is coming back in.*

MD: *Taking the time to notice the ache in the hips.... and, at the same time, notice what else is happening in your body ... Maybe feel what it's like to connect back to the Big Cat energy as it moves in your shoulders.*[30] *Maybe you can begin to track the movement really slowly, seeing if you can feel into the pre-movement impulse there ... while taking all the time in the world to be in the pleasure of the movement.*[31]

   [I move briefly, but going at slow pace in an attempt to activate Sam's mirror neurons, paying attention to the stirrings of movement, helping Sam re-align herself with the spontaneous initial impulse and sensation in her shoulders.]

Sam: (Sam closes her eyes and waits, then slowly begins to lean into one shoulder, making very small movements with head, neck and shoulder.) *It's sweet. It's delicious to feel the movement in my neck and the stretch come into the shoulder and travel down the arm.*

[Sam's head is gently rotating from side to side. It seems her head is turning more in one direction than the other. I suggest she move with her eyes open and allow her head to turn very slowly toward that direction,[32] just as far as is comfortable, pause there, and then come back to the centre—and to repeat that movement to the other side, again, just as far as is comfortable. The movement of the muscles of the head, face, eyes, jaw, neck and shoulders encourages Sam's social engagement system to open up, which brings more flow to the whole system as it directly connects to and acts on the ventral and dorsal vagus. Levine points out that it is only possible to "access the social engagement system when the nervous system is no longer hijacked by immobilization and the hyperarousal systems" (2010, p. 107). In the first session, Sam moved out of immobility and into sympathetic arousal to motor through the self-protective defence reflex of pushing out through her shoulders, arms, and hands. In the gentle rotation of the head we access the social engagement system which will restore an even greater rhythmic balance between the sympathetic and parasympathetic systems.

[Sam continues to move in the room at a deliberately slow pace, enjoying a greater fluidity in her movements. Her face is relaxed, she is more *in* her body, more connected.]

Sam: *I'm not jammed up. It's all moving through me in a flow. It's just doing what it's meant to do, it's just being **cat**.*

[An integration and coherence is beginning to happen: when the body moves to its own rhythm it is inclusive; the flow of energy is not bounded in one place, but wants to flow through to the perimeters from the core.

[I prompt Sam to be aware of her hips and legs as she moves. Staying in one position, she begins to shift her weight slowly through her pelvis from one leg to the other, raising one foot at a time off the ground and stepping back down again. The movement comes through the spine and her shoulders and arms join the synchronized walking movement. As she breathes out, her exhale gets longer with each downward movement; her hips are more open.[33] Sam is dropping her breath, weight and energy deeper down through her hips and legs and feet and into the ground. She moves as one animal body: that of a Big Cat.]

Sam: *It's like it's coming from my centre. All of me is moving in flow. It's not complex. It just does what it's meant to do in terms of everything, in terms of movement, in terms of what it's meant to do, it's just being Big Cat.*

MD: *It sounds like it's being its instinctual self.*

Sam: *Totally instinctual. Being Big Cat is being exactly what it needs to be. They don't move as if in fear. They move in an uninhibited way ... true unto themselves. It puts me in touch with my **still point**.*

[Sam has reached a point of deep integration, where image, movement, emotion and meaning coincide. By not overriding the physical discomfort she had felt in her hips, we stayed more in tune with the initial impulse. This allowed the energy to find its own pathways on which to move through the body, eventually incorporating the hips in the new pattern and rhythm.

[Initially, given Sam's excitement at experiencing her *cat* body, we might easily have overridden the resistance or activation in her painfully "jammed up" hips that indicated a block, trauma or complex lodged in that part of the body. Ignoring the body's warning might have induced us to go "over threshold", failing to integrate the blocked shadow energy in the body, which would then remain locked in the nerve endings of the tissue, joints or organs. Encountering resistance in the body indicates a *threshold moment*. If we bring our attention to its opposite, to where the energy is flowing naturally, and track the pre-movement sensation and impulse in that body part slowly and sensitively, the energy intensifies, opening new neural circuits that are inclusive of the part of the body in which the energy is stuck. It is crucial to slow the pace to allow sufficient time to support the work of building new neural circuits which in turn open new possibilities, enabling a new impulse. In this example, Sam reconnected with the impulse for movement in the shoulders. In its own time, a new impulse followed—she lifted her legs slowly and rhythmically, first one foot, then the other, placing each in turn back on the ground. Unblocking energy in the hips in this measured way supports the flow of energy to move freely and prompt the upper and lower body to join together in the dance. The integration brought into awareness something of the archetypal significance of Big Cat energy – "*being Cat is exactly what it's meant to be*". Her dream indicated the potential—what wants to come to consciousness—the instinctual energy of Big Cat, that lay in the shadows on the periphery of the back garden. Her moving, sensing body is dreaming the dream into consciousness.]

To summarize: In the first of these two sessions, our work was to release Sam from the *freeze/collapse* response to the shock of the news from home. The resource of the baby's smile allowed Sam to access her social engagement system, soothing the activation and facilitating the completion of the self-protective defensive response (pushing away and saying "it's enough!"). The session ended with an exquisite sequence of hand movements suggesting a deep integration taking place in Sam's system. The dream which immediately followed, showing where the energy wants to go, seemed to continue the process of consolidation, integration and transformation.[34] The series of images (baby's smile, glowing dog, powerful Big Cats) moves from human child to domesticated animal, the glowing dog to Big Cat—or, we might say, from the immediate, human problem at the forefront of consciousness, to the body (imaged in the domesticated instinct of the dog) to the fascinating, powerful, untamed realm of archetypal energy (the Big Cats). Significantly, Sam's focus shifts as her body resonates with the images. She moves from a warm, open emotional response to the baby's smile, to a sense of comfort, protection and security evoked by the dog's inner glow. Her response to the Big Cats is more complex: at first there is fear, then reassurance (she knows the dog will protect her). Then comes fascination, followed by curiosity as Sam's body is affected by the energy of the Big Cats and she embodies something of their potential in her imitation of their sinuous movement. In the first of these two sessions we worked slowly with the impulse that moved in her shoulders to complete the self-protective reflex of pushing away. The dream followed on from the opening in her system. She found her Big Cat movements in the 'open' shoulders and began to move in the room, titrating the blockage she felt in her hips, and slowly incorporating the released energy throughout her Big Cat body. The alignment between the dream image, impulse and body movement brought Sam into her 'truth and power', her cat body awakened. Sam was able to embody the Big Cats' power and stealth and simultaneously reach their deep capacity for stillness, arriving at her 'still point'. The cat, Marie-Louise von Franz reminds us, apart from being fiercely independent and resourceful, is an exceedingly tough, vital creature that is able to survive the most terrible things: "A cat goes its own way. It knows what it wants and goes its own way" (1999, pp. 59–60).[35]

By the end of our two sessions, the initial negative emotion had been "subdued", to use Damasio's term, by the emergence of the impulses arising in her body, which she then moved to as image. Imagination, emotion and sensation became embodied in the unfolding form. Her witnessing self and her social engagement system provided the constant drum beat that kept time for the pendulating dance between the sympathetic and parasympathetic systems. Sam is in the midst of a time of change and uncertainty in which she faces the challenge of serious personal and family difficulties. Sam's early childhood had left its mark on her nervous system's state of immobility and collapse, carrying a chronic lifelong illness. Finding her 'secure base' in her sensing moving body, as she dreamed her dream on, brought her a felt sense of coherence, fluidity and meaning – arriving at her 'still point', a deep state of homeostasis. She had found her support, needed to meet the challenges in her life, without being hijacked by the patterned nervous response of freeze/collapse. Schore comments, "The role of regulation is so important that I now see attachment theory primarily as a theory of emotional and bodily regulation" (in conversation with Sieff, 2015, p. 116). BodyDreaming highlights the importance of building a learned secure attachment to the body as a means to shift deep entrenched nervous system responses, complete self-protective defense reflexes and heal insecure attachment patterns. Our work together, a regulating alignment of dream, body and impulse, calls to mind for me the echo of the warm glow of the interior body in response to the image of the baby's smile, the dog's orange light and the gradual illumination of the passage way at Newgrange receiving the sunlight, as it creeps steadily toward the inner chamber during the Winter Solstice. Sam's work continues in Chapter 9.

Notes

1 Coleman Barks, "Birdwings", in *The Essential Rumi: Translations by Coleman Barks,* with John Moyne, A.J. Arberry, Reynold Nicholson (New Jersey: Castle Books, 1997), 174.

2 C.G. Jung, Lecture V, 21st February 1934, in *Visions: Notes of the Seminar Given in 1930–1934,* ed Claire Douglas (in two volumes – 2) (Bollingen Series XCIX) (Princeton, NJ: Princeton University Press, 1997; London & New York: Routledge, 1998), p. 1316.

3   A *complex,* according to Jung, is the sum of all the associated ideas and feelings that are attracted to an archetype [e.g., the archetype of the mother, the father, the sister, the brother, the hero, the victim, etc.]; the complex gives the archetype a form of expression. The complex is powered by affect. It is feeling this affect that tells us we are experiencing an archetype.

(Wilmer, 2013, p. 57)

4 "The same self-regulating, homeostatic process works in the psyche providing it is free to operate naturally and has not been damaged. Like the body, the unconscious psyche has an instinctive wisdom which can correct the errors and excesses of consciousness if we are open to its messages" (Edinger, 1972, p. 61).

5 "The ability to sense the psyche—which is often traditionally defined as soul, the spirit, the intellect, or the mind—is at the heart of what it means to perceive the inner world" (Siegel, 2012, pp. 43–44).

6   Never apply any theory, but always ask the patient how he feels about his dream images. For dreams are always about a particular problem of the individual about which he has a wrong conscious judgment. The dreams are the reaction to our conscious attitude in the same way that the body reacts when we overeat or do not eat enough or when we ill-treat it in some other way. Dreams are the natural reaction of the self-regulating psychic system.

(Jung, 1935, par. 248)

7 Jung meant by *individuation*:

In the last analysis every life is the realization of a whole, that is, of a self, for which reason this realization can also be called "individuation". All life is bound to individual carriers who realize it, and it is simply inconceivable without them. But every carrier is charged with an individual destiny and destination, and the realization of these alone makes sense of life.

(Jung, 1936, par. 330)

8 See Chapter 1, p. 65, n. 33
9 See Chapter 1, pp. 46–49, on Memory.
10 "The *circuitry* system of our own *nervous system* is such that if we attune, we come to create *resonance* in which our observing *self* takes on some of the features of that which we are observing. ... [T]his creates an *interpersonal resonance* in which each person *feels felt* by the other. When this joining is with respect and care, this *interpersonal attunement* is the basis of *secure attachment*" (Siegel, 2012, p. 23).
11 "Orientation is a proxy for the social engagement system which affects the ventral vagus directly" (Steven Hoskinson). Personal notes taken in Somatic Experiencing Training in Northern Ireland, 2013–2016.
12 Hoskinson describes a *Free Association* conversation as a means of self-regulating: "It's attuning to the person and the content that they bring, and selectively reinforcing around those more positive aspects of their psychic production, their associative

network aspects that are going to be disproportionately organizing" (Prengel, 2016, p. 6).

13 "The early affective mother-infant interaction that allows for the 'programming of prosody,'" that is, the "lilting, singsong, emotional communicative dance between mothers and infants, where high-pitched melodic 'motherese' prevails" (Wilkinson, 2010, pp. 48–49).

14 "With the sense of danger, we cannot activate ... the social engagement system. ... Instead of being present with mindfulness, we become removed, alone, and paralyzed. This is how we move from being receptive to being reactive" (Siegel, 2010a, p. 23).

15   The Social Engagement System is an integrated system with both a somatomotor component regulating the striated muscles of the face and a visceromotor component regulating the heart via a myelinated vagus. This system is capable of dampening activation of the sympathetic nervous system and the HPA axis. By calming the viscera and regulating facial muscles, this system enables and promotes social interactions in safe contexts.

(Porges, 2009, p. 41)

16 Fechner, 1873.

17 Of Jung's extensive comments on the concept of the *anima*, perhaps the most pertinent in the present context is his use of the term to designate the inner personality in the man:

The inner personality is the way one behaves in relation to one's inner psychic processes; it is the inner attitude, the characteristic face, that is turned towards the unconscious.... The anima usually contains all those common human qualities which the conscious attitude lacks.

(Jung, 1921, par. 803–804)

In this sense, the anima connects the man to his innermost self as she shows him an aspect of his unconscious. In his *Commentary on The Secret of the Golden Flower*, Jung writes: "I have defined the anima as a personification of the unconscious in general, and have taken it as a bridge to the unconscious, in other words, as a function of relationship to the unconscious" (1962, par. 62).

18 When curiosity and humour enter the field, we know that the social engagement system is more available and the vagus nerve begins to loosen its defensive position; as muscle tension relaxes there often follows laughter and sometimes great big yawns.

19 Cho's system is relaxing and Cho is feeling a degree of safety which could mean that the *medial prefrontal cortex* is secreting the gel-like substance, GABA or gamma-amniobutyric acid, which "is a neurotransmitter that plays an important role in the prefrontal inhibition of subcortical firing ... a kind of gel to soothe the limbic eruptions" (Siegel, 2010b, p. 28).

20 "The projection of the controlling, devouring parent can gradually be withdrawn as the analyst demonstrates again and again [her] own reflective function, the awareness of the patient as a separate psychological and emotional being" (Knox, 2011, p. 161).

21 "When aroused to fight or flight (sympathetic arousal), our guts tighten, and the motility of the gastrointestinal system is inhibited" (Levine, 2010, p. 122).

22 "The primitive unmyelinated vagus nerve of the immobilization system connects the brain with most of our internal organs. ... [T]his nerve largely serves our gastrointestinal system, including ingestion, digestion, assimilation, and elimination. It also significantly affects the heart and lungs" (Levine, 2010, p. 123).

23 See Fechner, Introductory chapter, *n*. 35, and Chapter 1, p. 65.

24 "Observing spontaneous (intrinsic) postures gives the therapist a vital window into the state of a client's nervous system and psyche. The body benevolently shows us when

we are preparing to act and precisely what incipient pre-movement action is being prepared for" (Levine, 2010, p. 146).

25 The Social Engagement system controls the voice, ear and facial muscles (Levine, 2010, p. 106).

26 "Where the reaction is not taking place, there's a lack of cellular awareness or ... cellular absorption of the information. It's like the cells are stimulated but they don't take it in" (Bainbridge Cohen, 1993, p. 12).

27   [T]he visual information we receive when we watch another act gets mapped onto the equivalent motor representation in our own brain by the activity of ... mirror neurons. ... We experience the other *as if* we were executing the same action, feeling the same emotion, making the same vocalization, or being touched as they are being touched.

(Stern, 2004, p. 79)

As clients observe the therapist demonstrating a somatic resource, they experience it in the brain as if they were executing the same action and experiencing the same emotional affect, essentially 'rehearsing' the movement themselves.

28 "This reflex is a defensive (fight) reflex and underlies all extension movements of the total arm or leg that are initiated from the hand or foot, such as the extensor phase of kicking, creeping, walking, climbing and equilibrium response" (Bainbridge Cohan, 1993, p. 130).

29 "An individual who has been able to move out of immobility, and then through sympathetic arousal, begins to experience a restorative and deepening calm" (Levine, 2010, p. 106).

30 Raja Selvam, Somatic Experiencing instructor, in conversation with Serge Prengel, emphasizes that in order to be able to work with what the body is holding and to tolerate the unbearable affects we need to open up more space in the body. He cautions against focusing on sensation alone and tracking it in one particular area in the body that is constricted, stressing the need to locate space that *is* available, where energy is flowing easily. This open space allows the blocked energy a space to flow into. "[T]he more intense an experience is in the physical body, more of the body needs to be involved in generating and holding it" (Prengel, 2014, p. 15).

31 Mary Starks Whitehouse, founder of Authentic Movement and Jungian analyst, discusses the impulse for movement:

Where does movement come from? It originates in ... a specific inner impulse having the quality of sensation. This impulse leads outward into space so that movement becomes visible as physical action. Following the inner sensation, allowing the impulse to take the form of physical action is active imagination in movement, just as following the visual image is active imagination in phantasy.

(Cited in Chodorow, 1991, p. 28)

32 Levine quotes Sir Charles Sherrington, the grandfather of modern neurophysiology: "much of the reflex reaction expressed by the skeletal musculature is not motile, but postural, and has as its result not a movement but the steady maintenance of an attitude." Levine then cites A.E. Gesell, a student of Sherrington, who adds that "'the requisite motor equipment for behavior is established well in advance of the behavior itself.'" Gesell "underscores how important posture is in the generation of new behaviors, sensations, feelings and meanings" when he writes: "'the embryogenesis of mind must be sought in the beginnings of postural behavior'" (Levine, 2010, p. 145). In BodyDreaming, we invite the client to slow down the gesture and go back to track the first stirring of a movement because this focuses our awareness on an internal process, namely, the *pre-movement movement*.

33 "Most of us keep our breath shallow because the eruption of feeling is too intense if we inhale deeply. Breathing is very important because it is a matter of receiving and that is the feminine principle incarnate" (Woodman, 1993, pp. 16–17).

34 Jung refers to the dream as a "spontaneous self-portrayal, in symbolic form, of the actual situation in the unconscious" ([1916] 1958, par. 505).

35   The cat in our country [Switzerland] stems originally from Egypt, where it was once a divine animal. There, they had a cat goddess who was the goddess of music, sexuality, pleasure in life, and life-embracing feminine fertility. The cat, in contrast to the dog, has never sold his soul to man. It has a kind of egocentric reserve. The cat says: "You may stroke me and you may serve me", but it never becomes your slave. And if you annoy it, it just walks out on you. In women's dreams, therefore, the cat is often an image of something feminine, independent and sure of itself, just what modern women so often lack. That's why the cat comes up in women's dreams as a positive model of feminine behaviour.... It is feminine, and at the same time, very firm, very identical with itself. The cat is not very amiable, but very true to itself.

(von Franz in conversation with Fraser Boa, 1988, p. 157)

References

Bainbridge Cohen, B. (1993) *Sensing, Feeling, and Action: The Experiential Anatomy of Body-Mind Centering*, Northhampton, MA: Contact Editions. Excerpts published in Hanlon Johnson, D. (1995), *Bone, Breath, and Gesture: Practices of Embodiment*, Berkley CA: North Atlantic Books.

Barks, C. (1997) "Birdwings," in *The Essential Rumi: Translations by Coleman Barks*, New Jersey: Castle Books.

Boa, F. (1988) *The Way of the Dream: Conversations on Jungian Dream Interpretation with Marie-Louise von Franz*, Boston, MA and London: Shambala.

Chodorow, J. (1991) *Dance Therapy and Depth Psychology: The Moving Imagination*, London: Routledge.

Damasio, A. (2003) *Looking for Spinoza: Joy, Sorrow, and the Feeling Brain*, Orlando, FL: Harcourt Books.

Edinger, E.F. (1972) *Ego and Archetype: Individuation and the Religious Function of the Psyche*, Boston, MA: Shambhala.

Fechner, G.T. (1873). *Einige Ideen zur Schöpfungs - und Entwickelundsgechichte der Organismen [Ideas in the History of Organism Creation and Development]*, Leipzig: Breitkopf und Härtel.

Jung, C.G. (1912) *Symbols of Transformation*, Collected Works 5, Princeton, NJ: Princeton University Press.

Jung, C.G. ([1916] 1958) *The Transcendent Function*, Collected Works 8, Princeton, NJ: Princeton University Press.

Jung, C.G. (1921) *Psychological Types*, Collected Works 6, Princeton, NJ: Princeton University Press.

Jung, C.G, (1935) *The Tavistock Lectures: On the Theory and Practice of Analytical Psychology*, Collected Works 18, Princeton, NJ: Princeton University Press.

Jung, C.G. (1936) *Individual Dream Symbolism in Relation to Alchemy*, Collected Works 12, Princeton, NJ: Princeton University Press.

Jung, C.G. (1962) *Commentary on "The Secret of the Golden Flower"*, Collected Works 13, Princeton, NJ: Princeton University Press.

Jung, C.G. (1997) *Visions: Notes of the Seminar Given in 1930–1934*, Claire Douglas (ed.), in *two* volumes, Bollingen Series XCIX, Princeton, NJ: Princeton University Press (London & New York: Routledge, 1998).

Knox, J. (2011) *Self-Agency in Psychotherapy: Attachment, Autonomy and Intimacy*, London: W.W. Norton and Co.

Levine, P. (2010) *In an Unspoken Voice: How the Body Releases Trauma and Restores Goodness*, Berkeley, CA: North Atlantic Books.

Ogden, P., Minton, K. and Pain, C. (2006) *Trauma and the Body: A Sensorimotor Approach to Psychotherapy*, London and New York: W.W. Norton & Co.

Porges, S.W. (2009) "Reciprocol Influences Between Body and Brain in the Perception and Expression of Affect: A Polyvagal Perspective," in *The Healing Power of Emotion: Affective Neuroscience, Development and Clinical Practice*, D. Fosha, D. Siegel, and M. Soloman (eds.), London and New York: W.W. Norton & Co., pp. 27–54.

Prengel, S. (2014) In conversation with Raja Selvam. "Raja Selvam: Integral Somatic Psychotherapy." https://relationalimplicit.com/somatic-perspectives/. Accessed 31 August 2018 at: https://relationalimplicit.com/zug/transcripts/Selvam-2014-07.pdf, pp.1–18.

Prengel, S. (2016) In conversation with Steven Hoskinson. Relational Implicit, https://relationalimplicit.com/somatic-perspectives/. Accessed 31 August 2018 at: https://relationalimplicit.com/zug/transcripts/Hoskinson-2016-05.pdf, pp.1–10.

Sieff, D.F. (2015) *Understanding and Healing Emotional Trauma: Conversations with Pioneering Clinicians and Researchers*, Hove, UK and New York: Routledge.

Siegel, D.J. (2010a) *The Mindful Therapist: A Clinician's Guide to Mindsight and Neural Integration*, New York: W.W. Norton & Co.

Siegel, D.J. (2010b) *Mindsight: Transform your Brain with the New Science of Kindness*, London: One World Publications.

Siegel D.J. (2012) *Pocket Guide to Interpersonal Neurobiology: An Integrative Handbook of the Mind*, New York: W.W Norton & Co.

Stern, D.N. (2004) *The Present Moment in Psychotherapy and Everyday Life*, New York: W.W. Norton & Co.

van der Kolk, B. (2014) *The Body Keeps the Score: Mind, Brain and Body in the Transformation of Trauma*, St Ives, UK: Penguin Random House.

von Franz, M-L. (1999) *The Cat: A Tale of Feminine Redemption*, Toronto: Inner City Books.

Wilkinson, M. (2010) *Changing Minds in Psychotherapy: Emotion, Attachment, Trauma and Neurobiology*, London and New York: W.W. Norton & Co.

Wilmer, H.A. (2013) *Practical Jung: Nuts and Bolts of Jungian Psychotherapy*, Wilmette, IL: Chiron Publications.

Woodman, M. (1993) *Conscious Femininity: Interviews with Marion Woodman*, Toronto: Inner City Books.

Chapter 4

Attunement

Learned Secure Attachment in the Body

"I'm yielding to it"

John Bowlby, psychiatrist, psychoanalyst and psychologist, was the driving force behind the development of Attachment Theory (1969). Bowlby placed the relationship between the child and the caregiver, in their particular environment and circumstances, at the centre of his theory of child development. Based on his relationship with his caregiver, the child develops an inner working model of selfhood and an inner working model of others that then influences his thoughts, feelings, expectations and behaviour patterns in subsequent relationships.[1] Psychoanalytic thinking in the 1970s was largely opposed to Bowlby's views, preferring to understand child psychology in terms of the fantasy life of the child. However, Bowlby's colleague, Mary Ainsworth, supported Bowlby's Attachment Theory with her evidence-based research, which addresses both a child's "stranger wariness" and his behaviour, focusing on how the child responds to rupture, i.e., the absence and subsequent reappearance of the mother after a period of separation. She devised a technique called Strange Situation Classification (SSC) in order to investigate how attachment styles might vary between children (Ainsworth and Wittig, 1969). Secure infants are very upset by the separation but are easily comforted by their mother's return and can resume play. As a child grows, he uses his mother/caregiver as a secure base from which to move away and explore the world. In 1979 Ainsworth, Blehar, Waters and Wall classified three different attachment styles: *secure attachment, insecure avoidant attachment*, and *insecure ambivalent attachment*. Later, in 1990, Mary Main and Judith Solomon identified a fourth pattern: *disorganized disoriented attachment* (1990). I will look in more detail at these patterns below.

Bowlby ([1969] 1981) envisaged that changes in attachment patterns could occur in an individual's lifetime, given the presence and timing of both positive and negative life events. He believed that children could rise above the effects of negative childhood experiences to some degree and attain *earned* secure relationships in their adult lives. Attachment theory shows that dependency is part of being human and the need for a connection with an attachment figure is an innate survival instinct. The presence of an attachment figure provides comfort and security, regulates emotions and provides a secure base from which one can explore the world, take risks, learn new things. Marion Solomon points out that Bowlby's theory of

an 'earned' secure attachment "confirms other research demonstrating that connections among neurons can be directly altered and shaped by current experience,
thanks to the neural plasticity of the brain" (in Fosha *et al.*, 2009, p. 232). Bowlby
viewed secure attachment as adaptive and normal and all forms of insecure attachment as deviations. More recently, evolutionary research demonstrates that "we
cannot designate certain behaviours as adaptive, others as maladaptive. Rather
their adaptiveness depends on the environment in which that individual is living"
(Sarah Blaffer Hrdy in conversation with Sieff, 2015, p. 196).[2]

Secure attachment—Bowlby reflects on the impact of separation on the mother/
infant relationship:

> From time immemorial mothers and poets have been alive to the distress
> caused to a child by loss of its mother; but it is only now in the last fifty years
> that, by fits and starts, science has awoken to it.
>
> (Bowlby, [1969] 1981, p. 46)

With the help of neuroscience, fMRIs and pet scans we can now measure the
effects of separation, chronic stress and trauma on the development of the infant's
brain. Bowlby stresses that the basic task in the first year of life is for the infant
to form attachments. The infant's primary relationship, usually formed with the
mother, determines how the infant's neural wiring is encoded and establishes
the pattern for all future relationships and attachments. The mother accomplishes the
task of creating secure attachment:

> through reciprocal, attuned somatic and verbal communication with her
> infant. The child engages in exploratory behavior in the presence of her par-
> ent, shows signs of missing the parent upon separation, approaches the parent
> without ambivalence upon reunion, and often initiates physical contact.
>
> (Ogden, Minton and Pain, 2006, p. 47)

Schore's extensive research in the fields of psychoanalysis, neurobiology, infant
development theory, and attachment theory underline the importance of the
attachment relationship since the mother is "the hidden regulator of the infant's
endocrine and nervous system" (Schore, 1994, p. 17). His findings conclude that
attachment is "fundamentally a process of psychobiological attunement, and ...
stable attachment bonds are vitally important for the infant's continuing neuro-
biological development" (*ibid.*, p. 23).

In the relatively recent past, research in neuroscience has clearly identified the
neural patterning that takes place during the formation of the infant's brain and
the role the mother–infant dyad plays in the inter-regulatory dynamic that shapes
the infant's developing autonomic nervous system. Beebe and Lachmann (2002)
emphasize the infant's innate capacity for regulation, and neuro-imaging shows us
the infant's ability to regulate herself *in utero*. Beebe and Lachmann point out that
mutual engagement between mother and infant creates bi-directional regulation:

> Regulatory interactions and self-regulation proceed hand-in-hand and shape each other. Rather than viewing interactive regulations as transformed *into* self-regulations, existing self-regulation is altered by, as well as affects, interactive regulations. Both infant and environment continuously construct, elaborate, and represent the regulations. ... [B]oth partners bring to the interaction organised behaviour and mutually constructed modes of regulating their joint activity. These dyadic modes include interactive as well as self regulation.
>
> (Beebe and Lachmann, 2002, pp. 181–182)

Beebe and Lachmann's insights are clearly relevant when we consider the dyadic regulatory process that is the work of psychotherapy, especially the work of body-focused psychotherapy, and leave us in no doubt that the body has a central role to play in affect regulation. In the past twenty years, work on adult attachment issues has "validated and expanded original formulations of attachment theory and made it clear that this theory is, at one and the same time, a theory of intrapsychic affect regulation and a systemic theory of relatedness" (Johnson, 2009, p. 262). A sense of a secure relationship with a partner acts as an emotional regulator: "it tranquillizes the nervous system" (Schore cited in Johnson, 2009, p. 262) and "fosters the ability to be able to deal with extreme negative emotions such as trauma, war, imprisonment" (Susan Johnson in Fosha, 2009, p. 262). Fonagy suggests that secure attachment is *knowing* that you exist in the mind of the other (Fonagy, Gergely, Jurist and Target, 2004). In secure relationships the connection to the partner provides "a form of comfort and creates a sense of emotional homeostasis" (Susan Johnson in Fosha *et al.*, 2009, p. 264).

Insecure Avoidant Attachment Pattern—Emotion is fundamental to the development of a secure attachment pattern. A mother may be physically present yet emotionally absent; and Panskepp argues that when there is a loss of connection with an emotionally unavailable attachment figure, a certain type of panic is provoked in the infant—a primal fear (cited in Johnson, 2009, p. 263). Attachment theory provides us with a "way to identify key recurring moments of palpable emotional disconnection, wherein reactive moments spark negative cycles, such as demand and withdraw, which then take over the relationship" (*ibid.*, p. 266).

Children who develop *insecure avoidant attachment patterns* invariably have mothers/caregivers who are emotionally unavailable: they avoid mutual eye contact and are rejecting and unresponsive, usually by withdrawing or pushing the child away. Over time, the child develops an internal model of the mother/caregiver as unable to give comfort and learns to become self-sufficient: "I don't need you" is the message she projects. The child holds an unconscious belief that she is unworthy to be loved. Following a separation from the mother, she will actively ignore or avoid the mother/caregiver by moving or pulling away when the mother/caregiver attempts to pick her up (Ogden, Minton and Pain, 2006, p. 49). Such behaviour indicates a breakdown in communication in which the mother/caregiver has failed to read or pick up the signals of the infant and has not responded in a timely or appropriate manner. The infant learns that if she reaches out, she will not receive a response. Consequently, adults with an insecure avoidant attachment pattern are likely to exhibit a dismissive attitude toward attachment to others, undervaluing and mistrusting relationships. They tend to withdraw under stress and avoid seeking emotional support from others. Preferring auto- to interactive regulation, they often find dependence frightening (*ibid.*, p. 50).

Insecure Ambivalent Attachment occurs when the mother/caregiver is inconsistent and unpredictable in her emotional response. When such a mother/caregiver returns after an absence, the child is inclined to cling to the parent but is not easily soothed. The child is never certain of the dependability of the mother/caregiver's response as she is sometimes allowed proximity, sometimes not. The mother/caregiver may at times be withdrawn, at others overly intrusive, driven by her own needs rather than acting in response to the child's. This pattern describes a failure in the contingency of mother/caregiver and child communication, and frequently "results in infants who appear cautious, distraught, angry, distressed, and preoccupied throughout both separation from, and reunion with, the mother. Upon reunion, they typically fail to be comforted by the mother/caregiver's presence or soothing, often continuing to cry" (Ogden, Minton and Pain, 2006, p. 50). As adults, these children "are preoccupied with attachment needs, overly dependent on others, and might have a tendency toward enmeshment and intensity in interpersonal relationships, with a preference for proximity" (*ibid.*).

Disorganized Disoriented Attachment Pattern—if trauma is experienced in the context of a child's earliest attachment relationships, it becomes "burned into the developing limbic and autonomic systems of the early maturing right brain, to become part of implicit memory, and leads to enduring structural changes that produce inefficient stress-coping mechanisms" (Schore, 2002, p. 9). In this group the attachment figure repels or terrifies the child, whose survival instinct causes it to pull away. In terms of neuroscientific theory, the autonomic nervous system's response is that of *flight*: "Her survival circuits are screaming, 'Get away from the source of terror. You are in danger!' But the attachment circuits are crying out, 'Go towards your attachment figure for safety and soothing!'" (Siegel, 2010, p. 185). The child is drawn toward the very one he is dependent on for regulation. The "self of the child is not *disconnected*, as in avoidance, or *confused*, as in ambivalent attachment. Instead the child's sense of self becomes *fragmented*" (*ibid.*,). When the distress is overwhelming, or the mother/caregiver is the cause of distress, the child is unable to regulate her arousal, which disables her ability "to process, integrate, and categorize what is happening. At the core of traumatic stress is a breakdown in the capacity to regulate internal states. If the distress does not ease, the relevant sensations, affects and cognitions cannot be associated—they are dissociated into sensory fragments—and, as a result, [children with this attachment pattern] cannot comprehend what is happening or devise and execute appropriate plans of action" (van der Kolk, 2008, p. 48).

The nervous system of the child belonging to this attachment group is caught in a biological dilemma: when the child perceives danger in the form of frightening or frightened caregivers, both hyper- *and* hypoarousal occur and the social engagement system is predominantly in *switched-off* mode; the child's system is disorganized, swinging between chaos and rigidity, leaving the child unable to hold onto a coherent sense of himself. Heller and LaPierre comment that, without necessarily developing a personality disorder, "[m]any individuals ... use fragmentation as a coping mechanism to manage overwhelmingly high levels of arousal and painful emotions. On a biological level, fragmentation creates a lack of coherency in all systems in the body" (2012, p. 152). I will speak more about this pattern of fragmentation as a coping mechanism to manage overwhelmingly high levels of arousal and of attachment in Chapters 5, 6 and 7 on Dissociation and Disorientation.

My clinical experience in infant observation in the 1990s impressed on me the importance of non-verbal, moment-to-moment, body-to-body communication between mother and infant, and the inter-regulation and proto-conversations[3] that take place in the mother/infant dyad. Mother and infant regulate each other, enlivening, soothing, calming and stimulating each other by turn-taking. This turn-taking is based on attunement, each to the other. It allows for mismatches of attunement and for re-attunement to take place. Tronick refers to this process as "rupture and repair" (Gianino and Tronick, 1986). Moments of misattunement provide opportunities for the infant to resolve the disruption or break in communication, which in turn contributes to the development of self-agency and the building of new neural pathways in the brain. Moments of misattunement encourage contingency and teach that repair is possible. Through the action of the mirror neurons the infant becomes aware that the mother's intention was not to harm or injure. On the basis of such moments of repair, trust is built: trust in oneself and trust of the other. Such moments constitute the building blocks of attachment and the emotions connected with it. They are essential to the internalization of a system that enables the child to regulate stressful affects, and return infant and mother to a state of homeostasis. Neuroscience demonstrates that "in a secure attachment relationship the interactions with the attuned mother support right hemisphere brain development, promote efficient affect regulation, and ... [enable] ... adaptive infant mental health" (Schore, 2001, p. 204). Schore emphasizes that through interactive regulation with the mother the child's immature brain is stimulated to create synapses that shape the orbitofrontal cortex, the part of the brain that has a profound effect on regulating emotional autonomic arousal.

Learned secure attachment occurs when an attachment pattern ruptured at an early stage of development is repaired through the therapeutic relationship and a secure attachment is formed, which Wilkinson describes as *learned*:

> Affective neuroscience is encouraging in that the emphasis on plasticity, with its possibility of the remaking of mind, means that the empathic analyst may be experienced in a new way, leading to change in the very nature of basic attachment, meriting a new category of attachments, that of 'learned secure'.
> (Wilkinson, 2006, p. 183)

Wilkinson clearly emphasizes the empathic and attuned therapist as fundamental to the creation of conditions in which new neural pathways may form to "allow for secure attachment, emotional well-being, healthy relationships, and the full realization of potential" (in conversation with Sieff, 2015, p. 332). She emphasizes that affective engagement, including affect regulation and attunement in therapy, enables new emotional learning to occur:

> As mind changes through the interaction with the therapist, acting in the role of secondary care-giver, so the nature of early attachment, the response to early trauma, can change. Therapy offers the possibility of the emergence of this new kind of attachment.
>
> (Wilkinson, 2006, p. 182)

Daniel Siegel argues that neural integration and the expansion of one's *window of tolerance* through an empathetic, attuned therapeutic relationship can help one attune to oneself and foster self-compassion and love, and that this enables the development of secure attachment through one's relationship to oneself. "We become our own best friend and develop an attachment status of earned security" (Siegel in Sieff, 2015, p. 158).

Learned secure attachment is the focus of BodyDreaming. I would like to propose that BodyDreaming offers an effective way to develop a learned secure attachment to the body, foster a sense of *coming home to oneself*, and promote a conscious alignment with the self-regulating principle of the psyche which Jung called the Self. In my own experience of integrating somatic practices into psychotherapy sessions, I find that, over time, both client and therapist are able to nurture a "learned secure attachment" relationship to their bodies. Through the sensing body we develop an ability to return to homeostasis by attuning to the felt sense experience of our responses, paying attention to the nervous system's cycles of activation and deactivation and actively enlisting the architecture of the social engagement system to help regulate. In this way a 'learned' secure attachment relationship begins to take root in the body within the context of the inter-regulatory dyadic therapeutic relationship.

By paying attention to and working with both the body's responses and the patterns of activation and deactivation particular to the client's attachment behaviours, the therapist is afforded an opportunity to change the attachment pattern, develop a secure attachment style and also increase the client's capacity for compassion and empathy towards his or her body. The body may then be experienced as ground or container, providing a safe refuge from the tyranny of an insecure attachment pattern. According to Stern (1985), a sense of core self is "not a cognitive construct" but is made up of activities and experiences that are sensed, lived: "the emphasis is on the palpable experiential realities of substance, action, sensation, affect, and time" (p. 71). Fostering a new relationship to the sensing body forms the fundamental building block from which to grow a sense of a core self. Over time, a learned secure attachment to the body is created, contingent on the client's consistent sensate experience of both inner and outer attunement within the container of the inter-regulatory therapeutic relationship, and leads to what Stern describes as an "experiential integration" (*ibid.*).

Over and over again in the therapeutic setting, we find ourselves at threshold moments of activation which require us to orient *outward* to seek a calming influence or still point in the turbulence. Learning to attend to inner attunement through interoception while also attuning to the outer field through neuroception and proprioception develops the capacity for a dual awareness within the holding environment of a non-judgmental therapeutic container. Inevitably, there will be repeated experiences of "disruption and repair",[4] especially when old defences are mobilized against new possibilities. Any new way of being initially threatens established defences developed as survival strategies in the face of overwhelm, anxiety and unbearable pain at the time of the original trauma. When one attempts to create new neural pathways, old defences mobilize against any perceived threat of change. The internal self-care defence system[5] kicks in and reactivates the nervous system in an attempt to return it to an old pattern, albeit a dysregulated old pattern. The work to establish new neural connections is consequently slow, measured, and calls for the deliberate, conscious building of the client's embodied experience of her body as living grounded container. When we experience an embodied, felt sense resonance to a positive resource, we find that our attunement to the body is reassuring; the body offers refuge and safety, guiding the autonomic nervous system's return to homeostasis. In this way, the resonating body may become the secure m/other. Building a connection to the body brings with it a sense of one's core self and of empowerment grounded in the security in one's cellular being. The forging of a learned secure attachment to the body deepens one's appreciation of the body as the loving container of all inner experience. Attunement to a positive resource and its felt sense resonance also enables turn-taking—the back and forth between body and image, body and conversation—together with an openness to receive whatever is pushing to emerge from the unconscious psyche or somatic unconscious. During this work, the attunement of the therapist with her client is as vital as the engagement of the mother–infant proto-conversations of attunement and misattunement.[6]

Before turning to the cases I have selected for this chapter, I wish to draw on Donald Kalsched's writings on what he calls the *inner self-care system* and how it functions in the psyche. Kalsched's insight into the dyadic self-care system that develops as a result of early relational trauma will serve as a framework for understanding the client work that follows. Kalsched developed the concept of the inner self-care system from his extensive clinical experience as well as a comprehensive review of psychoanalytic literature, including the work of Klein, Winnicott, Fairbairn, Guntrip, Grotstein, Kernberg and others (Kalsched, 1996). His model describes the psychological and biological impact of developmental trauma. It explains how defences imprinted on the psyche and encoded in the neurological wiring of the brain operate from the very beginning of an infant's life to ensure survival at all costs.

Kalsched argues that in the face of ongoing early relational trauma, the infant's defence system is so underdeveloped that there are few, if any, options open to him: he cannot utilize a *fight* or *flight response*. As a result, a psychological survival system is established which causes the psyche to split and a part of the nascent self withdraws or regresses while another part progresses or grows up too quickly.[7] Kalsched describes this initial moment of psychological dissociation as:

> a miraculous moment in that this defensive splitting saves the child's psychological essence in an encapsulated state, but it is also a tragic moment because with this splitting the child steps out of the reality and vivacity of his or her life.
> (In conversation with Sieff, 2008, p. 2)

These extremes—the "progressed vs. regressed parts" of the personality—together make up the psyche's *archetypal*[8] self-care system, which will go to any length to protect the vulnerable, innocent core of the individual in the face of danger or threat. Once this self-care system is organized, it functions as the psyche's self-regulator, screening all relations with the outside world as a defence against trauma. Intended to protect the individual from further trauma, it becomes a major defence against "any unguarded spontaneous expressions of self in the world" (Kalsched, 1996, p. 4). What initially served as protector becomes "the unwitting and violent inner persecutor" (Kalsched in conversation with Sieff, 2008, p. 4). This inner figure, "an internalized version of the actual perpetrator of the trauma", is frequently more sadistic and brutal than any outer perpetrator, indicating that we are dealing here with a *psychological* factor set loose in the inner world of trauma" (Kalsched, 1996, p. 4). The tragedy of this system is that it is not tempered by life events but remains stuck at the same level of reactivity as when the original trauma occurred, the "protector's" role being the "protection of the traumatized remainder of the personal spirit and its *isolation from reality.* ... Each new life opportunity is mistakenly seen as a dangerous threat and is therefore attacked" (*ibid.*, pp. 4–5). In this way, a defensive cycle of retraumatization becomes the norm, in both the nervous system and psyche: "the traumatized psyche is self-traumatizing. The self-defence system turns against the very person it is supposed to be protecting" (Kalsched in Sieff, 2008, p. 194). Instead of expressing what should be normal anger and rage toward her abusers, the innocent child who has suffered developmental trauma through abuse or neglect, turns her anger on herself, blaming herself for her pain: "I am no good, I'm bad, I'm at fault." She cannot tolerate the possibility that her caregivers are at fault; somehow, she must be responsible for her own suffering. The shame she feels as a result becomes so profound that it must be hidden at all costs. Anger, turned into self-blame, is responsible for "splitting the system into the supposedly inadequate inner child and the critical inner protector. This splitting of the psyche is a violent process, just like the splitting of the atom, and the fall-out is equally deforming and toxic" (*ibid.*, p. 193).

*

In this section, I will focus on one type of insecure attachment pattern: the ambivalent kind. In 1985, Mary Main developed the Adult Attachment Interview[9] and proposed that early forms of attachment have their counterparts in adult attachment patterns. She classified the insecure avoidant or anxious avoidant infant attachment pattern as the "dismissing" attachment pattern in adults; the insecure anxious resistant/ambivalent pattern in infants as the "preoccupied" pattern in adults; and the disorganized/disoriented attachment pattern in infants as the "unresolved" attachment pattern in adults. The insecure anxious/ambivalent pattern on which I focus in the following client session would therefore be considered by Main as an example of the "preoccupied" adult attachment pattern.

Researchers into adult attachment patterns have associated particular behaviours with each attachment style. West, citing Slade, categorizes the dismissive attachment pattern with behaviours that are *avoidant* and *deactivating* as well as *dismissive*, while behaviours associated with the preoccupied attachment style are *anxious* and *hyperactivating* as well as *preoccupied* (2016, p. 52). In the excerpts from the sessions that follow, I will highlight the activation triggered in the nervous system of a client with an anxious/resistant attachment pattern. We will discover the dominant style of response of this attachment style, which has been encoded in the nervous system from infancy. The role of the BodyDreaming therapist is firstly to recognize the nervous system's habitual response to activation, and to work to regulate affect, helping to establish greater homeostasis and coherence in the system, using interventions similar to those employed with clients in earlier chapters. Over time, implicit memory, dream images, body processes and impulses may help to identify the cause of the original activation. When the client becomes aware of his attachment behaviour, and the dysregulation of his nervous system that accompanies it, he can with time learn to self-regulate in the face of future activation. This learned regulatory practice, in turn, creates a sense of there being more *space* in the body in which to uncover early implicit memories and to explore dream images. The attuned therapist knows that the body holds the key to unraveling the knot of locked-in trauma that is disguised in attachment behaviors. Over time, with the practice of inner and outer attunement along with felt sense resonance, the client is released from the grip of out-dated defensive strategies that are highly dysregulating. The plasticity of the brain lends itself to new patterns of response, supporting new impulses for healing. In this manner, we work to develop an embodied *learned secure attachment* to the body within the context of the inter-regulating dyad of therapist and client.

*

David: "My pain is in my joy ..."
"I am held hostage my whole life by that needy part of me"

David and I had been working together for 5 years. We began our work face to face but at the time of the session excerpted below we had been using Skype for some time. From the beginning, our work had incorporated a somatic approach. Our focus was on David's intimate relationship with his partner on whom he felt overly dependent. We worked to realign his nervous system as his habitual response to conflict in the relationship was one of hypervigilance, a constant state of heightened activation, the typical response of someone, like David, with an early insecure attachment pattern.

David loved his partner and yet was caught in very painful dynamics that held him prisoner to the patterned responses of his early ambivalent style of attachment. His current relationship triggered an early wounding, keeping him trapped in an *old complex* which had developed when, as an infant, he had desperately wanted his mother's attention while at the same time anticipating her rejection—"it was as if she could not bear to look at me." He felt he was too much for her, then raged at her in defence. Consequently, as an adult, David could not find a comfortable way of being with his partner. Ogden, Minton, and Pain describe children with insecure ambivalent attachment patterns as having nervous systems dominated by a sympathetic arousal response of *fight* or *flight* as they struggle to maintain the arousal within their window of tolerance: "[T]hey cling to relational contact, becoming overly dependent on interactive regulation but simultaneously experiencing a lack of ability to be easily calmed and soothed in a relationship" (2006, p. 56).

When we first met, David was held captive by his ambivalent feelings. His hyper-vigilance meant that he was constantly over-extended and in emotional overwhelm, easily tipped into hopelessness or agitation. Bonnie Bainbridge Cohen reminds us that bringing awareness, or felt sense, to the body can offset emotional flooding: "Sensing is not an emotional space. ... Sensing is related to the nervous system through perceptions and can be a support and counterbalance to emotions." She describes herself as having been "chaotically emotional at one point in her life" and found *sensing* to be "a *haven* from that. And a way to get insight. Through the senses we get insight" (1995, pp. 188–189). We will see that sensing, using felt sense, proves foundational for David in helping him to shift his position from being tossed in the stormy waters of emotion to finding ground in his day-to-day living: by learning to sense and perceive, David gains greater insight into the dynamics of his interactions with and patterns of attachment to his partner.

Through inner and outer attunement, and inter-regulation with his therapist, David is developing a capacity to recognize threshold moments of activation, catching himself as he yearns for more attention from his partner. By directing his attention away from the source of activation and orienting it toward a nourishing resource, he is learning to interrupt his usual pattern of seeking increased closeness at the same time as he anticipates rejection. The pendulating rhythm of experiences of activation followed by deactivation changes the neuronal wiring of his autonomic nervous system's responses, enabling David to be less preoccupied with the other and attune to a felt sense experience of himself. This slow process describes the measured work of self-regulation and building a learned secure attachment to the body. David had to develop a nervous system response that could support him to stay with, rather than flee, his feelings of unreciprocated longing. He also came to recognize the speed at which his nervous system could flip into a state of hyperarousal or *flight* mode, causing him to blame his partner for not making him feel better. BodyDreaming work has enabled David to find more ground to be within himself, resulting in greater homeostasis in his system. This, in turn, has facilitated his increased focus on artistic pursuits, which had previously been hijacked by David's "needy, clingy infant self", a complex triggered by ambivalent attachment issues. David has found more ease within himself and within his relationship with his partner; his window of tolerance has expanded and both he and his partner are able to enjoy "shared moments of meeting"[10] as well as live separate and creative lives.

In the session that follows David recalls a recent incident with his partner during which he felt himself re-triggered and thrown back into despair and hopelessness.

David: *We are standing in the kitchen. My partner approaches me. I feel her hand on my back. I am filled with joy ... I feel alive. And immediately I feel sadness. I dissolve into the needy one: "I just want her to let me love her."*

[Almost as soon as David registers the pleasurable feeling of his partner's touch on his back ("*I am filled with joy ... I feel alive*"), he is triggered by an implicit memory of longing for touch. The pleasure of receiving his partner's touch is immediately replaced by his longing ("*I just want her to let me love her.*") David's autonomic nervous system switches, instantaneously, from pleasure to sadness.

MD: (I mirror his words.) *I just want her to let me love her.* (Then I ask a crucial question.)
         Whose voice is that?

David: *It's the needy one, the 'poor me' voice, the victim ... I can't show that side, or I will drive her away. If I tell her, she will feel it's the familiar voice that nags and pulls at her: 'I'm not getting enough. You don't love me.' And all that it does is drive her further away and make her angry with me.*

[David has learnt to recognize his needy self and how it plays out in the relationship. He is critical of his 'needy' side, judging it ("*it drives her away*"). His persecutor/protector attitude is dominant and shuns this needy side of himself. He dissociates from it—projecting it into the other who in turn will reject him for his clinging, needy behaviour. Kathy Steele emphasizes the need to bring the different parts together in working with attachment.[11]]

David: *I think maybe I should leave her ... I am never going to get any love from her. I blame her for being unloving, cold, and shut down.*

[In an instant David swings into disowning his harsh self-criticism by projecting it into his partner, whom he anticipates will reject him as being needy and nagging. He feels he is "*too much*" for her and that she is "*cold, shut down*".

David: *My pain is in my joy. As soon as I feel the joy of her touching me, I feel the pain. I want more—whether it's for her to give me more, or to allow me to give her more ... it's not enough!*

[He has plummeted into a trauma vortex, tormented by his simultaneous feelings—shame and blame–in a limbic overwhelm, which triggers a *fight, flight* or *freeze* response.]

MD: *Yes, you are naming the cycle, the pattern. Notice how quickly you have feelings of blame in response to the deep shame you are feeling about your hunger—your desire to be touched and to give touch. You judge yourself for those feelings thinking that you are "too much", that you want too much from her.*

David: *I want to leave her* [a *flight* response].

    She is no good; she can't love me in the way I need. She can't love me, she is cold, unloving, frozen [a *fight* response of anger and blame].

MD: *You feel your hunger for contact has not been met by your partner, like the infant whose mother is not attuned to him, and this leaves the infant with the feeling that there is something wrong or bad about his hunger, that he is unlovable. I imagine that you have the feeling there is something 'wrong' with you, that you feel you are 'too much' for her. Shame comes in and fills you with feelings of self-loathing. Shame can trigger intense activation in your nervous system, causing a* fight *or* flight *response. This response is your self-care system's defence against the shameful feelings, and it protects you by shifting you from shame to blame. This is the self-care system's way of ensuring your survival.*

[We had worked this pattern in previous sessions, and in offering *top-down* processing at this point I am appealing to David's neo-cortex to join with me in understanding the pattern which has been triggered once again. Cognitive understanding can have a calming effect on the limbic arousal, strengthen the collaboration between us[12] and enable David to develop a sense of self-agency and empowerment or, as Knox writes, "an awareness of the mental and emotional separateness of self and other".[13] David then recalls a recent visit to his elderly mother who is living in residential care, an occasion on which they shared a meal.]

David: *She wants food all the time. She ate the food on my plate even though her own plate was still full. She disgusts me.*

[David's visit with his mother has re-awakened the early implicit memory of the lack of attunement between them.[14] When implicit memory is stirred, it does not feel as if it is something recalled from the past, "instead we feel it as our present reality" (Siegel in conversation with Sieff, 2015, p. 143). Consequently, in the present, David is repelled by his mother's invasiveness, lack of boundaries and what appears to be an insatiable appetite. I recognize that he is in a heightened sympathetic activation; his ambivalent attachment pattern has been triggered, which causes him simultaneously to push his mother away and yet want more from her.]

David: *Her behaviour is despicable.*

[Clearly David is in a state of intense rage against his mother's invasive hungry self. He has reached a *threshold moment*: his rage, no longer held in implicit memory is now accessible, offering us the possibility to *rewire* his habitual response to a reactivation of the original trauma by creating new neural connections.]

The pleasure of the touch of his partner's hand on his back awakened David's unmet hunger and stimulated the memory of his mother's insatiable appetite. The *ambivalent* m/other—at one moment invasive, at the next unavailable—leaves him in a state of heightened arousal, an anxious attachment pattern that never allows him to take in the *good-enough* nourishment or the *good-enough* touch, for fear of its imminent withdrawal. The misattunement of David's early attachment relationship made a profound impact on his nervous system. The infant's limbic brain is encoded with the messages of early attachment patterns and will fire when something in the present triggers the complex, in David's case, leaving him overwhelmed and flooded by the chemicals and deep feelings of shame associated with his unmet hunger. In the scenario presented in our session, his partner's gesture brings instant pleasure and at the same time triggers the implicit memory of the needy hungry infant. Pleasure is inextricably linked to pain: to receive the touch is to feel the hunger for what threatens to be withheld by the m/other, and David's patterned response of ambivalence plunges him into shame and hopelessness, followed by rage and blame.

In this session David's system failed to regulate: he remained caught between the two contradictory experiences, swinging back and forth between states of hyper- and hypoarousal, between a sympathetic response (blame and rage) and a parasympathetic dorsal vagal response (shame and hopelessness).[15] As noted above (see Chapter 1, p. 41; p. 45), Hebb's Law states that "cells that fire together, wire together". The feelings elicited by the initial trauma were both pleasure and pain ("*my pain is in my joy*") and these contradictory emotions created the original neuronal wiring. Thereafter, when either pleasure or pain is activated, *both* feelings *together* trigger the same early-established pattern and limbic response. David's response to his partner's touch triggers an implicit memory and confirms the link between *positive* sympathetic arousal (receiving pleasure from his partner in the present) and *negative* shameful feelings held in the body as a result of the misattunement between the hungry infant self and the mother. This combination of opposing feelings needs to be *uncoupled*, the wiring re-set. Our work is to uncouple this unlikely pair: feeling fed—satisfaction, and feeling hungry—shame. We will work to create new pathways and possibilities for interacting using both top-down and bottom-up processes: that is, through understanding the complex and how it is retriggered; and through learning to self-regulate *interoceptively* by observing the autonomic nervous system's responses, and related emotions, and *proprioceptively* by orienting to the surrounding environment. This process should open David to receive new possibilities, new impulses for a more integrated life.

David returns to his story of conflict with his partner:

David: *As soon as I told her that I liked her touching me, she stopped doing it. I told her this because I didn't want her to stop doing what she was doing.*
        [I suspect that she froze as she unconsciously picked up the right brain to right brain *implicit* communication in his statement, that is, David's

anticipation of being rejected, of feeling that he is "too much" for her, and this hangs like a fog between them in the field. David's self-care defence system has been triggered in the face of the anticipated rejection.]

MD: *Your statement stops your partner in her tracks. It's like an arrow shot from your self-care system that wants to protect you from the antici-pated painful feelings of rejection. I suspect that the arrow contains the unwanted feelings that have been triggered, the implicit early memories of "not being good enough". In the moment, they are projected uncon-sciously onto your partner. As a consequence, she feels that her loving is "not good enough" for you, that she can never satisfy your hunger. She stops, pulls away and, in so doing, confirms your self-care system's belief that she is the problem, the one who is depriving you of the love you want to receive and to give.*

[David is familiar with the model of the self-care system. The example makes it powerfully present as it clearly illustrates the way in which the defence system and early complexes "work". We take our time to track David's responses to the changes and shifts that are occurring in response to our top-down *processing* conversation about the unconscious dynamic between him and his partner. We take time to resource him, connecting him to the environment which at that moment feels nourishing: the play of light on a plant, the cat curled into a ball on the sofa, the log burning in the stove. David's autonomic nervous system settles. He shifts position in his chair, moves his spine in a familiar, spiraling motion, gently rolling his head, letting his shoulders drop. His system is regulating, enabling him to receive the beauty and pleasure around him; this, in turn, supports his understanding and our "uncoupling" of the opposing emotions.

David: *I am more able to be myself now. I haven't felt this heaviness for some time and I recognize that I have lived with it forever. When I feel the heaviness I can't do anything* [the *freeze* response]. *Now, I can locate the heaviness right here in my chest, a little lower than my heart.*

[David's description of his experience of heaviness tells me that he is feeling into the dorsal *freeze* which lies beneath the sympathetic response. I wait, giving his system time to release blocked energy, and find greater fluidity and ease overall, as new pathways are forming.]

David: *I am feeling a high-pitched level of anxiety, a shivery sensation mixed in with the heaviness. I am noticing energy in my solar plexus ... and it's radiating down into my abdomen ... and now pulsing through to my back.*

[The ventral vagal system is coming on line as the symptom of heavi-ness or *freeze* is beginning to thaw, and the released energy is finding its way into David's back, his spine.

[David's eyes are closed now. His spine begins to move, spiraling in an upward direction. The movement continues through his neck and his head rolls gently toward one shoulder and then the other. This suggests to me that the ventral vagal system and the muscles of the social engage-ment system are also connecting. The movements are slow and fluid and then come to a stop. David's eyes open and continue the same circular movement. After some time the movement slows down and David seems to be deliberately and slowly scanning the room.[16] By spontaneously rolling first his head and then his eyes, David may well have opened the *tentorium*, which Heller and LaPierre claim enhances vision and will have the effect of energizing David's entire system.]

David: *I have been less affected by the winter this year, the greyness is different now.*

[In the past David suffered from Seasonal Affective Disorder.[17] I am hoping that the BodyDreaming work, in affecting his perception of light, will enable him to take in more light which, in turn, will affect his auto-immune responses and SAD. Letting in more light will also enhance David's social engagement system, which is key in modulating the sympathetic arousal of the ventral vagal system. He will be able to self-regulate better through his eyes. Heller and LaPierre are again helpful on this topic: "To the degree that there is contraction and disengagement in the eyes, we do not see the reality of our environment" (2012, p. 159).]

(David's cat comes close to him at this point and he strokes her back.)

David: *The cat is quieting my body. I can feel my body, mobile and fluid. It feels so good. The hairs down my back are kind of tingling, with a kind of prickly, tingly sensation. As I pay attention to it, the sensations increase.*

[I am wondering at this point whose back is being stroked—the cat's or David's? Cedrus Monte uses the term *corporal mutuality* to describe such "precious microseconds of genuine receptivity to life" (p. 19).[18] David's capacity to receive is increasing—the light in the room, and the touch of his hand on the cat are each contributing to an expansion of consciousness in this slow process of "uncoupling".[19]]

MD: *How does it feel to stroke your cat?*

David: *It feels very good.* (He is smiling.)

MD: *When you hear yourself say "it feels very good", how does your body respond? What do you notice?*

David: *It says 'Yes,* (exhaling with an audible sigh) *medium to good.'* (He laughs aloud, looking at me, including me in the humour as we are both aware that up till now he had a limited *window of tolerance* when it came to receiving pleasure.)

MD: *Humour is good ... And sadness may be in there too.*

[I name the sadness to show David that he can include it without triggering activation in his system: he may be feeling joy coupled with sadness and it may be okay to feel both.]

David: *Yes, and I am observing that I have less of an impulse to talk about my partner.* (Time passes ...) *And now I can see that my hands have become sweaty since I said that.*

[It is important for the therapist to be aware that when we are on the threshold of new possibilities, and engaged in the final stages of a cycle of re-wiring a neural pattern around a complex, the client is often suddenly thrown, disoriented. The conservative self-care system is being challenged directly and will almost inevitably respond with one *last stand* remark, threatening a reactivation of the complex in a final attempt to maintain control. In David's case, the mention of his partner triggers him and interrupts the moment of pleasure and ease. His sweaty hands reveal the dysregulation and activation in the autonomic nervous system— his anxiety has been triggered.]

David: *I am fearful, fearful of following my own impulses* [that is, fearful of staying with the new energy].

If I pay attention to my inner world, my pleasure, then I may lose connection with my mother. I have to keep attending to her to ensure my own survival.

[David is making meaning for himself, integrating what we have discussed concerning the self-care system, and seeing how it "plays out" in his life. He recognizes his hypervigilance around the mother/partner, his need to ensure that his mother is alive, his high dependency that guarantees his survival. However, this means that he leaves his core self behind, and becomes separated from his inner life and the pleasure he feels in being creative in his own company.

[David's primal need for survival triggers the trauma complex underlying his insecure ambivalent attachment style and throws him into hypervigilance, anxiety and dependency behaviour (the need to cling and seek attention from the other). However, his capacity to reflect (that is, to use the integrative circuit of the cortex) has increased, as this *top-down* process of *meaning-making* indicates.]

MD: *You're scared that she won't be there when you get back from what you're doing* (i.e., following his own creative impulses).

David: *Maybe I had to pay attention to my mother the whole time.*[20] *I do that to my partner and it drives her crazy.* (Sigh.) *I can feel a huge sense of relief.* (He sighs audibly and takes a big cat-like stretch, spreading his body slowly in all directions.) *It really feels good to go slowly and just to be in my body with this.*

[David is clearly in touch with himself, feeling compassion for himself and, at the same time, empathy toward his partner. This marks a big shift from the earlier victim position, with its self-pity, and that of the chronically demanding child. The opening of this neural pathway, enabling empathy and compassion, allows David to experience the deep pleasure of his big sigh of relief and the cat-like stretch of down-regulation.

[We have reached a critical threshold moment. David's whole system is realigning. He is experiencing what in neurophysiological terms would be described as a release from previous dorsal and ventral vagal activations— the dyad of hopelessness/*collapse* and blame/*fight*; and, as a consequence, a more regulated flow of energy and harmonious rhythm in his body enables new synapses to fire which support *meaning-making*. We are slowly re-negotiating and re-patterning responses and behaviours constellated by the original attachment style deeply entrenched through trans-generational trauma. When he names his hyper-vigilance and recognizes his dependency on the other, David is experiencing more compassion for himself and empathy for the other. Meeting the self-care system (his need to monitor the m/other, a strategy that guaranteed his life) releases David from a state of hyper-vigilance. He finds himself increasingly free to make connections and draw meaning from his statements: the integrative circuits of the brain are functioning.

[David recognizes that the hyper-vigilance of the persecutor/protector self-care system, directed towards both his mother and his partner, has enabled him to survive but at a cost. Energy fuelling the hyper-vigilance has not been available to him. He has made the m/other the centre of his universe and this has kept him out of alignment with himself and his creative pursuits and made his 'hunger' insatiable.]

David: *I feel sadness in that.*

MD: *Do you mean the sadness of having to pay attention to your mother and partner the whole time? Has that state of hyper-vigilance meant the loss of attention to your own creative pursuits?*

David: *Yes ... (sigh).*

MD: *Notice the sigh, the exhale.*

David: *It's a relief to come back to my body. I feel tinges of headache at the base of my skull. I feel that if I could slow down enough, I wouldn't get the headache.* (He rolls his head slowly, letting it fall right back. This spontaneous action may help release the constriction in the diaphragm at the base of his skull.)[21]

MD: *What is happening now?* (His head is arched back and rolling very slowly to one side and then back again).

David: *I can breathe more easily. I can feel my chest opening. It feels open and yet constricted at the same time.* (His head continues to roll slowly and it seems like it is arched backwards. This reminds me of the infant's head that spirals its way out of the birth canal and into life and then leans back, lifting its mouth to latch onto the mother to feed.)

David: *I can feel a slower pulsing in my thighs and a sense of weariness in my body. This feels replenishing. It's like a letting go. I'm yielding to it.*

MD: *Yes, I can see that you are yielding to it.* (His whole body is relaxing, softening, yielding to pleasure.)

[We have arrived at another threshold moment in which the body's impulses are leading the way. We are tracking, through interoception, the release of energy as it moves through David's body at its own pace. This is a moment in which top-down and bottom-up information is being exchanged, creating new neural circuits, greater coherence and integration in his entire system—physical, emotional, cognitive and, we may perhaps anticipate, spiritual. David's body is providing him with an experience of a secure base, allowing him to feel at home in himself and affording him a place in which he can experience both pleasure and pain. While David embodies this feeling of a secure base his 'field' of consciousness expands to include a curiosity about what surrounds him.

[Synchronistically, David's cat arrives back into his space and settles her body close to David's thigh, curling up tightly against him, reminding him of the warm connection they shared earlier. David allows himself to be touched, to receive the touch and to be present in that shared moment. The pleasure is mutual: there is an experience of reciprocity, without activation. David's body softens and relaxes into the physical exchange and a big smile breaks over his face.]

David: I'm yielding to it.

MD: Yes, you are yielding to it. [Together cat and David, body and psyche, co-mingle and give birth to Pleasure or Joy—the child born of the mythological Psyche and Eros.]

Commentary

David's overall capacity to let go, to yield in order to perceive and receive through his senses has increased. In BodyDreaming work, when we discover our secure base in our bodies we notice that we are more receptive to the living world around us, as Abram describes: "Whenever I quiet the persistent chatter of words within my head, I find this silent or wordless dance always already going on—this improvised duet between my animal body and the fluid, breathing landscape that it inhabits" (1997, p. 53).

When we have worked to realign the nervous system and open the senses, we become more amenable to participate in what already exists within our field of perception. Consciousness expands to include what is around us and we find ourselves influenced by what is already there and by what is drawing our attention and inviting us into participatory relationship. David Abram, drawing on Merleau-Ponty's work, describes participation:

> [a] defining attribute of perception itself. By asserting that perception, phenomenologically considered, is inherently participatory, we mean that perception always involves, at its most intimate level, the experience of an active interplay, or coupling, between the perceiving body and that which it perceives.
>
> (Abram, 2011, p. 57)

Coincidentally, or perhaps synchronistically, David's cat meets David in a precise manner that mirrors the symptom with which David presented at the beginning of the session. His wife's touch had triggered him; paradoxically, he can now receive and yield to the cat's touch without being triggered. "As soon as we acknowledge that our hands are included within the tactile world, we are forced to notice this reciprocity: whenever we touch any entity, we are also ourselves being touched *by* that entity" (*ibid.*, p. 58). David's perception of the field in which he is embedded is now participatory. He is open to receiving the touch of the cat and finds himself yielding to it, accepting the comfort it offers. This shift, I would argue, is largely enabled by the combined somatic approach and attachment work incorporated into BodyDreaming practice. While the focus is on building a learned secure attachment in our body selves, at the same time, the work opens us to a reciprocal exchange with "a living field of intelligence in which we participate" (*ibid.*, p. 273). This living field offers itself to us as an even greater container in which our body-mind-soul can feel resonant and "at home". With David's attachment system less activated, his exploratory system is now more available for his creative pursuits which find expression in the reciprocal life of the community.

Notes

1 "Encoded as procedural memory, these patterns manifest as proximity seeking, social engagement behaviour (smiling, movement toward, reaching out, eye contact) and defensive expressions (physical withdrawal, tension patterns, and hyper- or hypo-arousal)" (Ogden, Minton and Pain, 2006, p. 47).

2   But although pregnancy, labour and delivery alter a woman's brain to make her more sensitive to her newborn, a mother's commitment to her infant ... is, as with other mammals, biologically designed to be contingent on circumstances.
       ... [i]t is hardly surprising that babies evolved to be hypersensitive to any indication that their mothers are reluctant to commit to them, and to do everything in their power to counteract such reluctance.
                                    (Blaffer Hrdy in conversation with Sieff, 2015, pp. 194–195)

3 Mary Catherine Bateson, writer, linguist and cultural anthropologist, refers to the intimate engagements between a mother and her 9-week old infant as "proto-conversations" (1979).

4 Beebe and Lachmann, 2002, pp. 160–169. "The expectation develops that it is possible to maintain engagement with the partner in the face of strains and mismatches" (*ibid.*, p. 168).

5 Kalsched in conversation with Sieff, 2015.

6 "Similar to the child's caregiver, the therapist must be sensitively attuned to the client as well as to be able to weather the storms of difficulty and provide interactive repair when the inevitable empathetic failures occur" (Ogden, Minton and Pain, 2006, p. 117).
       See also Beebe and Lachmann, the principal of disruption and repair (2002, pp. 160—169).

7 Kalsched, in conversation with Sieff, 2008.

8 Jung writes about the power of an *archetypal* experience in an essay completed shortly before his death:

       Archetypes are images and at the same time emotions. One can speak of an archetype only when these two aspects coincide. When there is only an image, it is merely a word-picture, like a corpuscle with no electric charge. It is then of little consequence, just a word and nothing more. If the image is charged with numinosity, that is with psychic energy, then it becomes dynamic and will produce consequences. It is a great mistake in practice to treat an archetype as if it were a mere name, word, or concept. It is far more than that: it is a piece of life, an image connected with the living individual by the bridge of emotion.

(Jung, 1961, p. 257)

9 George, Kaplan and Main (1985) "The Adult Attachment Interview Protocol (AAI)". Unpublished manuscript held at the University of California, Berkeley.

10   The meeting is also intersubjective in the sense that each partner recognizes that there has been a mutual fittedness. Each has captured an essential feature of the other's goal-oriented motive structure. To state it colloquially, each grasps a similar version of 'what is happening, now, here, between us.'

(Stern *et al.*, 1998, pp. 907–908)

11 Kathy Steele discussed the outcome of continued dissociation between the different parts of the personality:

[It] maintains dependency on the one hand, and disgust about dependency on the other hand. The relationships among parts must be a target of direct intervention in order to change these systemic dynamics that occur when the attachment system is activated.

(2016)

12 Kathy Steele distinguishes between caregiving and collaboration:

Caregiving is a response to attachment seeking behaviour—a stronger wise person cares for a less strong person, a less wise person. Collaboration involves understanding and caring ... compassion without caregiving (or very limited). Collaboration is based on a co-operative sharing of (often implicit) affective cues and empathetic understanding of the client's mind, and helping the client understand the minds of others.

(2016)

13   So, the experience of agency in therapy is also the foundation for the capacity to experience strong emotion without fearing it as destructive—in other words, the capacity for self-regulation. Self-agency is also the capacity for self-reflection and awareness of the mental and emotional separateness of self and other.

(Knox, 2011, p. 161)

14 "Although social engagement is sought, the person becomes biased toward hyper-arousal, in part due to hyper-vigilance developed from previous experience of intrusive behavior by the primary attachment figure" (Ogden, Minton and Pain, 2006, p. 56).

15 Ambivalence (which is key to David's response) or avoidant attachment stems from the infant's early encounter with the mother: the baby's instinct is to 'latch on' to the breast while the mother whose own trauma is encoded in her body often remains blocked from being able to meet her infant and receive his need for nourishment, comfort and touch in an attuned manner. David's family survived the Jewish pogroms in central Europe. The resultant trauma was clearly trans-generational and, amongst other patterns of behaviour, was expressed in ambivalent attachment styles, as evident in the relationship between David and his mother.

16   Hans Selye and his ground-breaking research on the stress response documented
        that with high levels of psychological stress, there is a narrowing of the visual
        field. ... [The eyes] are windows into the nervous system: in the eyes we can
        see aliveness, availability, enthusiasm, joy, or, on the contrary, we can see fear,
        deadness, absence, distance, dullness, depression, or disconnection ... In Reichian
        theory, what is called the 'eye block,' [describes the] actual blocking of the dia-
        phragms at the cranial base, the *tentorium*, and in the region where the optic
        nerves cross. ... [this] engenders a depression of all bodily functions and systemic
        reduction of energy available to the organism.

(Heller and LaPierre, 2012, p. 158–159)

17   Seasonal affective disorder (SAD) is a type of depression that comes and goes in
        a seasonal pattern. SAD is sometimes known as "winter depression" because the
        symptoms are more apparent and tend to be more severe during the winter.

("Overview: Seasonal Affective Disorder (SAD)")

18 Abram, 1997: "Perception, in Merleau-Ponty's work, is precisely this reciprocity, the
    ongoing interchange between my body and the entities that surround it" (p. 52).
19 Somatic Experiencing teaches that:

        Coupling refers to an association between a stimulus and a response. In SE,
        coupling dynamics refers to the relationship that different aspects of SIBAM [sen-
        sation, image, behaviour, affect and meaning] have with one another. It also refers
        to the response of the nervous system to a stimulus that is perceived as similar to
        a prior trauma experience.

(Somatic Experiencing Trauma Institute, 2007)

20 "In evolutionary terms the infants [in prehistoric times] were the first to be abandoned
    often when resources were scarce. An infant then was vigilant with the mother since her
    non-commitment meant literal death" (evolutionary anthropologist Sarah Blaffer Hrdy
    in conversation with Sieff, 2015, 182–202). "It would be adaptive for infants to become
    connoisseurs of their mother's emotions and intentions" (*ibid.*, p. 198). David's hyper-
    vigilance may be understood in terms of his attachment pattern and transgenerational
    trauma —see *n.* 15 above.
21 Heller and LaPierre describe symptoms related to stress and trauma in the following
    terms: "In addition to the eyes, the diaphragms at the crown of the head and cranial base
    are extremely constricted. ... Tension in these diaphragms causes headaches, one of the
    most common physical complaints [of trauma victims]" (2012, p. 158).

References

Abram, D. (1997) *The Spell of the Sensuous*, New York: Vintage Books.
Abram, D. (2011) *Becoming Animal*, New York: Vintage Books.
Ainsworth, M.I.S. and Wittig, B.A. (1969). "Attachment and the Exploratory Behaviour
    of One-Year-Olds in a Strange Situation," in B.M. Foss (Ed.), *Determinants of Infant
    Behaviour* (Vol. 4), London: Methuen, pp. 113–136.
Ainsworth, M., Blehar, M., Waters, E., and Wall, S. (1979) *Patterns of Attachment: A
    Psychological Study of the Strange Situation*, Hillside, NJ: Erlbaum.
Bainbridge Cohen, B. (1993) *Sensing, Feeling, and Action: The Experiential Anatomy of
    Body-Mind Centering*, Northhampton, MA: Contact Editions.

Bainbridge Cohen, B. (1995) "Excerpts from Sensing, Feeling and Action," in D. Hanlon Johnson (ed.) *Bone, Breath, and Gesture: Practices of Embodiment*, Berkeley, CA: North Atlantic Books, pp. 185–204.

Bateson, M.C. (1979) "The Epigenesis of Conversational Interaction: A Personal Account of Research Development," in Bullowa (ed.), *Before Speech: The Beginning of Human Communication*, London, Cambridge University Press, pp. 63–77.

Beebe, B. and Lachmann, F. (2002) *Infant Research and Adult Treatment: Co-constructing Interactions*. Hillsdale, NJ: The Analytic Press.

Bowlby, J. ([1969] 1981) *Attachment and Loss: Volume 1, Attachment*. Harmondsworth, UK: Penguin Books.

Fonagy, P., Gergely, G., Jurist E. and Target, M. (2004) *Affect Regulation, Mentalization and the Development of the Self*, London: Karnac Books Ltd.

Fosha, D. (2009) "Emotion and Recognition at Work: Energy, Vitality, Pleasure, Truth, Desire, and the Emergent Phenomenology of Transformational Experience," in *The Healing Power of Emotion: Affective Neuroscience, Development and Clinical Practice*, D. Fosha, D.J. Siegel and M. Solomon (eds.), New York: W.W. Norton & Co., pp. 172–203.

Fosha, D., Siegel, D. and Soloman, M., eds. (2009) *The Healing Power of Emotion: Affective Neuroscience, Development and Clinical Practice*, New York: W.W. Norton & Co.

George, C., Kaplan, N. and Main, M. (1985) "The Adult Attachment Interview Protocol (AAI)." Unpublished manuscript held at the University of California, Berkeley.

Gianino, A. and Tronick, E.Z. (1986) "Interactive Mismatch and Repair: Challenges to the Coping Infant," *ZERO TO THREE, Bulletin of the National Center for Clinical Infant Programs* 5: 1–6. Reprinted in: Tronick, E.Z., (2007) *The Neurobehavioural and Social–Emotional Development of Infants and Children*, New York: W.W. Norton, pp. 155–163.

Heller, L. and LaPierre, A. (2012) *Healing Developmental Trauma: How Early Trauma Affects Self-Regulation, Self-Image, and the Capacity for Relationship*, Berkeley, CA: North Atlantic Books.

Johnson, S. (2009) "Extravagant Emotion: Understanding and Transforming Love Relationships in Emotional Focused Therapy," in *The Healing Power of Emotion: Affective Neuroscience, Development and Clinical Practice*, D. Fosha, D.J. Siegel and M. Solomon (eds.), New York: W.W. Norton and Co., pp. 257–299.

Jung, C.G. (1961) *Symbols and the Interpretation of Dreams*, Bollingen Series XX, Collected Works 18, Princeton, NJ: Princeton University Press.

Kalsched, D. (1996) *The Inner World of Trauma: Archetypal Defences of the Personal Spirit*, London: Routledge.

Knox, J. (2011) *Self-Agency in Psychotherapy: Attachment, Autonomy and Intimacy*, London: W.W. Norton and Co.

Main, M. and Soloman, J. (1990) "Procedures for Identifying Infants as Disorganized/ Disoriented During the Ainsworth Strange Situation," in M.T. Greenberg, D. Cicchetti and E.M. Cummings (eds.), *Attachment in the Preschool Years: Theory, Research, and Intervention*, Chicago, IL: Chicago University Press, pp. 95–124.

Monte, C. (2015) *Corpus Anima: Reflections from the Unity of Body and Soul*, Ashville, NC: Chiron Publications.

Ogden, P., Minton, K. and Pain, C. (2006) *Trauma and the Body: A Sensorimotor Approach to Psychotherapy*, London and New York: W.W. Norton & Co.

"Overview: Seasonal Affective Disorder (SAD)." Accessed August 28 2018 at: http:// www.nhs.uk/conditions/seasonal-affective-disorder. NHS Choices.

Schore, A.N. (1994) *Affect Dysregulation and the Origin of the Self: The Neurobiology of Emotional Development*, Mahwah, NJ: Lawrence Erlbaum Associates.

Schore, A.N. (2001) "The Effects of Early Relational Trauma on Right Brain Development, Affect Regulation, and Infant Mental Health," *Infant Mental Health Journal*, 22 (1–2): 201–269.

Schore, A.N. (2002) "Dysregulation of the Right Brain: A Fundamental Mechanism of Traumatic Attachment and the Psychopathogenesis of Postraumatic Stress Disorder," *Australian and New Zealand Journal of Psychiatry*, 36 (1): 9–30.

Sieff, D.F. (2008) "Unlocking the Secrets of the Wounded Psyche: Interview with Donald Kalsched," *Psychological Perspectives*, 51: 190–207.

Sieff, D.F. (2015) *Understanding and Healing Emotional Trauma: Conversations with Pioneering Clinicians and Researchers*, Hove, UK and New York: Routledge.

Siegel, D.J. (2010) *Mindsight: Transform your Brain with the New Science of Kindness*, London: One World Publications.

Somatic Experiencing Trauma Institute (2007) *Somatic Experiencing Professional Training Course Manual*, Boulder, CO: Foundation for Human Enrichment (B1.27).

Steele, K. (2016) "Lean on Me—Dependency and Collaboration in the Psychotherapy of Relational Trauma", 33rd ISSTD Conference, San Francisco, CA, 31 March 2016

Stern, D.N. (1985) *The Interpersonal World of the Infant: A View from Psychoanalysis and Developmental Psychology*, London: Karnac.

Stern, D., Sander, L., Nahum, J.P., Harrison, A.M., Lyons-Ruth, K., Morgan, A.C., Bruschweiler-Stern, N. and Tronick, E.Z. (1998) "Non-Interpretive Mechanisms in Psychoanalytic Therapy: The "Something More" than Interpretation," *International Journal of Psychoanalysis*, 79 (Pt 5): 903–921.

van der Kolk, B. (2008) "The John Bowlby Memorial Lecture 2006. Developmental Trauma Disorder: A New, Relational Diagnosis for Children with Complex Histories," in *Trauma and Attachment*, S. Benamer and K. White (eds.), London: Routledge, 2008, pp. 45–60.

West, M. (2016) *Into the Darkest Places: Early Relational Trauma and Borderline States of Mind*, London: Karnac.

Wilkinson, M. (2006) *Coming into Mind: The Mind-Brain Relationship: A Jungian Clinical Perspective*, London and New York: Routledge.

Chapter 5

Working with Dissociative and Disoriented Attachment Patterns (1)

"The child fell off the chair ..."

Think, dear friend, reflect on the world that you carry within yourself. And name this thinking what you wish. It might be recollections of your childhood or yearning for your own future. Just be sure that you observe carefully what wells up within you and place that above everything that you notice around you. Your innermost happening is worth all your love. You must somehow work on that.

("The Sixth Letter", Rainer Maria Rilke, 2000)[1]

*

In the previous chapter, the excerpt from a BodyDreaming session focused on David's insecure ambivalent attachment pattern. In this and the following chapter, I will focus on the third type of insecure attachment, the ***dissociative and disoriented attachment pattern***. To illustrate my work with this attachment pattern, I will use excerpts from notes on sessions with two analysands. The first case, presented in this chapter, allows me to present an overview of a long-term therapeutic process during the time in which I integrated the neurobiology of attachment theory and various somatic modalities into my psychoanalytic practice. With the second case, presented in Chapter 6, I concentrate on a critical session during the final six months of a 15-year analysis and the dream the session generated which in many ways confirmed, resolved and brought closure to the work.

In this chapter, I introduce Luke, an analysand with a ***dissociative and disoriented attachment pattern*** with whom I also worked for 15 years. My focus will be on a critical session shortly before the analysis terminated.

Before coming to see me, Luke had worked with a body-focused therapist with whom he experienced memory retrieval of being sexually abused as a very young child. He suspected that further memories might emerge while in therapy with me; he was searching for a means of integrating his early trauma, and felt that a psychoanalytical container might help him find words—a language—to frame something of his experience.

Luke was the youngest child in a large family. In his early years, he was cared for largely by older siblings as Luke's mother had been prescribed SSRI tranquillizers for many years prior to and during the time she was pregnant with Luke, and her dependency continued through much of Luke's childhood.[2] Years later, Luke's mother told Luke this after hearing a radio discussion about babies born of mothers addicted to heroin, noting that the symptoms of distress exhibited by those babies were reminiscent of Luke's own distress as an infant. When Luke was born he had cried incessantly and no one had known what was the matter. We may imagine both the unborn and infant Luke as the helpless victim of his mother's addictive cycle, activated at the cellular level by his mother's own psychobiological dysregulation.

> On the other side of the mother-infant dyad, interdisciplinary evidence indicates that the infant's psychobiological reaction to traumatic stress is comprised of two separate response patterns: hyperarousal and dissociation. In the initial hyperarousal stage, the maternal haven of safety suddenly becomes a source of threat, triggering an alarm or startle reaction in the infant's right hemisphere, the locus of both the attachment system and the fear motivational system. This maternal stressor activates the infant's hypothalamus-pituitary-adrenal (HPA) stress axis ... resulting in significantly elevated heart rate, blood pressure and respiration—the somatic expression of a dysregulated hypermetabolic psychobiological state of fear/terror.
>
> (Schore, 2009, p. 120)

There would have been no opportunity for the foetus to experience "the maternal haven of safety" to which Schore refers, which develops from the capacity of a non-addictive, psycho-biologically healthy mother to self-regulate and *inter*-regulate (i.e., regulate the relation between her own nervous system and that of the baby). Heller and LaPierre affirm that infants who have experienced prenatal trauma are already in a disorganized and dysregulated state at birth (2012, p. 137). The trauma lives on in a persistent high-arousal of the nervous system, with hyper- and hypoarousal occurring at the same time, resulting in a deep dorsal vagal *immobility/freeze* and hyperarousal. Heller and LaPierre describe the effects of this combined state:

> The vulnerable infant, who can neither fight nor flee, cannot discharge the high arousal and responds to threat with physiological constriction, contraction, core withdrawal, and immobility/freeze ... [all of which responses are] ... the primitive defense mechanisms infants utilize to manage the high arousal of terrifying early trauma. ... [T]his combination of high arousal, contraction, and freeze creates systemic dysregulation that affects all of the body's biological systems. The underlying biological dysregulation of early trauma is the shaky foundation upon which the psychological self is built.
>
> (Heller and LaPierre, 2012, p. 128)

The effect on the system is 'global' such that Somatic Experiencing refers to this state of activation as Global High Intensity Activation (GHIA).[3]

Pierre Janet, pioneer in neurology and psychiatry in Paris, first drew attention to the difference "between 'narrative memory'—the stories people tell about trauma—and traumatic memory itself ... [He] coined the term 'dissociation' to describe the splitting off and isolation of memory imprints" (van der Kolk, 2014, p. 180). Janet continues:

> [U]nable to integrate their traumatic memories, they lose their capacity to assimilate new experiences as well. It is ... as if their personality has definitely stopped at a certain point, and cannot enlarge any more by the addition or assimilation of new elements. The sensations, thoughts, and emotions of trauma are stored separately as frozen, barely comprehensible fragments.
>
> (*ibid.*)

Following his traumatic pre- and postnatal experience, Luke grew up in a chaotic environment: the family business was run from home and involved all the siblings. Surrounded by turmoil, Luke developed a dissociative/compartmentalized way of coping, a *self-state*[4] of control which allowed him to *manage* the world around him. At one point in his analysis, Luke drew an image of a number of cardboard boxes. He recalled there always being cardboard boxes in the home; from a very young age he had enjoyed playing with these boxes and would find safety by hiding in and playing in a box. His self-care system created a sense of safety and gave him control over his environment, regulating him within the defined, boundaried space of the cardboard box.[5] This powerful image of the many boxes poignantly captures how Luke's dissociative states existed independently, side by side, and how essential to his survival was the capacity of the psyche to dissociate. Bromberg reminds us that the normal personality structure is shaped by dissociation as well as by repression and intrapsychic conflict: "Dissociation, like repression, is a healthy, adaptive function of the human mind. It is a basic process that allows individual self-states to function optimally (not simply defensively ...)"[6]

Tronick (2007) reminds us that the interactive states between mother and infant are mutually regulatory, each affecting the other and the quality of the interaction is central to building a core sense of self in the infant. Regulation, co-regulation, inter-regulation, "has a fundamental effect on how the infant feels about himself— that is, on the child's feeling of effectance: the sense of what he can or cannot accomplish. ... If I can't affect you, I don't exist" (cited in Knox, 2011, p. 113). Luke's earliest experiences were heavily influenced by the tranquillizers in his mother's system, leaving him highly dysregulated and, following his birth, crying incessantly in a 'cold turkey' state of withdrawal. His early experiences left him in a "profound experience of defeat, accompanied by experiences of powerlessness and annihilation" (West, 2016, p. 276). This lack of a core self is central to the dissociative and disorganized attachment pattern. When the mismatches between infant and mother are not repaired, the infant develops a "negative affective core" (Gianino and Tronick, 1986, p. 156).

Marion Woodman writes this about the unmothered child:

> A mother who cannot welcome her baby … into the world leaves her …
> [baby] … groundless. Similarly, the mother's mother and grandmother were
> probably without the deep roots that connect a woman's body to the earth.
>
> (Woodman, 1990, p. 74)

At the beginning of our work together, I found Luke to be ungrounded, living less in his body than in his mind, the control centre out of which he *managed* the world around him. Power and control had replaced love as a primitive defence against the absence of a positive maternal container which would have given Luke a connection to his body. Luke's self-care system, constructed to guarantee survival at all costs, generated a dynamic to ensure he remain in control, protected from unbearable feelings of chaos, helplessness, and despair. Consequently, Luke controlled intolerable feelings by disavowing them and projecting them onto family, friends and business clients, whom he saw as vulnerable and needy. Luke worked hard and strove always to keep others content—never 'rocking the boat'—with the inevitable result that he was left feeling exhausted, neglected and rageful because of always dancing to the other's tune. Although he left school early, Luke later graduated from university with a professional training and embarked on a successful career which guaranteed him a position of power and control. Marcus West (2013) describes the 'dual' aspect of the complex:

> being both the passive, traumatized, 'victim' aspect, as well as the aggressive, traumatizing, 'abusive' aspect. I will describe how these two aspects fit together in a particular, characteristic, masochisto-sadistic way which, I suggest, until it is 'mastered' (a contentious phrase in the literature), ensures that the complex continues to dominate the individual's psyche and way of relating. The aggressive aspect of the complex is almost always split off, disavowed, denied and projected yet, characteristically, its manifestation by the individual becomes justified and legitimized by the trauma itself. … I have reversed the usual ordering of this term to indicate that the masochistic aspect is primary, and that the sadistic element emerges secondarily as a result of and in response to the wounding that has occurred.
>
> (West, 2013, p. 75)

Luke's self-care system ensured that a victim/controller dyad, reflecting Luke's inner psychic structure, remained in place. 'Victims'—family, friends and business clients—held the split-off woundedness that Luke was committed to 'managing'. Our work was to enable Luke to acknowledge the dual aspect of the victim/controller complex before he could begin to recognize his own vulnerable, helpless, wounded self currently projected onto the 'other' and to disidentify from the controller self that managed his inner world and his outer relationships.[7]

In actuality, the 'controller' and the 'vulnerable infant-self' appeared to operate independently of each other although they constituted two aspects of the same
complex. Jung argues that split-off or dissociated parts of the personality operate
as 'sub-personalities' with the capacity to act independently of the central ego;
thus "complexes are in fact 'splinter psyches'" (1934, par. 204). And in the early
1900s, Eugene Bleuler, whose influence on both Freud and Jung was highly significant, wrote the following about the dissociability of the psyche:

> In every case, we are confronted with a more or less clear-cut splitting of
> the psychic functions. If the disease is marked, the personality loses its
> unity; at different times different psychic complexes seem to represent the
> personality ... one set of complexes dominates the personality for a time,
> while other groups of ideas or drives are 'split off' and seem either partly
> or completely impotent.
>
> (Bleuler, cited in Krieger, 2014, p. 20)

For a long time in my work with Luke, there seemed to be little continuity
between our sessions and Luke's life, just as there was little continuity or coherence between the self-state of controller and that of the vulnerable infant-self
revealed to him in his previous therapy.[8] However, after some time in analysis,
Luke became conscious of the fact that he would disconnect, or dissociate, at
the end of each of our sessions. As he reached for his keys, which lay on the
side table, he would 'cut off' from his vulnerable self and once again assume
the self-state of 'controller' in order to cope with the outside world. I was left
holding the shameful, needy baby.

Children with a dissociative disorganized attachment pattern typically switch
from one state to the other and do not have a coherent sense of selfhood for,
as Bromberg points out, "[w]hen the illusion of unity is too dangerous to be
maintained there is then a return to the simplicity of dissociation as a proactive,
defensive response to the potential repetition of trauma" (1996, pp. 509–535).
Initially I felt objectified by Luke's highly functioning 'controller' self—as if I
were one of his busy, demanding clients whom he *had* to see, if only to pay. He
controlled the payments—when and how I would be paid—often forgetting his
cheque book or having his secretary write me the cheque. In the countertransference, I felt some shame that I had to ask for my fee, that I needed something
from him. I felt that I had not acted professionally, accompanied by a sinking
feeling in my stomach that I was getting it wrong somehow.[9] At other times I felt
frustrated and manipulated—a feeling of being controlled. I understood Luke's
behaviour as a way of splitting from his vulnerability by 'controlling' the payments in an unconscious show of 'aggression' or power over me, a replay of
the victim/controller dyad. As West states, see above p. 152, the 'dual element' of
victim/controller, "until it is mastered ... ensures that the complex continues to
dominate the individual, their psyche and way of relating" (West, 2013, p. 75).

Kalsched argues that the

negativity and destructiveness that take over the inner landscape [of the traumatized child] seem to result from the infant's natural aggression which cannot be expressed outwardly or processed with its love-objects. Instead, ... this aggression is re-directed into the interior where it becomes the energy behind dissociation and splitting.

(2013, p. 187)

Chronic shame is the most common response to feeling 'unlovable', with the accompanying behaviour of wanting to hide, disappear, camouflage ourselves or shut down entirely. Shame is what fuels the disconnection, fragmentation and deep dissociation. This helps us understand how the natural dissociability of the psyche was fundamental to Luke's survival: from the very beginning he was wired to the highs and lows of his mother's medication and thus experienced trauma at the pre-natal and pre-verbal stages of development, as well as throughout his childhood. Winnicott (1962) asserts that "at the early stage there is no external factor; the mother is part of the child. At this stage the infant's pattern includes the infant's experience of the mother, as she is in her personal actuality" (p. 61). He had little *in utero* and *perinatal* experience of interregulation and subsequently no-one with whom he could express or regulate his feelings and natural aggression. Tronick emphasizes the mutual regulation that takes place in the mother/infant conversations. "They are both participants with rules and goals and turn-taking which govern their communications" (2007, p. 250). When the goals are met between mother and infant, a "confirmation of self takes place" (*ibid.*, p. 261). When the mother fails to follow the rules of reciprocity, a core negative sense of self is built from the repeated mismatches and the infant learns helplessness. If their efforts to elicit the mother's attention have no effect "then the goals of mutuality must be given up" (*ibid.*). Tronick concludes that "the infant develops a pattern of behaviour that precludes human interchange, and in such withdrawal a denial of the child's self is produced" (*ibid.*). Denial of the child self lay at the core of our work and ultimately motivated Luke to retrieve this part of himself.

Through infancy, childhood and into adulthood, Luke's aggression turned inward; he experienced himself as toxic, 'bad', hopeless and helpless, feelings accompanied by a deep sense of shame.[10] He defended against such vulnerability with splitting. Bromberg confirms that

the key quality of a highly dissociated personality organization is its defensive dedication to retaining the protection afforded by the separateness of self-states (their discontinuity) and minimizing their potential for simultaneous accessibility to consciousness, so that each shifting 'truth' can continue to play its own role without interference by the others, creating a personality structure that one of my [Bromberg's] patients called 'having a whim of iron'.

(1996, p. 5)

If, in the course of our early work, I offered an interpretation attempting to create a link between the different self states, this seemed to bring Luke into a state of confusion, threatening his sense of comfort and fusion with me. He would immediately become disoriented, with eyes wide open in a startle response, and in a hesitant, frightened voice he would seek reassurance at the end of the session: "I don't know where we stand. Are we ok?" In the moment, it seemed that his experience of shame might cripple him. My interpretations and attempts to link self states seemed to trigger dissociation, throwing Luke into confusion while up to the point of my intervention he had related to me as a self-object, merging with me and insisting that I mirror him to the extent of fusing with him. When his professional work was not going well, when clients were not paying, then it seemed I should suffer too, and be kept waiting for payment.[11] Knox describes such extreme forms of defence as those that "prevent any new experiences being taken in, because all new events threaten the fantasy of total merger with, and control of, one's love objects" (2011, p. 147). Knox's interpretation reflects the degree of Luke's merger with his self-object, and the lack of a capacity for separation in his system.

Given the extreme toxicity of the prenatal environment, we may assume that the capacity of Luke's neocortex to override and regulate the degree of sympathetic hyperarousal he regularly experienced remained under-developed. This, in turn, would result in the significant impairment of Luke's capacity for self-regulation as an adult. For example, during therapy we might succeed in establishing an inter-regulatory communication—a new, shared understanding and meaning—the effect of which was evident to both of us during the session. However, Luke's dissociative pattern would quickly override the 'good feelings' and his appreciation of what we had built together, often "wiping it out". Just as his mother had been unable to keep Luke in mind, so Luke was unable to hold what we had co-created in the session. He was left, once again, in a state of disorientation. Bion (1959) refers to this form of defence as an attack on linking.[12] Regularly, in the first months of our work together, Luke would begin the session with, "I split off from our session last week. I can't sustain it." He described these times as though he had "blanked out". It felt to him, and to me, as if memory had been erased and "nothing would get laid down" between us. Perhaps this rhythm of connection and disconnection has echoes in the implicit memory bank of a drug-induced intoxication in the womb. This pattern of memory erasure and dissociation was consistent with the dynamics of Luke's intimate relationships. It seemed as though Luke could not assimilate new positive experience, failing to transition from deintegration to reintegration.[13] There was little experience of a core self to integrate the new experiences. As previously stated, in cases of intrauterine trauma there is no neocortex available to regulate the responses of the amygdala and limbic system. Hence the dorsal vagal system, with its more primitive defence mechanisms of dissociation, collapse and freeze, dominates responses to any on-going high arousal of the sympathetic nervous system, and this leaves the subsequent development of the ventral vagal and social engagement systems "severely compromised".[14] One's sense of self is built on implicit experiences of body-based emotions and interactions. If one is shut down, cut off, in a dorsal freeze, then the sense of self has no physical body base and is left fragmented. Allen *et al.*

comment: "dissociatively detached individuals are not only detached from the environment, but also from the self—their body, their own actions, and their sense of identity" (1999, 165).

Winnicott speaks to the early relationship of infant and mother, and the "continuity pattern of going-on-being" that is present when "the good enough mother (in respect of the unthinkable anxieties) enables the new human person to build up a personality on the pattern of a continuity of going-on-being" (1962, p. 60). He adds that "all failures (that could produce unthinkable anxiety) bring about a reaction in the infant; this reaction cuts across the going-on-being". If this reaction becomes persistent, then a fragmentation of being results (*ibid.*). The state of fragmentation described by Winnicott seemed to be the experience Luke and I shared in the early years of the analysis.

Schore points out that "[s]hame is the emotion elicited during a rapid transition from an excited positive state to a deflated negative one" (in conversation with Sieff, 2015, p. 122).[15] The subjective experience of shame is psychobiologically mediated by a sudden shift from sympathetic-dominant to parasympathetic autonomic nervous system activity (Schore, 1994, p. 205). Periods of hyperarousal evident in Luke's 'running' to satisfy the endless demands of those onto whom he projected his vulnerable, needy child self, would inevitably be followed by periods of extreme collapse or hypoarousal, during which Luke's aggression, anger and disappointment would be turned on himself. At such times of physical exhaustion, Luke would be overcome by negativity, shame and hopelessness, falling into a dorsal vagal *immobilized state* or *collapse.*[16]

During therapy, when traumatic events in his life were recalled or current stresses became insupportable (i.e., at times of heightened sympathetic arousal), Luke would often go into a state of high alert, risking re-traumatization. Schore suggests that the neurobiology of a person with such a response is wired in such a way that leaves no option except to flee from a state of hyperarousal "by the only means possible—that is inwards, through collapse and hypoarousal" (Sieff, 2015, p. 124).

On the first of these occasions, Luke's eyes rolled in their sockets, his head leant backward and he lost contact with me for a short period. He became disoriented and exhausted. Initially I was alarmed and alerted to the risk of re-traumatization and further disassociation. I felt protective of Luke but unable to reach him or prevent his sudden shift into this dissociative state. In the countertransference I felt frightened, helpless and paralysed. I had to sit and wait it out. Luke would become totally disconnected and exhausted during and after such an episode of heightened arousal and dissociation.[17] Luke had experienced one such major collapse, resulting in surgery to his spine, approximately 10 years before we began working together. My question to myself then was how to work with these 'intrusive' episodes that seemed to replicate the early chemical invasion of Luke's fragile embryonic and infant state with toxic substances?

Later when I came upon Schore's extensive study of neuroscientific research it helped me make an invaluable connection between Luke's dissociative episodes and the early trauma he had suffered in the toxic environment of the womb. Schore points out that extreme early trauma or stressful post-natal contexts results in "permanent alterations in opiate, corticosteroid, cortico-trophin releasing factor, dopamine, noradrenaline and serotonin receptors" (2003, p. 290). He notes that such changes may result in a permanent physi-ological reactivity in the immature limbic system:

> Elevated corticotrophin releasing factor is known to initiate seizure activity in the developing brain ... so this circuit hyperactivity may be expressed at later periods with 'psychogenic nonepileptic seizures,' ... [or] ... [P]artial seizure-like symptoms.
>
> (*ibid.*)

The description matched the dissociative episodes that Luke experienced as described above.

Schore points out that "the neo-natal brain is more prone to excitotoxicity than the adult brain" (*ibid.*) and emphasizes the long-term impairment to the develop-ing limbic system (and consequently to the development of the right brain) of persistent toxicity caused by early adverse experiences:

> Because the early maturing right hemisphere is more deeply connected into the limbic system than the left, this enduring reactivity is 'burnt' into corticolimbic circuits of the right brain, the hemisphere dominant for the reg-ulation of the stress hormones cortisol and corticotropin.
>
> (*ibid.*)

At the time Luke's mother was pregnant with him, there was little understand-ing of how drugs administered to the mother penetrate the placenta, reach and adversely affect the foetus. Dissociation is the body's response to intolerable stress and pain, and triggers the release of high levels of opiates which block the experience of pain. When Luke was born, he would not have received treat-ment to support his withdrawal from the tranquillizers upon which his mother was dependent. He would have been left to go 'cold turkey'. Luke's dissociation and subsequent splitting from his vulnerable infant self-state served as a life-saving mechanism to ensure his survival in the face of intolerable odds.[18]

In the course of our sessions when we inadvertently triggered a trauma state, it would send Luke beyond his window of tolerance into dissociation. These moments seemed to be connected with a state of overwhelm, and bringing atten-tion to that overwhelm in his body exacerbated the limbic arousal rather than causing it to abate, sending Luke over the threshold into the dissociative state. He described the process as inducing "a feeling of being inundated. Terror is coming in and I feel like I'm drowning." In hindsight, during those initial years of Luke's analysis, I realize that in moments of high activation, by being asked questions that brought him into his body, the sensation field, he was catapulted into the sea of chemical overload, drowning in toxicity, replicating the original trauma. At the time, I did not have the training to know how to titrate the trauma and support his system. In order not to recreate the powerful dissociative and seizure-like states, the trauma would have required an equal and opposite experience of a positive affective orientation in the 'here and now' to hold the balance and not tip him overboard.[19]

After some years of our working together, I trained in Peter Levine's Somatic Experiencing,[20] and began to integrate this somatic focus into my practice. Training in Somatic Experiencing, together with my understanding of Gendlin's felt sense exploration, enabled me to acquire new skills—namely, the capacity to build resilience in the client through the regulation of affect by using positive resourcing, and to titrate high levels of activation. Soon I began to notice a change in Luke: his swings between sympathetic highs and parasympathetic lows reduced. Schore writes that in a state of dissociation "the individual is cut off (disassociated) from both the external *and* the internal environment" (2003, p. 213—my italics). Learning to choose, focus on and relate to a positive resource gradually helped Luke to develop the capacity to remain present in the 'here and now' of the internal and external environment and in the moments of interaction between us. The acute episodes of dissociation, as described above, almost disappeared. This marked a crucial and significant step in Luke's healing. Luke and I spent a great deal of time exploring the body-sensation interface until he was no longer triggered when asked to focus on his body. Eventually, we were able to use the body-sensation feedback as a positive resource when Luke found himself on the edge of dissociation. His growing capacity to focus on what was happening in his body that was *not* traumatic helped him to open more space, attain greater fluidity in his body, and eventually maintain body awareness.

The first occasion on which Luke successfully maintained body awareness, when he might otherwise have fallen into "psychogenic nonepileptic seizure", occurred in a moment of activation: he was suddenly seized by terror—eyes fixed and wide open, body rigid. I drew his attention to his body with the question, "What do you notice happening in your body right now?" His attention was drawn to his head—the pain behind his eyes. "Is there anywhere in your body you are not feeling pain?" I asked. In response, Luke began to notice his nostrils. He could feel the air moving in and out. His eyes locked in terror with mine. It felt to me as if he was begging me to stay present with him, to keep him from falling into a 'hell'.[21] I kept speaking to him in a low-pitched, steady voice, drawing his attention to the air moving through his nostrils and the space that was opening up in his nostrils.[22] After a while I noticed Luke's breathing deepening; he was no longer panting, the glazed look had left his eyes. "That was so frightening," he said. In spite of his terror, Luke had not fallen into a trance state or a "psychogenic nonepileptic seizure". Instead, by focusing on the movement and sensation of his breath in his nostrils, Luke was able to withstand the pull to dissociation. He was supported to stay present in the 'here and now' of his body sensation while listening to my voice and watching my face. This regulatory moment proved highly significant for Luke, empowering him to meet, head on, his familiar self-care system's tendency to dissociate. The support he felt afforded him a *Perseus's shield*,[23] helping him withstand the terror of annihilation, enabling him to remain present through felt sense body awareness. Consequently, this particular resource—the sensation of breath in his nostrils—came to serve as a *pause* button which Luke could use whenever he found himself on the threshold of overwhelm and dissociation. Luke had discovered a capacity to remain present to his activated self rather than 'go out of' his body in *fight, flight* or *freeze*. The critical threshold moment successfully negotiated in this particular session marked a palpable shift in our establishing what Winnicott calls a "pattern of continuity, of going-on-being" (1962, p. 60):[24] supported by my presence, Luke's sensing body had helped him remain present to himself, a capacity seminal to his work to develop a learned secure attachment to the body.

Slowly, over time, Luke began to *take root* in himself, take in positive experiences, and develop a new, independent standpoint distinct from the default positions of activation, fragmentation or *freeze*. Luke's growing capacity for inner attunement and his development of a language to describe the sensations and emotions he experienced in his body emerged in tandem and brought Luke into a living and soulful relationship to his body—his physical container. Joan Chodorow, Jungian analyst and dance therapist, suggests that by paying attention to the "world of bodily felt sensations the ... [client] ... creates a situation that is in many ways similar to that of an infant who swims in a sensory world" (1986, p. 97). Chodorow's comments are particularly poignant in Luke's case as he learnt to titrate not only current emotions but particularly those triggered by early implicit memory. We achieved this through a slow and sensitive oscillation between activating symptom and deactivating resource, avoiding both overwhelm and retraumatization. This process of titration ensured that the dorsal vagal *freeze* response exerted less and less control of Luke's system while, at the same time, it enabled Luke to develop tolerance and compassion for himself and for some of his defensive strategies and behaviours. Self-blame, shame and self-hatred triggered by perceived failures in relationship diminished significantly and were replaced by self-care and the pursuit of creative interests. Luke began to feel less the victim of limbic activation as he practised interoception and felt sense awareness, developing his ability to titrate emotional overwhelm and manage dysregulation without dissociating.   We were coming to the end of the analysis. Luke had become less identified with his controller self and seemed to have found greater cohesion between his different 'states'. He was functioning well in his life, and had begun to train in a new profession.[25] We had started to discuss bringing the analysis to a close, so it came as a shock when we went headlong into a crisis: I failed to anticipate Luke's response to an extended Christmas holiday I was about to take. In the last session before the break, my pending absence and its impact on Luke were discussed. Luke, for the first time, was able to own his extreme vulnerability and sense of abandonment.

This event marked a significant development step for Luke. With hindsight, and in light of what happened during the Christmas holiday, I realize that we had needed more time than had been available to integrate and assimilate the experience. In the moment, however, Luke was able to remain present to his feelings and articulate his neediness, vulnerability and anger without dissociating or turning his negative emotions inward on himself. We had opened a core issue of abandonment in the session with which I resonated in the countertransference. I had the feeling that I was the all powerful m/other abandoning him, recklessly shattering the safety of the *temenos* we had created. Davies and Frawley (1992) speak to the three key players in the cycle of abuse in early developmental trauma—victim, abuser, and an omnipotent idealized rescuer (West, 2013, p. 26). I was no longer in the idealized position of safeguarding the *temenos* but felt responsible for abandoning Luke. It was my role "to bear and embody the feelings corresponding to the 'aggressor' in the original trauma" (*ibid.*, p. 186). To dare to express his emotions about our imminent separation required that Luke consciously recognize me as an independent being who had agency, who was choosing to go on an extended holiday. I was no longer fused with him as a self-object. Instead, Luke was rendered powerless, feeling unwanted, exposed, abandoned and shamed.

In the days following the session, implicit memories of Luke's early infant self were activated, triggering a trauma response that exploded into the outer world, shattering Luke's newly acquired resilience, pushing him over his threshold, and stimulating the type of "psychogenic nonepileptic seizure" referred to earlier. At the time, Luke was over-extended on many fronts and felt as though he were on the verge of collapse: his body could not tolerate the level of pressure that was building up in his system. His old self-care system of hyperactivity had been activated in the face of the pending holiday, protecting him from feelings of abandonment, vulnerability and anger. The hyperactivity (sympathetic activation) of Luke's controller self left him in a state of exhaustion. In the session, Luke realized the cost to himself of maintaining a high level of control and caretaking of the 'other' and found that he no longer wanted to cut himself off from his vulnerable and needy child self. However, he was frightened that he would not be able to care for his child self while his analyst was away.

We agreed that Luke's commitment to staying present to his child self would require him to be assertive and, in a show of "healthy aggression",[26] say 'No' to his partner regarding their joint plans for the holiday period. However, Luke was extremely anxious about the break: "*I want to hold myself and I don't know if I can do it on my own.*" In hindsight, I see that in the countertransference my feelings of guilt at leaving him drew me away from staying with his feelings of anger, helplessness and abandonment at the impending break. Instead I remained in the role of *idealized rescuer*, colluding with Luke's more able controller self, joining him to find practical solutions to some of the needy demands that threatened to engulf him in my absence. The old self-care system re-established itself and, with my help, he shifted out of his shame-based dorsal collapse (i.e., he is *bad* and I abandon him because he is *bad*). Instead, Luke's sympathetic/*fight* response is mobilized and he readies himself to tackle what he perceives as his partner's unreasonable demands. In this way the persecutor-protector defence is mobilized and Luke's sympathetic system's *fight* response is re-established in the guise of the controller self. I later realized that we might have worked with the helplessness and rage of Luke's child self in response to the threat of abandonment to help titrate the *healthy aggressor* toward me, without seeking active solutions.

Saying 'No' to the plans he had previously agreed with his partner, in a bid to protect his child self, threatened the established relationship balance on which Luke's emotional life-line had depended for many years. It required him to act in a way that ran counter to his recognized identity and role in the partnership; it required him to override the demands of his self-care system and his attachment style behaviour. The ensuing encounter with his partner proved too great an assault on Luke's self-care system. When his proposal was rejected, Luke was pushed beyond his window of tolerance and he went into a full-blown *fit*—an episode similar to a psychogenic nonepileptic seizure, followed by total immobility— a dorsal *freeze* that manifested in a major physical collapse, for which he was hospitalized. Soon after he was discharged from hospital, Luke suffered a further collapse when he fell off a chair and slipped a disk, losing mobility on his right side. It seemed that Luke's abandoned inner child was fighting back; not content to be ignored any longer, he was making his presence felt through eruptions of unconscious processes manifesting in Luke's bodily collapses.[27] The right side of Luke's body—symbolically associated with consciousness and masculine energy—was impaired, as was Luke's ability to rule both his inner and outer worlds. His body 'received' attention through daily physiotherapy. He remained in a cast for nine months—the incubation term needed to reconstitute himself in the 'womb' that he would create around him. Significantly, nine months later Luke reported to me: "*The inner child is the one who fell off the chair.*"

As Jung reminds us, what we do not make conscious we meet as fate in the outer world. This, it seems to me, is what happened to Luke. His immobility meant that he was relegated to a prone position for some time. Although his controller self continued to run his office from his day bed, Luke was nevertheless forced to slow down. He had no alternative but to relinquish his habitual mode of over-extension and hyperactivity that had for so long ensured a profound dissociation from his child self. As a result, Luke's collapse slowly metamorphosed from misfortune to resource, a deep well from which he could draw nourishment and, most importantly, in which he could learn to meet himself. Ursula Wirtz argues that "like cures like":

It takes trauma to heal trauma. Voluntary sacrifice is the antidote to involuntary sacrifice. The trauma of the sacrifice of the False Self (i.e., Luke's controlling self-state), experienced in the safety and security of the therapeutic relationship, can bring about the healing of the trauma of physical and psychic violation.

(Wirtz, 2014, p. 291)

Little by little, Luke admitted into consciousness the exhaustion and helplessness that had underpinned his lifelong self-care pattern of hyperactivity and control, and accepted his system's vulnerability, now undeniably at the forefront of consciousness. Luke continued for some time to serve the 'victim', who by now had become the 'oppressor' outside himself, at the cost of his own health, putting himself at risk of permanent immobility. This ensured that the dissociation would continue until the *other* ceased to carry the projection of Luke's own helplessness and aggression.

We worked hard to integrate the *child state* which had *collapsed* in Luke's bid to be taken seriously by his partner. Luke's symptoms—a cry for attention from and recognition by his child state—made it clear that Luke must sacrifice his controller self. This constituted a major show-down and challenge to his self-care system. Luke felt as if there were two people, each manifesting on opposite sides of his body—his left side holding flexibility and the right rigidity and pain. He was in a lot of pain and suffered from exhaustion. At one point, Luke said: "*I'm divided. I divide myself constantly. I feel very split. I don't know who I am.*" His lack of a sense of a core self sent Luke into orbit, triggering his self-care system: "*I'm free falling. My partner is my satellite. I am constantly orbiting around her.*" At this time, the defence of controller/hyperactivity was no longer operating with the same effect—the pain and symptoms in Luke's body kept him alert to the splitting. Luke began to pull back the projections of neediness from his partner and started to identify his own neediness. This was akin to restructuring his self-care system by bringing attention and care to his vulnerability, his body, his child state. The life-long exile of the inner child was not reversed without a major struggle. In what felt like a role reversal, the child self began to make demands on the controller self and we witnessed the confrontation taking place in the body and psyche. The right side of Luke's body, holding the symptom, asked his left side for help: "*Carry me.*" In response, the left side felt threatened, frightened that it was "*being dragged back somewhere*". It took refuge in the familiar but persecutor-protector role and became the *aggressive controller* to the child self, shouting at it, "*Get off me, I want to be free.*" Luke could appreciate that the child/victim was exhausted from the struggle and the lack of acknowledgement by his controller self. On one occasion, Luke exclaimed:

> *I don't have the strength in me for this. It takes all my strength to stay paralyzed. ... It feels like it's in the right side of my body and I'm not able to move it.*

Luke's experience of paralysis may have been the result of an implicit memory of the drugs flooding his infant's system and immobilizing him in the womb.

In this session I was anxious that the battle between the two sides was in danger of overwhelming Luke's consciousness and compromising him further physically. Luke was desperately trying to stay present to the inner drama, played out in his body. He let out a big sigh and slowly the tears came. He sobbed, head down, collapsing inward onto his chest.

Luke: *The child in me is crying. He has had to hold it for so long.*

As witness, I felt such grief in my heart for this exhausted infant self and, simultaneously, compassion for the ever-strident controller self who had managed to survive. Indeed, Luke was a divided self. Adrienne Rich's words ring true:

> But there come times—perhaps this is one of them—when we have to take ourselves more seriously or die.
>
> (1993, p. 74)

It felt as though the stakes were high. I was not sure how it would resolve. Would Luke manage to sacrifice the old pattern to heed the cry of the child self? And what would it take?

*

At this time, I had the opportunity to train with Steven Hoskinson and I began to incorporate his approach, Organic Intelligence, in which affect regulation is introduced by focusing awareness on the immediate environment.[28] As Luke and I were working via Skype at this time, the creation of a safe container needed to include an embodied awareness of the environment. It required that we co-create a living *temenos* which would embrace the room where Luke was sitting and also the image on the screen of me, sitting in my room. Later, while reading this chapter in preparation for publication, Luke recalled that during our Skype sessions he had also been able to see a small image of himself at the bottom of his computer screen, and this had played an important role as it served as *self-witness* to his own process. He acknowledged that this image provided a *"reflective mirror for me, which brought me deeper into the experience. I was seeing myself and that made me feel even more present."*[29] One of my roles was to hold intact the physical or, more accurately, the *virtual* container, should the outside world threaten to invade.

In the following sequence of sessions, I will trace the developmental steps that Luke and I negotiated and which led to Luke's completion of his long-term analysis, the individuation process to which he had committed so many years before. It will become clear from the sequencing of the body work, the dreams and the process that the work is incremental, each step preparing Luke for the next, loosening the grip of his complexes and self-care system and bringing him to a greater sense of his own potential.

Our challenge came in the form of an attack on the container/*temenos*, which seemed to mirror Luke's pre-natal experience of invasion and flooding by his mother's prescribed tranquillizers. Luke's partner, who held the 'needy, demanding' energy, tried to interrupt a session and enter Luke's room, the *temenos* we had created together on-line. The intrusion was highly activating for Luke and replicated the early trauma when his delicate embryonic system was overwhelmed and invaded by chemical substances, *knocking him out*. On this occasion, my challenge was to support Luke to stay present by regulating the inflow of stress chemicals so that he could withstand the intrusion on all levels—physiologically, biologically and psychologically. We titrated the overwhelm, enabling him to withstand familiar patterned responses and the pull to dissociate. This was accomplished by supporting Luke's inner witness to register the opposite: the pull to dissociate and lose consciousness, on one hand, and the need to remain aware of the complex emotions he was feeling, on the other—i.e., terror of his partner's (the other's) rage if he continued to refuse her entry into the room, and the dread of being abandoned. Would his partner still be there for him after the session? Would there be a furious and catastrophic outburst?

I consciously aligned with Luke's inner witness and neocortex to soothe the limbic overload and orient him in the environment of his room. For the first time, Luke's attention was drawn to a blanket that lay beside him on a chair. He instinctively reached out for the blanket and wrapped himself in it, cocooning himself from the intruding presence outside his room. By drawing his attention to the felt sense experience of his skin in contact with the texture of the blanket, Luke could begin to distinguish *inside* from *outside*. His sensing body felt safe, swaddled like a newborn: his system eased, his breathing deepened, his eyes became less startled and he grew less hyper-vigilant. In this instance, Luke's body was able to receive comfort and, as a result, generate more space to enable him to tolerate the intensity of activation. He found he could remain present both to his inner experience and the menacing presence of the *other* outside his room. This event affirmed Somatic Experiencing teacher Raja's Selvam's insistence on the importance of finding a way to gain more space in the body to diffuse a difficult physiological and psychological experience, so that it becomes tolerable and does not overwhelm the individual.[30] Awareness of the interface between the two surfaces—skin against blanket—helped Luke discover his boundary, which was a pivotal moment in our work out of which the next sequence of sessions evolved. In the moment, it provided Luke with an embodied sense of his *Perseus's shield* that protected him from the external interloper and the intrusive toxic chemicals in his system.[31] The pleasure of feeling himself safely inside his own skin, boundaried by the touch of the blanket, enabled Luke to tolerate the separate space that opened up between him and the demanding 'other' who eventually withdrew. This was a significant developmental step. Luke was able to relinquish his need to be in control, trusting he would neither *drown* in overwhelm nor be annihilated if he remained separate from the 'other'. He seemed more receptive to his experience, his body visibly softened. He reported that he felt warmth spreading throughout his body, his breath dropping deeper into his belly. Bonnie Bainbridge Cohen comments, "When you feel that deep breath, something has been repatterned into the nervous system" (in Hanlon Johnson, 1995, p. 191).[32] This particular session with Luke marked the beginning of the ending of his work with me. Luke had found a home inside his skin—a secure base, albeit temporarily.

In the following session, Luke presented with pain in his scapula—the winged part of the shoulder blade—which he understood to be connected both to his fear of intrusion and the work from the previous session. While bringing attention to the symptom in this part of his body, Luke recalled the image of a large white bird that had served as an important creative resource at a crucial point in his analysis. We had worked with this image and it had a numinous charge. Luke had experienced the image as numinous in the past and now, recalling it, he felt a strong resonance to it in the muscle group in his upper back or scapula. Bainbridge Cohen describes this group of muscles:

> [e]ssential to survival and to the infant's ability to separate safely from the mother … [containing] movement patterns of flexion and extension … these patterns underlie withdrawal and approach, fight and flight, bringing toward and pushing away.[33]

I encouraged Luke to sense into that place in his back where he felt a resonance with the image and to allow the energy there to begin to move. I encouraged him to go at a slow pace, listen for any impulse for movement, and allow himself to be guided by the energy. I watched as movement began in his shoulder blades, extending out into his arms as they began to stretch. His palms were open and pushing away from his body. He gradually extended the gesture as he drew a complete circle around his body at arm's length.[34] It looked as if Luke had created a clearly defined container and that he stood right at its centre. He looked more fully himself, strong, sitting upright, his spine extended. With eyes still shut, arms extended, he stayed connected within himself, taking time to complete the self-protective movement. Then he opened his eyes, looked around slowly and turned to face me, taking me in. In that moment I felt our separateness— two separate beings. Luke had created the external container which defined his boundaries further than the skin boundary he had encountered with the blanket. With this new boundary in place, he looked more resilient, more present. I had a sense of his 'arrival'. The image of the white bird had awakened Luke's self-protective responses and in completing the movement he had defined a space that was separate, a space in which he could be in the world and feel safe. Luke was inhabiting his body, boundaried by skin and his musculature. Levine states that "resolving trauma through embodied interoceptive awareness, and the completion of unresolved (i.e., thwarted) procedural memories of defence, restores vital self-protective impulses, here-and-now orientation, coherence, and a confident sense (and expression) of flow" (2015, p. 146). Luke had defined an external space in which he felt protected from intrusion.

By completing the protective defensive movement, Luke is repatterning his defence system and affirming his sense of agency, as well as the ability to protect himself and to separate safely from m/other. The symptom of the painful scapula evoked the numinous image of the white bird, an image key to the unfolding of Luke's developmental movement sequence. Image and body worked together to align with the innate drive toward wholeness. As Woodman and Dickson remind us, "if you want to live your own life, your images and your body are your individual guides. Together, they strengthen your inner core. ... The imagination moves ahead of the action" (1996, p. 195). The 'other' would always carry the threat of impending intrusion and violation for Luke unless he could find the key to activating defensive structures both physically and psychically. Creating a sense of himself as embodied, regulated and protected within his own boundaries, and able to defend against intrusion, was an essential first step before Luke could begin the work of tolerating and exploring his powerful feelings of rage.

Up to this point in his life, Luke had found himself predominantly in relationships that were enmeshed, symbiotic minefields which kept him in a constant state of hyper-vigilance, prepared to ward off blows and protect himself against invasion or abandonment. Heller and LaPierre explain how internal dysregulation, encoded in the system from early trauma, becomes projected onto the environment:

> Not realizing that the danger they once experienced in their environment is now being carried forward as high arousal in their nervous system, traumatized individuals have the tendency to project onto the current environment what has become an ongoing internal state. ... The mind attempts to make sense of this internal biological dysregulation by finding an external cause for the continuous state of inner turmoil.
>
> (2012, pp. 142–143)

Luke lived with the fear that he might accidentally set off an angry explosion in the 'other', a fear that felt primal, as the dangerous, uncertain environment echoed the toxic pre-natal environment in which his mother's medication posed a constant threat to Luke's fragile organism. Luke became more aware of instances when he would find himself in bondage to that part of himself that "*won't rock the boat*", afraid of the 'other's' rageful outburst. His feelings of being the powerless victim were on the surface but in the countertransference I was picking up an underlying rage. Luke was caught in an internal battle-ground between different self-states: he admitted to feeling that his child self was in a rage for Luke's failing to protect him from the intrusive demands of the 'other'. His self-care system was activated by the newly found 'voice' of the child self and retaliated, calling the child a bully. "*He is holding me to ransom. He is a bully.*" Luke had the image of a big black ball suspended from a crane, like a pendulum that knocks houses down. The child self felt utter isolation—being stuck inside "*the black ball place, in absolute darkness alone, no language, no thought, just a pitch-black dark feeling inside my body.*" This image was extremely potent for Luke. His child self blamed him: "*you are not good enough, you are not doing enough for me.*" In response, the persecutor/controller self retaliated against the tyranny of the bullying child and left Luke hanging in a black ball of rage. However, Luke slowly began to recognize that there was some connection between his fear of his partner's outbursts of rage and the controller self's fear of the child self's rage. We were at a new threshold, although Luke was not yet able to own the projection or begin to embody some of his rage.

Luke came to our next session looking defeated, exhausted. He recalled a dream:

> *I was trying to take my children and put them up in the attic because my father was going to get them. I was stabbing my father in the back, right where my pain is, but he wouldn't die.*[35]

Luke: *I need to say "back off" to my partner and I'm exhausted. I don't have the energy in my "No." Normally I don't feel the pain in my back. But now I can feel the pain. I'm bending over backwards to meet her—it's back-breaking.*

Luke's exhaustion, a dorsal vagal collapse response, is coupled in this instance with the idea of saying "No" to his partner. He fears the rageful outburst and rejection that might ensue. Luke's self-care system's protector/persecutor is successful in stopping him saying "No," thereby protecting him from the imagined toxic attacks of his partner. However, the effect is a dorsal collapse—exhaustion which renders Luke impotent, powerless, ineffectual (as in the dream when his stabbing of his father has no effect). Chronic physical pain is not always about there being something wrong. It is more likely to tell us about a pattern of holding or bracing oneself. It serves the survival instinct and in this way has ensured Luke's survival.

Luke's relationship with his father is highly problematic. Luke's father controlled his large family and the business with his violent temper. He used Luke to his own ends—emotionally and physically abusing him. Consequently, Luke's relationship to his own rage is highly complex, as Luke does not want to identify himself with his angry father. His dream shows a break-through in his father complex as Luke demonstrates his use of newly developed defensive and protective responses by removing his children from his father's reach, in this way creating a boundary and a safe haven for them. A very different relationship to the complex is evidenced in Luke's attempt to stab his father in the back. Roget's *Thesaurus* defines the expression "to stab someone in the back" as an attempt to deceive or betray the other person. In order to protect his children (his child self), Luke would have to betray or "stab to death" the father, in this case everything his actual father stands for, and the inner father complex that holds Luke captive; in other words, what needs to die is the abusive controller in the psyche.

Linda Hartley[36] points out that a client who needs to develop a sense of a core self "will need to further her muscular strength, her agency, her ability to direct her energy in a focused and intentional way that importantly achieves the results she seeks" (2004, p. 150). Luke's symptoms and dream image are drawing my attention to a particular group of muscles in his back. Luke needs to find a secure base, a core sense of self *in and through his musculature* to empower him to say "No" to his partner and begin to change his patterned, or default, dorsal vagal collapse response.

I initiate a movement sequence to help stimulate and strengthen the muscle group in the thoracic spine between the shoulder blades,[37] the area in the dream where Luke was stabbing his father and from whence the image of the white bird had earlier evoked the self-protective action of creating a boundary around himself. This area has been the centre of chronic pain for Luke since the beginning of our work together.[38] I invite Luke to stand close to and face the wall, with his hands extended in front of him and placed on the wall. At first I invite him to notice any sensations in his body in response to holding this position. He observes the muscles in his neck beginning to tighten. I wait a moment and enquire if he notices anything else that is happening in his body. Luke's posture shifts slightly as his spine realigns itself. Luke stands taller. Next I invite him to notice the area where the shoulder blades move and to be curious about any pre-movement movement[39] in that area, and then to bring his attention to his arms and hands as his open palms lightly press against the wall. I encourage him to notice any bodily sensations. At first his attention is drawn to the pain in his back.

MD: *Allow your attention to go where you feel the pain in your back ... and then see if there is anything else happening in your body?*

In the gentle pushing action, Luke can feel the sure, firm connection between his back, his arms and hands as he pushes against the wall, confirming the strength in his muscles and that his energy has moved just as he intended it to move. Luke stands straighter, taller, his spine extended, his legs strong. He has experienced his own sense of agency. He feels more empowered. In contrast to the dream image in which his attempt to stab his father was ineffectual, Luke now experiences an embodied sense of efficacy: he can attain his goal. He looks at me directly and speaks in a clear voice, his head nodding with a sense of achievement.

Luke: *I feel my feet are solid on the ground.*

The movement sequence has opened a connection between his upper and lower body and has enabled Luke to experience a direct relationship between his intention and the completion of his action, giving him a sense of self that is rooted and strong.

Our next session begins with yet another cry of exhaustion.

Luke: *I'm not able to fight any longer, I'm so exhausted, I'm full of despair. I want to die. If I go into my body I will feel pain.*

This is clearly a moment where we need to employ pendulation, a term Peter Levine uses to remind us of the "continuous, primary, organismic rhythm of contraction and expansion" (2015, p. 55). We recognized an experience of expansion and strength in the previous session. But now the body has again collapsed, swung toward its opposite, a self-care retaliation for the expansion he experienced, now he is locked in a "state of fixity ... [in which] ... it seems nothing will change" (*ibid.*). In such a state, an individual will usually do anything to avoid confronting the feelings in the body. "The body has become the enemy. The sensations are perceived as the feared harbinger of the entire trauma reasserting itself. However, it is just this avoidance that keeps people frozen, stuck, in their trauma" (*ibid.*).

To counteract the collapse, I invite Luke to orient outward in order to engage his social engagement system. The trees and the play of light coming through their branches attract his attention. We chat about the trees for some time to establish greater flow in Luke's system. His body relaxes, his breath deepens. His eyes are open, taking in more of his environment. Luke is engaged with me, sharing what is a pleasurable experience for both of us. He turns towards me.

Luke: *I feel more expansive. I feel I'm part of the universal energy. Things are bigger than me. [Pause]. A voice is saying, "Yes, you are being held by the trees and healing can pass through your body." And another voice is saying, "I have been here before. It doesn't work. Get a grip."*

Luke's response marks a new threshold moment. He is able to witness the speed at which his divided self is activated, his self-care system interrupting the establishment of new experiences, new pathways in the healing process. I hear the intrusion of the familiar voice of the persecutor/protector that will not risk any change: "*It doesn't work. Get a grip.*" Freud recognized that the psyche is conservative and does not welcome change; old defences die hard and challenge change. He named this aspect of the psyche the *negative therapeutic reaction.*[40] Marion Woodman describes the same psychic phenomenon in terms of the archetype of the *death mother* which can dominate the psyche as a result of the failure of the early relationship and, like the gaze of the Medusa, turn us to stone. "Death mother's gaze penetrates both psyche and body, turning us into stone. It kills hope, it cuts us dead. We collapse. Our life energy drains from us, and we find ourselves yearning for the oblivion of death" (Woodman in conversation with Sieff, 2015, p. 69). The death mother fights against "anything that might precipitate meaningful change. Potentially vibrant energy is locked into cold, rigid, unchanging, lifeless form" (*ibid.*, p. 71).

I recognize the death mother's voice as I hear Luke cut off the pleasurable conversation. In an effort to titrate this overwhelming sense of hopelessness, I draw his attention away from the trauma vortex. I suggest that he look out at the trees again, with the light playing through their branches. He looks out, taking his time to be present, the tension easing from his shoulders, his face softening, his breath dropping. He describes his response:

Luke: *I feel a warmth, a flow of energy moving up from my pelvis. I'm breathing more into my belly. I'm feeling tired, and when I breathe deeply I feel the tiredness.*

MD: *How do you register your tiredness? What do you notice?*
Luke: *There's pain in the front of my face, in my cheekbones, a numbness in my nose.*

I suggest that Luke make some movements with his jaw, part of the social engagement system that can calm the ventral activation. I demonstrate chewing movements. He mirrors me and starts to yawn. I encourage him to allow the yawns. Loosening the jaw muscles in a yawn can help to open a healthy parasympathetic response.[41]

Luke notices that his chin feels floppy after yawning, and he starts to rotate his head in what appears to be a loosening of the whole area of the head and shoulders. He feels a sadness in his thoracic spine area, the part of the back where we had been working. Next, Luke's head leans backward and rests in a backward position. He senses a movement of heat between his head and his solar plexus. His head begins to move forward and backward, slowly at first, then speeding up with some force. I invite Luke to notice this movement and ask what it would be like to slow it right down and continue to observe what is happening. The forward-backward movement of his head continues at a slower pace for some time and then he speaks:

Luke: *I am being shaken by the shoulders, my head is flying back and forth, unravelling my neck.*
       [Luke's experience has the feel of an implicit memory and I am reminded of the dream image of the big black ball suspended from a crane like a pendulum that knocks down houses. Luke releases a sigh.]
Luke: *The breath is going down into my belly now.*
MD: *What is it like to breathe into your belly?*
Luke: *It's like drowning. I feel so sad.*

The word *drowning* alerts me to how close Luke might be to falling into a dissociated state or even a fit, a psychogenic nonepileptic seizure. I suggest he keep looking at me and that he might find it helpful to try the 'voo' breath, blowing his breath out and making a 'voo' sound from deep in his belly. This should give him some sense of control over the feelings that threaten to drown him. I demonstrate the breath: I inhale, filling my belly with air, pause, and then, on the exhale, I gently make the sound 'voo' from the belly and through my mouth on an easy exhalation.[42] I do the breathing with him for a few breaths. Then Luke calls out to me in a fearful voice.

Luke: *Stay with me!*
MD: *I am right here. You are doing really well.*

As we are on a Skype session, I speak reassuringly with a gentle but firm and low tone of voice. Intermittently I mirror his breathing.

Luke stops using the 'voo' breath. His head continues to make a rocking movement, and his spine joins in so that his whole torso sways forward and backward, accompanied now by waves of sobbing and tears. Slowly, over time, the movement becomes lighter, smaller and slower until it finally ceases altogether. The tears and sobbing subside. Luke stretches himself out until he is lying on his back on the couch. Though he remains quiet and still for some time, I imagine an internal shaking continuing in his body. He is giving his body time to settle and soothe. Finally, I notice Luke's hand as it moves onto his belly; he strokes himself, using his hand in a circular motion. I watch for some time and mirror the action, letting him know that I am witness to this moment of self-soothing. Minutes pass.

MD: *What are you noticing?*
Luke: *The heat of my hand on my belly. It's so comforting. I'm touching myself.*
        After some time, Luke's body settles even more, his breath quietens. Luke sighs in a healthy parasympathetic response, deeply relaxed. He looks spent but at ease.
Luke: *I am full with myself. I am full of possibilities.* (Luke's voice sounds strong but quiet. He smiles gently and looks toward me).
        And I can comfort myself.[43]

We are both deeply touched by what has happened. There is joy and a sense of awe at Luke's newfound attitude. Nietzsche's words resonate with me: "out of [the] lack of order, a dancing star should be born."[44] Luke has managed to stay present and work with high levels of arousal and terror that might have easily triggered dissociation, collapse and seizure-like episodes, as in the past. However, given the sequencing in the work in recent sessions, his system was now more able to withstand the possible overwhelm and stay present to re-experience the implicit memory. The 'voo' breath opened the pathway of the vagal nerve connecting the mouth, head, neck, respiratory system and belly, eliciting the movement of the head backward and forward, reminiscent of an early traumatic memory. Luke's whole torso was engaged in the rocking movement while releasing sounds and tears of grief in order to find resolution. The movement had its own rhythm which allowed the energy to discharge and come to completion, with time for settling and integration. In the resting time, naturally governed by the healthy parasympathetic system response, Luke lay quietly recovering. "You have all the time in the world. Trust the lull," I hear Ann Skinner encourage BodySoul Rhythms workshop participants. The 'lull' allows for a 'hovering' period and has an altogether different feeling tone from that of a parasympathetic *immobilization*. It has the quality of an incubation from which something new may emerge in its own time. Mary Hamilton also comments that new impulses, like dreams, "arise out of the same source, a visceral inner source resonating with unknowable fields" (2009, p. 152).[45] Out of this restorative calm, deep in Luke's belly and nervous system, a new impulse arose. Luke's hand began to massage his belly rhythmically and his words punctuated the silence, announcing the new impulse: "*I am full with myself. I am full with possibilities.*" Luke spoke from a new place, with a sense of his own potential.

The work of these last few sessions laid the foundational steps to facilitate the necessary repair work to Luke's nervous system and attachment patterns, as well as his completion of self-protective developmental movements. Over the course of his long-term analysis, Luke attained greater resilience and capacity to be present as witness to his own process. Working with BodyDreaming—attuning to his somatic unconscious, his dreams, self-care system and relationships—enabled Luke to repattern his disorganized disoriented attachment pattern. In this way Luke 'earned' what West calls a "good ego-core relationship."[46] Luke now senses that his body, no longer trapped in the past, holds the future and feels "full of possibility". The BodyDreaming process has rooted Luke in a secure attachment to his own *living* matter: "In reality, there is nothing but a living body. That is the fact; and psyche is as much a living body as body is living psyche: it is just the same" (Jung, 1988, p. 396). I found it deeply moving to witness Luke's arrival at this point where he could experience the 'living body' of his own matter alive with expanded awareness of strength and potential ("I am full with myself. I am full with possibilities.").

At the beginning of our next session, Luke arrived in an excited state.

Luke: *It's a miracle. I no longer need my back brace to support me. I'm free. I have been walking.*
         He proudly shared with me notes he had made after the last session.
Luke: *Remember to blow it out—the utter grief and terror, the feeling of drowning and being overwhelmed. Stay with myself—by rubbing my belly and I will know what to do and what to say.*

The previous session had marked an important milestone in the long process of our work together, clearly showing Luke's capacity to tolerate and remain conscious to a level of emotional activation that would earlier have caused him to dissociate. We might say that the session constituted a re-enactment of an implicit memory of a life-threatening invasive experience that Luke needed to re-negotiate, both on a psychological and a physiological level, so that he might create new neural pathways and re-align his 'original' experience. Levine, summarizing Nadar and LeDoux's neuroscientific research, throws new light on the functioning of memory:

> [Memories] are not formed and then pristinely maintained, as was previously assumed. Rather, memories are formed and then rebuilt anew every time they are accessed, i.e., remembered. ... [M]emory comes with a natural updating mechanism. ... The purpose of the very act of recall is to provide the molecular opportunity to update a memory based upon new information. ... [B]y changing our present time sensations and images, the memories that are accessed will become more empowered.
>
> (Levine, 2015, pp. 140–141)

Levine stresses that inner strengths and resources not available at the time of the trauma can be "accessed, embodied, and allowed to fully complete and express themselves" (*ibid.*). We witnessed this happening with Luke when the energy locked in the implicit memory was released. There followed a parasympathetic resting time, out of which arose a new impulse—the self-soothing massage to the belly and the realization of being full of possibility. Levine comments that if the new impulse is "adequately engaged, supported and sequenced ... the newly reconsolidated experience then becomes the new updated memory" (*ibid.*, p. 142). Luke's "miracle" was his experience of attuning to body and psyche, dream image and body impulse, symptom and felt sense experience, to bring about a resolution of early implicit traumatic memory. The session had consolidated the work of the development of a securely embodied core self, a moment of indwelling, when the 'living body' takes precedence and leads the way to healing—psyche and soma at one in the dance. Luke's finely tuned process enabled him to re-navigate the waters of early trauma, and repattern his early attachment style. He reached a point at which his energy—his life force—no longer needed to defend against the threat of annihilation with fragmentation and dissociation, and instead was able to support him to relate to his 'living body', which had become his home.

It is my hope that my discussion of Luke's case demonstrates how the psychoanalytic frame and somatic modalities together enhance each other's potential for healing.

Notes

1 "The Sixth Letter", in *Letters to a Young Poet*, Rainer Maria Rilke, 2000, pp. 52–53.
2 A paper on Neonatal Abstinence Syndrome, JAMA Pediatrics, 2006, concludes:

> Neonatal Abstinence Syndrome [NAS] occurs in 30% of neonates exposed to SSRIs [Xanex, Ativan, Valium, Klonopin] in utero. These babies should be monitored for at least 48 hours after birth. The long-term effects of prolonged exposure to SSRIs, particularly in neonates who develop severe symptoms, has yet to be determined.
>
> (Levinson-Casteil *et al.*, 2006)

3 See Chapter 2, *n.* 21. "The earlier the trauma the more global the impact on the physiology and psychology" (Heller and LaPierre, 2012, p. 121).
4 In 1946, Jung spoke of the natural dissociability of the psyche at Eranos:

> [Dissociation] arises from the fact that the connecting link between the psychic processes themselves is a very conditional one.... As the plurality of psychic components at the primitive level shows, the original state is one in which the psychic processes are very loosely knit and by no means form a self-contained unity. Moreover, psychiatric experience indicates that it often takes only a little to shatter the unity of consciousness so laboriously built up in the course of development and to resolve it back into its original elements.
>
> (Jung, 1946, par. 365)

Frequently, a dissociative or "secondary consciousness represents a personality-component which has not been separated from ego-consciousness by mere accident, but which owes its separation to definite causes" (*ibid.*, par. 366) which we might argue affords an accurate description of the origin of Luke's dissociative mode of coping.

5   "The purpose of the self care system is to keep an innocent core of the self out of further suffering in reality by keeping it 'safe' in another world. Further, this innocent core of the self is a sacred something within the human personality that is often referred to as the soul" (Kalsched, 2013, p. 24).

6   Dissociation, like repression, is a healthy, adaptive function of the human mind. It is a basic process that allows individual self-states to function optimally (not simply defensively) when full immersion in a single reality, a single strong affect, and a suspension of one's self-reflective capacity is exactly what is called for or wished for. As Walter Young {1988} has succinctly put it: 'Under normal conditions, dissociation enhances the integrating functions of the ego by screening out excessive or irrelevant stimuli. ... Under pathological conditions ... the normal functions of dissociation become mobilized for defensive use.

(Bromberg, 1996, pp. 35–36)

In other words, dissociation is primarily a means through which the psyche maintains for the human being an experience of personal continuity, coherence, and the integrity of a sense of selfhood.

7   What people call love is often an unconscious and addictive quest for power. How often are we nice to somebody—burying our anger and disappointment and professing our love for them—when we are actually trying to ensure they stay with us because we are terrified of abandonment and loneliness? Paradoxically, an overwhelming desire to please is rooted in an addictive quest for control—by pleasing others we are better able to manipulate them, albeit unconsciously.

(Woodman in conversation with Sieff, 2015, p. 67)

8   "I am ... inclined to think that autonomous complexes are among the normal phenomena of life and that they make up the structure of the unconscious psyche" (Jung, 1934, par. 218).

9   Jacqueline Gerson writes: "Embodied countertransferential feelings reflect the state of the life process in an analysand as evoked in the body of the analyst" (2005, p. 209).

10   Shame is not like other affects. It is a global affect that colours the individual's core sense of self, so that the person does not feel that they have done something bad or wrong, but rather that they *are* bad or wrong. ... Shame is the visceral essence of feeling bad about yourself ... [and] is a key factor in the individual getting stuck in states of regression. [It] is associated with the profound threat reaction of freezing and collapse, associated with the activation of the unmyelinated dorsal polyvagal nerve (Porges, 2011, Schore, 2003), where the individual dissociates from their normal sense of self just prior to death (in the same way that the gazelle collapses just before the lion strikes).

(West, 2016, pp. 223–224)

11   The splitting that occurs [i.e., in a case such as Luke's] has other features related to the frustration of the early expression of the self (de-integration), which now 'requires' the object to mirror and not be separate from the subject, thus there is an attempt to use the analyst as a self-object and a narcissistic form of love may come

into play. This can mirror the early experience of the patient where they were used as a self-object by the abuser.

(West, 2013, p. 76)

12 "Bion hypothesizes that sadistic superego perversely attacks not only the child's ego, but all 'linking' processes in the mind which allow the child to have an experience of a coherent self" (Kalsched, 1996, p. 123).

13   In essence, the deintegration and reintegration describe a fluctuating state of learn-ing in which the infant opens itself to new experiences and then withdraws in order to reintegrate and consolidate those experiences. During a deintegrative activity, the infant maintains continuity with the main body of the self (or its centre) while venturing into the external world to accumulate experience in motor action and sensory stimulation.

(Fordham and Heath, 1989, p. 64)

14   Because the ventral vagal system fails to develop, ... traumatized infants favor freeze and withdrawal over social engagement as a way of managing states of arousal. This pattern has lifelong implications. On the physiological level, since the vagus nerve innervates the larynx, pharynx, heart, lungs, and the enteric nerv-ous system (gut), the impact of early trauma on these organ systems leads to a variety of physical symptoms. On the psychological and behavioral level, the capacity for social engagement is severely compromised, leading to self-isolation, [and] withdrawal from contact with others.

(Heller and LaPierre, 2012, p. 101)

15   When shame hits, usually unexpectedly, we feel that a spotlight is focused on us, revealing all that is wrong with who we are. We want to bury our head and disap-pear from view. We feel as if we could die. Shame is the subjective experience of inner collapse.

(Schore in conversation with Sieff, 2015, p. 122)

16 "The activity of the dorsal vagal complex is associated with intense emotional states and immobilization, and is responsible for the severe hypoarousal and pain blunting of dissociation" (Schore, 2009, p. 120).

17 The body undergoes "sudden and rapid transition from an unsuccessful strategy of struggling requiring massive sympathetic activation to the metabolically conserva-tive immobilized state mimicking death, associated with the dorsal vagal complex" (Porges, 1997, p. 75).

18   [T]he right brain strategy of dissociation represents the ultimate defense for blocking conscious awareness of emotional pain. If early trauma is experienced as 'psychic catastrophe' the autoregulatory strategy of dissociation is expressed as 'detachment from an unbearable situation,' 'a submission and resignation to the inevitability of overwhelming, even psychically deadening danger' and 'a last resort defensive strategy.'

(Schore quoting himself from an unpublished work in Fosha, Siegel and Soloman, 2009, p. 127)

19 See Damasio in Chapter 3.
20 See www.traumahealing.org.
21 I.e., into a dorsal vagal collapse, a death-like, immobilization trance. The terror in Luke's eyes was caused by his recall of a dream image of his hanging on for dear life to the side of a cliff.

22   [O]ne way to work with the feeling state, to generate it, sense it more fully, and even tolerate it, is to open the whole body to the experience as much as is possible through awareness, movement, breath, or self-touch in different directions.
(Raja Selvam in conversation with Serge Prengel, in Prengel, 2014, p. 5)

23   Levine, 1997, p. 67. Perseus's shield is a metaphor for a healthy defence against the threat of overwhelm which supports Luke to withstand his patterned response of dorsal vagal collapse, immobilization and annihilation.

24   "If reacting that is disruptive of going-on-being recurs persistently it sets going a pattern of fragmentation of being" (Winnicott, 1962, p. 60).

25   Luke's change of profession reflected his successful integration of inner states. It also meant that he would have to relinquish his controller self to some degree in order to fulfill his new role and bring greater consciousness to his dynamic interactions.

26   Levine defines healthy aggression as an innate somatic drive to overcome adversity and move forward in life:

[W]ith this instinct engaged, transformation becomes possible as the client gradually meets and embraces trauma. I further speculate that the instinct operates through activating the coordinated, procedurally based systems for motivation, reward, and action. This convergence of motivation and action systems (dopamine and noradrenaline) is what I call 'healthy aggression.'
(Levine, 2015, p. 69)

27   Margaret Wilkinson (2010, p. 141) cites Jung (1928, par. 267) to remind us that "dissociated content, which he [Jung] described as a traumatic complex, may suddenly return to consciousness: 'It forces itself tyrannically upon the conscious mind. The explosion of affect is a complete invasion of the individual. It pounces upon him like an enemy or a wild animal.'" It may, of course, equally well manifest in illness or physical collapse.

28   The client is invited to allow the senses, often the eyes, but not necessarily the eyes, to discover what it is that stimulates their curiosity in the environment. This process of discovery is then followed by a conversation about the 'chosen' object. The process awakens the social engagement system, modulating the ventral vagus and consequently calming the nervous system—the heart and respiratory rates. I like to include interoception by exploring the body's resonance with the object, actively engaging the sensing body in the moment.

29   Janet Adler, co-founder of Authentic Movement with Mary Starks Whitehouse and Joan Chodorow, writes:

In the practice of Authentic Movement the mover's internal witness has developed in relation to a gradual internalization of ... [his] ... external witness. Originally, the external witness held consciousness so that ... [he] ..., the mover, could open to the unconscious. Now ... [his] ... internal witness holds consciousness for ... [him] ... as ... [he] ... finds more space to open to other sources of energy.
(Adler, 1999, p. 184)

30   "[T]he more intense an experience is in the physical body, more of the body needs to be involved in generating and holding it" (Raja Selvam in Prengel, 2014, p. 15). Implicit memory *is held* in the body (see Chapter 1, pp. 46–48, *n*. 15; *n*. 16; *n*. 17; *n*. 19).

31   If we attempt to confront trauma head on, it will continue to do what it has already done—immobilize us in fear. Before Perseus set out to conquer Medusa he was warned by Athena not to look directly at the Gorgon. Heeding the goddess's wisdom, he used his shield to reflect Medusa's image; by doing so, he was able to cut off her head. Likewise, the solution to vanquishing trauma comes not through confronting it directly, but by working with its reflection, mirrored in our instincts."

(Levine, 1997, p. 65)

"... so many traumatized people [may] use their shield—equivalent of sensation, the 'felt-sense,'—to master trauma. The felt sense encompasses the clarity, instinctual power, and fluidity necessary to transform trauma" (*ibid.*, p. 67).

32 Bonnie Bainbridge Cohen makes an important distinction between sensing (perception and the nervous system) and the fluid systems in the body, including breath.

Sensing is related to the nervous system through the perceptions. Feeling and flow are related to the fluid system including the circulatory, lymphatic, and cerebral spinal fluids.... The fluids are a counterbalance to the perception of the nervous system.... [T]here comes a time when you want the perceptions (felt sense) to go quiet ... let the fluids become the mover.... I mean letting them go unconscious and letting the fluids take control. What happens when you go into sensing is that you retard the breathing, respiration, because you are retarding the fluids. ... All of a sudden someone will take a deep breath and you know the fluids have been released. The fluids are the internal respiration. By sensing, we release the restriction, whether it's muscular or whatever, which releases the blood. The breath follows. When you feel that deep breath, something has been repatterned into the nervous system.

(Bainbridge Cohen in Hanlon Johnson, 1995, p. 190)

33 This group of muscles is used developmentally by the infant to reach, to take, to push away. The infant gains a sense of agency when he activates these muscles—in evolutionary psychology we appreciate that they are essential to survival and to the infant's ability to separate safely from the mother. "Two early reflexes are the flexor Withdrawal and the extensor Thrust. They involve simple flexion and extension and underlie our gathering into ourselves and reaching out into the environment from our hands and feet" (Bainbridge Cohen, 1993, p. 130).

34 "[A]ctive imagination in movement tends to develop a relationship to both sensory and imaginal realms. When felt body sensation emerges as physical action, an image may appear that will give the movement meaning. Or, when an inner image emerges as physical action, the proprioceptive, kinaesthetic experience may lead the mover toward connection to his or her instinctive body" (Chodorow, 1999, pp. 260–261).

35 This is the thoracic spine area, including the shoulder blade, which is where Luke suffers chronic pain and where he imagined the healing image of the white bird.

36 Linda Hartley is founder of the Institute of Integrative Bodywork and Movement Therapy.

37 "How we use our muscles affects the way they function, and this influences the way we feel, which in turn affects the way we use the muscles: cycles develop which can be beneficial or limiting to different degrees" (Hartley, 2004, p. 150). The sequence I explored with Luke helps the client to open the muscle group in the thoracic spine and feel into the strength and power of that area of the back without straining or indeed without much effort at all.

38 "Muscular tension is not 'bad' in itself, and it is not always appropriate to release tensions. It may be more important to explore the function of the tension. For example, is it helping to support us because there is not enough support in our life, or do we need the tension because we need to get more of a grip on our life, not release it?" (Hartley, 2004, p. 151).
39 See Chapter 3, p. 111, *n.* 32, for an explanation and illustration of *pre-movement movement* as the place where the impulse for movement begins in the body.
40 S. Freud, "The Ego and the Id", [1923] 1961.
41 "We work with the arms and the face and neck areas with awareness, movement or self-touch to expand the experience into these areas as well as to minimize the dysregulation or excess load in the chest area" (Raja Selvam in Prengel, 2014, p. 7).

42   The salubrious sensations evoked by the combination of breathing and the sound's reverberations allow the individual to contact an inner security and trust along with some sense of orientation in the here and now. They also facilitate a degree of face to face, eye to eye, voice to ear, I-Thou contact and thus make it possible for the client to negotiate a small opening in the "social engagement system," which is then able to help him or her to develop a robust resilience through increasing cycles of sympathetic arousal (charge) and discharge and thereby to deepen regulation and relaxation.

(Levine, 2010, p. 127)

43 "Securely attached children learn what makes them feel good; they discover what makes them (and others) feel bad, and they acquire a sense of agency that their actions can change how they feel and how others respond" (Van der Kolk, 2014, p. 119).
44 Cited in Jung, 1988, p. 106.
45 Ann Skinner, Mary Hamilton and Marion Woodman co-founded BodySoul Rhythms. See the introductory Chapter, "A Note to the Reader."

46   I believe the ability to shift between the reality-oriented certainty of the known self and the openness to somatic-affective reactions and communications from the core self is what is meant by a good ego-self relationship (Edinger, 1972; Neumann, 1966), or as I would put it, a good ego-core relationship. When the individual's ego is functioning broadly and inclusively, it can then be open to the continuous, spontaneous flow from the core self, which will inevitably, at times, introduce new experiences that will challenge the current organization of the ego (self-knowledge, self-experience, and functioning) and require an expansion as the new experience/knowledge/functioning is accommodated.

(West, 2016, p. 121)

References

Adler, J. (1999) "Body and Soul," in *Authentic Movement: Essays by Mary Starks Whitehouse, Janet Adler and Joan Chodorow*, Patrizia Pallaro (ed.), London and Philadelphia, PA: Jessica Kingsley Publishers, pp. 160–189.

Allen, J.G., Console, D.A. and Lewis, L. (1999). "Dissociative Detachment and Memory Impairment: Reversible Amnesia or Encoding Failure?" *Comprehensive Psychiatry*, 40, 160–171.

Bainbridge Cohen, B. (1993) *Sensing, Feeling, and Action: The Experiential Anatomy of Body-Mind Centering*, Northampton, MA: Contact Editions. Excerpts published in Hanlon Johnson, D. (1995), *Bone, Breath, and Gesture: Practices of Embodiment*, Berkeley, CA: North Atlantic Books.

Bion, W.R. (1959) "Attacks on Linking," *International Journal of Psychoanalysis*, 40: 308–315. Reprinted in: *Second Thoughts* (1967), New York: Jason Aronson, pp. 93–109.

Bromberg, P. (1996) "Standing in the Spaces: The Multiplicity of Self and The Psychoanalytic Relationship," *Journal of Contemporary Psychoanalysis*, 32: 509–535.

Chodorow, J. (1986) "The Body as Symbol," in *The Body in Analysis*, Nathan Schwartz-Salant and Murray Stein (eds.), Illinois: Chiron Publications, pp. 87–91.

Chodorow, J. (1999) "Joan Chodorow," in *Authentic Movement: Essays by Mary Starks Whitehouse, Janet Adler and Joan Chodorow*, Patrizia Pallaro (ed.), London and Philadelphia, PA: Jessica Kingsley Publishers, pp. 209–311.

Davies, J.M. and Frawley, M.G. (1992). "Dissociative Processes and Transference-Countertransference Paradigms in the Psychoanalytically Oriented Treatment of Adult Survivors of Childhood Sexual Abuse," *Psychoanalytic Dialogues*, 2, 5–36.

Fordham, M. and Heath, B. (1989) "The Infant's Reach: Reflections on Maturation in Early Life," *Psychological Perspectives: A Quarterly Journal of Jungian Thought*, 21 (1): 59–76.

Fosha, D., Siegel, D., Soloman, M., eds. (2009) *The Healing Power of Emotion: Affective Neuroscience, Development and Clinical Practice*, New York: W.W. Norton & Co.

Freud, S. ([1923] 1961) *The Standard Edition of the Complete Psychological Works of Sigmund Freud. Volume XIX, 1923–1925, The Ego and the Id and Other works*. London: The Hogarth Press: The Institute of Psycho-Analysis.

Gerson, Jacqueline (2005) "Wounded Instincts, Weeping Soul: Working with Embodied Countertransference," *Spring, A Journal of Archetype and Culture*, Body & Soul: Honouring Marion Woodman, 72: 205–217.

Gianino, A. and Tronick, E.Z. (1986) "Interactive Mismatch and Repair: Challenges to the Coping Infant," *ZERO TO THREE, Bulletin of the National Center for Clinical Infant Programs* 5: 1–6. Reprinted in: Tronick, E.Z. (2007) *The Neurobehavioural and Social-Emotional Development of Infants and Children* New York: W.W. Norton, pp. 155–163.

Hamilton, M. (2009) *The Dragon Fly Principal: An Exploration of the Body's Function in Unfolding Spirituality*, London; Ontario: Colenso Island Press.

Hanlon Johnson, D., ed. (1995) *Bone, Breath, and Gesture: Practices of Embodiment*, Berkeley, CA: North Atlantic Books.

Hartley, L. (2004) *Somatic Psychology: Body, Mind and Meaning*, Berkeley, CA: North Atlantic Books.

Heller, L. and LaPierre, A. (2012) *Healing Developmental Trauma: How Early Trauma Affects Self-Regulation, Self-Image, and the Capacity for Relationship*, Berkeley, CA: North Atlantic Books.

Jung, C.G. (1928) *The Therapeutic Value of Abreaction*, Collected Works 16, Princeton, NJ: Princeton University Press.

Jung, C.G. (1934) *A Review of the Complex Theory*, Collected Works 8, Princeton, NJ: Princeton University Press.

Jung, C.G. (1946) *The Psychology of the Transference*, Collected Works 16, Princeton, NJ: Princeton University Press.

Jung, C.G. (1988) *Nietzsche's Zarathustra: Notes of the Seminar Given in 1934–1939*, James L. Jarrett (ed.), in two volumes, Bollingen Series XCIX, Princeton, NJ: Princeton University Press (London & New York: Routledge: 1989).

Kalsched, D. (1996) *The Inner World of Trauma: Archetypal Defences of the Personal Spirit*, London: Routledge.

Kalsched, D. (2013) *Trauma and the Soul: A Psycho-Spiritual Approach to Human Development and its Interruption*, London: Routledge.

Knox, J. (2011) *Self-Agency in Psychotherapy: Attachment, Autonomy and Intimacy*, London: W.W. Norton and Co.

Krieger, N. (2014) *Bridges to Consciousness: Complexes and Complexity*, London: Routledge.

Levine, P. (1997) *Waking the Tiger: Healing Trauma - The Innate Capacity to Transform Overwhelming Experiences*, Berkeley, CA: North Atlantic Books.

Levine, P. (2010) *In an Unspoken Voice: How the Body Releases Trauma and Restores Goodness*, Berkeley, CA: North Atlantic Books.

Levine, P. (2015) *Trauma and Memory: Brain and Body in a Search for the Living Past: A Practical Guide for Understanding and Living with Personal Trauma*, Berkeley, CA: North Atlantic Books.

Levinson-Castiel, R., Merlob P., Linder N., Sirota L. and Klinger G. (2006), "Neonatal Abstinence Syndrome After In Utero Exposure to Selective Serotonin Reuptake Inhibitors in Term Infants," *Arch Pediatr Adolesc Med*, 160 (2): 173–176. 10.1001/archpedi.160.2.173.

Porges, S.W. (1997) "Emotion: An Evolutionary By-product of the Neural Regulation of the Autonomic Nervous System," *Annals of the New York Academy of Sciences*, 807: 62–77.

Prengel, S. (2014) In conversation with Raja Selvam. "Raja Selvam: Integral Somatic Psychotherapy". https://relationalimplicit.com/somatic-perspectives/. Accessed 31 August 2018 at: https://relationalimplicit.com/zug/transcripts/Selvam-2014-07.pdf, pp.1–18.

Rich, A. (1993) "Transcendental Etude," in *The Dream of a Common Language: Poems 1974–1977*, New York and London: W.W. Norton & Co.

Rilke, R.M. (2000) *Letters to a Young Poet*, trans. J. M. Burnham, Novato, CA: New World Library.

Schore, A.N. (1994) *Affect Dysregulation and the Origin of the Self: The Neurobiology of Emotional Development*, Mahwah, NJ: Lawrence Erlbaum Associates.

Schore, A.N. (2003) *Affect Dysregulation and Disorders of the Self*, London and New York: W.W. Norton & Co.

Schore, A.N. (2009) "Right Brain Affect Regulation: An Essential Mechanism of Development, Trauma, Dissociation, and Psychotherapy," in *The Healing Power of Emotion: Affective Neuroscience, Development and Clinical Practice*, D. Fosha, D. Siegel and M. Soloman (eds.), New York: W.W. Norton & Co., pp. 112–144.

Sieff, D.F. (2015) *Understanding and Healing Emotional Trauma: Conversations with Pioneering Clinicians and Researchers*, Hove, UK and New York: Routledge.

Tronick, E.Z., (2007) *The Neurobehavioural and Social–Emotional Development of Infants and Children*, New York: W.W. Norton.

van der Kolk, B. (2014) *The Body Keeps the Score: Mind, Brain and Body in the Transformation of Trauma*, St Ives, UK: Penguin Random House.

West, M. (2013) "Trauma and the Transference-Countertransference: Working with the Bad Object and the Wounded Self," *Journal of Analytical Psychology*, 58 (1): 73–98.

West, M. (2016) *Into the Darkest Places: Early Relational Trauma and Borderline States of Mind*, London: Karnac.

Wilkinson, M. (2010) *Changing Minds in Psychotherapy: Emotion, Attachment, Trauma and Neurobiology*, London and New York: W.W. Norton & Co.

Winnicott, D.W. ([1962] 1990) "Ego Integration in Child Development," in *The Maturational Process and the Facilitating Environment: Studies in the Theory of Emotional Development*, London: Karnac Books.

Wirtz, U. (2014) *Trauma and the Beyond, The Mystery of Transformation*, New Orleans, LA: Spring Journal.

Woodman, M. (1990) *The Ravaged Bridegroom: Masculinity in Women*, Toronto: Inner City Books.

Woodman, M. and Dickson, E. (1996) *Dancing in the Flames: The Dark Goddess in the Transformation of Consciousness*, Dublin: Gill & MacMillan.

Chapter 6

Working with Dissociative and Disoriented Attachment Patterns (2)

"It's all about trusting your gut"

The time will come
when, with elation,
you will greet yourself arriving,
at your own door, in your own mirror,
and each will smile at the other's welcome,

and say, sit here. Eat.
You will love again the stranger who was your self
(From Derek Walcott, "Love after Love")[1]

*

I have found that the integration of somatic modalities into psychotherapy has a profound and immediate influence on the functioning of the nervous system, the body, mind and psyche of the individual in the context of the regulating therapist-client dyad. I have also found that interventions grounded in somatic practice are particularly effective with clients who have a dissociative and disoriented attachment style, as they enable the therapist to work with dissociative content buried in the somatic unconscious. Heller and LaPierre support my experience with the remark

> [a]lthough there is valuable confirmation and support from the neurosciences on the impact of inadequate attachment and attachment failure on the brain, there has been a significant disconnect between neuroscientifically based Attachment Theory and somatically oriented psychotherapies.
> (Heller and LaPierre, 2012, p. 136)

My focus on the core issues of two long-term cases in this and the previous chapter will, I hope, demonstrate the impact of somatic intervention on the progression of the therapy for each analysand over time. First, however, I would like to highlight the research of Bessel van der Kolk, which I found most useful to my understanding of the progress made by both analysands.

Bessel van der Kolk discusses Ruth Lanius's pioneering work with people suffering from post-traumatic stress disorder (PTSD) who had also experienced severe early childhood trauma. Lanius's work shows how trauma affects self-awareness, in particular sensory self-awareness. Her studies on the Default State Network (DSN), the idling brain, reveal very interesting data: subjects were asked to lie in a brain scanner and to think about nothing at all. In the so-called 'normal' group, it was found that participants think about themselves—indicating a capacity for self-awareness. The scans showed that the principal pathways on the mid-line of the brain lit up from behind the eyes through the neocortex to the base of the reptilian brain. This mid-line of awareness Bessel van der Kolk calls the *Mohawk of Awareness*; it contains the structures involved in our sense of self:

> The largest bright region at the back of the brain is the posterior cingulate, which gives us a physical sense of where we are—our internal GPS. It is strongly connected to the medial prefrontal cortex (MPFC), the WatchTower … (this connection does not show up on the scan because the fMRI can't measure it). It is also connected with brain areas that register sensations coming from the rest of the body: the insula, which relays messages from the viscera to the emotional centres; the parietal lobes, which integrate sensory information; and the anterior cingulate which coordinates emotions and thinking. All of these areas contribute to consciousness.
>
> (van der Kolk, 2014, p. 90)

However, when those suffering from PTSD and early childhood trauma underwent the scanning, it was discovered that there occurred a shut-down on the self-awareness mid-line pathway in the brain.

> There was almost no activation of any of the self-sensing areas of the brain. The MFPC, the anterior cingulate, the parietal cortex, and the insula did not light up at all; the only area that showed a slight activation was the posterior cingulate, which is responsible for basic orientation in space.
>
> (van der Kolk, 2014, p. 90)

Van der Kolk, reviewing Lanius's research, insists that the mid-line circuit is what needs to be repaired in order for those suffering from early childhood trauma to acquire a sense of self or sensory self-awareness. In BodyDreaming, the therapist works to rehabilitate or repair this mid-line circuit by attempting to bring awareness to the analysand's inner experiences through such questions as "where do you feel the resonance with that emotion, image or experience in your body?" We attempt to get 'below' the emotion to explore the physical sensation of an experience.[2] The physical body is our 'home', our matter and we make it *matter* by listening to it, paying attention to how it receives and responds to the world. In turn, the body supports our developing self-awareness so we become more grounded in the 'here and now' as our *matter*—body *and* mind—fully 'inhabits' a particular moment in time, a 'present moment'.[3] It can take a long time for an individual to discover a comfortable body-sensation connection, especially if the body has been the location of trauma or abuse. In such cases the development of a capacity for sensory self-awareness must be approached with great caution.[4]

*

Teresa was in analysis with me, twice weekly, for almost 15 years. She and her twin brother, the eldest siblings of a large family, were each born with a severe genetic physical disability. In addition to this, Teresa suffered developmental trauma, emotional, physical and sexual abuse. At the age of 8 the twins were separated and sent away to single sex institutions far from the family, returning home only for the annual holidays. Understandably, Teresa's early history and her separation from her twin brother manifested in the form of a *disorganized disoriented attachment pattern*.

Teresa had a close relationship with her mother, identifying with her mother's role as the carer, a role which Teresa adopted from birth by looking after her twin brother, who was considered the needy baby. The role of *benign carer* ensured Teresa's survival, granting her meaning and connection throughout her life. However, her needs as an infant and, later, as a young child left unprotected by the mother when exposed to the violence and sadism of the father, were recorded in the somatic realm in the form of skin complaints, weeping sores and painful joints.

When Teresa felt overwhelmed, either from outer threatening forces or internal persecutory objects, she sought refuge in her mind. It is worth noting here that the primary cell from which the skin and nervous system develop is called the ectoderm, i.e., both our brain and our skin are made of the same primary cell (Green, Stout, Taylor and Soper, 1984). This was evident in how Teresa's symptoms manifested. Under threat from severe emotional overwhelm, Teresa would retreat to her head or brain, pressing her hands against her head, trying to keep the persecutory objects under control, whether they were experienced as *inside* or *outside*. Teresa's skin acted as the membrane, the boundary wall with which she defended herself and held herself together, serving as an affect regulator in the absence of an inner caretaker. Her skin would dependably flare up when she felt under provocation or outright attack (Bick, 1968).

Joyce McDougall considers the consequences of a lack of identification with an internal caretaker, writing that this

> often gives rise to the conviction that one is not responsible for one's bodily well being. The fantasy of not truly possessing one's own body or (which often amounts to the same thing) the unconscious fantasy that one's body is under the control of another plays an important role. Thus somatic expression tends to arise in place of unrecognized psychotic fears and wishes.
>
> (McDougall, 1989, p. 48)

In Teresa's case, the constant presence of symptoms reflected both the unprocessed explicit memory and the implicit memory of her painful past.

From infancy, Teresa developed a capacity for self-regulation through *mothering* first her twin brother and later, in the institution, a much younger child suffering from multiple disabilities. Initially, Teresa managed her adult and professional life well by living in a community environment similar to that of her school years, but now professionally in the role of carer. By this time, the climate was changing: abuse and institutional violence were no longer the taboo subjects they had been, and had started to make the headlines. Teresa found that she was disturbed by the public airing of such topics, and this was reflected in an exacerbation of her symptoms, namely, extreme skin irritability and inflammation of the joints. At the beginning of our work together, when Teresa spoke about her childhood, the extremity of her early suffering was palpable. Although her communication was largely non-verbal, my body picked up the distress and I found myself imaging the wordless spaces, as Teresa had as yet no words for her unutterable pain. I bore witness to the psychic numbing of her child body petrified with fear, which Ferenczi describes as "the actual child, of whom the awakened ego knows absolutely nothing".[5] I would watch, helpless, not able to reach her, as Teresa sat in a trance-like state, her body once again petrified, still and rigid.[6] Afterwards, she would be unable to recall anything that happened during these episodes of deep dissociation. The following poem by American poet Emily Dickinson speaks eloquently of this experience that gripped us both:

> There is a pain – so utter –
> It swallows substance up –
> Then covers the Abyss with Trance –
> So Memory can step
> Around – across – opon it –
> As One within a Swoon –
> Goes safely – where an open eye –
> Would drop Him – Bone by Bone.
>   (Emily Dickinson)[7]

A dissociative trance such as that described above would hold Teresa back from the abyss of pain that threatened to engulf her. I found myself caught, too, participating in the non-thinking place of the trance-state; time would pass, feeling like 100 years, as in the fairy tale. It felt to me as though a disturbance in chronological time had occurred and I found myself angry that I had succumbed, powerless once again in the face of such a defence.[8]

The trance won out each time, until, some six years into my work with Teresa, I began to integrate into my psychoanalytic perspective a somatic approach based on my training in BodySoul Rhythms and, later, Peter Levine's Somatic Experiencing trauma training. Both Woodman and Levine use the image of Medusa to describe the death-like trance that turns us to stone in the face of trauma. Woodman describes Medusa as the *death mother* who kills off life. After each dissociative episode in my sessions with Teresa, I felt defeated and persecuted ("no good, a failure"), experiencing a state of *freeze* and immobility which Woodman attributes to the energy of the archetypal *death mother*, epitomized by the petrifying stare of Medusa: "Death Mother's gaze penetrates both psyche and body, turning us into stone. It kills hope. It cuts us dead. … We collapse. Our life-energy drains from us, and we find ourselves yearning for oblivion" (Woodman in conversation with Sieff, 2015, p. 69). Understanding Teresa's episodes from the perspective of Woodman's *death mother* and Kalsched's self-care system enabled me to feel more compassionate and hopeful, and, most importantly, less persecuted and defeated.

Levine highlights the physiological aspects of the self-care system, describing the immobility response as a key part of the nervous system's circuit breaker:

> Without it, a human being might not survive the intense activation of a serious inescapable situation without risking energetic overload. Indeed, even the symptoms that develop out of the freezing response can be viewed with a sense of appreciation and gratitude if you consider what might happen if the system did not have this safety valve.
>
> (Levine, 1997, p. 105)

Together Teresa and I developed a shared perspective which enabled us to hold the experience with compassion. However, it was only when we began to integrate the approach to trauma which Somatic Experiencing teaches that we were able to develop a *Perseus's shield* to protect against the overwhelming ferocity of the dissociative trance-state. The somatic approach afforded a means of staying present in the here and now, and in touch with each other. With time, the trance-state no longer swallowed Teresa and 'took her off', and I was able to remain more present in my body as a witnessing ego; through speaking, mirroring and orienting I could bear witness to the process as it was unfolding.[9] In time, the shield we created helped Teresa to regulate the unbearable affect, and weaken the power of the trance, psyche's place of refuge from unutterable pain. We managed to curb the immediacy and power of the trance-state at threshold moments, slowing it down while, at the same time, tracking the dissociative process. The pace of the work was necessarily measured as we titrated the affects that repeatedly threatened to engulf Teresa. Over time, Teresa gained a sense of *coming home to her body*, a body-sensation connection which enabled her to self-regulate, learn to manage arousal and threshold moments, and remain more present with me in the room.

The capacity to develop a body-sensation connection and to hold awareness when threatened with dissociation strengthens the parasympathetic response of the nervous system—the 'down beat'—and supports the formation of new pathways in the mid-line of the brain. However, the difficulty in attempting to heal the mid-line of the brain and develop sensory awareness is made clear by Damasio, who points to the deep divide that exists between our sense of self and the sensory life of our bodies. Damasio describes how the mind uses screens to hide "the body—our own body, by which I mean the ins of it, its interiors … the inner states of the body, those that constitute the flow of life as it wanders in the journey of each day" (2000, p. 28). With Damasio's words in mind, my therapeutic aim was to help Teresa track the felt sense of her experiences such as the smell of a rose, the texture of a fabric, a favourite recording of music, the memory of the touch of a child's hand, which increases one's capacity to stay present when feeling activated. Learning to regulate *positive* affect is essential in order to face attachment and early trauma issues. The development of a capacity for interoception (attuning to the felt sense response to a resource) helps one gain an inner sense of groundedness, a 'secure base' which allows one to 'take in' good experiences and develop a learned secure attachment to the body.[10]

*

I now want to focus on a few sessions which mark the beginning of the end of Teresa's long analysis with me and a transition from 14 years of twice-weekly analysis to a new rhythm of once-weekly sessions.

When Teresa arrived for her session, I met her outside the building and apologized that the workroom was occupied by a locksmith repairing the lock of the office door. I asked her to wait while the locksmith completed his task. She took herself for a walk round and round the block while she waited. We began the session, 20 minutes late, and spoke about the synchronicity of this 'lock out' occurring at the time when we were changing the sessions from twice-weekly to once-weekly: the boundaries were shifting, an intruder was in *her* space, Teresa was left outside, waiting, vulnerable, unprotected. I later understood that Teresa's system had initially been triggered into sympathetic arousal and she had stepped into self-regulatory mode, needing to take control and manage me. She wanted to look after me, worrying what this was like for me and how I would manage with the external door unlocked, leaving me vulnerable to intrusions. Then, when we finally sat together in the office, her system swung from high sympathetic activation to the dorsal vagal response of freeze, probably a global high intensity activation (GHIA) with both sympathetic and parasympathetic systems being triggered at the same time (see Chapter 2, *n.* 21).

As noted earlier, when trauma happens between 0 and 3 years, there is as yet no regulating orbitofrontal cortex sufficiently developed to calm the limbic brain's activated system; the hippocampus, which records explicit memory, has not yet fully developed. As a result, the trauma is exacerbated by both the (outer) absence of the regulating m/other and the (inner) memory of an absent regulating m/other; there is no memory of an early repeated experience of *rupture and repair* to help the infant navigate the current trauma. Woodman comments on the early defence of collapse or freeze:

> If, while growing up, we sense that we are unacceptable to our parents, carers or teachers, or if we intuit that we threaten them, then our nervous system becomes hyper-vigilant. Our cells are imprinted with a profound fear of

abandonment; as a consequence our body numbs out the moment we feel threatened. … We experience a collapse of both our psychological and physical energy. I call this possum mentality.

(Woodman in Sieff, 2015, p. 70)

The male 'intruder' in the office, blocking access to Teresa's intimate space, our shared *temenos*, constituted a repetition of the original trauma, the implicit memory of which was buried in Teresa's body. The analyst/mother had, once again, failed to protect her. This time, however, Teresa was able to make and verbalize connections to past material and seemed to be actively engaged in the process of making meaning of the current situation. She felt present in our exchange. Nevertheless, as soon as we explored how her *body* was experiencing the situation things shifted dramatically.

MD: *What do you notice is happening in your body right now?*
Teresa: *I'm not aware of anything in my body. I'm in my head.*
MD: *Where in your head are you?*
Teresa: *Outside my head.*
        (Teresa recognizes this pattern and names it.)
        This place my body knows so well.
        [Teresa was seeking refuge in a familiar dissociative defence by being "outside her body". Joyce McDougall (1989, p. 28) refers to this phenomenon as follows: "The body like the mind is subject to repetition compulsion in the somatic sphere; a complex body-mind reaction also tends to be inexorably repeated whenever the necessary stimulus arises." When her trauma response of dissociating is triggered, Teresa becomes split off from her physical body, replicating the means she used in childhood to ensure her survival by 'going to her head'. I decided to focus on Teresa's changing relationship to her body as a resource: we had been working to develop in Teresa a more *positive* relationship to her body, slowly establishing her awareness of the felt sense resonance of her inner experiences. Consequently, I drew attention to her breath.]
MD: *See what it's like to pay attention to where your breath is moving in your body.*
Teresa: *I can feel it in my throat.*
        [At this point, as soon as I had invited Teresa to reconnect to her body as positive container, she stopped abruptly. I waited, feeling as if something had intruded upon her and 'cut her dead'. She seemed to have fallen victim to Medusa's gaze which had dropped her into a *freeze*. She sat petrified, staring fixedly, silent, barely breathing. All of this happened in a split second.]
MD: *What do you notice is happening now, Teresa?*
        [I was using my voice to maintain contact with Teresa in the face of the dissociative *freeze* (i.e., addressing her by name, having her open her

eyes, etc.) although, at this point, I wasn't sure of the depth of Teresa's dissociation and whether she would in fact be able to hear me and communicate with me.]

MD: *What's happening, Teresa?*

Teresa: *It's no good what is happening. It's no good. I feel stupid.*

[We were back to a familiar defence of the persecutory self-care system that turns against Teresa, shaming her with name-calling ("you're stupid").[11] This is the voice that had kept Teresa hostage to the dissociative state for so many years. Kalsched points out that the shaming voice creates the belief:

> there must be something wrong with me ... I am not lovable. These beliefs constitute shame—a core conviction of our own defectiveness. ... [B]laming beliefs are protective in that they prevent us from becoming angry with our parents and blaming them, and because we depend on our parents for survival we cannot afford to do that. This self-blaming, shameful belief system is the best that our psychological self-care system can do.
>
> (Kalsched, 2015, p. 13)

Teresa's circumstance of being born with a disability carried a shameful stigma in the family and further fuelled her sense of self-blame, her self-identity bearing the label 'faulty goods'. Overwhelmed by shame, stripped of her capacity for speech, Teresa had very few words. She could only repeat words of hopelessness and despair.]

Teresa: *It's no good. It's no good.*

[Because Teresa was still *frozen*, I tried to connect with her again by taking a different focus, intervening this time with a specific question about the demonic inner voice that tells her that everything is hopeless, 'no good.']

MD: *Whose voice is that?*

Teresa: *It's my father's.* (Teresa's father had shamed Teresa in her body as a child, in a viciously sadistic manner.)

[When Teresa was able to state "it's my father's", I knew that her witnessing self was present and had not been petrified; it retained enough autonomy to enable her to hear my question and respond from the midst of the activation. This told me that the orbitofrontal cortex was functioning, that Teresa was sufficiently grounded in her body not to dissociate completely. Teresa had developed a strong sense of what it feels like to remain *present* in the body when activated and this had created a 'Perseus's shield' to protect her from the *death mother*. Hearing herself in her *own voice* respond to my question with the statement "it's my father's" enabled Teresa to start the process of dis-identifying from the grip of the original trauma and the activated self-care system. She could now recognize her father as the intruder who had kept her dissociated, locked out of her body, and frozen into a place of shame; the tyrannous voice she hears is not only the voice of her own persecutory self-care system but, at a deep, implicit level, the voice of her father. Kalsched describes the shame-based splitting that we witness in Teresa as:

> [a] split between a critical inner protector and a supposedly inadequate inner child. The splitting of the psyche is a violent process. The split is cemented into the fabric of our being and a (false) shame-based identity becomes the filter through which we see our life.
>
> (Kalsched, 2015, p. 13)

[Teresa had discovered a context for the negative voice that had shadowed her all her life and caused the extreme splitting in self-defence; this discovery made the implicit explicit, conscious. While the disclosure rooted her in her story, her history, it also made her more present in the 'now' moment.[12] Stern speaks to the 'now' moment when both the therapist and the client "grasp a similar version of what is happening, now, here, between us" (Stern et al., 1998, p. 908). When working with BodyDreaming we are working with implicit memory, and the work is not a linear process nor is it goal-oriented. We are not *trying* to make the repressed unconscious material conscious; instead we attune in the dyadic conversation between therapist and client, listening to the 'hints and guesses' emerging from the body, mind and soul. This is not *repair* in the sense of making something bad good, but creating new synapses and new pathways for the emerging life force to flow. In the 'now' moment with Teresa, the past and present meet; body, mind and soul are present, witnessed by both client and analyst.[13]]

The disclosure now held between us expanded our shared implicit relationship, allowing for greater compassion. In neurophysiological terms, we might argue that for Teresa to recognize and name the destructive voice as the voice of her father opened up new neural connections between the right hemisphere where the implicit memory is stored, and the left hemisphere with its facility for naming; between the orbitofrontal cortex and the limbic brain and brain stem, representing both a *top-down* and a *bottom-up* regulatory and integrative experience.

Following Levine's observation that "[t]he sensation is ultimately what will help you move through the trauma" (1997, p. 79), I returned Teresa's attention to the movement and sensation of warm breath as it moved in her body, particularly in her throat, from where she had spoken "it's my father's" voice. Grounding Teresa's spoken words in her body through a felt sense experience supported Teresa to stay present to the activation and dysregulation and name the feelings that arose. The right brain holds the impression, sensation, and implicit memory of the traumatic event. At the point we had reached in her analysis, Teresa felt sufficiently supported to be able to withstand the Medusa freeze and stay present to her experience with me, witnessing herself and being witnessed. With the neo-cortex operating in this way she could tolerate the previously 'intolerable' feelings and sensations, and access her left brain in naming and blaming her father. She was engaged with making meaning, integrating her present and past experiences. This session with the synchronistic event of the locksmith/intruder provided Teresa with an empowering response to her activation, while uncovering the implicit memory and trauma. We were attentive to the deep, primitive response that had manifested in the dorsal vagal immobility or freeze and could feel into and ease the level of trauma that had lain buried in Teresa's lower belly, the site of the dorsal vagal immobility. Teresa and I slowly titrated the cycles of activation and deactivation, tracking the felt sense experience, knitting together sensation, emotion and meaning.[14] We were actively making links where before there had been dissociative splitting in the psyche and intense immobility in the ANS and musculature of Teresa's body. This painstakingly slow process enabled Teresa to acquire greater trust in her system, confirming the connections she had formed in herself (while building a secure attachment to her body) and which could now support her. Kalsched describes "how the saving and protection of a vital core of selfhood seems to be the 'goal' of what I have called the self-care system" (2013, p. 269). Our session confirmed that *vital core of selfhood* which Teresa could now acknowledge and embody, no longer requiring the defences of freeze, splitting and dissociation. Levine emphasizes that it is the integration of contraction and expansion—the regulating cycles of activation and deactivation—and the healing focus of felt sense that "supports us in orchestrating the marvel of transformation" (1997, p. 197). Teresa's transformative experience continued into the dream she presented at the next session.

Teresa's dream came directly from the work of meeting her *vital core of selfhood* in the previous session and reflected the critical transition period as we shifted the boundaries of the session from twice weekly to once a week in preparation for Teresa to leave analysis. Kalsched writes about the significance of dreams at such key points in therapy:

> Events that were so traumatic they could not be experienced would be encoded in somatic and, simultaneously, celestial forms—as embodied affects without images, or images without affects. As the capacity for symbolic experience developed, dreams would then bring these two poles together and make experience of unbearable realities possible for the first time. Such dreams would be true integrative events. It is an accomplishment to dream about them, to render the 'unspeakable horror' into symbolic language.
>
> (Kalsched, 2013, p. 314)

Teresa's Dream

My plane has crashed. There is a hole in the plane near where I am sitting and I climb out onto the ground. I go to tell a colleague all that happened. I feel she doesn't believe me. I have an idea and look at my watch and it is just 6 o'clock and I suggest we put on the TV to see the news and I am sure that they will show the crash. It is the first item on the news. It shows all the emergency crews and the people. My colleague turns to me and says, "But you weren't there." Inside I feel I am never going to convince her. I know now what I need to do. I need to go back to the scene of the crash. I know that when I talk to the people who are helping with the rescue they will believe me and they will tell me what to do because I feel all shaken up inside and very strange.

As we looked at the dream together Teresa realized that she was no longer caught in her old pattern of an immobility response. In fact, in the dream, the dream-ego is able to move and take action, getting herself out of the plane that has crashed. The disbelief of her colleague might formerly have triggered shame, putting her in a 'no thought', 'stupid' place, attacking her thinking[15] and rendering her stupid. That familiar response now gives way to a capacity to think, consider options and mobilize herself to take further action. The dream-ego decides to find support and have her experience confirmed by the observable objective data recorded on the TV news. This action describes the type of thinking that originates in the rational left brain of the orbitofrontal cortex with which Teresa and I had long worked, enabling Teresa to learn how to calm anxiety generated in the subcortical areas of the limbic system and brain stem. The reptilian brain prepares us for action or inaction—*fight, flight* or *freeze*—and is directly influenced by the calming orbito-cortex which determines the *course* of action we take. The work of the previous session had succeeded in bringing together *top-down* and *bottom-up* processing, facilitating a link between emotion, thought and action, as imaged in the dream: when faced with her colleague's disbelief, the dream-ego can *think*, and *chooses* to return to the scene of the crash. Also in the previous session we had success-fully 'revisited the crash', that is, revisited the memory bank of the early trauma which the locksmith's presence had activated. The dream shows how familiar trauma responses—immobility and dissociation—seem to have undergone repair which, in turn, suggests that a new pathway, or neurological change, has taken place. Energy previously trapped in the nervous system and musculature of her body is perhaps now available to enhance Teresa's sense of purpose and direction. Certainly Teresa as dream-ego found herself free to act, self-agency restored.[16]

Teresa's confidence grew as she remembered the dream and her increased con-fidence seemed to trigger further recall:

For the second time I get up and walk, this time back to the scene of the crash. This is in total contrast to the paralysis I felt in childhood; it was like finding a 'resource' in me. I know what to do and I am able to move now.

Teresa's immobility response imaged in the dream as 'the paralysis I (the dream-ego) felt in childhood' is giving way, *thawing*, and leaving her in a position to move, a critical development confirming Levine's observation that "the key to healing traumatic symptoms in humans is in our physiology. ... The important thing to understand about this function is that it is involuntary. This simply means that the physiological mechanism governing this response resides in the primitive, instinctual parts of our brains and nervous systems, and is not under our control" (1997, p. 17).

Teresa continued to recall more of the dream, her memory stimulated by the new-found mobility in her system. She remembered her dream-ego going to meet her analyst and "some dear friends" at the scene of the crash and saying confidently to them: "*It's about trusting your gut, a different way of knowing, separate from your brain, it doesn't feel like it's coming from the right place, it's like my head is in my stomach, inside, down there.*" She pointed to the area of the digestive system and continued, almost in reverie: "*You have to listen, to step back. This is out of sync with the mind. It's hard to believe because it wasn't coming from the right place.*"

Our work had opened up new neural pathways, strengthening Teresa's *core self* and growing her connection to the *gut brain* or gut knowing of which Candace Pert speaks.[17] Pert, who discovered neuropeptides and their receptors (see Chapter 2), uses the phrase the *network system of communication* (or *mobile brain*) that happens *throughout* the body.

> [I]t could be said that intelligence is located not only in the brain but in cells that are distributed throughout the body. ... [S]ince neuropeptides and their receptors are in the body as well, we may conclude that the *mind* is in the body, in the same sense that the mind is in the brain. ... [W]e need to start thinking about how the mind manifests itself in various parts of the body and, beyond that, how can we bring that process into consciousness. ... Mind does not dominate body, it becomes body—body and mind are one.
>
> (Pert, 1997, pp. 187–188)

It would seem that Teresa's dream image of the *head* in the *stomach* is indicative of a potential shift in consciousness which, in turn, would give Teresa the opportunity to develop a shift in her nervous system's response to activation.

> Teresa had journeyed from 'outside her head' down through her body into the gut's 'knowing'. In the first session described above, we had opened new neural pathways through the releasing of energy in the dorsal vagus and the mobilizing of a *healthy* sympathetic response by naming Teresa's anger and blame. The unblocking of energy in the dorsal vagus also affected Teresa's ventral system and the social engagement muscles in the larynx and pharynx, organs of the voice. Consequently Teresa's voice was 'opened' in naming her father and in the dream image of her speaking with a confident voice to her analysts and dear friends. Ann Skinner (BodySoul Rhythms co-founder and voice teacher) underscores the importance of finding one's authentic voice, the voice "coming from its own natural source with full resonance".[18] Teresa's analysis had begun with the deafening silence of the trance state. However, over time, Teresa has come to experience herself physically and

psychically in a manner that has shifted her centre of gravity from 'outside' her head to her gut. We hear Teresa articulate her body's truth in an authentic voice: "It's a different way of knowing ... like my head is in my *stomach, inside*, down there." Jung's words ring true at this critical point: Only if you first return to your body, to your earth, can individuation take place; only then does the thing become true.

(Jung, 1934, pp. 1313–1314)

In the course of working with Teresa, I found that her relationship to her body had altered. A fundamental change often takes place when we use the BodyDreaming approach in therapy. Our bodies (or *matter*) become animated by the positive attention that we bring to our sensing bodies—they "matter"—and, in turn, we are affected by the *matter* of our bodies. Through sustained focus on affect regulation, inner attunement, resonance and felt sense experience, we create an environment in which we can observe how matter and psyche interact, how the body, mind and soul meet and yet do not meet. As cited in the introductory chapter, "A note to the reader", (p. 12), Jung writes that "... the difference we make between the psyche and the body is artificial. ... In reality, there is nothing but a living body. That is the fact; and psyche is as much a living body as body is living psyche: it is just the same" (1988, p. 396).

We observed that the work of the earlier session with Teresa seemed to serve as a catalyst for the dream that followed. The psyche appeared to speak in the dream images that emerged in direct response to the bodywork; in such instances, we become aware that the body is alive with psyche, and that dream images speak to the individuating process taking place. Jung holds that "dream symbols are the essential message carriers from the instinctive to the rational parts of the human mind, and their interpretation enriches the poverty of consciousness so that it learns to understand again the forgotten language of the instincts" (1964, p. 52). In the months prior to the dream of the plane crash, Teresa had dreamt of the *inside* of the body, of buildings and containers that were filled with golden light. Jung argues that, in illness and at times of fragmentation and challenge, the Self, the guiding principle of the totality of the psyche, may provide powerful dream images that hold us and guide us through the dark times. Such images are analogous to the alignment of the sun during the Winter Solstice at Newgrange: they hold a promise of the return of light. At the time of her 'golden' dreams, Teresa was working with the somatic unconscious, through BodyDreaming, bringing to awareness the implicit memory of unspoken early trauma.[19] She experienced her body in a new way, directing her attention to her *matter* that had been despised, rejected and disabled ('no good') gradually sensing it filled with a golden numinous light; discovering a felt sense of her 'insides'—her belly, her chest, her tissue alive and filled with light.. She gradually came to embody, in Winnicott's terms, a sense of "indwelling",[20] a homecoming for her body, mind and soul.

Her experience of this archetypal energy, or spirit, was compelling, and Teresa quietly sought out times to sit, rest, and bring awareness to her 'golden' sensing body, nurturing the tentative relationship that held the seeds of a **learned secure attachment** to her body. Thus it was that when the incident with the locksmith occurred retriggering an early trauma Teresa managed to stay present in her body and withstand the pull to dissociation and collapse. We titrated the emotional shock with felt sense experiencing and top-down regulation, which offered us the possibility to work differently in the 'here and now' moment with this 'trauma'. The dream images, that came from the process of psyche and body working together, showed the situation as it was and the *lysis* pointing her in the direction of 'where the energy wants to go'. Woodman speaks to the power of the healing energy of the dream image that brings the psyche and the physical together:

> The psychic energy frees the physical, the physical illuminates the psychic. … Moreover, it is the contained energy of the images that constitutes what Jung, drawing upon an ancient tradition, called the *subtle body* or breath-soul. … The subtle body denies neither spirit nor soma, but brings them together in a *tertium non datur*, a third which holds the physical and psychic tensions and acts as a catalyst releasing energy to both sides.
>
> (Woodman, 1985, p. 63)

Elsewhere, Woodman writes of transformative moments during which we experience an interpenetration of psyche and matter: "Genuine spiritual experience for the woman must penetrate with passion into her body, and her yielding to that power brings forth the new creation, the new attitude to her immediate environment" (1980, p. 119) and, we might add, to her body.

After years of working with Teresa I felt privileged to witness her rebirth, a profound experience of "indwelling", carrying with it a sense of newfound freedom. Where there had been fragmentation and deep dissociation there now was a restored sense of physical and psychic wholeness. Her core self had been "*forge[d] in the smithy*" of her sensing body.[21] Just as at Newgrange, the winter sunlight arrives into the tomb, a moment of incarnation where the life force touches the rock and lights up the cairn, signalling the sun's return, so Teresa's closing dream of the long analysis announces the inner alignment that has grown and developed between her body sensing self and the Self, a matter of incarnation. She, too, is oriented to the sunlight.

Notes

1   Walcott, 2014, p. 227.
2   Essential to the repair of the mid-line circuit is the individual's capacity to "first notice and then describe the feelings in their bodies—not emotions such as anger or anxiety or fear but the physical sensations beneath the emotions: pressure, heat, muscular tension, tingling, caving in, feeling hollow, and so on" (van der Kolk, 2014, p. 101). I found van der Kolk's analysis very helpful to my understanding of the use of 'orienting'. When I invite a client to orient, no matter how traumatized he or she may be in the moment, I am drawing on the region of the brain, the posterior

cingulate, that lights up in such 'idle moments', that is responsible for our orientation in space and that positively affects the sympathetic nervous system (the heart and respiratory centres).

3 Stern explores our experience of 'present moments':

> Awareness or consciousness is a necessary condition for a present moment....
> The present moment is the felt experience of what happens during a short stretch of consciousness. ... It is the experience as originally lived. ... The felt experience of the present moment is whatever is in awareness now, during the moment being lived. ... Subjective awareness does not passively 'reach' or pop into awareness fully formed. It is actively constructed by our minds and bodies working together.
>
> (Stern, 2004, p. 33)

4 Siegel cites van der Kolk on this point:

> [T]raumatized individuals as a rule have serious problems attending to their inner sensations and perceptions. When asked to focus on internal sensations, they tend to feel overwhelmed or deny having any. When they finally do pay attention to their inner world, they usually encounter a minefield of trauma-related perceptions, sensations and emotions.
>
> (In Ogden, Minton and Pain, 2006, p. xxv)

5 Ferenczi speaks to the two sides of the self-care system: the one that is destroyed, the child-self, and the one that sees the destruction, the progressed intellectual side. He describes the destroyed child-part of the personality, in the aftermath of early trauma, as

> a being suffering purely psychically in his unconscious, the actual child, of whom the awakened ego knows absolutely nothing. This fragment is accessible only in deep sleep, or in a deep trance... It behaves like a child who has fainted or given up the ghost, completely unaware of itself, 'dead,' who can perhaps groan, who must be shaken awake mentally and sometimes physically.
>
> (Ferenczi, cited in Kalsched, 1996, p. 121)

6 [Traumatic flashbacks] are stored in more primitive circuits with less cortical and left-hemisphere involvement. ... they are ... somatic, sensory, and emotional, as well as inherently nonverbal. The lack of cortical- hippocampal involvement results in an absence of the localization of the memory in time, so when it is triggered it is experienced as occurring in the present (Cozolino, 2002, pp. 272–273).

7 Dickinson, [1863]1999, p. 233.

8   Children who suffer from problematic dissociation can often display symptoms that can be misinterpreted as other psychological problems. According to the International Society for the Study of Trauma and Dissociation, children with dissociative disorders are prone to trance states or *black-outs* where the child becomes unresponsive or has a lapse in attention. They may also stare at nothing, forget parts of their life or what they were doing a moment ago, or act as if they just woke up in response to being called to attention. Coupled with sudden changes in activity levels (like a child being lethargic one minute and hyperactive the next), these symptoms are often misinterpreted as Attention Deficit Disorder or Bipolar Disorder.

> (Muller, 2014)

9   If past experiences are to be changed, they must be rewritten or replaced by a new temporal experience occurring in the same time framework. The rewriting must also be lived through with its own temporal dynamics. ... Such new temporal experience re-writes not only the explicit past, but also the implicit past experience.

(Stern, 2004, p. 220)

10   "A secure attachment combined with the cultivation of competency builds an *internal locus of control*, the key factor in healthy coping through life" (van der Kolk, 2014, p. 113).

11   The prototypical conscious subjective experience of shame is psychobiologically mediated by a sudden shift from sympathetic-dominant to parasympathetic autonomic nervous system activity. Throughout the rest of the lifespan it is phenomenologically experienced as a blockage of vitality affects, a sharp gradient of change of emotion, a rapid, unexpected, uncontrollable transition from a 'crescendo' to a 'decrescendo,' an 'animate' to an 'inanimate' feeling state.

(Schore, 1994, p. 205)

12   The most intriguing now moments arise when the patient does something that is difficult to categorise, something that demands a different and new kind of response with a personal signature that shares the analyst's subjective state (affect, phantasy, real experience etc.) with the patient. If this happens, they will enter an authentic 'moment of meeting'. During the 'moment of meeting' a novel intersubjective contact between them will become established, new in the sense that an alteration in the 'shared implicit relationship' is created.

(Stern *et al.*, 1998, pp. 911–912)

13   "... such [intersubjective] meetings involve linking between organism and context, inside and outside, giving rise to a state that is more inclusive than what either system alone can create. Tronick has termed this more inclusive state the dyadic expansion of consciousness" (*ibid.*, p. 908).

14   "Organisms have evolved exquisite processes to heal the effects of trauma. These processes include the ability to unite, integrate, and transform the polarities of expansion and contraction" (Levine, 1997, p. 196).

15   Bion, 1959.

16   So the experience of agency in therapy is also the foundation of the capacity to experience strong emotion without fearing it as destructive—in other words, the capacity for self-regulation. Self agency is also the capacity for self-reflection and awareness of the mental and emotional separateness of self and other.

(Knox, 2011, p. 161)

17   The entire lining of the intestines ... is lined with cells—nerve cells and other kinds of cells–that contain neuropeptides and receptors. It seems entirely possible to me that the density of receptors in the intestines may be why we feel our emotions in that part of the anatomy, often referring to them as 'gut feelings' ... [Y]our brain is extremely well integrated with the rest of your body at a molecular level, so much so that the term *mobile brain* is an apt description of the psychosomatic network through which intelligent information travels from one system to another. ... Every one of the zones, or systems of the network—the neural, the hormonal, the gastrointestinal, and the immune—is set up to communicate with one another, via peptides and messenger-specific receptors. ... Imagine each of these messenger systems possessing a specific tone, ... if we

could hear this body music with our ears, then the sum of those sounds would be music that we call the emotions.

(Pert, 1997, pp. 188–189)

18   Few people hear their own voices because their fear and blocked rage keep the voice in the throat, unrelated to the real energy of their imagination and emotion. In those brief moments when we do manage to free our authentic voices, the whole being resonates with that truth, and a marriage of personal and transpersonal is palpable in the environment.

(Woodman, 1985, p. 64)

19   In each of us there is another whom we do not know. He speaks to us in dreams and tells us how differently he sees us from the way we see ourselves. When, therefore, we find ourselves in a difficult situation to which there is no solution, he can sometimes kindle a light that radically alters our attitude—the very attitude that led us into the difficult situation.

(Jung, 1933, par. 325)

20 Kalsched cites Winnicott's discussion ("On the Basis for Self in Body" in *Playing and Reality*, 1971) of the "'coming into being' that happens or fails to happen in transitional space".

As the mother continually introduces and reintroduces the baby's mind and body, Winnicott says, something mysterious comes to 'indwell' in the body, and as Winnicott describes it, we would be hard-pressed not to think of this 'something' as the human soul. Indwelling leads to 'personalization,' which ... has to do with feeling real and becoming a person. So hope has centrally to do with something ineffable—mind, psyche, spirit—taking up residence in the body and this, symbolically speaking, has always been known as the incarnation of the spirit in matter.

(Kalsched, 2005, pp. 174–175)

21 Joyce, 2000, p. 213.

References

Bick, E. (1968) "The Experience of the Skin in Early Object Relations," *International Journal of Psychoanalysis*, 49(2): 484–486.

Bion, W.R. (1959) "Attacks on Linking," *International Journal of Psychoanalysis*, 40: 308–315. Reprinted in: *Second Thoughts* (1967), New York: Jason Aronson, pp. 93–109.

Cozolino, L. (2002) *The Neuroscience of Psychotherapy: Building and Rebuilding the Human Brain*, New York: W.W. Norton & Co.

Damasio, A. (2000) *The Feeling of What Happens: Body, Emotion and the Making of Consciousness*, London: Vintage.

Dickinson, E. ([1863] 1999) "There is a pain – so utter –." No. 515. In *The Poems of Emily Dickinson, Reading Edition*, R.W. Franklin (ed.), Cambridge, MA and London: Harvard University Press.

Green, N.P.O., Stout, G.W., Taylor, D.J. and Soper, R., ed. (1984) *Biological Science*, Cambridge: Cambridge University Press.

Heller, L. and LaPierre, A. (2012) *Healing Developmental Trauma: How Early Trauma Affects Self-Regulation, Self-Image, and the Capacity for Relationship*, Berkeley, CA: North Atlantic Books.

Joyce, J. (2000) *A Portrait of the Artist as a Young Man*, Oxford and New York: Oxford World's Classics.

Jung, C.G. (1933) *The Meaning of Psychology for Modern Man*, Collected Works 10, Princeton, NJ: Princeton University Press.

Jung, C.G. (1934) *A Review of the Complex Theory*, Collected Works 8, Princeton, NJ: Princeton University Press.

Jung, C.G. (1964) *Man and his Symbols*. Conceived and edited by Carl G. Jung. New York: Doubleday.

Jung, C.G. (1988) *Nietzsche's Zarathustra: Notes of the Seminar Given in 1934–1939*, James L. Jarrett (ed.), in two volumes, Bollingen Series XCIX, Princeton, NJ: Princeton University Press (London and New York: Routledge: 1989).

Kalsched, D. (1996) *The Inner World of Trauma: Archetypal Defences of the Personal Spirit*, London: Routledge.

Kalsched, D. (2005) "Hope vs. Hopelessness in the Psychoanalytic Situation and in Dante's Divine Comedy," *Spring, A Journal of Archetype and Culture*, Body and Soul: Honouring Marion Woodman, 72: 167–188.

Kalsched, D. (2013) *Trauma and the Soul: A Psycho-Spiritual Approach to Human Development and its Interruption*, London: Routledge.

Kalsched, D. (2015) "Uncovering the Secrets of the Traumatised Psyche: The Life-Saving Inner Protector who is also a Persecutor," in *Understanding and Healing Emotional Trauma Conversations with Pioneering Clinicians and Researchers*, D. Sieff (ed.), London: Routledge, pp. 11–24.

Knox, J. (2011) *Self-Agency in Psychotherapy: Attachment, Autonomy and Intimacy*, London: W.W. Norton and Co.

Levine, P. (1997) *Waking the Tiger: Healing Trauma - The Innate Capacity to Transform Overwhelming Experiences*, Berkeley, CA: North Atlantic Books.

McDougall, J. (1989) *Theatres of the Body: A Psychoanalytic Approach to Psychosomatic Illness*, London: Free Association Books.

Muller, R.T. (2014) "Fragmented Child: Disorganized Attachment and Dissociation." *Psychology Today*. 20 June 2014. Accessed 28 August 2018 at: www.psychologytoday.com/ca/blog/talking-about-trauma/201406/fragmented-child-disorganized-attachment-and-dissociation.

Ogden, P., Minton, K. and Pain, C. (2006) *Trauma and the Body: A Sensorimotor Approach to Psychotherapy*, London and New York: W.W. Norton & Co.

Pert, C. (1997) *Molecules of Emotion: The Science behind Mind-Body Medicine*, New York: Scribner.

Schore, A.N. (1994) *Affect Dysregulation and the Origin of the Self: The Neurobiology of Emotional Development*, Mahwah, NJ: Lawrence Erlbaum Associates.

Sieff, D.F. (2015) *Understanding and Healing Emotional Trauma: Conversations with Pioneering Clinicians and Researchers*, Hove, UK and New York: Routledge.

Stern, D., Sander, L., Nahum, J.P., Harrison, A.M., Lyons-Ruth, K., Morgan, A.C., Bruschweiler-Stern, N. and Tronick, E.Z. (1998) "Non-Interpretive Mechanisms in Psychoanalytic Therapy: The 'Something More' than Interpretation," *International Journal of Psychoanalysis*, 79 (Pt 5): 903–921.

Stern, D.N., (2004) *The Present Moment in Psychotherapy and Everyday Life*, New York: W.W. Norton & Co.

van der Kolk, B. (2014) *The Body Keeps the Score: Mind, Brain and Body in the Transformation of Trauma*, St Ives, UK: Penguin Random House.

Walcott, D. (2014) "Love after Love", in *The Poetry of Derek Walcott: 1948–1913*. Selected by Glyn Maxwell. New York: Farrar, Straus & Giroux; London: Faber & Faber.

Winnicott, D.W. ([1971] 2005) *Playing and Reality*, London and New York: Routledge.

Woodman, M. (1980) *The Owl was a Baker's Daughter: Obesity, Anorexia Nervosa and the Repressed Feminine*, Toronto: Inner City Books.

Woodman, M. (1985) *The Pregnant Virgin: A Process of Psychological Transformation*, Toronto: Inner City Books.

Chapter 7

Working with Numbness, Shut-down, Freeze

"The bushes don't have panic attacks"

In the previous chapters, to continue with the metaphor of Newgrange, our focus has been to build the 'cairn', the structure, which is oriented outward to receive the light of the winter sun as it shines down the passageway at the 'right' moment to illuminate what we might describe as the 'inner sanctum'. In BodyDreaming we spend a long time building the psychobiological 'cairn' or container by repeatedly regulating the autonomic nervous system and thus widening the 'window of tolerance' by 'holding the tension of opposites' between activation and de-activation until the client is 'aligned with the winter sun' and open to the possibility of a new perspective, an expanded 'field'. We understand and experience the 'field' as a dynamic alignment between the inner world—the psychobiological self—and the outer world: the 'field' in which I find myself is both me and everything around me with which I am aligned, positively and negatively. When we build a strong container it makes us less likely to be 'triggered' and drawn into enacting early patterns of attachment behaviour and developmental trauma; it promotes an expansion of consciousness and, in this way, supports us to attune to our own inner regulatory nature, to others, to the world and nature around us. We become receptive to what presents itself in both the inner and outer worlds, that something 'new' which carries the potential to awaken our interest and open us to possibility.

In Chapter 3, I referred to Jung's essay, *The Transcendent Function* ([1916] 1958). Jung's understanding of psychic dynamics explains how psychic life develops when the ego is sufficiently strong to 'hold the tension of opposites' between conscious and unconscious content—that is, strong enough to tolerate conflict rather than try to avoid it. The something 'new', or 'new' third, that presents itself if ego-consciousness is strong enough to hold the often difficult and uncomfortable 'tension of opposites' is transformative, creating a more life-enhancing alignment between inner and outer realities, and expanding the reach of the conscious personality. If one cannot 'hold the tension of opposites', the result is psychological stasis and one-sidedness, with old complexes and patterns of behaviour reinforced. The experience, however, of a 'new' perspective, that is, a 'new' image, gesture, impulse, dream, or understanding arising spontaneously, enables one to recognize a vital core, and depth of awareness in the personality other than that of rational ego-consciousness. To establish an alignment with this 'Other'—whether experienced as originating in the inner or outer world—is, in Jung's terms, to establish a relationship with the Self, the term he used to describe the archetypal organizing principle of the psyche that appears to underlie and promote the development of all life, and out of which ego-consciousness emerges as the personality develops. It is also to recognize that the ego is not 'master in its own house'—an essential part but not the whole. Ego exists on the 'ground' of the Self and holds a position in the psyche that is relative to the larger dynamics and mystery of psychic life in its entirety.

Following Jung's argument for the relativity of ego-consciousness, Erich Neumann reminds us of the limitations of ego-centred consciousness and how there are numerous levels of consciousness beyond the reach of ego-consciousness. Neumann points out that a one-sided focus on the value and centrality of ego-centred consciousness has cost us our original awareness of 'alternate' levels of consciousness. He insists that reality demands a wider perspective and uses the term 'unitary reality' to describe what "can be no longer (or rather, which can be no longer exclusively) divided into an outer physical-biological world and an inner psychic world by means of the polarization of our consciousness" (1989, p. 4). In order to develop the capacity to experience reality as 'unitary', a viable conscious relationship must persist between ego and Self, ego and unconscious. In other words, sufficient psychic 'ground' must accrue to support a strong, flexible ego first to admit its own relativity in the face of both inner and outer worlds, and second, to admit and relate to the 'other' in whatever form the 'other' presents itself. BodyDreaming offers the opportunity to deepen one's connection to 'Other' through creating homeostasis, experiencing felt sense resonance, and encouraging relatedness and reciprocity.

In this chapter we will look more closely at the process of re-alignment between outer and inner worlds through the lens of BodyDreaming, as this constitutes the first step towards building a healthy, resilient relationship between ego and unconscious, I and Thou, or, in the terms of analytical psychology, a strong ego-Self axis. As discussed in earlier chapters, the practice and process of BodyDreaming aims to develop a capacity for interoception and inner attunement. As a method of tracking felt sense resonance within oneself and between oneself and 'other' phenomena in what is discovered to be a shared 'field', BodyDreaming works to enable us to witness the vital relationship pertaining between inner and outer, and experience an alignment between inner attunement (how we attune to our inner selves) and how we attune to the outer world. We are talking about a sense of *reciprocity* which engages the individual in a dynamic interchange—a lively interplay—between inner and outer, me and the world.

In the phenomenology of Merleau-Ponty, an experience of reciprocity between oneself and the world is indistinguishable from the act of perception—how we perceive ourselves and the world around us. According to David Abram, who draws extensively on the philosophy of Merleau-Ponty in his book, *The Spell of the Sensuous*, "the act of perception involves precisely this reciprocity between oneself and the objects that surround it. ... Our most immediate experience of things ... is necessarily an experience of reciprocal encounter—of tension, communication and commingling" (1997, pp. 55–56). Abram argues that in order to live and die well, we need to learn to experience ourselves, once again, as part of the larger community or 'field' of nature; we need to relearn a "spontaneous, sensorial engagement with the world around us" (*ibid.*, p. 57). Merleau-Ponty's work suggests that the act of engaging with the world at a *sensorial* level is an act of *intimate* perception, involving an "active interplay" or *reciprocity* "between the perceiving body and that which it perceives" (*ibid.*). Abram urges us to live our connection with "the matrix of earthly life in which we ourselves are embedded" *from within*, that is, through the vehicle of the *intelligent body* (*ibid.*, p. 65). In BodyDreaming we draw on the notion of reciprocity between self and other, self and world. Through focused attunement to the natural intelligence of the body, we work to open the client to a sense of living in a shared universe and participating in an ongoing interchange with the world, and to the discovery that *reciprocity*, although not always perceived, is continuously present below the level of conscious awareness. Conscious awareness of what Merleau-Ponty refers to as the 'perceptual reciprocity' between myself and what surrounds me brings me to a deep sense of connectedness and *at-one-ment* with my surroundings. In Abram's words, "I find this silent or wordless dance already going on—this improvised duet between my animal body and the fluid, breathing landscape that it inhabits" (*ibid.*, p. 53).

*

Kate is a new participant in a BodyDreaming workshop in which the majority of the participants are experienced in this work. It is Day 3 of a 4-day workshop, and Kate has volunteered to work her dream. I have observed that Kate has held herself apart in the group, and also that, when speaking, she makes poor eye contact. This indicates to me that her social engagement system might not be fully mobilized and that a dorsal vagal 'freeze' response monopolizes her system.[1] I was aware that this was a developmental trauma response and that she was in a heightened state of activation. I was therefore delighted when, after three days in the group, Kate made contact and volunteered to work a dream.

MD:	*Let's take a minute to find our ground before you begin to speak the dream.*
Kate:	*I feel a bit nervous.*
MD:	*It's good to hear you acknowledge the anxiety that is here.*

[I invite Kate to allow her eyes to wander in the room and she is drawn toward a painting that she has made. She is surprised by the appearance of the colour yellow that is now taking her attention. As she continues to pay attention, the image seems to change.]

Kate: *Something appears that was not there before...*

MD: *Something appears that was not there before. How is it for you to notice that?*

Kate: *It makes me anxious.*

MD: *There's a part of you that is holding anxiety and maybe we can all hold that with you in the room.*

[I am aware of Kate's anxiety about the changes she perceives in the image. I orient her to the group in a casual way to normalize her experience—"*we can all hold that with you.*" I notice that she is closing her eyes, a familiar 'shut down' response in the face of anxiety. By mentioning the group, I try to make her aware of the group's supportive presence. She opens her eyes to see the other participants, and I find myself hoping that she will feel met by the reassurance of the individuals comprising this warm, experienced container. I am at the same time awakening the group to the shared 'field of consciousness'[2] and to each participant's role as witness to Kate's process, as we are all active participants in this inter-regulatory process. We will see how Kate draws on the group field in a very positive way during the session. The group becomes an ally or, we might say, an alloy, if we think of our use of inter-regulatory skills in terms of the alchemical process as the ingredients that allow us to create and bind the container of the outer bowl].[3]

MD: *Maybe you can tell us the dream.*

[I'm picking up that 'waiting' to tell the dream is anxiety-provoking for Kate. We need to hear the dream and then orient her so she can settle into herself and calm her arousal levels].

THE DREAM: *I was on a course making a singing bowl. I had a bronze bowl, different from the brass one that I brought here to this workshop. Instead of its being a really hard metal which it is in reality, it's very soft. It's disconcerting as it should be a solid object. For no obvious reason it's soft, it's damaged. I show it to Antonius—he's the master bowl maker. He looks at it. There's a little tear in it as well, which is a big thing for a metal maker. They can crack but it's a big thing. It feels very special. It is vulnerable in a way that it ought not to be. So Antonius says "I think you should go outside and sit with it." I do that.*

I think when I'm walking it gets softer and it shouldn't do that. It's really disconcerting and I sit down. I put it on a table and it starts to dissolve, and it becomes like a flat circle. Then a little while after that it's completely gone. I'm wondering what I am going to say in the 'Make a Bowl Workshop' when they ask "Where is your bowl?" I've got no explanation. This shouldn't happen.

I can see myself and I have a much smaller version of the bowl—hard, distilled. It needs to be a hard metal to get the sound, a gold bowl wouldn't ring. In some way in the dream I get a glimpse of another reality, the 'future' bowl is not quite right.

MD: *You see this in the future?*

Kate: *I see a smaller version of the one I was holding. Occasionally one gets damaged if it is left in the fire too long. You can cut off the top part, and you end up with a perfect bowl but it's a smaller bowl.*

MD: *Now that you have spoken the dream, just take a minute to see how your body is doing in response to the dream and your recounting it. Are you noticing anything?*

Kate: *It's quite an effort to speak.*

MD: *Just notice that it's an effort to speak from this place.*[4]

Kate: *It's easier to be silent than to go on and on. I would miss out. I wouldn't be speaking but it's an attractive thing not to have to speak.*[5]

MD: *'Attractive' is a good word. It attracts you—the idea of not speaking ... it's attractive.*

Do you feel that like an energy? Do you feel a sinking, tired feeling that pulls you down or is it an enlivening thing? How does it register with you, 'the attraction not to speak'?

Kate: *I know you have spoken sense, but I actually can't follow it. I've lost it. I heard the word energy but I can't understand it.*

[I am losing connection with her. She is highly activated. She has closed her eyes, which indicates to me that the dorsal vagal response of 'freeze' is setting in. Kate's system is triggered and the link between us is temporarily broken. She is aware that a disconnection has happened. When she stopped telling the dream, she observed that she wanted to retreat into silence but this would mean her 'missing out,' with the social engagement system switched to 'off' position. In naming this retreat space, however, she disclosed her defence position to the group (perhaps unconsciously 'naming it to tame it'?), perhaps reaching out to the *vas* or containing group to help hold her anxiety. The ego is invariably challenged by change—"the psyche's conservative tendency takes over to defend a beleaguered ego against disruption and change, and rigidity sets in" (Yeoman, 1998, p. 128). The 'changes' Kate experiences (first the change in the image in the painting, then the impulse to retreat into silence) may have pushed her system beyond her window of tolerance and into its old defence line with the dorsal vagus activated. As a result, Kate dissociates, the 'Broca' area of her brain is incapacitated and she loses connection with my words. The early defence system which attacks her capacity to link things together—in this case, to stay connected with me—prevents her from receiving and understanding what I am saying.][6]

MD: *It's good that you notice you are not following my words and that you couldn't easily continue to speak once you had shared your experience with us. It's good that you notice all these shifts.*

[We are experiencing a 'threshold moment'. I hold a mirror for Kate, a thread of cognition, working to re-instate the function of the left hemisphere of the brain by tracking what I see happening, even though she may not be able to follow my language and logic due to high levels of arousal in her system. However, I trust that my witnessing the shifts Kate is experiencing may help to rebuild the link between us and engage her capacity for cognition, her orbitofrontal cortex. I am offering a 'top-down' explanation, acting as 'auxiliary cortex' by helping to soothe her activated feelings and make a conscious alliance with her orbitofrontal cortex, the seat of her witness/observer self. My words may also serve to keep the group conscious of its role as witnessing presence, as the disconnection that is happening to Kate will be mirrored in the 'field' of the room. By using the integrative function of the brain to 'name it to tame it' and to make meaning, I am attempting to regulate the limbic activation triggered by everything that is 'unpredictable', both in Kate and in the room. In this way, everyone and everything in the 'whole field' is strengthened. Together we are creating a holding environment that will allow Kate's nervous system to tolerate what previously lay outside her 'window of tolerance'. In this instance, a 'threshold moment' indicates the need to orient Kate outwardly to enable further down-regulation of the activation.]

MD: *I'm going to ask you to orient toward something in the room or outside the window. I know you like to close your eyes. However, in this particular way of working it's really important to orient ourselves with our eyes open or we will engage old pathways, revisit old retreats and repeat old defences. With BodyDreaming, we hope to rewire the brain and open new circuits.*[7]

(I notice that Kate is looking at the art work that is hanging on the wall.)

Are you finding yourself drawn to look at your art work, or would you rather look outside to orient?

Kate: *I'm looking at one of my pictures hanging up there.*

MD: *What are you drawn to in the painting?*

Kate: *It's blue and green. I haven't got my glasses, which I'm enjoy-
             ing. It's a bit yellow ... fuzzy. It feels like it's turning into a dif-
             ferent thing.*
MD: *It has the potential to change. It could turn into a different thing.*
             (I mirror some of her words and add a positive emphasis by
             using an upbeat, light voice.)
Kate: *It could turn into a different thing. It's not a picture of one thing.*
             (I'm aware that she is joining me in mirroring.)
MD: *It's not fixed. What is it about the yellow? You didn't realize
             there was that much yellow in it?*
             [The theme of change–that things don't stay the same—has
             echoes with Kate's dream. I maintain an easy manner and a 'free
             association' style of conversation.]
Kate: *Yes, I had been thinking that it was more blue.*
MD: *And today it is the yellow colour that is more apparent.*
             [If we support Kate's nervous system through an easy style of
             free association conversation and the curiosity of the right hemi-
             sphere, we may inhibit the familiar pattern of shutting down,
             which would previously have cut off her social engagement sys-
             tem. This is the first step or threshold at which we seem to be
             able to linger, taking our time in order to regulate the nervous
             system and facilitate a greater openness to the unpredictable, the
             unexpected.]
MD: *What's the feeling response you are having to 'it's not fixed ... it
             can turn into a different thing.' Do you notice anything happen-
             ing in your body?*
Kate: *I feel uncooperative. I can't answer that. I can't think of the
             right words.*
             [Kate's capacity to think, to make the link, is interrupted once
             again.)
MD: *'Uncooperative' is a good answer. It's good to say it, just how it is.*
             [In mirroring her, I affirm Kate's capacity for self-observation,
             which may help to maintain the connection between us. I'm reas-
             suring her that it's okay to feel 'uncooperative', that there is no
             'right or wrong' in this process. I do not want to get pulled into
             the 'negative' aspect of her 'uncooperative' side so I acknowl-
             edge it without giving it more or less importance.]
MD: *And it has potential for change. It's one of the things that's
             striking you.*
             [I return to the last link we shared which was positive—'*it*
             (the image in the painting) *has potential for change*'—while I
             am carefully watching her response to see if it is okay to hold
             that link between us. I take my cue from her body, her eyes,
             breath, and position in the chair. She looks comfortable, eyes

	open and engaged. Once I am reassured that her Kate has settled, I can then take another initiative.]
MD:	*I'm going to bring you back to your dream now.... What part of the dream are you drawn to?*
	[I'm reorienting her as what had seemed a positive exploration quickly turned into something different. I now focus on mirroring shifts in the dream image.]
Kate:	*If I had to pick a part—it's the whole process of it, the bowl not being what it ought to be. It's soft ... changing metal into soft stuff—that's an impossibility.*
MD:	*'An impossibility' ... it would be impossible to change metal into this soft stuff.*
Kate:	*Yes, it shouldn't happen.*
MD:	*Dreams can do that. They can suddenly turn something around, and bring in a completely different quality, even substance.*
	[In teaching a little about dreams, I am attempting to calm the limbic system, with top-down regulation, so she is not overwhelmed by her response to the dream image. I notice she has closed her eyes again. I follow this shift of energy and ask the question.]
	What's happening now?
Kate:	*I was thinking in the dream I haven't done anything wrong for something so drastic to happen to the bowl.*
	[This statement signals a threshold of activation: Kate may be hitting a self-blame pattern. I have the option to shift the attention away from the complex and to orient her in the right hemisphere 'here and now' exploration once again.]
MD:	*I'm going to invite you to open your eyes again. Let's go back to look at the painting. What strikes you about it now?*
	[A short interchange follows about the painting. I lead the way in free association conversation. We discuss the colours that Kate finds most effective but she says she feels 'uncooperative'. When I ask if she enjoyed making the shapes she says she cannot remember. It seems that we have not established a sufficiently strong resource in the shared viewing of the painting to counteract the tyranny of the complex that is surfacing and we struggle to withstand "being sucked into the trauma vortex", as described by Levine (1997, p. 199). As a consequence, Kate interrupts the conversation ...]
Kate:	*So while this is happening I'm feeling something... when you were working with other people I found the sessions enjoyable. To my surprise it felt like a safe thing happening, and now this feels like it's got holes in it. Suddenly it does not feel safe.* (She has closed her eyes again.)

MD: *It might help you to open your eyes, and we can have a talk about that. So you are not feeling safe?*

[Kate's patterned response is to withdraw, her self-care system stepping in to shut down the social engagement system by closing her eyes.[8] With her eyes open we can draw on her social engagement system to help regulate her emotions, keeping her present in the room. When she is formulating her dilemma, Kate maintains a link, a connection (between herself and me, and between her right and left hemispheres). Recognizing that she *was* able to be 'present to others' while they were doing their work enables her to contrast her own sense of disconnection while she is taking her turn at this point in the group–'*it feels like it's got holes in it.*']

Where do you notice the anxiety? How did you notice it coming in?

[I had intended an open question, which would enable Kate to reflect on her inner experience—e.g., "what do you notice is happening in your body when you say that? Where in your body do you notice the activation?" but her attention remained focused on the outside, in the room. Importantly, however, Kate's response highlighted for us 'the shared field' we were in, her perception of the room '*with holes in it*'—which mirrored her inner state.]

Kate: *It's all around the room. There are lots of blank bits in the room. It's not a complete circle.*

MD: *There are blank bits in the room?*

Kate: *Yes, holes, round holes.*

[The room, which had previously been safe, has now got 'blank bits ... round holes' in it. This image indicates the high level of anxiety in Kate's system.

[I do not focus explicitly on the activation expressed in Kate's perception that there are 'round holes in the room'. Instead, with a clear, steady voice, I invite Kate to orient. This time I do not go back to her painting. Instead, I draw her attention to nature. I am consciously orienting her to pleasure,[9] inviting nature to lead the way as a 'neutral' third that is outside of the therapeutic dyad or the container of the room. In this way we are expanding the vas/bowl/container by attuning to 'the field' that exists beyond it.]

MD: *Gently open your eyes again and take a moment to let them wander outside the room.* (The octagonal room has walls of glass on two sides.)

(I turn to the participants). *I invite everyone in the room to allow your eyes to wander outside and see what takes your attention.*

[This will ensure that the participants—who are asked to hold the tension in the room—do not, on the one hand, become too rigidly fixated or, on the other, escape into a state of day-dream but will themselves reorient and remain present.]

[It's as though Kate's phrase, 'holes in the room', images the dissociative shut-down that is happening as participants' mirror neurons respond to Kate's process and they begin to lose focus. (Perhaps you, as reader, may also be feeling a wave of dissociation?) When I invite the room to orient outwardly, beyond the room, to nature, there is an openness and ease in my voice, demonstrating that I can let go and yield in order to allow nature to regulate us. Each participant's mirror neurons will function to support everyone to 'join' my easy manner of orienting. Although I have no idea what Kate will be drawn toward, I have an implicit trust that the regulating 'other' in nature will present itself. As soon as everyone begins to allow their attention to be drawn to nature I notice an ease flooding the room. Breath flows more easily as we reconnect with the life force—with what the Chinese call *chi* energy—and bodies seem more relaxed. The shift of energy that is happening in the room will be a further support to Kate's system.]

MD: *Allow your eyes to rest on something outside.*

Kate: *I like the furthest trees. I can't see beyond them, but I like what I'm seeing.* (She is speaking in a quieter voice.)

          There's a horizon beyond the trees. You don't know what's there.

MD: *Or do you know what's there?* [I am trying to find out what is engaging her.]

Kate: *Yes, there's more green stuff.*

MD: *More green stuff.*

Kate: *Yes.*

MD: *Is it enjoyable to look at those trees?*

          [The pleasurable feeling that will down-regulate and connect Kate to what is engaging her.]

Kate: *It was okay for a minute, and then it's not enjoyable any longer.*

          [Kate is catching—or tolerating—the threshold moment where before she might have dissociated at this point. She may be signalling that she is going into shut down and hypoarousal. I hear it in her flat tone of voice and an unusual lack of differentiation in her language—'green stuff'.]

MD: *It seems like there's a feeling of resting into something that is okay, and then quickly coming out of it again. The room feels safe and then it's not. The trees are safe and then not. It seems as though we are moving very quickly between these extremes. We do not slow down sufficiently to allow us to be present to the new place. Notice how quickly the shift happens.*

[It seems that once Kate names something as okay the limbic system is triggered and she is immediately overwhelmed, the flight response her only option. I name the process as I see it, appealing to her neocortex, and reminding her that we can think together about this. She is not alone. We are not going to get lost in the 'round holes', in the emotional overwhelm, the hyperarousal of the flight response or the hypoarousal response of dissociation. By acting in the role of 'auxiliary cortex', top-down regulating, I describe what I see is happening, which engages her neocortex and in turn regulates the emotional limbic system. We are co-creating the field, and developing her curiosity and her capacity to witness herself in the moment-by-moment experience of the here-and-now.][10]

MD: *Are you noticing anything as you look out there?*
Kate: *The light green stuff* (vegetation) *is coming into focus, that's more friendly.*
MD: *Great, the light green stuff is more friendly.*
Kate: *Yes, I don't imagine it suffers from panic attacks ever.*

[In this statement, Kate is letting us know that there is a part of her that is safe from panic attacks which is now projected onto the bushes for safe keeping.[11] This is very helpful information since we are working together for the first time and I don't know her trauma history and, consequently, the patterns of her autonomic nervous system responses.]

MD: *The bushes seem to be able to go with the flow.*
          (Time passes.)
          There's a beautiful movement of the bushes in the wind, isn't there?
Kate: *Yes, they are not going to have a panic attack.*

[Kate is reinforcing that part of herself which is not going to go into overwhelm and suffer a panic attack.]

MD: *That's reassuring to know. See how your body responds to that. It's good to know the bushes are not going to have a panic attack.*

[The bushes, seemingly randomly chosen, now have the capacity to counteract Kate's terror and assuage her patterned response of panic. Nature is resourcing her; her limbic system is soothed by the precise attention she is giving to this particular image.

[Kate communicates her reassurance to all in the room. There follows a deactivation for everyone, a parasympathetic response, as a collective sigh is released into the room. Together we are creating a 'field' that will tolerate what was previously outside 'the window of tolerance', imaged in the words "the bushes don't have panic attacks". This represents a powerful coming together of left (meaning) and right (image) hemispheres—the metaphor of the bushes not suffering panic attacks bridging the two hemispheres.

[Time passes as Kate continues to look outside at the bushes.]

MD: *The bushes know how to move with the flow of wind; then they take a rest; then a gust of wind will come and they will move with it again. Is there anything in your body responding to that rhythm?*

Kate: *No, not in a direct response, but I do feel a tightness in my neck. A bit of humour about the bushes is coming in.* (She smiles.) *I can imagine having a conversation with them. The bushes can do 'chilled out'. 'Bush-ness' is all they've ever done, and they have an understanding that because I'm human that's not going to be my normal thing. So they're casual about it, and know I'm not going to be as good at just hanging out.* (She is quite animated and smiling).[12]

MD: *This is an interesting conversation you're having. It's very nice to hear that. How do you receive these words in your body? See if there is any part of you that can let that conversation with the bushes come right into your body.*

Notice any changes that might be happening.... See how your body is responding to the humour. Notice that you've smiled, that your eyes have relaxed a bit. That's really good. What do you notice when the humour comes in? and, by the way, "Thank you, bushes, thank you for sharing."[13]

(A big laugh rings out in the room.)

[I am joining Kate in her humour, letting go of the tension that I have been holding since the beginning of the session. The humour releases us from the tyranny of having to get something right, striving, or making too much of an effort. The humour in our conversation now bounces to-and-fro from one to the other, forming an interactive regulation and helping to maintain a link between us and the participants in the room.[14]

[The bushes have become the 'new third', enabling Kate to maintain contact with herself. Speaking about them and their effect supports her attempts at self-regulation and homeostasis. In playful interactions between mother and infant, the infant looks away as a means of controlling the level of stimulation and regulating arousal (Beebe and Lachmann, 2002, p. 158). Kate has managed to self-regulate by looking away from me to the trees, back and forth, at her own pace. She can connect with the bushes, converse with them, and humorously share that communication with the group. She has clearly negotiated a full cycle of deintegration and reintegration, which enables her to feel more stable within herself and to introduce humour in her engagement with the group.[15] The bushes serve as mediators of Kate's new-found stability. The capacity for humour and play is a healthy sign that Kate's social engagement system is coming 'on line' and her creativity is flowing.[16]

[Our slow, attuned work of tracking Kate's cycles of activation and deactivation allows Kate to be receptive to the image of the moving bushes with their 'bush-ness', which, in turn, opens new neural pathways and effects a transformation at a psychobiological level, 'shaping her sense of identity and value' (Stein, 1998, p. 45) and enabling her to remain present to her experience.]

MD: *Where do you notice the humour resonating in your body? In your face?... jaw?... lips?*

Kate: *It feels a bit outside of me. I can't find it in my body. At least I don't really notice.*

MD: *Maybe I can mirror a little to you what I notice. I saw that first you smiled. It looked like you were enjoying something before you spoke the words. It came into your face first, your cheeks lifted, your eyes opened up, your facial muscles first responded to your private joke. Then you were very generous and shared it with us and you got us all laughing. We enjoyed the joke too.*

(Kate is smiling and the group is responding with laughter. There is a real sense of everyone 'joining with' Kate.)

What did you notice in your face as you responded to the laughter just now? Did you notice that you were smiling as I was speaking to you?

Kate: *Yes ...* (She is smiling and laughing and again the room joins with her in laughter.)

MD: *Very good. Is that ok that you smiled?*

Kate: *Yes, it was ok, and then it stopped.*

MD: *Ok. And that's great that you notice the change, when it stopped.*

[Kate is aware of the point at which there is a change, a disconnection. Her inner 'witness' remains present and available, paying attention to the 'stops', which means that Kate is less likely to succumb to a 'freeze' response or dissociation.]

MD: *I'm going to slow things down.*

[I want to activate the right hemisphere so I orient to the bushes again to help reconnect Kate to the present moment.]

You may just want to look at the bushes, to bring your focus outside, allow yourself to orient to them again to see what they can do. They don't have panic attacks ... (pause) ...

They are really moving now, catching the wind, with a great flexibility of movement. Do you feel yourself resonate with the movement?

(Time passes.)

Kate: *It feels like if I stay with it, it makes it possible for me to stay in the room.* [17]

[Kate is clearly self-regulating; she knows her resource and how to use it. She recognizes that in orienting to the bushes she feels safe and the link between us does not have to be severed. Her social engagement system is absorbed with the bushes, and not with me or the group at this point. Practising self-regulation anchors her in the here and now, and facilitates her opening to the group to permit inter-regulation, so she has less need to dissociate. Fordham's description of the infant's cycles of deintegration and reintegration are useful to shed light on what is happening. The bushes enable Kate to 'remain' in the present moment by allowing the deintegration and reintegration process to unfold in a safe and continuous cycle. She gives herself time to recover from the recent 'deintegration' caused by the extraversion and laughter she herself generated in the room, and recuperates and reintegrates by allowing herself to 'hang out with the bushes'.][18]

MD: *That's great to notice that if you stay with the bushes 'it makes it possible for you to stay in the room.' I am sure that every-one here appreciates the power of the work you are doing. It is really touching us all deeply. We can each observe the effect of your orienting to the bushes and how it helps us all to stay present in the room and not dissociate. Our mirror neurons are picking up the shifts in the cycles of activation and deactivation. They so appreciate when you 'hang out' with the bushes.*

               'Thank you, bushes'. This is beautiful, powerful work. (I say this a little tongue-in-cheek but with feeling!)

Kate: *I've got a hotline to the bushes and I don't feel they need you to thank them.*

               (A big laugh is generated in the room.)

[Kate's witty response was instantaneous, and a great example of the sympathetic system coming back on-line once her energy had been released from a dorsal vagal 'freeze'. Knox makes the connection between turn-taking and the development of self-agency, "which has been defined as finding oneself through action and reaction in relationship" (2011, p. 10). Kate is safely engaged with the bushes—she has a hotline to them—which means the immobility response of the dorsal vagus is not needed to protect her. Consequently, she is able to respond energetically. Her social engagement system is free to connect to me and to play with the group. This lets us know that 'reintegration' is happening and a corresponding expansion of Kate's capacity for self-agency.]

MD: *They don't need my thanks. They just are.* [I mirror Kate.]

Kate: *They are not against it* per se. *They just say 'ah, there's Marian again, she always feels she has to say thank you.'*

(There is a big outburst of laughter.)[19]

[The ease and flow of the humour brings with it a release for everyone in the 'field'. Kate's quick humour enlivens and draws the group together, leaving 'no holes' in the room. Like the wind in the bushes, she becomes the animating factor in the room. By emphasizing the humour we couple activation (the sympathetic response) positively with humour and not with a disconnection.]

MD: *It's probably true what you say. Can you repeat that phrase?*

[I am encouraging her humour, giving even more time to the integrative circuit in her system to fire and establish itself.]

Kate: *I just imagine the bushes saying 'ah, there's Marian again. We love to move, but Marian doesn't really need to thank us.'*

(Again, the room laughs.)

MD: *What's it like to get the whole room laughing?*

Kate: *I can handle that.* (She laughs.)

MD: *That's lovely.*

[Kate's laughter has burst through the room like a bolt of lightning, freeing tension and the 'holding' pattern, and opening up further possibilities for creative play.[20] Kate's unconscious intervened by orienting her toward the image of the bushes, illustrating Jung's claim that the psyche, like the body, is self-regulatory. Jung also argues that psychic energy is teleological—that is, it appears to be purposive, driving us toward wholeness. How extraordinary and yet simple to find that natural phenomena—bushes moving in the wind—become the perfect antidote to activation of the autonomic nervous system, that is, to the psychological complex and dissociation associated with the psyche's old defence against activation. In remaining present to nature's resource—the movement of the bushes—Kate found a link to herself, a secure base which allowed her a sense of continuity and capacity for 'going-on-being'.[21] Through play, laughter and banter the process of self- and inter-regulation helped create a coherence and connectedness in the room, an intermingling between the one and the many, and between inner and outer realities.[22] We have journeyed with Kate through activation and deactivation, dysregulation and regulation, disruption and repair, deintegration and reintegration. From the oscillation between these opposites a 'new third' is emerging, a playful, creative, regulatory energy that is shaping 'the field'.

[The 'field' of perception has changed since we started the session—there is greater flexibility, curiosity and openness to meet Kate's dream than when she first spoke it in the room. We now have some intimation of a 'unitary reality'—an awareness that something bigger than our individual, ego-conscious selves is influencing the field, shaping our inner world and how we are interacting with the world around us. Neumann calls this a state of 'unitary reality,' in which we realize that the outer world is not separate from the inner world: they co-exist, commingle. Consciousness of the inter-connectedness of outer and inner introduces a quality of consciousness that stretches beyond ego boundaries and the supposed polarities of matter and psyche, a quality of consciousness in which things can shift and change, as in Kate's dream of the singing bowl. This is the 'field' in which we find ourselves as we continue with BodyDreaming to explore the dream proper.]

MD: *Maybe now is a good time to look at the dream image again. You said that the substance of the bowl could not change that dramatically.*

Kate: *Yes. It's not possible.*

MD: *Yet in the dream something is made possible.*

Kate: *Even if the fire damages a bowl, it wouldn't get soft. It's very disconcerting. It should be solid in your hand, and shouldn't change, unless you really hammer it.*

MD: *I hear the words 'disconcerting' and 'it shouldn't change'.*

Kate: *Usually the structure is firm, but something really different is happening here.*

MD: *When something new is wanting to come in, as portrayed by the image of the changing substance of the bowl, we observe that it triggers activation of the autonomic nervous system. The dream ego finds it 'disconcerting', warning 'this shouldn't be happening' and prompting the question, "Have I done something wrong?" It seems the dream ego does not want 'soft stuff' and so rejects the change. It wants to hold a firm, solid bowl. When change is looming, the self-care system fights to hold the 'old system' rigidly in place.[23]*

In the dream, however, despite being activated by the crack in the bowl, the dream ego does not remain stuck or frozen. On the contrary, it consults with Antonius, the master bowl maker, who might represent the part of you that holds the knowledge of the alchemical process of bowl-making. He advises you to go outside and sit with your bowl.[24] He has the capacity to hold the tension, while tolerating the changes in the substance.

[In the dream, the dream ego walks outside and the bowl changes into a soft, liquid substance.[25] There are stages in the alchemical process known as *dissolutio* and *coagulatio*, in which what was once solid is first dissolved into liquid, then coagulated once again into a solid but different substance. This process may be compared to a loosening of rigid views, the dissolution of old complexes accompanied by corresponding changes in neural pathways. In the dream, Antonius represents the alchemist, the individuating self, who works to bring about transformation.

[Antonius holds the contradictions and paradox,[26] representing an aspect of Kate's psyche, perhaps—in Jung's terminology, the Self—that holds the larger perspective and guides the process at a pace that is not shocking to the initiate. Antonius's regulatory advice to sit and contemplate the bowl helps to keep the dream ego from a panic response to its unexpected dissolution. Jung speaks about the psyche's capacity to hold the 'tension of the opposites' without polarizing an image or situation into right or wrong, until a new possibility or 'third thing' emerges as a product of the transcendent function of the psyche: "The transcendent function is not something one does oneself; it comes rather from experiencing the conflict of opposites" (Jung, 1973, p. 269).[27]

MD   *Let's look outside again at the flexibility of the bushes ... the 'bushes don't have panic attacks.' And now we can see that they are still, there is no wind....*

Kate: *It's a dynamic stillness. They are not rigid, even though they are not moving.*

MD: *What happens when you see that?*

Kate: *I'm back with the need to look at them, and not lose the connection.*

MD: *When you are connected with the bushes, how does your body feel?*

Kate: *I know your sentence makes sense, but it doesn't to me.*[28]

MD: *OK. Let's stay with the connection to the bushes.*

[Kate is aware of the threshold moment at which point she might lose her link with me, but she now knows how to hold her connection with the bushes. Whereas at the beginning of the session Kate closed her eyes when the link was lost, I notice that now she keeps her eyes open.]

It's really important to stay with that connection ... And while you do, I will talk to the group.

[While we wait with Kate, we remain conscious, openly curious but without an agenda. We are allowing time for the new neural pathways to form.]

MD: [I now address the group while Kate is looking out at the bushes, integrating what she is taking in:]

Jung understood that dreams have a prospective function in that they can orient us toward the future. We see this in Kate's dream of the future in which the small bowl the dream ego is holding isn't broken but is complete. It had been damaged but now it's complete as a smaller bowl. It's a lovely image to hold. See if you can all rest into that image, the bowl that has undergone changes and is now complete.

Through the dream, the psyche is pointing to something really important about the process of making a bowl, in particular, a bowl that changes. It's not perfect but it is complete. The image presents a paradox, a stage in the alchemical process during which substances can change and solidify again. And you, Kate, know about that from your knowledge of the process of making bowls.

Kate: *Yes. First you put it in the fire until it changes. It becomes like liquid in the fire and the colours are amazing. The process itself is amazing. It is the* Splendor Solis, *the feast of images. I studied it for my M.A.*

MD: *Then you know about trusting this process.*

[Her familiarity with alchemy confirmed the correlation of the dream process and the alchemical process. My reminding Kate of what she already knows will have the effect of strengthening the neocortex regulation and the integrative circuits of the cortex so that she may build more trust in the psyche's images and the process of transformation.]

Kate: *I suppose I do.*

MD: *And knowing that at each step in the process of transformation the substance changes—whether from* solutio *to* dissolutio *or from* rubedo *to* citronis—*you will know that at each step we meet another layer of a complex. The substance has to change again and again from a solid to a softness to a liquid until it disappears before transforming into a new, small, perfect bowl.*

Kate: *I thought something had corroded it, before it disappeared. There was something beautiful in the* dissolutio.

MD: *Stay with that memory in your body, that there was something beautiful in the* dissolutio.

          (Time passes.)

          You can feel that the changes–the dissolutio *is beautiful. You have been sitting with the bushes—and you're noticing that the process itself, the* dissolutio, *is no longer disconcerting but 'beautiful'.*

[I can feel that Kate has really taken in my words whereas earlier she could hear my words but not understand their meaning. There is a 'top down' and 'bottom up' integration happening. She has held the tension of the opposites between the tendency to dissociate, triggered by the 'changes' on the one hand and, on the other, staying with the bushes, sitting with the 'changing bowl' as Antonius advised ... and by holding the tensions of opposites a 'new conscious attitude' (a 'transcendent third') has emerged in Kate's phrase 'the *dissolutio* is beautiful.']29

You might want to look at the bushes again.

Kate: *They are casual, lovely. They have a casual 'Hi, mate, not doing too badly ... still here', feel. And alchemy doesn't have to be lightning bolts all the time!* Dissolutio *does not always have to happen with lightning bolts. It can happen when we are just 'hanging out'.*

I don't feel the same in my body as I did before we started. I feel comfortable to be, to be comfortably upright.

MD: *You feel comfortably upright. That's good. Keeping your eyes open, look around and see if there is anything you need, anything that needs to happen here. If so, might it have anything to do with your bowl?*

[In orienting Kate back into the room, encouraging her to maintain the link with her open *dissolutio* state, I am attentive to where this new energy wants to go. Mary Hamilton speaks to the importance of such a moment and the role of the 'educator' in serving as midwife to the direction of the energy flow: "The educator then questions where the underlying directive impulses want to go, how they want to be shaped and brought to life. She affirms new possibilities. She knows that if new life is not mirrored and affirmed it tends to re-encase its guiding intelligence in physical tension" (2009, p. 141).]

MD: *Is there anything coming to you?*

Kate: *Maybe it involves everyone standing and being still. I want you all* (addressing the participants in the room) *to be the bowl. Let's stand where we are, in a circle.*30

[Kate's direction is powerful and brings the field even more alive. Hamilton reminds us that "the Self in dreams and the felt impulses of deep inner guidance arise from the same source, a visceral inner source resonating with unknowable facts" (*ibid.*, p. 152).]

Kate: *I would like everyone to listen to the voice under the earth. I had to listen to the voice. I want everyone to listen to that.*

It's part of a great voice, but this is another greener, deeper voice.... I haven't got the words. If everyone would put one ear listening to that all the time no matter what else you are doing, then I would be able to breathe. (She laughs.)

The bowls are wonderful—they help. I have to make them. They are a deep process but they are only half way, they are indicating something deeper. The sound they make, that they

take me into, is really deep. But having listened to the sound it's the silence after the sound, that is the point ... It's the silence.
(Silence... a silence envelops the room.)

Kate: *The bushes are saying that they could make us stay here forever.*
(She smiles. The group breathes and smiles.)

Working with Kate in this particular vas shifted consciousness not only for Kate as the 'client' but for each person who was present in the field. Kate's realization that 'the bushes don't have panic attacks' regulated the field, and dissolved any separation between the participants as separate beings and the bushes outside, gathering us into an experience of the underlying unified field—the *unus mundus* (unitary world). Through BodyDreaming, the therapist aims to link the client and all group participants, if working in a workshop setting, to nature in order to promote participation with the environment through a felt sense engagement with our capacity for perception, neuroception, interoception and proprioception, that is, with the heart's knowing. This is not to induce an unconscious *participation mystique*: the intention is not to experience a state of unconsciousness or trance. BodyDreaming works with the slow, measured steps of orienting, affect regulation, and felt sense cellular resonance, to build the 'Mohawk of Awareness' integrative circuit in the midline of the brain (see Chapter 6, p. 183). Inner attunement and outer orientation, working in tandem, promote an enhanced level of consciousness that 'dissolves' or transcends formerly rigid ego boundaries to enable an experience of an interconnected field. The aim is to enable clients and participants to realize a heightened and more inclusive awareness of themselves, others and the world around them, which amounts to a lived experience of the 'transcendent function of the psyche' that has the power to transform our experience of opposites and difference. In the practice of BodyDreaming we walk the tightrope of the opposites—activation and deactivation, conscious and unconscious, matter and spirit, right hemisphere and left hemisphere, 'top-down' and 'bottom-up' processing—until a new attitude or understanding presents itself as a result of our 'experiencing the conflict of opposites'. It is precisely the development of our capacity to 'experience conflict' and tolerate the tension of opposites on which BodyDreaming focuses. Woodman refers to this way of working as the necessary path of 'building a conscious container' in our bodies and psyches which allows the ego to expand and to receive archetypal energy that can transform but not overwhelm it. Similarly, in the workshop or therapeutic space, the client's (or participants') experience of the 'field' expands through the regulation of affect in an attuned manner in order that the 'container' may become sufficiently strong to take archetypal energies in, as they present themselves. Kate experienced previously unconscious playful energy through the self-regulating relationship that she built with the bushes. In turn, the homeostasis filtered through to the field and, in so doing, transformed fear, dissociation and rigidity into the quicksilver mercurial energy of play and humour. Kate's anxiety and dissociative tendencies had transformed into playful engagement, and commingling with the regulatory bushes their combined presence altered the field – creating a new 'bowl', made up of each individual participant, and resounding with "the silence after the sound". It was an exquisite moment of alignment, similar we could say to the Newgrange image of the Winter Solstice penetrating its light into the depths of the cairn.

Notes

1 Heller and LaPierre (2012) point to signs indicative of when an individual's social engagement system is not fully mobilized as "directly observable in the lack of emotion and expressiveness in the face, the lack of contact and engagement in the eyes, and behaviourally, in the social anxiety and withdrawal they experience" (p. 154).

2 The 'field of consciousness' refers to the quantity of perceptual stimuli, both internal and external, that is included or excluded from awareness (Ogden, Minton and Pain, 2006, p. 68).

3 The bowl is the central image in Kate's dream and is equivalent symbolically to the 'vas', the term used in alchemy to describe the vessel in which the various substances are held and worked in the process of transforming base metal into gold—in psychological terms, in the process of transforming a leaden unconscious attitude into a more enlightened, conscious attitude.

4 The part of the brain known as 'Broca's area' is responsible for language. It lies in the left brain and is affected negatively by heightened limbic activation in the right brain, where implicit memory of trauma is stored (van der Kolk, 2014, p. 45)

> [O]ur scans clearly showed that images of past trauma activate the right hemisphere in the brain and deactivate the left.... Deactivation of the left hemisphere has a direct influence on the capacity to organize experience into logical sequences and to translate our shifting feelings and perceptions into words. (Broca's area, which blacks out during flashbacks, is on the left side.)
> (van der Kolk, 2014, pp. 44–45)

5 Kalsched (1996) writes of the protective function of the self-care system:

> [It] always seems to be the protection of the traumatized remainder of the personal spirit and *his isolation from reality*. Once the trauma defense is organized, all relations with the outer world are 'screened' by the self-care system. What was intended to be a defense against further trauma becomes a major resistance to all unguarded spontaneous expressions of self in the world.
> (Kalsched, 1966, p. 4)

6 The immobilization system all but completely suppresses the social engagement/attachment system. When you are 'scared to death' you have few resources left to orchestrate the complex behaviours that mediate attachment and calming; social engagement is essentially hijacked. The sympathetic nervous system also blocks the social engagement system, but not as completely as does the immobilization system (the most primitive of the three defenses).
> (Levine, 2010, p. 101)

"Attacks on linking manifest themselves in the attempted destruction of the inner mental functioning of patient and analyst, and on the verbal and nonverbal communication which is the link between them" (Bion, 1959, p. 308). Kalsched (1996, p. 36) refers to Bion's 'attacking the links' as an "attack on the very capacity for experience itself ... between affect and image, perception and thought, sensation and knowledge." "Bion's notion of 'attacks on linking' fits Freud's description in *Civilization and its Discontents* (1930) of the death instinct as an instinct seeking to dissolve units. It is also an elaboration of Klein's concept of splitting." Read more: https://www. encyclopedia.com/psychology/dictionaries-thesauruses-pictures-and-press-releases/ linking-attacks.

7 Cozolino addressing moments of heightened arousal, dissociation and trauma suggests "[B]eing simultaneously aware of inner and outer worlds may support a higher level of integration.... this process results in a memory configuration that is no longer 'implicit only' but instead becomes integrated with the contextualizing properties of explicit systems of integration" (2002, p. 277).

8 "The more primitive the operative system, the more power it has to take over the overall function of the organism. It does this by inhibiting the more recent and more refined neurological subsystems, effectively preventing them from functioning" (Levine, 2010, p. 101).

9 The therapist keeps in mind that in orienting to pleasure we are looking for a positive image to down-regulate the *activation.*

10   [S]tudies by David Crosswell and colleagues (2007) at UCLA have demonstrated that middle prefrontal areas including the ventrolateral prefrontal cortex are activated when we name an emotion accurately. This internal labelling is associated with diminished amygdala firing following the observation of an emotionally expressive face – 'name it to tame it.' All in all, the integrated middle of the prefrontal region plays an essential role in monitoring and modifying the firing patterns of the lower limbic brain stem areas. It is this regulation that we need in order to deal with coordination and balance of a nervous system.

(Siegel, 2010, p. 189)

11   Projection is one of the commonest psychic phenomena. It is the same as *participation mystique* ... We merely give it another name, and as a rule deny that we are guilty of it. Everything that is unconscious in ourselves we discover in our neighbour, and we treat him accordingly.

(Jung, 1931, par. 131)

12   According to Panskepp (1998) the hallmark of the play action system is laughter, which strengthens attachment and social bonds. Play reciprocally pairs increased arousal with pleasure and is associated with endorphin production, general well-being, and an increase in physical and mental health.

(Ogden, Minton and Pain, 2006, p. 119)

13 Winnicott (1971) has stated that a primary task of the therapist is to help clients learn to play.

14 "Tronick (1989) offers experiential evidence that the nature of interactive regulation is associated with the adaptiveness of the self-regulation" (Beebe & Lachmann, 2002, p. 158).

15   In essence the deintegration and reintegration describe a fluctuating state of learning in which the infant opens itself to new experiences and then withdraws in order to reintegrate and consolidate those experiences. During a deintegrative activity, the infant maintains continuity with the main body of the self (or its centre) while venturing into the external world to accumulate experience in motor action and sensory stimulation.

(Fordham and Heath, 1989, p. 64)

16   Play behaviour is often usurped by defensive tendencies: fear, agitated movements, freezing, tension or collapse.... The therapist meticulously tracks for incipient playful actions—the beginning of a smile, a joke, or a spontaneous action—and capitalizes on those moments, drawing them out and becoming appropriately playful. Inducing the state of play in clients allows them to begin to enjoy the process of healing, dis-identify with traumatic associations, and engage a new range of possibilities.

(Ogden, Minton and Pain, 2006, pp. 119–120)

17 Gianino and Tronick (1986) have made the integration of interactive regulation and self-regulation central to their work.

Their position is that self-regulation and interactive regulation occur at the same time. The same interactive repertoire with which the infant initiates, maintains, and modifies well-regulated interactions and repairs, avoids, and terminates disrupted interactions simultaneously performs self-regulatory functions.

(Beebe and Lachmann, 2002, p. 158)

18 See *n.* 15 above on deintegration and reintegration.

19   According to Panksepp (1998), 'The hallmark of the play action system is laughter, which strengthens attachment and social bonds.' [And, quoting Schore,] Play reciprocally pairs increased arousal with pleasure and is associated with endorphine production, general well-being and an increase in physical and mental health.

(Ogden, Minton and Pain, 2006, p. 119)

20 Winnicott stressed that psychotherapy must provide opportunities for:

... formless experience, and for creative impulses, motor and sensory, which are the stuff of playing... And on the basis of playing is built the whole of man's experiential existence.... We experience life in the area of transitional phenomena, in the exciting interweave of subjectivity and objective observation, and in an area that is intermediate between inner reality of the individual and the shared reality of the world that is external to individuals.

(Winnicott, [1971] 2005, p. 86)

21 Winnicott, [1962] 1990, p. 60.
22 "Inducing the state of play in clients allows them to begin to enjoy the process of healing, disidentify with traumatic associations, and engage a new range of possibilities" (Ogden, Minton and Pain, 2006, pp. 119–120).
23 "Each new life opportunity is mistakenly seen as a dangerous threat of re-traumatization and is therefore attacked" (Kalsched, 1996, p. 5).
24 Kate wrote her thesis on the alchemical text *Splendor Solis*. Her psyche is steeped in alchemical imagery and she has a deep knowledge of the alchemical process of transformation, which Jung equated with the psyche's natural process of individuation. Jung saw alchemy as a metaphor for the process of growth that an individual embarks on in analysis. I did not know about Kate's interest in alchemy at this stage of our work.
25 In alchemy this process is referred to as 'dissolutio'.
26   The tremendous role which the opposites and their union play in alchemy helps us to understand why the alchemists were so fond of paradoxes. In order to attain this

union, they tried not only to visualize the opposites together but to express them in the same breath.

(Jung, 1955, par. 36)

27   Jung, 1973, Letters Vol.1, Letter to M. Zarine, 1939, p. 269.

Old Heraclitus, who was indeed a very great sage, discovered the most marvellous of all psychological laws: the regulative function of opposites. He called it *enantiodromia*, a running contrariwise, by which he meant that sooner or later everything runs into its opposite.

(Jung, 1917, par. 111)

"There is no energy unless there is a tension of opposites; hence it is necessary to discover the opposite to the attitude of the conscious mind" (Jung, 1917, par. 78).

28   Here again we see an 'attack on linking' and how activation in the limbic system is affecting the Broca region of the brain, making it impossible for Kate to follow my thoughts or the meaning of my words. In this regard, Kalsched speaks to the relentless nature of the self-care system: "As much as he or she wants to change, as hard as he or she tries to improve life or relationships, something more powerful than the ego continually undermines progress and destroys hope" (1996, p. 5). "Over the years of my clinical practice I have observed how, repeatedly, this tyrannical 'system' seems to take over the personality after trauma.... The system constitutes an archetypal defense against new life and the urge toward individuation" (Kalsched, 2013, pp. 82–83).

29   How the harmonizing of conscious and unconscious data is to be undertaken cannot be indicated in the form of a recipe.... Out of this union emerge new situations and new conscious attitudes. I have therefore called the union of opposites the 'transcendent function.' This rounding out of the personality into a whole may well be the goal of any psychotherapy that claims to be more than a mere cure of symptoms.

(Jung, 1939, par. 524)

30   Kate addresses the participants directly, which is an interesting mirror or bracketing to what happened at the beginning of this session when I tentatively drew Kate's attention to the supportive presence of the group, saying to her, *"maybe we can all hold that (anxiety) with you in the room."* The group, which had developed holes, has in the process become a mirror image of the 'complete' dream bowl. She can sit and play with it, as 'bowl maker' Antonius advised.

References

Abram, D. (1997) *The Spell of the Sensuous*, New York: Vintage Books.

Beebe, B. and Lachmann, F. (2002) *Infant Research and Adult Treatment: Co-constructing Interactions*, Hillsdale, NJ: The Analytic Press.

Bion, W.R. (1959) "Attacks on Linking," *International Journal of Psychoanalysis*, 40: 308–315. Reprinted in: *Second Thoughts* (1967), New York: Jason Aronson, pp. 93–109.

Cozolino, L. (2002) *The Neuroscience of Psychotherapy: Building and Rebuilding the Human Brain*, New York: W.W. Norton & Co.

Fordham, M. and Heath, B. (1989) "The Infant's Reach: Reflections on Maturation in Early Life," *Psychological Perspectives: A Quarterly Journal of Jungian Thought,* 21 (1): 59–76.

Freud, S. ([1930] 2001) *The Standard Edition of the Complete Psychological Works of Sigmund Freud. Vol. 21, 1927–1931, The Future of an Illusion; Civilisation and its Discontents; and Other Works,* London: Hogarth Press and The Institute of Psycho-Analysis.

Gianino, A. and Tronick, E.Z. (1986) "Interactive Mismatch and Repair: Challenges to the Coping Infant," *ZERO TO THREE, Bulletin of the National Center for Clinical Infant Programs* 5: 1–6. Reprinted in: Tronick, E.Z., (2007) *The Neurobehavioural and Social–Emotional Development of Infants and Children,* New York: W.W. Norton, pp. 155–163.

Hamilton, M. (2009) *The Dragon Fly Principal: An Exploration of the Body's Function in Unfolding Spirituality,* London and Ontario: Colenso Island Press.

Heller, L. and LaPierre, A. (2012) *Healing Developmental Trauma: How Early Trauma Affects Self-Regulation, Self-Image, and the Capacity for Relationship,* Berkeley, CA: North Atlantic Books.

Jung, C.G. ([1916] 1958) *The Transcendent Function,* Collected Works 8, Princeton, NJ: Princeton University Press.

Jung, C.G. (1917) *On the Psychology of the Unconscious,* Collected Works 7, Princeton, NJ: Princeton University Press.

Jung, C.G. (1931) *Archaic Man,* Collected Works 10, Princeton, NJ: Princeton University Press.

Jung, C.G. (1939) *Conscious, Unconscious, and Individuation,* Collected Works 9/1, Princeton, NJ: Princeton University Press.

Jung, C.G. (1955) *The Components of the Coniunctio,* Collected Works 14, Princeton, NJ: Princeton University Press.

Jung, C.G. (1973) *Letters, Vol. 1, 1906–1950,* G. Adler (ed.), trans. R.F.C. Hull, Princeton, NJ: Princeton University Press.

Kalsched, D. (1996) *The Inner World of Trauma: Archetypal Defences of the Personal Spirit,* London: Routledge.

Kalsched, D. (2013) *Trauma and the Soul: A Psycho-Spiritual Approach to Human Development and its Interruption,* London: Routledge.

Knox, J. (2011) *Self-Agency in Psychotherapy: Attachment, Autonomy and Intimacy,* London: W.W. Norton and Co.

Levine, P. (1997) *Waking the Tiger: Healing Trauma – The Innate Capacity to Transform Overwhelming Experiences,* Berkeley, CA: North Atlantic Books.

Levine, P. (2010) *In an Unspoken Voice: How the Body Releases Trauma and Restores Goodness,* Berkeley, CA: North Atlantic Books.

Neumann, E. (1989) *Place of Creation,* Bollingen Series LX1 – 3, Princeton, NJ: Princeton University Press.

Ogden, P., Minton, K. and Pain, C. (2006) *Trauma and the Body: A Sensorimotor Approach to Psychotherapy,* London and New York: W.W. Norton & Co.

Siegel, D.J. (2010) *The Mindful Therapist: A Clinician's Guide to Mindsight and Neural Integration,* New York: W.W. Norton & Co.

Stein, M. (1998) *Transformation: Emergence of the Self,* Texas: A&M University Press.

van der Kolk, B. (2014) *The Body Keeps the Score: Mind, Brain and Body in the Transformation of Trauma*, St Ives, UK: Penguin Random House.

Winnicott, D.W. ([1962] 1990) "Ego Integration in Child Development," in *The Maturational Process and the Facilitating Environment: Studies in the Theory of Emotional Development*, London: Karnac Books.

Winnicott, D.W. ([1971] 2005) *Playing and Reality*, London and New York: Routledge.

Yeoman, A. (1998) *Now or Neverland: Peter Pan and the Myth of Eternal Youth: A Psychological Perspective on a Cultural Icon*, Studies in Jungian Psychology, 82, Toronto: Inner City Books.

Chapter 8

The Matter of Self-Regulation
"The sun is coming out of her face"

> *How*
> *did the rose*
> *ever open its heart*
> *and give to this world all of its beauty?*
> *It felt the encouragement of light against its being,*
> *otherwise we all remain too*
> *frightened.*
> (Hafiz, "How Did the Rose?", translated
> by Daniel Ladinsky)[1]

*

In previous chapters, the emphasis has been on repatterning nervous system responses largely established by early attachment patterns and encoded in the wiring of the brain (Ainsworth, cited in Schore, 2003).[2] I selected examples of work with clients to demonstrate how the incorporation of a somatic approach when working with attachment patterns is often effective in *uncoupling*, over time, habitual responses and their resultant behaviours. In BodyDreaming, we work to build the client's capacity for *self*-regulation through the *interactive* regulation promoted in the therapeutic relationship. To enable the release and constructive *expression* of energy that has been locked in body symptom, attachment pattern or psychic disturbance, we emphasize attunement (mirroring, prosody, social engagement); affect regulation (resourcing through positive experiences and images); titration of affect; and interoception, coupled with felt sense body scanning. The aim is to restore the *whole* system (psyche *and* soma) to homeostasis, and to create new neural pathways to realign the nervous system and transform its habitual responses to both inner and outer stimuli. The work enables us to attune to unconscious processes moving in body-mind-psyche and supports the growth of a learned secure attachment to the body and the development of a strong dialogue with the regulating 'Other' as found in the field in which we engage.

In this and the following chapter, I will explore the idea that as we develop a learned secure attachment to the body, we become aware of the "living body"—our instinctual nature—and understand that our matter *matters*, and through it we are brought into greater alignment with that regulatory Other, which Jung refers to as the Self. Quoting from Nietzsche's *Thus Spake Zarathustra*, Jung writes: "out of that living body everything originally has come … Zarathustra says to go back to the body, go into the body, and then everything will be right, for there the greatest intelligence is hidden" (1988, p. 370). We come to experience our own matter as part of a greater consciousness guided by the same laws of coherence and order that David Bohm calls the *Implicate Order* (1980), and that underlie all life forms and natural processes. We can align with this 'greater consciousness', the organic intelligence of the planet, or the Self, in Jungian terms, when we bring awareness to our nervous system's natural stabilizing rhythm that is innate and that offers us an entry to a wider consciousness and a greater sense of interconnectedness.

When working with early trauma to restore the autonomic nervous system's organic rhythm of expansion and contraction, we may tune into this larger, regulating consciousness. We may begin to sense the invisible hand of Self-regulatory[3] guidance in an individual's system as it presents in the form of healing gesture, image or emotion and felt sense reciprocity with what is around us. We may feel resonance at a level at which body, psyche, emotion and meaning seem to coalesce and, in that moment, experience the felt sense of an alignment with something greater than ego-consciousness, an embodied consciousness of the ego-Self axis (Edinger, 1972). Scientist, inventor and author Itzhak Bentov pointed out in 1988 that the micro-rhythm of our pulse reflects the rhythm of the planets orbiting the sun in our universe. "We are," he writes, "energy—pure energy—pulsing cell to cell" (cited in Reeves, 2003, p. 23). Bentov argues that the 'pulsing' of the human organism synchronizes with the vibrational patterns of the earth. He describes all matter as comprised of atoms which have orbiting electrons that create a vibrational pulse. In this way, the body mirrors the universe: as the planets orbit the sun, so the electrons orbit the nuclei of the atoms in each cell. Reeves comments that "constant motion of all matter, not just the body, is both solid matter that you can see and feel and energy fields that can only be seen and measured by machines" (*ibid.*). Bentov points out that the planet 'oscillates' at around 7.5 cycles per second, as does the micro-motion (the cellular pulse) of the body, the alpha rhythm of the brain and the low-level magnetic pulsation of the earth (cited in Reeves, *ibid.*). This continuous electromagnetic pulse links each individual body to the rise and fall of the beat of the planet and is met, in response, by the entire solar system. Bentov states that "[t]he universe and all matter is consciousness in the process of developing" (*ibid.*, p. 23). We are part of that greater consciousness and bringing this rhythmical connection to awareness in the body in a focused way enhances homeostasis, stimulating health and well-being.

In BodyDreaming we work to create the conditions in which we may experience our body-mind-psyche in relation to an 'expanded consciousness', or sense of wholeness, that is, as part of a larger dynamic field. Anne Baring, Jungian analyst and author, describes this sense of wholeness as "… a holographic quantum universe … [in which] … everything is connected to everything else in what is virtually a stupendous intelligent field of information and a unifying web of life" (2013, p. 350). Baring claims that this "returning concept of wholeness or unity is at a new level of the spiral of evolution ..." (*ibid.*). I would like to think that BodyDreaming plays a small part in the development of the evolutionary spiral about which Anne Baring speaks, facilitating a greater sense of connection and interconnection through the attunement process which enables us, at times, to experience "a participatory awareness of the unified nature of all cosmic and planetary life" (*ibid.*) as we experience our matter, our body, infused with psyche and *vice versa.*

The Chinese story of the Rainmaker,[4] which Jung loved to tell, addresses a situation where there is a lack of underlying order—resulting in a drought in the land. The rainmaker was invited to help and he withdrew to a retreat saying "*Here they are out of order*". He had to wait three days until he "was *back in Tao and then naturally the rain came.*" To be back in Tao is to experience a restoration of the sense of oneness with the natural order—*unus mundus*. The story illustrates the inherent possibility of alignment between ourselves and the natural world. In BodyDreaming when we bring our nervous systems back into homeostasis through pendulating between the opposites, we can attain a state, in Fechner's (1873) terms, of "greater harmony and pleasure", both in ourselves and between ourselves and the world around us. As a result, we may find ourselves more open to our dream images and the stirrings of the somatic unconscious as we recognize ourselves as participants in a BodyDreaming universe that is living, breathing, and dreaming itself through us. Abram writes of this essentially participatory engagement with the world when he writes: "We come to know more of this sphere not by detaching ourselves from our felt experience but by inhabiting our bodily experience all the more richly and wakefully, feeling our way into deeper contact with other experiencing bodies, and hence with the wild intercorporeal life of the earth itself" (2011, pp. 143–144). In this way, we uncover our innate potential for a conversation between inner and outer that, in turn, fosters a sense of alignment, flow and participation with and in the world of which, of course, we are a part. In terms of the metaphor threaded throughout this text, we might call this evolving conversation 'a Newgrange moment'.

For the past century, physicists have been exploring a quantum level of interconnectedness that is both inner and outer, material and psychic, particle and wave, and that implicates both perceiver (scientist) and perceived (object). David Bohm teaches that the "present approach of analysis of the world into independently existing parts ... in interaction ... does not work" and that "the primary emphasis is now on the undivided wholeness ... of the universe ... in which the observing instrument is not separable from what is observed" (1980, p. 192). It is in the context of such groundbreaking changes in our world-view that Jung developed his map of the unconscious, including what he called 'the collective unconscious':

> [T]he mighty deposit of ancestral experience accumulated over millions of years, the echo of prehistoric happenings ... the collective unconscious is, in

the last analysis, a deposit of world-processes embedded in the structure of
the brain and the sympathetic nervous system.

(Jung, 1928, par. 729)

Jung firmly situates the contents of the archaic collective unconscious in both
psyche and body, brain and nervous system, of the modern-day individual. In
the somatic and psychic unconscious, we are implicitly connected to 'prehistoric
happenings'. And through BodyDreaming, we may develop the possibility of
experiencing a connection to this deeper layer of consciousness as we discover
the capacity to resonate with the wider field, the *unus mundus*.[5] We may recall
Kate's session in Chapter 7, and her comment that "the bushes don't have panic
attacks". The external world was at hand to support Kate's activation, enabling
her to remain present in a room full of participants as we worked on her dream.
Just as she had listened to the bushes and had been affected by their presence, at
the close of her session Kate invited the group to listen to the silence that was
beneath the ground, to commune with the silent pulsating rhythm of the universe.
The silence felt palpable and full.

Eric Neumann reminds us that Western consciousness has tended to become
polarized, validating ego-consciousness over more instinctual, intuitive forms
of awareness, distinguishing inner from outer, matter from psyche. He argues
that we can no longer afford to polarize outer physical, biological matter and the
inner psychic world, and are in need of a new image of ourselves and our position in the world to "counterbalance the atomization … [that has happened to our
sense of] … our outer reality" (1989, p. 4). Neumann's proposed image or picture
of ourselves and the world recognizes "reality" as "unitary", an undivided field
in which matter and psyche are seen as indivisible or, as Jung writes, "it is not
only possible but fairly probable, even, that psyche and matter are two different
aspects of one and the same thing" (1947, par. 418). While Neumann does not
underestimate the importance and necessity of ego-consciousness, he points out
that "ego-consciousness only represents one particular form of knowledge whose
clarity, precision, and applicability to the ego is dearly paid for with its one-sidedness"
(1989, p. 7). He recognizes that consciousness is in fact multi-layered, comprising
"differing intensities of consciousness" (*ibid.*, p. 6) and opening to "extraneous
knowledge … [and] … other forms of knowing" that lie beyond the reach of a
rational ego which dismisses such knowledge as false or illusory (*ibid.*, p. 7). In
this brief reference to Neumann's argument, I can only suggest the richness and
complexity of his model of an essentially undivided human being in relation to
an indivisible world, that "unitary reality" which structures and sustains all forms
of life. I can, however, take from it Neumann's reminder that we do not have
to be shamans or mystics to experience "other forms of knowing", as we intuit
and connect to powers and "knowing" beyond the reach of the conscious mind
through active imagination, attending to our body's resonances and listening to
new impulses, exploring dreams and participating in creative process. Particularly
relevant to the practice of BodyDreaming is Neumann's point that differing

intensities of consciousness lying outside the focus of ego-consciousness may, if ego-consciousness turns "toward a previously unknown or unconscious content", be lifted "into the light of consciousness" (*ibid.*, p. 6). I believe that the process of BodyDreaming allows us to begin to chart the territory of which Neumann speaks—a territory in which there is no sharp distinction between psyche and matter, and where "boundaries between inner and outer, psychic and physical realms melt away" (*ibid.*, p. 24). In moments when we recognize that we are in the previously uncharted waters of "extraneous knowing", we may expect the unexpected—a felt sense experience of awe or fear or communion, perhaps, indicative of an encounter with the numinous.

In these final two chapters, I will further develop the ideas introduced above—namely, that our matter and all matter is alive, and that by developing a more regulated secure base within our own matter we may discover ourselves to be in a participatory relationship with the matter around us. In such moments, we may find that the world is not inanimate but alive, interactive and reciprocal: we may find ourselves participating in what Neumann refers to as a "unified field … [whose] biological and psychologically deeper layers … are alive in every person-ality … where psychical and physical matters are no longer polar opposites, the firm outline, defining a person or form, becomes blurred" (1989, p. 21). In attach-ment terms this experience of a unitary reality deepens our regulatory field; we discover ourselves attached in our living bodies to all matter. I suggest that such 'moments of recognition' are threshold moments when, as at Newgrange, an outer and inner experience coincide, and open us to an experience of the numinous.[6]

By recognizing the dynamic reciprocity alive between all matter, we uncover our 'living body' as participant in the matter around us. We experience ourselves as intrinsically part of where we stand rather than as separate, alienated, fragmented or dissociated. We reach beyond the boundaries of the ego to touch, and be touched by, the phenomenal world 'outside' ourselves. In Chapter 7, Kate's recognition that "bushes don't have panic attacks" while regulating her also expanded 'the field'. Her social engagement system employed both play and humour to further regulate herself and the group, ultimately leading to an expansion of conscious-ness, repairing the bowl, making the circle whole again. We stood, experiencing a silent reality that was 'unitary', participants in a unus mundus.

The numinous quality of such an experience may be highly activating, arous-ing feelings of awe and fear. The BodyDreaming therapist, firstly, regulates the emotions, titrating between expansion and contraction, giving all the time that is needed to titrate this 'expanded state'. The possibility of an experience of the numinous is intrinsic to our nature and, as Cedrus Monte would claim, to our very flesh: "The numen is within the flesh as the flesh, and accessible to us if we allow ourselves the opportunity to discover it" (2015, p. 78). By establishing an embod-ied home for our soul in our body, we begin to realize that our body and soul, psyche and matter, are indivisible, each reflectors of the *numinous*, the "hint of the god."[7] The flesh (our matter) serves as a conduit for psyche; it is the concrete aspect of the soul through which we encounter the *numinous*.

Following Jung's claim that "the distinction between mind and body is an artificial dichotomy" (1931, par. 916)," I will focus on my work with two clients
whose experiences provide poignant images of the "intimate ... intermingling of
bodily and psychic traits" (*ibid.*). The transcripts track the moment by moment
interactions that in many ways may be seen to prepare us for the embodied realization of our participation in a "unitary reality".

*

Ana was a participant in a short, introductory course on BodyDreaming that I
offered to students in an analytical psychology training programme. I led an exercise on Levine's use of a resource as a self-regulating tool and invited members of
the group to orient toward a positive resource—a memory, person, animal, activity,
object or place—whatever made them feel good. They were asked to spend some
time with their experience of the chosen resource and later register any changes
that might have taken place in their bodies as a result. At the end of the exercise,
Ana was clearly animated and shared her experience with the rest of the group. She
had chosen *food* as her resource. She had been excited to do the exercise, to *feed*
on her resource but the positive image had flipped into its opposite and activated an
old complex.[8] She had been reminded of her early experiences of *lack* while being
fed by her mother. (As a therapist, it is important to be prepared for a situation such
as this. Introducing an orienting or resourcing exercise is intended to support the
process of *de*activation but the opposite—activation—may just as easily result: an
archetypal dynamic can flip from one extreme, or pole, to the other in an instant.)

Below is the dialogue that followed Ana's disclosure that an old complex had
been triggered:

Ana: *When you asked us to find a resource, I realized I saw an image of my*
         mother with a bag. She had a brown handbag ... it smelt of tobacco, not
         filter cigarettes as there were none available in those days. It was full of
         loose tobacco. The first image that followed was of smoking ... then came
         food. I was taking in all kinds of food.

MD: *How did that image feel in your body?*

Ana: *My muscles felt tense and sore. I felt the familiar pain in my stomach,*
         and I know I used to dissociate trying not to feel the pain, using food and
         cigarettes to medicate myself.[9]

MD: *You are describing for us an experience of activation. Perhaps the image*
         of food triggered the memory of your mother who may not have fed you
         the food your body wanted and needed. The body memory may be held in
         your sore, tense muscles.

         It's not that you didn't do the exercise correctly now. This is just
         what came up for you. You have been activated, an implicit memory was
         triggered, perhaps bringing with it the body memory. And you brought
         meaning to it. You made a story ... understanding that you ate food—any
         food—as a means to cut yourself off from the pain you were feeling.

[I join with Ana in meaning-making, top-down processing, using the neocortex to calm the limbic arousal while still allowing just enough space for emotion. If we were to move too quickly into the emotion at this stage, we would be following the familiar, well-worn pathways of the complex, finding ourselves pulled into the trauma vortex. Instead, I mirror the trajectory of Ana's experience back to her in a clear manner, addressing the emotion but ensuring the meaning-making circuit of the neocortex remains engaged].

[Discussion draws in the witnessing self, which is distinct from the complexed self, and this seems to settle Ana's nervous system; she is no longer activated so I invite her to notice how she is in her body. She reports that her breath has dropped, her heart rate has decreased, and she is feeling less over-heated. She is present, curious and open to what is happening in the 'here and now' in her body and psyche. She picks up the conversation.]

Ana: *When you introduced the exercise and said 'resource', the word 'food' came to mind. I love to eat food, to be together with friends, eating—that is the resource that food is for me.*

MD: *What do you feel in your body when you think of food as a resource?*

Ana: *I feel good. It's something I enjoy. I can do right. I have the image of being with friends in a restaurant.*

MD: *Is there a particular restaurant that you have in mind?*

[I am opening a Free Association right hemisphere conversation, allowing Ana's associations to form and to further the regulation.]

Ana: *The pizza place on the corner.*

MD: *Let's take some time to see yourself sitting there with friends in the pizza place on the corner.*

   What do you notice happening in your body as you see yourself there?

Ana: *I can feel the place; people are happy to serve us. They ask us what we want to eat. I can say 'this is what I want' and not feel bad. I feel good when I can choose what I want to eat.*

   They ask me what I want and I can tell them exactly what I want.

MD: *How does your body respond to that?*

Ana: *This sensation, this pleasure goes right down into the stomach.*

   [Ana is tracking the felt sense of the pleasure in the experience.]

MD: *That's great, and you can feel the pleasure now down in your stomach?*

Ana: *Yes, and I see my grandmother.* (The sensation of pleasure evokes a memory.)

MD: *You feel the pleasure in your stomach and you can see your grandmother.*

Ana: *Yes, and she is making schnitzels.*

MD: *She is making schnitzels.*

[In repeating her phrase, I mirror back to her the sound, emotion, and resonance of how I heard those words in my own body. I notice that there is a shift from the negative end of the 'archetypal pole' of the mother complex—the pain of the empty stomach with the failure of the mother's feeding—to the opposite, the positive end, that is, to what will become the full stomach with the grandmother's loving feeding.]

MD: *Take a minute to really smell the schnitzels.*

Ana: *Yes. I feel happy.*

MD: *Where do you feel the happiness in your body?*

Ana: *In my stomach ... it feels warm.* (Pause.) *It feels full of love.* (She smiles.)

MD: *That's beautiful.*

Ana: *I feel the sheer love of this woman.*

MD: *You can feel the sheer love of this woman. ... That's beautiful.*

Ana: *I tell her that her schnitzels are going right down into my kidneys. I used to say that as a child to my granny—that her schnitzels are going into my kidneys.* (She is smiling.)

MD: (I join with her pleasure and smile.) *You used to tell your granny that her schnitzels are going right down into your kidneys ... Allow yourself to really feel that ... the goodness of the schnitzel going down to your kidneys.*

Ana: *And her love, too, her smile, the pleasure that she had in feeding me.*

MD: *And let your whole body respond to that pleasure she had in feeding you ... do you feel your tummy warm with the love she is feeding you?*

Ana: *Yes, I feel my tummy warm and every bone in my body, every cell is feeling this love. I can see the sun is coming out of her face.*

MD: [As I repeat "the sun is coming out of her face" and "every bone in your body is drinking it up, she is feeding every bone with love" ... I am noticing Ana's face—her face is smiling and filled with light.]
      What do you notice about your own face?

Ana: *I keep smiling. I see my grandmother's white hair, blue eyes, full of love.*

MD: *Your grandmother's face is 'full of love' and that makes your face smile. She is full of love for you, Ana. What a treasure! Feel into and enjoy how your whole body responds to her love.*

[Observers and observed in the shared field—we each participate in the archetypal force of the grandmother's love for Ana, experienced at a cellular level. A smile radiates around the room.]

At the beginning of the exercise, Ana had been caught at one extreme of the activation/deactivation spectrum by the negative feelings that arose with the image of her mother; she also suffered physical pain with the accompanying tightening of her tummy muscles. We allowed space for the recognition of her pain and feelings: the memory of the brown bag, the smell of tobacco, and the meaning Ana drew from the recollection that she ate food ("no matter what") to "medicate" herself against the pain of her mother's not feeding her the food she wanted. By tracking body sensation, emotion and linking it to meaning, the memory remained available to Ana but did not further activate her. We acknowledged the triggering complex, and with top-down processing Ana was able to regulate. Without any conscious direction on my part, her energy was drawn quite naturally towards the opposing positive image, the resource she had discovered in 'food'. The result was the pleasurable image of being with friends in a favourite restaurant, asking for what she wanted to eat and receiving it from a waiter who was happy to serve her. This stage in the process must not be hurried or over-looked; allowing the body to respond to the image is integral to the natural, healthy process of oscillation between activation and deactivation. We need to remind ourselves, that body and psyche are inseparable, two aspects of one and the same thing. What we witnessed with Ana amounts to a reciprocity between body sensation and psyche (image/memory) in receiving an experience of pleasure; in Fechner's terms, it amounts to the 'just noticeable difference' that fires new synapses and opens new neural pathways. The body needs time to open itself to receive the pleasure of the image, and the attunement of the therapist is crucial to titrate any activation that results. As in a homeopathic process, in BodyDreaming the new feelings that will counteract the presenting issue need to be incorporated drop by drop, otherwise the new pathways will not be laid down. Schore comments: "You have to be *in* the emotion to learn how to regulate it in a new way—talking about it is not enough" (in conversation with Sieff, 2015, p. 132). The slow focused tracking and mirroring of Ana's positive experience amplifies her emotional experience and creates just the right degree of emotion to lessen the original wounding experienced in the attachment relationship.[10] The pain of the developmental trauma (her traumatized and imprisoned parents in the time of her country's invasion) is slowly being titrated in the 'here and now' experience of receiving her grandmother's pleasure at a cellular level within the mutuality of their exchange—the giving and receiving of love in the schnitzels. In this way, we are slowly laying down new pathways in the attachment circuit and creating a learned secure attachment to her sensing body. Woodman and Dickson comment, "If you want to live your own life, your images and your body are your individual guides. Together they strengthen your inner core" (1996, p. 195).

As Ana inhabited the memory of being fed by her grandmother, the effect on her sensing body took on a numinous quality in herself and in the field. The group both witnessed and were participant in the 'expansion of consciousness'. Through the aid of mirror neurons and heart to heart, cell to cell communication, Ana's experience was received and felt by each sensing body present in the room. Ana's smile became more radiant, her skin was filled with light ("every bone in my body, every cell is feeling this love"). By slowing down the process of attunement, we allowed Ana's body to experience fully the sensation of pleasure, ushering in what Cedrus Monte refers to as the healing '*numen of the flesh*' (2015, p. 78). The numinous experience forges a participation in the group; each person is touched at a cellular level. Ana's radiant smile reflects both the inner love she receives now from her grandmother and that love which is mirrored back to her from the participating field. As Woodman and Dickson state, "what is going on in the heart and mind of the perceiver will be picked up in the body of the perceived" (1996, p. 197). Reciprocity between image and body (psyche and soma), as well as the sensing, resonating 'body' of the group, is powerfully shared by all. The *temenos*, or container, that we had created was attuned to the radiance of Ana's smiling face, and through the resonating body each, in her own way, was able to participate in something of the mystery of the numinosity of the flesh.

In terms of the metaphor of Newgrange, the winter sun penetrates matter—the depths of the cairn—as it illuminates the chamber at the end of the passageway, revealing the architecture and carvings and the powerful mystery present in the stone. The inner chamber reveals the hidden treasure of the standing stone with the triple spiral carving, concealed from light except during the solstice days of midwinter. At the heart of BodyDreaming lies the hope that the work may support the body to open to its own 'Winter Solstice' experience, when the body's self-regulating system reveals its 'hidden' nature, the *numen* of its flesh. Monte affirms that "the nature of matter itself [is] to embody and transmit the numinous experience" (2015, p. 78), a truly relational energy that is participatory, bringing us into an expanded state of consciousness in a moment of reciprocity.

As we have seen with Ana, an experience of reciprocity does not always occur between the living matter of a human body and the living matter of something outside that body, in nature. It may occur between our own matter and a memory or an image originating in and arising from the body, as is often experienced in the practice of *active imagination*.[11] When we locate where, in the body, there is resonance with the image, we experience a felt sense of a *conversation* between image and body—psyche and soma—as we notice how the body responds to the image. In this reciprocal way, image brings light—awareness—to flesh, matter, and matter, body, enlivens the image. Reciprocity and insight occur in the shared field, the in-between space of the resonating body and the image. Awakening our flesh in this way to its inherent *numinosity*, its own power to be fully alive with *Chi*/spirit, is the ultimate goal of the BodyDreaming process. We are creating what in Jungian terms is called the 'subtle body'. Woodman and Dickson comment, "With concentrated work, opaque matter gradually transforms toward more subtle matter. Jung understood the subtle body as the soul body or energy present in matter" (1996, p. 196). The work necessitates the creation of a safe space or *temenos* in which the body feels respected, safe, and attuned to; only then can it retrieve its self-regulating function, relinquish its defensive strategies, extend its consciousness beyond the boundaries of the six senses, and open itself, perhaps, to receive an experience of the *numen* in the flesh, a reciprocity of spirit and matter.

A week later Ana and I met on the street. She said, with a big knowing smile, "I get it. In BodyDreaming, the resource, the positive image, is the mother, the good mother. It *is* like having a good feed." Jung maintains that it is through an encounter with the *numinous* that "real therapy" is possible, and that "inasmuch as you attain to the numinous experience you are released from the curse of pathology."[12] Ana's experience in BodyDreaming had helped to establish new neural pathways in her attachment circuit and when we met, a week later, she was delighted to tell me that she had the capacity to give herself a good feed, to be a good 'grandmother' to herself. The real healing happened individually for Ana and collectively through the group's witnessing and participation in the recognition of the love that radiated through the 'numen' of the flesh; in Ana's words "*I feel the sheer love of this woman.*"

Notes

1 Ladinsky, 2002, p. 161.
2 "[A]ttachment is more than overt behaviour, it is internal, 'being built into the nervous system in the course and as a result of the infant's experience of his transactions with the mother'" (Ainsworth, 1967, p. 429, cited in Schore, 2003, p. 12).
3 Jung's term the 'Self' was adopted from Nietzsche's coining of the term in his *Thus Spake Zarathustra*. Jung's development of the concept in his analytical psychology was influenced by Eastern religion, Gnosticism and alchemy, as well as his encounters with indigenous communities in America, Africa and India. Jung writes:

> My definition of the self is as a non-personal center, the center of the psychical non-ego—of all that in the psyche which is not ego—and presumably is to be found everywhere in all people. You can call it the center of the collective unconscious.
>
> (Jung, 1988, p. 783)

4 Jung, 1970, pp. 419–420, para. 604.
5 Marie Louise von Franz, quoting Jung, reminds us that Jung postulates:

> the reality which we seek introspectively to describe as the collective unconscious might be the same unknown and uncognizable reality that atomic physics seeks to describe from the 'outside as material reality.' Therefore Jung even asserted he would have no objection to regarding the psyche as a quality of matter and matter as a concrete aspect of the psyche, provided that the psyche was understood to be the collective unconscious. This is just simply nature, 'nature that contains everything, therefore also unknown things … including matter.'
>
> (von Franz, 1988, p. 40)

Note also: "Synchronistic events … seem to point toward a *unitary aspect of existence* which transcends our conscious grasp and which Jung called the *unus mundus*" (*ibid.*).
6 Jung describes the *numen* (or *numinous*) as:

> a dynamic agency or effect not caused by an arbitrary act of will. On the contrary, it seizes and controls the human subject, who is always rather its victim than its creator. The *numinosum*—whatever its cause may be—is an experience of the subject independent of his will … The *numinosum* is either a quality belonging to a visible object or the influence of an invisible presence that causes a peculiar alteration of consciousness.
>
> (Jung, 1938, par. 6)

7 "[I]n the least the greatest will appear—such is your expectation. And that is the *numen*, the hint of the god" (Jung, 1997, p. 919).
8 Jung borrowed the term *enantiodromia* from Heraclitus. It means "running counter to" and Heraclitus used it "to designate the play of opposites in the course of events—the view that everything that exists turns into its opposite" (1921, par. 708). Important to us is Heraclitus's tenet, "It is the opposite which is good for us," and we will see that the negative image into which Ana's positive image flips is the precise counterpole; the 'necessary' resource, needed in order to effect healing and insight. This shows us, as James Hillman argues in *The Dream and the Underworld*, that opposites are not, in fact, irreconcilable, but two polar forces of one and the same power:

> [O]nly similars can be opposites. Only those pairs having something material, essential in common can be sensibly opposed. A turkey cannot be opposed to a

theorem, unless we can discover in what way they are like each other. ... [We may regard] ... opposition as an extreme metaphor, a radical way of saying one thing as though it were two violently differing things in sharp war ... Oppositionalism distinguishes by drawing to extremes. These extremes must touch, because they need each other for the distinction to become apparent.

(Hillman, 1979, p. 84)

In the language of BodyDreaming, Hillman's term, 'oppositionalism', describes the compensatory dynamic of the unconscious psyche when the client is 'presented' with the precise image (resource) that is required to initiate the process of self-regulation, insight and healing.

9 Ana was born during a time when the Soviet army invaded her country. Her parents were politically active in protests and both suffered imprisonment during her early childhood. Ana was cared for by her grandmother.

10 "An affect cannot be restrained or neutralized except by a contrary affect that is stronger than the affect to be restrained" (Spinoza cited in Damasio, 2003, p. 12).

11 "In its most basic sense, active imagination is opening to the unconscious and giving free rein to fantasy while, at the same time, maintaining a conscious viewpoint" (Chodorow, 1999, p. 223). Murray Stein describes active imagination:

[as a] major tool that Jung and Jungians and Post-Jungians ... use for setting up a *path of communication* between the conscious and the unconscious ... between the known and the unknown ... trying to come into contact with it, bring it into the light of day, look at it and assimilate it ... so it is part of the project of assimilating conscious and unconscious, bringing them together, letting them interact.

(Personal notes from a lecture on Active Imagination
by Murray Stein, ISAP, Zürich, 2010)

12 "[T]he main interest of my work is not concerned with the treatment of neuroses but rather with the approach to the numinous" (Jung, 1973, p. 377).

References

Abram, D. (2011) *Becoming Animal*, New York: Vintage Books.

Baring, A. (2013) *Dream of the Cosmos: A Quest for the Soul*, Dorset, UK: Archive Publishing.

Bohm, D. (1980) *Wholeness and the Implicate Order*, London, Boston, MA, and Henley, UK: Routledge and Kegan Paul.

Chodorow, J. (1999) "Joan Chodorow," in *Authentic Movement: Essays by Mary Starks Whitehouse, Janet Adler and Joan Chodorow*, Patrizia Pallaro (ed.), London and Philadelphia, PA: Jessica Kingsley Publishers, pp. 209–311.

Damasio, A. (2003) *Looking for Spinoza: Joy, Sorrow, and the Feeling Brain*, Orlando, FL: Harcourt Books.

Edinger, E.F. (1972) *Ego and Archetype: Individuation and the Religious Function of the Psyche*, Boston, MA: Shambhala.

Fechner, G.T. (1873). *Einige Ideen zur Schöpfungs - und Entwickelungsgechichte der Organismen* [*Ideas in the History of Organism Creation and Development*], Leipzig: Breitkopf und Härtel.

Hillman, J. (1979) *The Dream and the Underworld*, New York: William Morrow Paperbacks Harper Collins.

Jung, C.G. (1921) *Psychological Types*, Collected Works 6, Princeton, NJ: Princeton University Press.

Jung, C.G. (1928) *Analytical Psychology and 'Weltanschauung'*, Collected Works 8, Princeton, NJ: Princeton University Press.

Jung, C.G. (1931) *A Psychological Theory of Types*, Collected Works 6, Princeton, NJ: Princeton University Press.

Jung, C.G. (1938) *Psychology and Religion*, Collected Works 11, Princeton, NJ: Princeton University Press.

Jung, C.G. (1947) *On the Nature of the Psyche*, Collected Works 8, Princeton, NJ: Princeton University Press.

Jung, C.G. ([1955–56] 1970) *Mysterium Coniunctionus: An Inquiry into the Separation and Synthesis of Psychic Opposites in Alchemy*, Collected Works 14, Princeton, NJ: Princeton University Press.

Jung, C.G. (1973) *Letters, Vol. 1, 1906–1950*, G. Adler (ed.), trans. R.F.C. Hull, Princeton, NJ: Princeton University Press.

Jung, C.G. (1988) *Nietzsche's Zarathustra: Notes of the Seminar Given in 1934–1939*, James L. Jarrett (ed.), in two volumes, Bollingen Series XCIX, Princeton, NJ: Princeton University Press (London & New York: Routledge: 1989).

Jung, C.G. (1997) *Visions: Notes of the Seminar Given in 1930–1934*, Claire Douglas (ed.), in two volumes, Bollingen Series XCIX, Princeton, NJ: Princeton University Press (London & New York: Routledge, 1998).

Ladinsky, D. (2002) *Love Poems from God: Twelve Sacred Voices from the East and West*, New York: Penguin Compass.

Monte, C. (2015) *Corpus Anima: Reflections from the Unity of Body and Soul*, Ashville, NC: Chiron Publications.

Neumann, E. (1989) *Place of Creation*, Bollingen Series LX1 – 3, Princeton, NJ: Princeton University Press.

Reeves, P. (2003) *Heart Sense: Unlocking your Highest Purpose and Deepest Desires*, Boston, MA: Conari Press.

Schore, A.N. (2003) *Affect Regulation and the Repair of the Self*, London and New York: W.W. Norton & Co.

Sieff, D.F. (2015) *Understanding and Healing Emotional Trauma: Conversations with Pioneering Clinicians and Researchers*, Hove, UK and New York: Routledge.

von Franz, M-L. (1988) *Psyche and Matter*, Boston, MA: Shambhala.

Woodman, M. and Dickson, E. (1996) *Dancing in the Flames: The Dark Goddess in the Transformation of Consciousness*, Dublin: Gill & MacMillan.

Chapter 9

Intimations of the Numinous

"It feels like a visitation from the lady in red in here"

Awake, my dear.
Be kind to your sleeping heart.
Take it out into the vast fields of Light
And let it breathe.
(From Hafiz, "Awake Awhile",
translated by Daniel Ladinsky)[1]

*

The body, in Cedrus Monte's view, is not only the receiving vessel of the *numen* ... but, by the nature of matter itself, it also "contains its own capacity for generating" the numinous experience (2015, p. 69). I would add that a learned secure attachment relationship to the body brings with it a quality of attunement to the body that awakens it to its natural organismic intelligence, including its potential to open itself to numinous experience. As noted in the previous chapter, Monte writes that the *numen* is not extraneous to flesh: "it is within the flesh as the flesh and accessible to us if we allow ourselves the opportunity to discover it" (*ibid.*, p. 78). When we regulate our nervous system's responses, bringing greater fluidity to oscillations between contraction and expansion, and attune to our sensing bodies, we open ourselves to moments of recognition in which self meets body, body meets self, in a reciprocal relationship. Conscious recognition of the body affects the body and promotes an expanded consciousness which stimulates a level of awareness beyond that of the ego: at a cellular level, it may open us to an experience of the *numen*—that is, to feelings of awe, bliss, wonder or terror in the face of the Other. An experience of the numinous is an experience of an unknown Other beyond the present reach of the ego. Any such experience originating beyond the purview of the ego feels as though it comes from outside of us, a 'visitation' from elsewhere; and we have no way of knowing whether this 'elsewhere', the mysterious *locus* and generator of all experience and knowledge *extraneous* to the ego, lies *beyond* the body or *in* the body, or both. We do know that, to varying degrees, any encounter with the *numinous*, the utterly Other, impacts us in and through the body, as the emotions also assail us physically, in and through the body: we tremble, sweat, suffer palpitations, shortness of breath; we are overcome by awe, terror, joy, bewilderment.[2] When we learn to work with the nervous system's responses, as we attune to the inner world of the somatic unconscious and the dream world of the psyche in tandem with an attunement to our physical surroundings, we strengthen both body and psyche to meet and sustain an experience of the *numinous*, integrate it, and work to discover its possible significance and meaning.

Neumann defines different layers of consciousness, and points to the limitations of the dominance of ego-consciousness:

> [Ego consciousness] only represents one particular form of knowledge ... a restricted knowledge in which the multiplicity of other forms of knowledge is renounced. ... Unconsciousness signifies merely unconsciousness of knowledge, not its absence ... [and] there are various forms of unconscious knowledge.
>
> (Neumann, 1989, p. 7)

Neumann (see Chapter 8), describes "extraneous knowledge" as a state of consciousness beyond the range of ego-consciousness that "is nevertheless of decisive importance for human life, possibly even more so than the knowledge of ego-consciousness" (*ibid.*, p. 17). I am proposing that the work of BodyDreaming shifts the locus of consciousness from the ego to a body-centred knowing—redeeming what lies culturally in the shadows and making it foreground—and that the numinous quality that can accompany this shift of consciousness forges a deep attachment to our sense of Self, a core self that is rooted and embodied, akin to a realignment of an embodied ego-Self axis.

In the transcripts from a BodyDreaming session that follow, we track my client, Sam, whom we have already met in Chapter 3, as she works to bring greater consciousness to her body and her dream, opening herself in the process to an experience of the *numinous*. Sam's experience constellates the opposites: awe and fear, attraction and repulsion, and we see how the process of working with those opposites guides her towards an integration of the new and previously unknown which, in turn, supports her to move forward in her life.

The following session took place when Sam was about to return to her homeland after spending a number of years overseas engaged in the study of depth psychology. Family circumstances necessitated that she end her studies prematurely. Sam felt ambivalent about this and extremely anxious about returning to the considerable demands of her family. It seemed timely to participate in a BodyDreaming session in the hope that it might help her align herself in a grounded connection to her body's dreaming. Sam had some understanding of the work because she was a participant in a small group to which I was teaching the basics of BodyDreaming. The excerpt below is from a private session.

Sam began the session by saying that she had had a deeply disturbing dream. As we have seen in earlier chapters, when a client wants to speak a dream, I first settle both my client's and my own nervous systems. To regulate affect, I take time to orient my client and myself in the here and now, and in the space in which we find ourselves. I initiate a free association right hemisphere conversation with a positive bias towards pleasure. I pay attention to the client's threshold of activation, noticing the extent of her window of tolerance, and what her default position might be—*fight, flight* or *freeze*. I notice what "*complex du jour*"[3] might be playing out in the client's psyche—what is occupying the client's thoughts, emotions, energy. I may register expressions that carry emotional valence—both positive and negative—as my client describes her current state of being. I will mirror back to my client positive responses to gestures, words and sounds.

By regulating affect and the nervous system in this way, I am creating greater fluidity in the client's system, allowing more available space in the body to receive the emotions of the dream. I focus the client's attention on the body as a resonating dynamic field ready to serve as a resource should the client be highly activated by the dream content and go 'over threshold'—that is, beyond his or her window of tolerance. Marion Woodman assures us that the *body* dreams the dream onward:

> The two work together because they belong together. The body is the unconscious in its most immediate and continuous form; the dream is also the unconscious, though as a body of images it lacks both the immediacy and continuity of the physical body.
>
> (Woodman, 1982, p. 79)

However, first we need to have established homeostasis in the system in order to support the body to dream the dream onward. I begin the session with Sam by preparing the body to create an optimal state of homeostasis before exploring the dream image itself.

I invite Sam to orient by looking around the room.

MD: *Maybe take a moment to look around the room, let your eyes fall on anything that they might be curious about, not searching for anything, just see what they rest on.*

   (I use *invitational* language, which helps to maintain a fluidity in the questions as well as in my attitude, opening up the right hemisphere exploration rather than wanting the client to focus on something specific.)

   What are you drawn to? What draws your attention?

Sam: *I see an image of two hearts that is hanging on the wall.*

MD: *Is this image one of your drawings?*

Sam: *Yes.*

MD: *What do you notice about it as you look at it now? What strikes you?*

   [It is a drawing of three concentric hearts. Each heart is connected to the other by a fine chain: the outer and largest heart is red; at the centre is the second largest golden heart, and the third, white heart forms the connection between the two. This line is red in the outer heart, gold in the second, and white in the third, in the centre.]

Sam: *What strikes me about it now is the colour gold, the heart within the heart. It's dependent, so dependent on the red heart. In a way it becomes attached to the bigger heart by that little thing that holds it.*

MD: *It looks like there might even be another heart there?*
        [I register the language and metaphor but I keep the conversation light and open-ended at this point.]

Sam: *Yes, there is a third heart, one that I rubbed out—a white heart in the middle. I didn't actually rub it out. I put a bit of colour into it, after I hooked it to the other one.*

MD: *What is it like when you look at it, what happens in your body as you look at it now.*
        [I ask a question that will stir the body's resonance to the image and to the accompanying emotion.]

Sam: *There's a little bit of anxiety in me when I see it, there's a sadness. I'm not sure what it is. I haven't worked out what the image is about. I haven't worked with it as yet.*

MD: *How do you register sadness when the sadness comes in?*
        [I am asking about the felt sense experience of the sadness.]

Sam: *It's a feeling of heaviness, almost as heavy as lead, the shield that the dentist puts on for an X-ray, a sort of pulling down of my energy.*
        [This suggests a dorsal vagal collapse or *freeze*.]

MD: *Is there anything about the image that doesn't pull down your energy?*
        [I consciously avoid the pull of the activating image of the dentist's shield, which could bring her into the dorsal collapse/immobility of the trauma vortex. Instead, I ask an open question, arousing her curiosity to determine if there is a positive feeling connected with the image of the hearts that might act as a resource.]
        Do you notice anything in the image that doesn't pull your energy down?

Sam: *Yes. The colours don't pull it down and I like the lightness of the gold.*
        (She is smiling and is more alert.)

MD: *What does it feel like when you say that?*

Sam: *Because of the lightness of the gold I feel a lightening in my upper chest, the opposite of the sadness and heaviness. I feel an uplifting in my chest.*
        (She sits more upright.)

MD: *Is that in response to the gold in particular?*

Sam: *Yes. I feel it with the gold, the light in the centre of the gold in particular. The bigger heart is the overall container but the one in the middle with the gold has a lightness to it.*

MD: *Lovely. Let's stay with the lightness of the gold heart and maybe you might like to bring your attention to how your body is responding, being aware of your chest and any other changes that you notice.*

(Sam closes her eyes.)

You may wish to have your eyes closed, but you don't necessarily have to keep them closed.

[I am encouraging her to remain open to the possibility of a different experience of internal attunement—or interoception—with eyes open—which will enable Sam's social engagement system to be more available to her.]

Sam: OK. (Sam opens her eyes at first but then closes them again. After a while she makes a movement with her hands.)

I just feel drawn to doing this for whatever reason ... (Her hands open out in a gesture as if they are touching something.)[4]

MD: *How would it be to continue to let the hands do exactly what they want to do?*

Sam: *I probably want to get up and touch the image. I have to feel what's going on there. As I'm looking at it, it's flat, but I see it as a three-dimensional rounded form.*

(Sam is engaged in a right hemisphere exploration which may change her perception of things. She gets up and goes over to touch the image very gently; her hands outline the shape of the three hearts.)[5]

MD: *What's it like to do that?*

Sam: *It brings tears to my eyes as I touch it. ... And I'm also aware of the flatness and coldness of the actual paper... .*

(Sam is gripped by emotion as she engages in active imagination with her image; touching the heart expands her emotional and imaginative experience while, at the same time, she witnesses herself concretely touch the actual paper. She sits down and continues to move her hands and fingers gently as if they are still moving over the heart. I notice that her gesture has the quality of soothing, maybe even of caressing.)

MD: *What's it like for your fingers to be making that action; is it like a caress? Do they want to be doing this?*

[I introduce curiosity to Sam's exploration to help her register her pleasure which, in turn, enhances the formation of pleasure circuits.][6]

Sam: *Yes. They do want to caress it. It's as if they are almost willing something into being.*

        ... I'm wanting to feel it, all of it—the whole of it. There is in me a sense of my wanting it to know that it is seen and held.

MD: *You really want this heart to know that it's seen, and that it's held.*

Sam: *Yes. I want this heart to know it's seen and, yes, that all of it is held. I feel compelled.*

MD: *You feel compelled.*

[I mirror Sam's choice of word "compelled", demonstrating the strength of her desire to make connection with the heart.]

Sam: *Yes, for it to be seen and held, all of it, not only the surface—but all of it. I want to do this.* (Sam moves her hands in a very particular rolling motion, each hand *rolling* over the other, gesturing three dimensionality—the front, back and sides of the heart.)

MD: *Is it as if you are holding the heart in your hands, feeling all of it in the space between your hands?*

Sam: *It makes my own heart seem like it's pumping harder, I imagine there is a pulse in this heart as I'm holding it—there is some weight to it. ... Now that I have it here, I don't know quite what to do with it, either. I have the feeling of its becoming more flesh or having more substance. It's not a hard object.*[7]

[The quality of Sam's embodied attention has brought about a reciprocity between herself and the image. The boundary is blurred in this expanded state of "extraneous knowing". Sam is engaged in what Anita Greene refers to as "embodied processing", an active imagination with the image. Through the careful attention Sam has given it, something has come into being, transforming the image into a living symbol.[8]

MD: *It's not a hard object, it's becoming more like flesh.*

Sam: *You know, there's a 'give' to it.* (i.e., unlike the "cold, hard surface" of the paper she described at the outset.)

MD: *How is that for you to feel that is becoming more 'flesh,' that it comes alive in this way?*

Sam: *I feel okay and it makes me feel that I don't know what to do with this.*[9]

[The exploration is bringing Sam to an edge—a new threshold of experience—a different kind of knowing is happening and I observe a slight tension coming into her body.]

MD: *Maybe it's just about holding it, feeling its heartbeat, just letting it be as it is right now.*

[I reassure Sam, encouraging her to feel into the pleasure she is experiencing with the image.

In hindsight and in the light of what happens next, it might have been wiser to have slowed down the process, titrating the new experience incrementally, by accessing the social engagement system and orienting her outward in the here and now of her physical surroundings.]

(There is silence while Sam gazes down at the image, holding the heart between her hands.)

The image seems to have revealed its nature to you, its 'gold'. It has substance, a heartbeat, three-dimensionality. What are you feeling as you are holding it?

Sam: *It's bringing tears to my eyes, a mixture of awe and fear, I don't know what to do, not sure it's fear.*[10]

[There is a numinous, awe-inspiring feeling in the 'field', a sense of a 'visitation' by an archetypal energy, which Jung refers to as the quality of the *numinosum.*]

MD: *What do you notice happening in your body as you feel the awe and perhaps fear?*

Sam: *I feel like I'm jamming up.*
         [The act of naming "awe and fear"—qualities associated with a numi-nous experience—has activated Sam, triggering her default position of *freeze*—"jamming up".]

MD: *It's really helpful that you notice this "jamming up". You have your wit-ness present and your witness knows that something wants to "jam up" in your body just as you are also feeling the emotions of awe and fear.*
         [I attempt to down-regulate Sam's arousal as I provide a map of what may be happening, a top-down processing.]

Sam: *Yes.*
         [The experience of holding the image of the heart in her hands and feel-ing the heartbeat of that image as it resonates with her own heartbeat has caused a shift in Sam's ego-consciousness. She does not *know* or under-stand what has happened but she realizes that something has aroused the emotions of *awe* and *fear*, which she recognizes as evidence of the *numen*. Sam's autonomic nervous system is activated, which risks putting her *over threshold* and triggering the possible shut-down of a dorsal vagal freeze—"*I feel like I'm jamming up.*"]

MD: *Let's take a moment to feel your feet on the ground.* (In a previous ses-sion, having her feet on the ground proved a key resource for staying present and not going into *freeze*.) *And maybe find your sitz bones and feel your buttocks and thighs on the chair.* ... (I wait, giving Sam time to respond to the invitation.) ... *You might like to take a moment to look around the room, maybe have a little stretch—stretching your arms and shoulders, perhaps, opening more space for the energy to move so it doesn't jam up.*
         [I take my time to give these directions and I make the appropriate movements, gently stretching my upper body—shoulders, head and neck—with the intention of stimulating Sam's mirror neurons and reac-tivating her social engagement system. Slowly she follows my initiative, her head and neck begin to move as she begins to scan the room with her eyes, loosening her shoulders and stretching her arms into the space. I see that the movement has calmed her system; she is breathing more easily, her muscles relax in her face, a sense of relief comes into the room.[11]]

MD: *Perhaps it's okay to have an emotional response and to "not know" what the experience is about ... simply to receive its presence.*
         [I reassure Sam in a soothing but firm voice, appealing to her neocortex, a top-down processing.]

Sam: *I can feel my heart beating harder.*
         [Rather than reassuring her, it seems Sam is more activated. In hind-sight, perhaps I could have enquired about her orienting response as she had been looking around the room, using her social engagement system. This might have drawn her attention to her decreased heart rate and cre-ated more space in her body to receive the emotion.

[Sam is now looking at her image of the hearts on the wall, resourcing herself. I leave her to self-regulate for some time until I notice a shift in her skin colour and her breathing; her whole body relaxes. I join with her in contemplating the image.]

MD: *You felt your heart beating earlier alongside the beat of the heart you held in your hands. There's something about the heart here.*[12]

[I recall the pleasure of her engagement with the image and stir her curiosity.]

Sam: *Yes. There is.* (She softens visibly.)

MD: *There is something heart-full here, a heart to heart connection ... and it brings tears.*

[I am referring to the emotion that was stirred by the numinous experience without over-interpretation; with a soft brushstroke, we can hold the powerful affect in a regulating way.]

Sam: *Yes.*
      (Silence.)

MD: *Is there anything that you notice happening in your body right now?*[13]

[I want to ground the emotion—the awe and fear in Sam's body—seeing the "direct effect in the body" (Harding, [1947]1973, p. 314).]

Sam: *Yes, there's a gut reaction to that, a tightening.*

[The gut is wired to the vagus nerve and its millions of connecting 'wires' feed back directly to the brain. My question about her body's response at this stage may have been premature, not leaving enough space and time for the down-regulation, the parasympathetic response, to settle. Inadvertently, I have been 'jamming up' Sam's space—by not allowing her enough 'down time' to settle with the new experience before asking her to notice her body's response, in my too eager search for the *just noticeable difference* factor.[14]]

MD: *It's good that you notice the "tightening" in your gut.*

[Here I am affirming and mirroring Sam's interoceptive skills, strengthening her alliance with her witnessing self. In the moment, I decide to orient her again to the room, bringing in the social engagement system to avert the vagal arousal of her tightening gut.]

While you are noticing your gut, maybe at the same time see what it would be like to bring your attention outward into the room, gently moving your head from side to side, very slowly... .

[Sam's body relaxes—her shoulders drop, her breathing is deeper, her face relaxes, a noticeable ease of tension, generally. Her eyes are naturally drawn back to the image on the wall.]

(Time passes.)

While you are taking the time to look at your image, what is it that you notice?

Sam: *It's okay now.* (She sighs, nodding her head. She is breathing easily. Her system is further down-regulating.)
      (Silence.)

MD: *Is it okay to have your heart beat in response to this image?* (I speak in a soft voice, joining Sam in the down-regulation, allowing space for emotion.)

Sam: *Yes, and it's okay for the 'not knowing' to be present.*

[This marks a threshold moment in which Sam is staying within her window of tolerance, whilst remaining present to her 'not knowing' self.[15]

[Just then I observe that Sam's hands begin to make a gesture: with palms open, facing each other, swaying, they move rhythmically. Sam is following an impulse. Her body leads the way in this exploration; she is attending to the moment-to-moment process, sensing into where the fluid body wants to move.[16]

[I mirror the movement of Sam's hands and affirm her acceptance of 'not knowing.']

MD: *And it's okay for the 'not knowing' to be here while you move.*[17]

(The movement with her hands continues.)

Witnessing your hands as they are moving—is it comforting to have your hands move in this way?

Sam   *Yes. It is comforting.*

MD: *What do you notice happening for you?*

Sam: *I feel it's really grounding me. I can feel my thighs.* (She begins to rub her thighs.) *I feel energy like a tingling going right down my legs; I can feel my feet on the floor, which I couldn't feel before. I am aware of the energy there now.* (Big sigh, a release of breath—the fluid body's response.[18])

MD: *That's great that you can feel your feet on the ground and the energy coming right down through your legs, and with that comes a big release of breath.*

[The big release of breath and the accompanying opening in the lower half of Sam's body tells me that the dorsal vagus has released its deep hold and that Sam is experiencing more space and greater fluidity, not only in her hands but in her gut and throughout her whole system, right down to her feet. Her whole body is more receptive to receiving energy, which gives her the sensation of feeling grounded. Without this ground she is in danger of 'jamming up', being overwhelmed by 'not knowing', and remaining stuck in the familiar pathways of the complexes.]

Before we begin to focus on Sam's dream, I would like to summarize the work we have done so far. At the outset Sam's response to the 'living symbol' of the beating heart opened her to a sense of a reality other than that of the ego, in other words, to an experience of "extraneous knowledge" (Neumann, 1989, p. 7). This, in turn, triggered an experience of the *numinous*, evoking feelings of awe and fear, coupled with a dorsal response of 'jamming up' in the body. Because, as Neumann reminds us, the ego is not competent to deal "with phenomena relating to a reality-field other than its own" (*ibid.*, p. 14), we habitually shut out experiences of the 'other' that lie beyond our conscious understanding. As Sam engaged with the image, we titrated each cycle of activation, by accessing the social engagement system, e.g., orienting to the space around her, calming the ventral arousal. Supporting her system to remain open and fluid helped Sam to stay present to her body's responses and to the transformational power of metaphor as paper heart became beating heart.[19] In the conversational style of top-down processing Sam was learning to stay present and curious, which facilitated the emergence of the totally new impulse in the form of movement—a rhythmic swaying of her two hands. The movement could be viewed as a metaphor for a dance of opposites: 'knowing' and 'not knowing', 'ego knowledge' and 'extraneous knowledge'. We called on Sam's observing self to witness her hands moving and to witness the felt sense experience of the movement. At this point, Sam was capable of letting go of an ego 'knowing' state and surrendering to the flow of energy expressed in the 'not yet known' movement. Aware of the energy moving throughout her body, Sam has developed the capacity to witness the experience of the numinous, the living symbol in her sensing, gesturing body.[20] The movement slowed down and Sam looked content and steady within herself, an overall appearance of coherence.

Needless to say, the process described above is fraught with difficulties, as an influx of archetypal energy, or the *numinous*, may easily overwhelm a body, psyche and nervous system not yet capable of tolerating the process that might support conscious integration of the experience. As Woodman and Dickson caution, "in whatever ways the process of bringing the body to consciousness develops, a strong container in which the energies can transform, physically and psychically, is essential" (1996, p. 196). Patient, focused work that slowly titrates each new emotional experience at a felt sense level, is needed to ensure that an individual's container (body and psyche) is strong and flexible enough to withstand an influx of archetypal energy and able to integrate such an experience. Otherwise, the potential meaning of an invaluable experience is lost and new neural pathways are not established; consciousness fails to expand and things remain unchanged.

In Sam's case, our work strengthened Sam to allow her to open to the numinous; by titrating activation, expanding her capacity for feeling the strong emotions of awe and fear, her system found greater fluidity to move with new impulses and experiences. We had been preparing what Irene Dowd calls "a more spacious and ecologically rich inner land to move through" (1995, p. 86).[21] Sam had the flexibility now to move between extremes, to expand into unknown territories and to trust her body as a source of inspiration and consciousness. We had laid the foundation, the inner knowing and 'grounded' support from which to explore her dream.

Sam's Dream

I need first to situate Sam's dream in the context of her actual situation. Sam was on the verge of moving back to her hometown in North America after a period of study abroad. The programme of study had proven a truly transformative experience and one she was reluctant to leave. Outer circumstances, however,

required that she return home to an as yet uncertain future. The somewhat rare-
fied, cloistered life of the student that Sam had enjoyed had to be sacrificed. She
had no sense of what the future might hold and found herself at a difficult transition in her life. However, as Jung writes, in an "abstract, ideal state" (which we
might understand as the protected life of the student):

> one does not *live* in the true sense of the word. ... In order for it [life] to come
> alive it must have 'blood,' it must have what the alchemists call the *rubedo*,
> the 'redness' of life. Only the total experience of being can transform this
> ideal state ... into a fully human mode of existence.
>
> (Jung, [1952]1977, p. 229)

Drawing on the symbolism of the alchemical process, Jung explains how transformative change or a 'new dawn' (the *albedo* stage in the alchemical process) follows a
struggle with the darkness (the *nigredo*, understood psychologically as a confrontation with the shadow or the unconscious 'other' side of the personality). Symbols in
alchemical writings, in art and in dreams present the *rubedo* or 'reddening' stage of
the process in images such as blood, the phoenix, the rose, a crowned king, a figure
wearing red. This alchemical symbolism informs the imagery of Sam's dream, and
the dream, as Jung reminds us, is "a spontaneous self portrayal, in symbolic form,
of the actual situation in the unconscious" ([1916] 1958, par. 505).
    Sam speaks her dream:

Sam: *A woman is in the room with me. We had been talking, we had tea together.
Then she leaves and I go to lock the door after her only to find that the
lock doesn't work. I open the door a little bit and I see a woman standing
on the other side of the door, on the landing, wearing a long red robe, a
housecoat, actually. She turns around slowly. I can see the front of her
robe. She looks at the lock with me. I have a feeling she does something to
the lock and the door doesn't lock any more. I'm lying in the bed and I can
feel a presence on the other side of the door. I'm pushing and punching
against the door but I know there is no point since the lock doesn't work
any more. I am terrified when I wake up out of the dream.*

MD: *"The door doesn't lock any more."*
    [Sam's words resonate for me with the phrase "jammed up" that she had
    used previously in the work with the paper hearts.]

Sam: *She is out there.*

MD: *Did you draw her?*
    [Jung often invites his patients to "dream the dream onward" by draw-
    ing, painting or modeling.][22]

Sam: *No. She is the second woman in red I've dreamt of in the last two weeks.
Who is she? is the question I ask myself.*
    [The fact that the image has appeared a number of times tells me that
    Sam's unconscious wants her to pay close attention to this image.]

MD: *How does it feel now to have spoken the dream?*

Sam: *I don't know what the dream is about. I have a feeling in my body it may be an important dream.*

MD: *What do you notice in your body?* (Sam spontaneously maintains the link to the body that we have created in the first part of the session, allowing the body to resonate with the dream. The question slows down the process and steers Sam away from moving too quickly into her thoughts and associations, which would be a more usual way of working the dream.)

Sam: *I feel a shimmering, like a feeling of shaking.*

[I ask myself the question: 'Is Sam activated, on a threshold of overwhelm, or is there a release of energy happening in her system?']

MD: *Where do you feel it?*

Sam: *It's not an all-over feeling. Right now I'm feeling it way deep down in my belly somewhere. I'm not settled and I have been in this space since I had the dream. There's an unsettledness in me.* [I note this as a sign of activation.]

MD: *Somewhere deep in the belly there is a shaking, an unsettledness.* (I mirror her words.)

Sam: *Yes.* (Sam rubs her thighs, drawing on the earlier gesture when she had felt the energy move down her legs. She is resourcing herself spontaneously.)

MD: *As you rub your thighs, you might like to bring your awareness there, and perhaps notice if it helps you to feel the comfort, or whatever is going on there. This is a great way to ground yourself while you are sensing the energy in your thighs. And maybe you might see what it's like to keep your eyes open.*

[I evoke the body memory of the grounding work we did earlier, and invite Sam to keep her eyes open; this will ensure her social engagement system becomes available, and helping her meet her dream with curiosity and greater fluidity.]

You may want to take a look again at your image of the hearts on the wall.

[I invite Sam to orient back to the image at this point to enlist her social engagement system, opening the right hemisphere and slowing down the left hemisphere which might want to rush into interpretation and 'knowing' what the dream is about.]

Sam: *When I worked on the dream, that's the drawing I made* (pointing to the image of the hearts on the wall). *The image just came out of me. It is the image of the heart within the heart. The image is of a wallhanging suspended on the door of an adjacent apartment. It's just outside the door of my room, and my room in the dream is the one that is unlocked and can't be locked again.*

And there is a woman in red who appeared while I was doing some active imagination work and who spoke to me saying that I have to 'open my heart'. To access her now, the lady in red, I have to leave the room. She didn't come into the room. She is out there, she is literally outside (the door), *waiting for me.*

[I don't offer any reflection or elaborate on the possible meaning of the image at this point but wait in the uncertainty.]

I don't know ... (she reaches with her hand to the top of her head).

I don't know. (Sigh.)

MD: *Feel how your whole body is now, as you say, "I don't know."*

Sam: *In a way, I feel spent, I'm tired.*

[The 'not knowing' may be triggering a dorsal freeze or Sam may be tired from the work we opened earlier.]

MD: *Where do you feel the tiredness coming into your body?*

Sam: *I want to go to sleep, I don't want to know. I don't want to go on.*

[These words speak to me of a dorsal freeze/collapse, a hopelessness, a giving up.]

MD: *I notice that your left hand is raised in a gesture. What does it want to do?*

Sam: *It's pushing.* (She gestures with some force.)

MD: *How far does it want to push?* (I offer my hands for her to push against.[23] She pushes with force against my hand. Pushing helps to stir her protective reflexes and evokes healthy aggression, stimulating a sympathetic ventral response which may open the way out of a dorsal collapse.)

Sam: *I don't want ...* (Her voice stirs with emotion.)

MD: *"I don't want." It's great to find that push and those words.*

[It feels as though Sam may be mobilizing rage that can often underlie the dorsal freeze. Her words and gesture mirror the pushing gesture she made at the end of the dream, trying to keep the door locked even though she knew "the lock doesn't work any more."]

Sam: *I can feel myself knotting up in the solar plexus.* (Sam has stopped pushing.)

MD: *It's good that you notice the activation that comes into the solar plexus with the push and the energy of the "I don't want." Let's take some time with that.*

[I counteract the limbic activation by enlisting the neocortex, calling on Sam to witness the sequencing of gesture, voice and emotion.]

Let's really slow down and take time with this.

What is happening in the belly, where you feel yourself tightening up?

Sam: *I can feel it all the way down.* (She draws her hand over the length of her torso.)

MD: *What do you feel?*

Sam: *Pain in my shoulder and a cramping in my gut. I'm hunching over. I need to sit up straight.* (She straightens herself in her chair.)

MD: *How does it feel to sit upright?*

[When the client makes a spontaneous readjustment to settle or support herself, we bring attention to what has just occurred; this awareness can strengthen the effect of the self-soothing.][24]

Sam: *I feel stronger, somehow.*

MD: *Where in your body do you feel the strength coming in?*

[I am drawing Sam's attention to the strength she is beginning to feel: to where she notices any small change, the *just noticeable difference*

(Fechner, 1873).[25] This will increase the support she feels within herself and enable her body to call up the memory of this experience in the future as a felt sense resource.]

Sam: *I feel it in my back. I can feel the difference.* (She makes the 'pushing' gesture with her hands once again.)

I don't know what the hands are saying. It could be they are saying, "don't come any closer" or maybe, "I surrender."

[The opposites are apparent in her body's response: is it a gesture of defence or collapse?]

MD: *What's it like to feel into those hands with the strength in your back now to support you? Do you notice that the belly has any more space when you are upright?*

Sam: *Yes, it does.*

[I mirror her posture—her hands raised and her supported upright back.]

What is it like to have my hands mirroring yours?

Sam: *I can feel energy in this hand.*

[The mirroring seems to have energized her. She begins to make a fist and push the air. I mirror the strength of the pushing. We continue for a while before she stops.]

MD: *What is happening? What are you noticing? It seems as if there was a lot of energy in that pushing.*

Sam: *Yes. My hands got tired. I had to bring them down. They don't feel like doing that right now.*

MD: *The hands have their own story, their own rhythm of energy flow – "They don't feel like doing that now." Notice how your whole body feels now, right down to the feet.*

[I take my cue from the hands, then bring Sam's attention to her whole body, allowing for the process of down-regulation to expand.]

Sam: *I don't feel quite so tight here in my belly.*

MD: *Great. How are the shoulders doing? And your back?*

Sam: *I can feel the support of the chair for my back, but it's further back than I like it to be. Can we get a cushion?*

MD: *Yes.* (I hand her a cushion.) *And just notice what it's like for the back to get this support.*

Sam: *It likes that it feels supported; it's not needing to hold itself up. I can relax into it without collapsing down too far.*

[Support versus collapse: a healthy parasympathetic response without falling into freeze or collapse of the dorsal.]

MD: *How does your whole body feel when it's being supported?*

Sam: *It doesn't hurt so much. I don't need to worry about it. It's taken care of.*

MD: *It feels taken care of and it doesn't hurt so much—wonderful. Really allow yourself to feel into this—how your body responds when it feels taken care of.*

Sam: *It knows that Sam is held ...and I don't need to do anything extra.*

MD: (I mirror Sam's words.) *"You don't need to do anything extra"! Sam is held. Allow yourself to explore this feeling of being held in your body.*
       [When the body feels safely held, the whole system relaxes, letting go of hyper- vigilance or hyper-sensitivity.]

Sam: *I can feel some ease. I don't need to worry about it. It's taken care of.*

MD: *Beautiful. Really feel into how your body responds to that experience of being taken care of.*
       (Silence.)
       [Sam is dropping deeper into the experience. I notice her face soften, her shoulders drop, and her breathing eases ... .]
       How gorgeous for your body to feel that it is taken care of, that it's held and you don't need to do anything extra.
       [I am deliberately slowing down and mirroring the emotional experience, remembering Damasio's appreciation of Spinoza's argument that we need an emotional experience that is strong and powerful as a counterpoint to shift the familiar complex or default nervous system response.]
       Notice any changes that may be happening. (I can see that Sam's breath has changed.)

Sam: *I have a deeper breath. I am feeling a little more relaxed.*

MD: *Let's give some time to this response in the whole body.*
       [I am watching the deeper breath, the easing of muscle tension in the shoulders and back, the release in the gut. It is important to give time for the new neural connections to become established. We are in the process of rehabilitating the parasympathetic *freeze/collapse* response, and learning that surrender is not the same as collapse.]

MD: *Where do you feel a 'little bit' more relaxed?*

Sam: *It's always in here for me, in my tummy.*

MD: *How would it be to allow your tummy to feel this little bit of letting down ... and maybe to notice the rest of your body?*
       (Sam is stroking her thighs.)

Sam: *I still need to calm the flesh—the shimmering, trembling.*

MD: *Beautiful—calming the flesh—see how the flesh is responding while you are calming it.*

Sam: (Sigh. Sam's breath deepens.) *It feels a little bit like the heart earlier. It's about becoming aware of the flesh, the resistance and the shaking.*

MD: *What's it like for your body to become aware of itself?*

Sam: *It's new, in a way. It's a different relationship to flesh, somehow. It is a different relationship to flesh. And it needs the touch of my hands to calm it down.*
       [Sam is self-regulating by using touch to soothe her newfound connection to flesh, witnessing how she is keeping herself from going over threshold and jamming up.]

MD: *Your touch is self-soothing, calming, just like when you were holding and stroking the heart earlier.*

Sam: *Yes, to calm it down.*

MD: *Really beautiful. Let's just give it space.* [That is, space for the emotion to come in and time for the neural pathway to establish connection throughout the body. I notice Sam's tears.]

        Where do you feel the emotion?

Sam: *Around my eyes and neck.*

MD: *What are you noticing?*

Sam: *A pain that's gripping me under my jaw, where my jaw is held tight.*

MD: *Good that you're noticing the jaw. What else do you notice in your body as you continue to stroke those thighs?*

        [I acknowledge the discomfort, the bracing in her jaw, and I bring her attention to the place of ease, the comfort that she is receiving from rubbing her thighs. She continues to stroke her thighs, her body feels supported, and release comes with her tears.]

Sam: *I didn't expect this* (more tears).

        I can feel myself ... I can ...

        [I notice that Sam's eyes are closing and her voice dropping. It feels like she is retreating, ... a freeze coming in after the wave of emotion, perhaps.)

MD: *See what it would be like to keep the eyes open while you are receiving the self-soothing touch, reassuring your flesh that you will stay with it even when the emotion comes in. The emotion may signal the amygdala, and its quick defensive response could jam up the flow of energy. So, instead, let's see what it is like to stay with eyes open and to be aware of the self-soothing touch on your thighs.*

Sam: *Yes.*

MD: *Your body knows how to let the emotion through without tightening.*

Sam: *That's right. It's not tightening and it's not trembling.* (She continues to stroke her thighs. She sighs and her breath drops deeper.)

MD: *That's great. Beautiful.*

Sam: *I am reminded of Marion Woodman's familiar gesture of stroking her arms, and "loving those thighs".*

MD: *Yes. I remember that.*

Sam: *It's only now that I 'get' that gesture. I appreciate what that gesture really means. I know it now, but in a different way.*

        [The 'extraneous knowledge' of the body's innate wisdom is being consciously integrated into Sam's entire system—in a coherency of body, mind and soul.]

MD: *As you are soothing your body—stroking your thighs—the body opens in response, cell by cell, the breath drops, tears flow. The energy releases and frees up the jammed place; the room which was locked is now open.*

        [Here I am referencing the dream image of the locked door; the body is dreaming on the dream.]

Sam: *Yes, and nothing will stop it.* (Sam means that the energy that is flowing won't be jammed up again. Perhaps she is referring to her fear of leaving this place of study which has opened up so many locked doors in the body, mind and psyche.)

MD: *The door is not going to be locked again.*

Sam: *Yes.*

MD: *The inner lock around the clenched jaw is not going to lock again.*

Sam: *Yes, I have to get over that fear.* (She laughs.)

MD: *You are getting over it, step by step.*

Sam: *How did I ever manage to do anything when this body is so afraid, clenched shut all the time?*

MD: *It's about growing a different relationship to flesh.*

Sam: *Yes. I know about that part of it.*

MD: *Psyche is speaking to you through the flesh.*

Sam: *Yes, that's the way the Self comes through to me.* (We are engaging the integrative/ meaning-making circuit of the brain, bringing in further coherence between body and psyche.)[26]

MD: *How is your jaw now?*

Sam: *It's loosening a bit.*

         [I notice a stifled yawn.]

MD: *Let's just have a few yawns ... Annie-style yawns.*[27]

Sam: *Thank you, Annie, you are here with us, making the whale sounds and waiting with us, hovering, until the impulse comes, trusting the lull, not forcing it, just waiting ... until it comes. And great slobbery lips, and consonants, kkkkk ggggaaaa, ffffff ...*

         [Sam is playfully recalling her BodySoul Rhythms mentor, Ann Skinner, and taking herself through the familiar exercises that encourage the jaw and mouth and lips to loosen and make sounds. These muscles form the architecture of the social engagement system, which directly impacts the ventral vagus. Annie encourages the attitude of hovering, trusting that the new impulse will arrive.]

         (Sam brings the sound-making to a close and looks around the room.)
         And the sun is shining. I need to move. I have been finding myself doing more movement recently, enjoying my tai chi *practice.*

         (Sam's expression is open, her face is smiling, her back upright.)
         It feels like a visitation from the lady in red (the woman in the red housecoat in her dream). *I am noticing the red of the candle, and the red spiral wall hanging, all the red energy in my room.*[28]

         [Sam's positive memory of the voice work prompted her to play with her sounds and this freed her up, enhancing her curiosity and receptivity and triggering the integrative circuit. There is a moment of linkage—a recognition during which inner and outer elements meet, as the colour red in the dream is reflected and matched by the red Sam now sees for the first time in so many things around her.[29] Sam looks livelier, alert, full in herself. She speaks with a sense of conviction.]

I want to meet her (the woman in the red housecoat). *And I have to go out of the room, through the door, if I want her. If I want to embrace that aspect of my life, then I have to go out of this room.*

The new impulse has arrived: Sam is clear that she has to go out of the room to embrace the energy of the woman in the red housecoat. Levine (2015) comments, "When one's body is able to experience a relaxed sense of strength, one's mind is able to experience a relaxed sense of focused attention" (p. 119). Where before there was terror and *freeze*, now there is a congruence, a flow to Sam's energy and she has a sense of agency about her. The slow pace of the work has enabled the numinous dream image to take shape in her body, mind and soul, and its meaning has become self-evident. Embodied meaning has become an imperative for Sam. "[I]mage and meaning are identical; and as the first takes shape, so the latter becomes clear" (Jung, 1947, par. 402). Now emboldened, Sam is able to surrender to the call of the dream. This time, her surrender is driven not by fear of collapse but by a sense of *recognition* of a body-psyche connection, an integration and alignment of body, mind and soul. Fosha describes such moments of recognition as almost invariably involving "two things fitting together, … it is not necessarily relational or interpersonal—the fit can be between self and other, but it can also be between self and self, or self and process, or self and experience" (2009, p. 179). Certainly, a visible ease, reflecting a new sense of alignment, was evident in Sam's system—in her voice and breath, her facial muscles, her shoulders, her spine.[30] Woodman comments on these *threshold moments of alignment* as bringing "ease and wholeness … through reconnection with soul as friend, listening to what it has to say in our [*sic*] body. It's a question of *consciousness*—without consciousness nothing changes" (in conversation with Ryley, 1998, p. 89). The BodyDreaming work has helped awaken consciousness in Sam's body, a somatic consciousness that brings greater coherence between her body, mind and soul. Sam's initial reaction to the dream image of anxiety and freeze reflects the overwhelm operating in her system. Sam's window of tolerance has widened and she has become more capable of remaining present to moments when the impulse to freeze threatens. BodyDreaming has helped to mitigate the old patterned response and allows her to go on dreaming the dream through the attunement to and titration of the powerful and numinous emotion arising in her body.[31]

Central to BodyDreaming work is the understanding of how the *quality* of attention we bring to our bodies affects our cells. "Whether we know it or not, we experience at a cellular level the love or lack of love that is directed toward us" (Woodman and Dickson, 1996, p. 197). Candace Pert refers to *neuropeptides*, the communication receptors in the cells: "It is these peptides and their receptors that make the dialogue between conscious and unconscious processes possible."[32] They form a communications network of emotion that operates throughout the body at the cellular, molecular level. Monte argues that "it is the bonding of particular receptors with cells that initiates the experience of a certain feeling state. … These feeling states not only include sadness, disgust, anger, joy, fear, surprise, *and also* awe, bliss, wonder and other states of consciousness that have been up until now physiologically unexplained" (Monte, 2015, p. 76, emphasis mine). Pert's discovery of receptor cells (*neuropeptides*) initiated a radical shift in our understanding of cell function. Neuropeptides carry emotion throughout the whole body as well as transmit information "from the surface of a cell deep into the cell's interior, where the message changes the state of the cell dramatically ... and can translate to large changes of behavior, physical activity, even mood" (Juhan, cited in Monte, *ibid.*). The knowledge that we have the ability to effect changes in cell structure which, in turn, may initiate dramatic shifts in mood throws the essential role of attunement in the therapeutic setting into strong relief. Attunement becomes the corner stone of any successful alliance: attunement between therapist and his body, client and her body, and between therapist and client, *living body* to *living body* through direct right-hemisphere communication. A therapist's appreciation of the importance of attunement will consequently have a profound impact on the way in which he or she works with embodied transference and countertransference.[33] When Sam became overwhelmed by her body's response to the numinous image of the heart which she felt was beating in her hand, she knew that she had encountered an energy beyond the reach of her present state of consciousness—hence the *numinosity* of the image conveyed to her in and through her body. In the countertransference I too was affected. Excited to be in the numinous territory with her, my questions about how she was experiencing this moment in her body had the effect of a dorsal freeze—"jamming her up". Once I became aware that, at this point, by drawing attention to her body I was activating her further, I realized I had to abandon my line of questioning and repair the misattunement. I followed her body's responses, gently titrating what was happening and allowing her system time to settle and continue the work on the dream. Jung believed that "[d]reams are the natural reaction of the self-regulating psychic system" (Jung, 1935, par. 248). Sam was triggered by the recurrent and numinous dream image of the woman in the red housecoat. Once again we titrated the emotions and Sam tracked the gradual release of energy—the tingling and shimmering sensations in her arms, shoulders, jaw, gut, hips and legs. Ultimately the playful voice work provided the vital cue that enabled her to settle into a parasympathetic down-regulation. Out of this lull or resting time the image or impulse arose and Sam was now in a position to receive the new impulse and act: "*I know I have to follow her*"—that is, follow the *rubedo* or life blood represented by the figure of the woman in red. Jung, speaking of the rubedo, states that "the blood alone can reanimate a glorious state of consciousness ... [and] rejoins the profound unity of the psyche."[34]

The last section of the dream, the lysis, indicates the direction in which the energy wants to move (Woodman, 1990, p. 88). Jung reminds us that the *numinous* heals: "the fact is that the approach to the numinous is the real therapy and inasmuch as you attain to the numinous experiences you are released from the curse of pathology."[35]

Just as the people gathered at Newgrange at the Winter Solstice over 5,000 years ago to honour the sun's return to the earth, Sam's body and psyche have aligned in an expanded state of consciousness which has brought her deep healing and hope.

As I come to the close of this final chapter, I hope that the therapeutic aims and practice of BodyDreaming have been clearly illustrated through the transformative experiences of my clients, expressed so poignantly in their own words. It has been my intention to demonstrate the underlying tenet of BodyDreaming, namely the 'unified field' and interconnectedness of spirit and matter; psyche and soma; body, mind and soul. When we align ourselves in our sensing bodies with this unified field, we access our deepest knowing and sense of participation with a Self-regulating drive. The embodied relationship to our flesh roots us in relationship to our core self, an inner and outer orientation to 'Wholeness', which can change the patterns of developmental trauma little by little.

Notes

1 Ladinsky, 2006, p. 38.

2 "In our struggle towards a genuine encounter with the 'soul of the world', ... the secret may be the body—body as it is expressed in the individual person, physical, concrete, ensouled" (van Loben Sels, 2003, p. 221).

3 *Complex du jour*: a term used by Steven Hoskinson (Organic Intelligence- https://organicintelligence.org/) to describe the client's presenting issue or complex on that particular day. It is a complex as best described by Jung that is wired in the nervous system, and when it is triggered then the corresponding circuit of activation will be operating. Jung talks about the archetypal core of a complex, the organizing *idea* or *principle*, of which the complex is a personal and individual representation. Similarly, Hoskinson refers to the complex as part of the fractal system, the form of which will be repeated in each constellation wherever it is triggered.

4   The gesture is spontaneous and immediate. It is not an arbitrary sign that we mentally attach to a particular emotion or feeling; rather, the gesture *is* the bodying-forth of that emotion into the world, it *is* that feeling of delight or of anguish in its tangible, visible aspect.

(Abram, 1997, p. 74)

5   If he/she [referring to the client] can be encouraged to play with the imagery, allowing it to take whatever form it happens to come up with, the energy locked in the shadow will emerge, bringing with it the buried creative fire. In that new integration, the Self brings healing for the soul and energy for the art.

(Woodman in interview with Stromstead, 2005, p. 19)

6   The brain, motivated to learn from experience, responds plastically, for plasticity and motivation are linked (Doidge, 2007). Positive affects, that is, the reward aspect ... light up the way. Whether we are talking about the secretion of dopamine and acetylcholine, or of oxytocin, or about the down-regulation of the amygdala as states of fear are replaced with exploratory states ... the brain registers and marks the positive nature of experience and seeks to reengage it. In the process we change and grow.

(Fosha, 2009, p. 176)

7 Woodman might describe the embodied process we are engaged with as a waking dream.

> Body movements, I realized, can be understood as a waking dream. In its spontaneous movements the body is like an infant crying out to be heard, understood, responded to, much as a dream is sending out signals from the unconscious.
>
> (Woodman, 1982, p. 79)

8   Although … [embodied processing] … begins with a physical sensation, it often transforms that sensation into a feeling or image so that the border between imaginal and embodied modes of experience is blurred, at which point their reciprocal relationship becomes apparent. *Both* are symbolic ways of working. Each mode complements the other. The imaginal approach to psyche needs the grounding effect of embodied awareness to bring intuitive insight into the present moment of actual experience.

> (Greene, 2005, p. 202)

9 "A symbol does not define or explain; it points beyond itself to a meaning that is darkly divined yet still beyond our grasp, and cannot be adequately expressed in the familiar words of language" (Jung, 1926, par. 644).

10 The *numinous* is "accompanied by the ego's sense of being seized by a mysterious power greater than or 'beyond' itself, over and against which it stands in awe, fascination, or dread" (van Loben Sels, 2003, p. 17).

"The idea of God originated with the experience of the *numinosum.* It was a psychical experience, with moments when man felt overcome" (Jung, 1988, p. 1038).

Derived from the Latin *numen,* meaning hint or sign, any experience of the *numinous* provides a hint or sign of an energy and power that originates beyond the reach of ego-consciousness.

11 "[T]he molecules of our emotions share intimate connection with, and are indeed inseparable from, our physiology. It is the emotions, I have come to see, that link body and mind" (Pert, 1997, pp. 18–19).

12   Your body is always dreaming. By this I mean your body has a rich symbolic existence that assembles all the sensations and experiences that your conscious mind is ignoring, and then, instead of drawing you a picture as your dreaming psyche does, it offers you a symptom or a spontaneous craving or a flood of tears that has a depth of meaning that goes far beyond the limits of the literal "picture".

> (Reeves, 2003, p. 63)

13 Esther Harding, Jungian analyst, writes of the numinous energy that resides in the shadow, and of its direct effect on our system when it is brought to consciousness:

> [T]hrough the bringing to consciousness of the shadow and of the soul figure, only a part of the energy they contain is made available for conscious daily life; another, and that the greater part, retreats into less accessible regions of the unconscious. This elusive part is the numinous element—that component which has power to move us with fear or dread, which can 'make us to quake.' … The emotions aroused by this numinous aspect of the unconscious act through the sympathetic or autonomous nervous system, which is not under the control of the voluntary centres or of the conscious will. They therefore produce a direct effect in the body, such as strange reactions and sensations in the intestines, or palpitations of the heart… .
>
> (Harding, [1947] 1973, p. 314)

14 Just Noticeable Difference—see Chapter 1, p. 65. My intervention is a good indica-
tor of the countertransference operating in the activated therapist. By staying with the
questions, we keep the sympathetic system dominant and obstruct a further slowing
down which might allow a full parasympathetic response. The therapist learns to recognize these threshold moments and when to let go of questions and wait —allowing
the time it takes for the full parasympathetic response—for Sam's body to soften, to
"unjam". It is helpful for me in these moments, where we need to 'hover', to remind
myself of a phrase that Anne Skinner (BodySoul Rhythms) uses: "we have all the time
in the world." My nervous system implicitly resets and opens itself again to the unexpected and, coincidentally, the process is mirrored in the client.

15 Recognizing when we are triggered by the 'not knowing' state, and being able to
increase our window of tolerance in the 'not knowing' state, are primary steps in
BodyDreaming work. As we expand consciousness, we bring our attention to and
then titrate the arousal that's triggered, to create more space for emotions. As we
expand the window of consciousness, we are pushing against the edges of the window of tolerance.

16 "The unconscious per se is unknowable; it is a reality that is inferred from such things
as spontaneous or involuntary body movement and dreams. Ultimately, we may come to
think of body movement or the dreaming state as a manifestation not of unconsciousness,
but as a consciousness that operates upon us and within us" (Woodman, 1982, p. 79).

17 "The moment when 'I am moved' is astonishing both to dancers and to people who
have no intention of becoming dancers. It is a moment when the ego gives up control,
stops choosing, stops exerting demands, allowing the self to take over moving the
physical body as it wills. It is a moment of unpremeditated surrender that cannot be
explained, repeated exactly, sought for or tried out" (Whitehouse, 1999, p. 82).

18 See Bonnie Bainbridge Cohen, this volume, Chapter 5, n. 32.

19 In many ways the work of BodyDreaming is similar to the process of "deintegration and
reintegration" as described by Michael Fordham and Bryan Heath: "In essence deintegration and reintegration describe a fluctuating state of learning in which the infant
opens itself to new experiences and then withdraws in order to reintegrate and consolidate those experiences. During a deintegrative activity, the infant maintains continuity
with the main body of the self (or its centre) while venturing into the external world to
accumulate experience in motor action and sensory stimulation" (1989, p. 64).

20 "The symbols of the Self arise in the depths of the body and they express its materiality
every bit as much as the structure of the perceiving consciousness. The symbol is thus
a living body, *corpus et anima*" (Jung, 1939, CW 9/1, par. 291).

21 Irene Dowd was a dance movement teacher, author and choreographer at the Juilliard
School in New York from 1968. Her studies included anatomy and neuroanatomy.

22   It does not suffice in all cases to elucidate only the conceptual context of a dream-
content. Often it is necessary to clarify a vague content by giving it a visible
form. This can be done by drawing, painting or modelling. Often the hands know
how to solve a riddle with which the intellect has wrestled in vain. By shaping
it, one goes on dreaming the dream in greater detail in the waking state, and the
initially incomprehensible, isolated event is integrated into the sphere of the total
personality, even though it remains at first unconscious to the subject. ... The
less the initial material is shaped and developed, the greater is the danger that
understanding will be governed not by the empirical facts but by theoretical and
moral considerations.

(Jung, 1916, par. 180)

23   As a therapist you will offer just enough resistance to allow the client to sense
herself pushing out from her centre. You will be asking her to feel how the

movement seems to originate from her belly and is expressed through her shoulders and arms and out through her hands.

(Levine, 2010, p. 118)

24 The chemical *acetylcholine* is released, ensuring that cells that fire together wire together, strengthening the connection between the self-soothing gesture and the feeling of relaxation that accompanies it. Heller and LaPierre, writing of Hebb's Law, explain that

> if two neurons are electrically active at the same time, they will automatically form a connection. If they are weakly connected, the synapse between them will be strengthened. Neural firings gather all aspects of an experience together into a neural ensemble that is encoded in memory. Indeed, it is believed that the firing *is* the memory.
>
> (Heller and LaPierre, 2012, p. 102)

25 See Fechner, this volume, introductory chapter, "A Note to the Reader", p. 24, *n.* 35; and Chapter 1, p. 65.
26 Siegel describes integration as that which:

> enables the coordination and balance of a system to unfold over time. A complex, nonlinear system has a natural push toward integration. In interpersonal neurobiology, we see integration as yielding the flexible, adaptive, coherent, energized, and stable (FACES) flow that is bounded on one side by chaos and on the other side by rigidity. ... [W]e see integration as the heart of health; impaired integration results in the chaos and rigidity that are the hallmarks of dysfunction. ... [The] maintenance of the differentiated qualities of the individual components of the system even while linking them together is an essential aspect of integration. Linkage does not mean addition or making the same. Integration is not homogenization. Both differentiation and linkage compose integration.
>
> (Siegel, 2012, 16, 3–4)

27 This is a reference to Ann Skinner, Sam's voice teacher and mentor at the BodySoul Rhythms workshops she attended.

28   The *Rubedo* announces the full awakening of the heart, and the creation of the body of light. ... Body, soul and spirit are unified and transfigured in this experience. As a triune whole, they in turn are united with the divine ground of being—what the alchemists called the *unus mundus*.

(Baring, 2013, p. 482)

29 "My usage of the term [Recognition] includes, but goes beyond, the relational experience of being known. It refers to all experiences that occur when there is a match, a 'click' between something inside and something outside, however inside and outside are subjectively defined" (Fosha, 2009, p. 178).

30   Moment to moment recognition is accompanied by and expressed through 'vitality affects' (Stern, 2000). These vitality affects have *positive somatic affective markers* (e.g., deep sighs, fleeting smiles, head nods, sideways head tilts); they tell us the transformational process is on track.

(Fosha, 2009, p. 178)

31   To ignore what we do to ourselves [our bodies] ... will cut us off from a richly connected source of embodied energy. It is as if we have welded shut the access to

the realm of the maternal—of *Mater*, of *matter*—of *Mattering*. If you truly wish to meet your heart, you have to be willing to receive its wisdom about what matters in your most private thoughts and feelings.

(Reeves, 2003, p. 49)

32 Pert, 1997, p. 189. See this volume, Chapter 2, p. 75.
33 See Jung's essay, "The Psychology of the Transference," 1946, par. 422, in which Jung provides a diagram of the unconscious dynamics active *between* therapist and client, as well as those operative *in* both therapist and client.
34 Jung, 1952, p. 229.
35 Letter to P.W. Martin, 20 August 1945, in Jung, 1973, p. 377.

References

Abram, D. (1997) *The Spell of the Sensuous*, New York: Vintage Books.
Baring, A. (2013) *Dream of the Cosmos: A Quest for the Soul*, Dorset, UK: Archive Publishing.
Dowd, I. (1995) *Taking Root to Fly: Articles on Functional Anatomy*, New York: Irene Dowd.
Fechner, G.T. (1873). *Einige Ideen zur Schöpfungs- und Entwickelungsgechichte der Organismen* [*Ideas in the History of Organism Creation and Development*], Leipzig: Breitkopf und Härtel.
Fordham, M. and Heath, B. (1989) "The Infant's Reach: Reflections on Maturation in Early Life," *Psychological Perspectives: A Quarterly Journal of Jungian Thought*, 21 (1): 59–76.
Fosha, D. (2009) "Emotion and Recognition at Work: Energy, Vitality, Pleasure, Truth, Desire, and the Emergent Phenomenology of Transformational Experience," in *The Healing Power of Emotion: Affective Neuroscience, Development and Clinical Practice*, D. Fosha, D.J. Siegel and M. Solomon (eds.), New York: W.W. Norton & Co., pp. 172–203.
Greene, A.U. (2005) "Listening to the Body for the Sake of the Soul," *Spring, A Journal of Archetype and Culture*, Body & Soul: Honouring Marion Woodman, 72: 189–204.
Harding, E. ([1947] 1973) *Psychic Energy: Its Source and Its Transformation*, Bollingen Series X, Princeton, NJ: Princeton University Press.
Heller, L. and LaPierre, A. (2012) *Healing Developmental Trauma: How Early Trauma Affects Self-Regulation, Self-Image, and the Capacity for Relationship*, Berkeley, CA: North Atlantic Books.
Jung, C.G. (1916) *General Aspects of Dream Psychology*, Collected Works 8, Princeton, NJ: Princeton University Press.
Jung, C.G. ([1916] 1958) *The Transcendent Function*, Collected Works 8, Princeton, NJ: Princeton University Press.
Jung, C.G. (1926) *Spirit and Life*, Collected Works 8, Princeton, NJ: Princeton University Press.
Jung, C.G. (1935) *The Tavistock Lectures: On the Theory and Practice of Analytical Psychology*, Collected Works 18, Princeton, NJ: Princeton University Press.
Jung, C.G. (1939) *Conscious, Unconscious, and Individuation*, Collected Works 9/1, Princeton, NJ: Princeton University Press.
Jung, C.G. (1946) *The Psychology of the Transference*, Collected Works 16, Princeton, NJ: Princeton University Press.

Jung, C.G. (1947) *On the Nature of the Psyche*, Collected Works 8, Princeton, NJ: Princeton University Press.

Jung, C.G. (1952[1977]) "Combat Interview," in *C.G. Jung Speaking: Interviews and Encounters*, W. McGuire and R.F.C. Hull (eds.), Princeton, NJ: Princeton University Press (1977), p. 229.

Jung, C.G. (1973) *Letters, Vol. 1, 1906–1950*, G. Adler (ed.), trans. R.F.C. Hull, Princeton, NJ: Princeton University Press.

Jung, C.G. (1988) *Nietzsche's Zarathustra: Notes of the Seminar Given in 1934–1939*, James L. Jarrett (ed.), in two volumes, Bollingen Series XCIX, Princeton, NJ: Princeton University Press (London and New York: Routledge: 1989).

Ladinsky, D. (2006) *I Heard God Laughing: Poems of Hope and Joy*, London: Penguin.

Levine, P. (2010) *In an Unspoken Voice: How the Body Releases Trauma and Restores Goodness*, Berkeley, CA: North Atlantic Books.

Levine, P. (2015) *Trauma and Memory: Brain and Body in a Search for the Living Past: A Practical Guide for Understanding and Living with Personal Trauma*, Berkeley, CA: North Atlantic Books.

Monte, C. (2015) *Corpus Anima: Reflections from the Unity of Body and Soul*, Ashville, NC: Chiron Publications.

Neumann, E. (1989) *Place of Creation*, Bollingen Series LX1 – 3, Princeton, NJ: Princeton University Press.

Pert, C. (1997) *Molecules of Emotion: The Science behind Mind-Body Medicine*, New York: Scribner.

Reeves, P. (2003) *Heart Sense: Unlocking your Highest Purpose and Deepest Desires*, Boston, MA: Conari Press.

Ryley, N. (1998) *The Forsaken Garden, Four Conversations on the Deep Meaning of Environmental Illness*, Wheaton, IL: Quest Books.

Siegel, D.J. (2012) *Pocket Guide to Interpersonal Neurobiology: An Integrative Handbook of the Mind*, New York: W.W Norton & Co.

Stromstead, T. (2005) Interview with Marion Woodman, "Cellular Resonance and the Sacred Feminine: Marion Woodman's Story," *Spring, A Journal of Archetype and Culture*, Body and Soul: Honouring Marion Woodman, 72: 1–30.

van Loben Sels, R. (2003) *A Dream in the World: Poetics of Soul in Two Women, Modern and Medieval*, Hove, UK and New York: Brunner-Routledge.

Whitehouse, M.S. (1999) "C.G. Jung and Dance Therapy: Two Major Principles," in *Authentic Movement: Essays by Mary Starks Whitehouse, Janet Adler and Joan Chodorow*, Patrizia Pallaro (ed.), London and Philadelphia, PA: Jessica Kingsley Publishers, pp. 73–101.

Woodman, M. (1982) *Addiction to Perfection: The Still Unravished Bride*, Toronto: Inner City Books.

Woodman, M. (1990) *The Ravaged Bridegroom: Masculinity in Women*, Toronto: Inner City Books.

Woodman, M. and Dickson, E. (1996) *Dancing in the Flames: The Dark Goddess in the Transformation of Consciousness*, Dublin: Gill & MacMillan.

Conclusion

"Let your hands touch something that makes your eyes smile"

I know a cure for sadness:
Let your hands touch something that
makes your eyes
smile.

I bet there are a hundred objects close by
that can do that.

Look at
beauty's gift to us –
her power is so great she enlivens
the earth, the sky, our
soul.
(Mirabai, "A Hundred Objects
Close By", translated by
Daniel Ladinsky)[1]

The image of the pearl provides a metaphor for the core of BodyDreaming work during the process of which we encounter, in the depths of the somatic unconscious, those irritants that initially disrupt homeostasis and disturb the natural flow of expansion and contraction of our autonomic nervous systems ... but with attunement and titration a pearl can form. These 'irritants' may include genetic factors, developmental trauma, early relationship deficits, complexes, physical or psychological trauma on a global or individual scale, all of which are held in implicit memory and wired into the autonomic nervous system's responses in the body. As with the process involved in transforming an irritant into a priceless gem, in BodyDreaming we work to restore homeostasis, evoking the body and psyche's innate self-regulatory rhythms. In the process we are repatterning nervous system responses, and creating neural pathways, ultimately opening space for new possibilities to present themselves. Often our work involves holding the tension of opposites, out of which tension a new 'third', new life, insight or possibility may develop. We demonstrate this movement between activation and deactivation in the early chapters with Cho, Maria, Sam and Helen. We titrate the emotion that is associated to the activation, with the corresponding emotion associated to the deactivating resource. We spend time experiencing and resonating with the opposite energies until the innate impulse for healing triggers a new image or gesture. As readers we are witness to a new alignment happening, a Newgrange moment, where inner and outer, image and body, couple in a new alliance. We, as readers, become active witnesses participating through attuning to the resonating matter of our connective tissue, muscle, bone, and nervous system. The individual 'client' is released from her anxiety, distress or concern and finds herself supported and strengthened at a core level by the engagement with the BodyDreaming process.

When we incorporate BodyDreaming into our therapeutic practice, we find ourselves working with, being guided by and bringing awareness to the deep layers of the somatic unconscious, where the autonomic responses of the body lie. We learn to attend to our nervous system responses and align with our natural capacity to self-regulate. The careful process of attunement slowly leads us into relationship with the images and dreams as they resonate in our sensing moving bodies. In Sam's case we worked with the energy of the Big Cats dream and saw how the BodyDreaming practice opened the field and expanded Sam's capacity to listen and attend to her body as it resonated with gestures and movements arising in response to the dream image. The energy of the dream became embodied as Sam gave free expression to the impulses arising out of her body in the movements of her muscles and joints, hips, legs, arms. Her matter and the matter of the Big Cats wove together in 'dreaming on the dream'. Sam reconnected to the axis that aligns her dreams and images with her body's wisdom, like at Newgrange where the sun penetrates the inner chamber at the Winter Solstice.

In BodyDreaming we may become aware of the relativity of our ego in relation to a growing intimation of a larger consciousness or reality inclusive of the world both within and without, and find ourselves participants in a reciprocal 'unified field'. We may experience moments of recognition during which we perceive that a 'pearl of great price' lies buried within our sensing, feeling matter and psyche. Through attending to our matter and psyche, we develop the capacity to align with the Self- regulating principal and the innate drive toward wholeness that Jung addresses, working toward the fulfilment of our human and spiritual potential. However, the 'pearl of great price' is to be honed with the material from the somatic unconscious, whose depths lie in the dark ocean, and must be brought into the light of day, into consciousness, through the meticulous regulatory work of attunement and regulation, before its luminosity may be revealed.

We begin to recognize and appreciate the reciprocity that is possible between our matter and the matter that surrounds us. With Kate we found ourselves engaged in a conversation with the bushes. Gradually, the body inside and the body outside were speaking to each other. We witnessed Kate not disconnect, not dissociate, not shut her eyes but keep them open and stay connected to the safety that the bushes offered. Kate's conversational exchange with 'the bushes that don't have panic attacks' awakened her humour and playfulness and became a way to make herself and the room whole again. We might say that, like at Newgrange where the passageway opened with the Winter Solstice light, the connection between Kate and the bushes opened the passageway for each member of the group to experience her participation in our shared nature. The group had come to an alignment; the ego with the wider field of the self, eager to welcome 'the silence beneath the sound'.

In conjunction with neuroscientific research, analytical psychology, developmental psychology and somatic practices Bodydreaming offers a therapeutic method of working with developmental trauma and other traumas that encompass self and inter-regulation, requiring both inner and outer attunement. In a world in which psychological fragmentation and disorientation are widespread, the aim of BodyDreaming is to enhance our sense of rootedness and participation in the world through attunement to the regulatory life force we meet in the body, in dreams and in relation to the 'other', the world in which we participate. Inner attunement promotes the growth of a steady secure base which enables us to feel our sensing bodies and psyche as participants in a wider dynamic field.

We recall the insecure attachment styles of David's anxious, and Therese and Luke's disorganized, attachment patterns that kept them prisoner to the developmental trauma still operating in their emotions, behaviours, beliefs and most importantly in their nervous system responses. Each of them was in long-term analysis with me. Over time, together, we built an attuned relationship to the sensing body that supported the work of repatterning the nervous system and the deep release from the underlying freeze/ immobility response of the dorsal vagus. BodyDreaming work fosters an attunement to the core body-sensing self, which widens the capacity to tolerate and witness the difficult and often shameful dynamics operating between the different parts of the self, e.g., protector/ persecutor, victim /controller. In focusing on self-regulation we were able to expand their window of tolerance for painful and opposite feelings, pull back the projections onto others of neglected and despised parts and find an alignment with the self-guiding principle of wholeness that is operating both within and around us.

With the BodyDreaming approach we may begin to experience our sensing bodies, our matter transform at a cellular level in response to the quality of attention we bring to it. In Ana's case the slow pace and mirroring of the work was critical to enable Ana to receive / take in at a felt sense level the memory that was evoked for her of a 'good feed' of schnitzels cooked for her by her loving grandmother. Her face lit up with delight and wonder, her tummy warmed, her bones drank it up, as she ingested the love in those schnitzels that reached right to her kidneys. The group witnessed Ana's deep cellular pleasure and the archetypal love of her grandmother was enjoyed by everyone present, as reflected in each participant's face. The quality of numinosity that came through the shared experience was palpable and healing.

Sam's dream in Chapter 9 also invites us to consider an experience of the numinous and its power to bring us into a deeper alignment with Self. Often, as in Sam's case, we can feel overwhelmed by emotion in the face of the numen, and can shut down or override the experience. However, the gradual process of titrating the emotions of awe and fear and the dorsal vagal freeze / immobility response brought Sam into an easier dialogue with the unfamiliar that was presenting itself to her firstly in the heartbeat of her image and latterly in the dream image of the woman in the red housecoat. Gradually we titrated the experiences to expand her 'window of tolerance' to include a new "extraneous knowledge" (Neumann, 1989, p. 7). The last section of the dream, the lysis, points the direction in which the energy wants to move (Woodman, 1990, p. 88). Sam's sensing body has released her from overwhelm and immobility, the legacy of developmental trauma. She can dream her dream on, knowing now how to respond to the invitation from the woman in the red housecoat. She is ready to take action. Body and psyche have aligned in a new and expanded state of consciousness, introduced by the numinous dream image, and her body is alive with a sense of agency and hope.

This returns us to the metaphor of the alignment at Newgrange at the time of the Winter Solstice, which presents an image of a largely forgotten world in which the cyclical alignment of inner and outer, body and psyche, matter and soul was held sacred. What if we were to establish self-regulation as the central axis of therapy? This would mean prioritizing an orientation to and alignment with our natural capacity for self- and inter-regulation, an inner attunement to the somatic unconscious and psyche's manifestations and an outer attunement to our surroundings. Self- and inter-regulation do not belong solely to human physiology and psychology but are shared by all living things. In discovering a secure base in our sensing body's core self we find we are participants within our natural world.

Neuroscience confirms what the construction of the cairn at Newgrange demonstrates and ancient traditions from many cultures worldwide have always known, namely, as previously cited in Chapter 1, "[h]ow the body can think beyond anything ever formulated before—how it senses on the edge of human thinking" (Gendlin, 1992, pp. 341–353). Perhaps we may dare to dream that our sensing body may already be leading us into a new paradigm in which our alignment with the self-regulatory principal in our matter and all matter may hold the remedy for our ailing planet. In the words of Mirabai, the renowned woman poet-saint of India, (c. 1495–1550):

> *her power is so great she enlivens*
> *the earth, the sky, our*
> *soul.*[2]

*

Notes

1 Ladinsky, 2002, p. 245.
2 Ladinsky, *ibid.*

References

Gendlin, E. (1992) "The Primacy of the Body not the Primacy of Perception: How the Body Knows the Situation and Philosophy," excerpt from *Man and World*, 25 (3–4): 341–353. Accessed 29 August 2018 at: www.focusing.org/pdf/primacy_excerpt.pdf.

Ladinsky, D. (2002) *Love Poems from God: Twelve Sacred Voices from the East and West*, New York: Penguin Compass.

Neumann, E. (1989) *Place of Creation*, Bollingen Series LX1 – 3, Princeton, NJ: Princeton University Press.

Woodman, M. (1990) *The Ravaged Bridegroom: Masculinity in Women*, Toronto: Inner City Books.

Bibliography

Abram, D. (1997) *The Spell of the Sensuous*, New York: Vintage Books.

Abram, D. (2011) *Becoming Animal*, New York: Vintage Books.

Adler, J. (1999) "Body and Soul," in *Authentic Movement: Essays by Mary Starks Whitehouse, Janet Adler and Joan Chodorow*, Patrizia Pallaro (ed.), London and Philadelphia, PA: Jessica Kingsley Publishers, pp. 160–189.

Adler, J. (2002) *Offering from the Conscious Body: The Discipline of Authentic Movement*, Rochester, VT: Inner Traditions.

Ainsworth, M.I.S. and Wittig, B.A. (1969). "Attachment and the Exploratory Behaviour of One-Year-Olds in a Strange Situation," in B.M. Foss (Ed.), *Determinants of Infant Behaviour* (Vol. 4), London: Methuen, pp. 113–136.

Ainsworth, M., Blehar, M., Waters, E. and Wall, S. (1979) *Patterns of Attachment: A Psychological Study of the Strange Situation*, Hillside, NJ: Erlbaum.

Allen, J.G., Console, D.A. and Lewis, L. (1999). "Dissociative Detachment and Memory Impairment: Reversible Amnesia or Encoding Failure?" *Comprehensive Psychiatry*, 40, 160–171.

Bacon, J. (2007) "Active Imagination and Focusing in Movement-based Performance and Psychotherapy," *Body Movement and Dance Psychotherapy*, March 2007, 2(1): 17–28.

Bainbridge Cohen, B. (1993) *Sensing, Feeling, and Action: The Experiential Anatomy of Body-Mind Centering*, Northampton, MA: Contact Editions.

Bainbridge Cohen, B. (1995) "Excerpts from Sensing, Feeling and Action," in D. Hanlon Johnson (ed.) *Bone, Breath, and Gesture: Practices of Embodiment*, Berkeley, CA: North Atlantic Books, pp. 185–204.

Baring, A. (2013) *Dream of the Cosmos: A Quest for the Soul*, Dorset, UK: Archive Publishing.

Baring, A. and Cashford, J. (1993) *The Myth of the Goddess: Evolution of an Image*, London: Arkana; Penguin Books.

Barks, C. (1997) "Birdwings," in *The Essential Rumi: Translations by Coleman Barks*, New Jersey, NJ: Castle Books.

Bateson, M.C. (1979) "The Epigenesis of Conversational Interaction: A Personal Account of Research Development," in Bullowa (ed.), *Before Speech: The Beginning of Human Communication*, London: Cambridge University Press, pp. 63–77.

Beebe, B. and Lachmann, F. (2002) *Infant Research and Adult Treatment: Co-constructing Interactions*, Hillsdale, NJ: The Analytic Press.

Beebe, B. and Lachmann, F. (2013) *The Origins of Attachment: Infant Research and Adult Treatment*, Hillsdale, NJ: The Analytic Press.

Bentov, I. (1988) *Stalking the Wild Pendulum: On the Mechanics of Consciousness*, Rochester, VT: Destiny Books.

Bick, E. (1968) "The Experience of the Skin in Early Object Relations," *International Journal of Psychoanalysis*, 49(2): 484–486.

Bion, W.R. (1959) "Attacks on Linking," *International Journal of Psychoanalysis*, 40: 308–315. Reprinted in: *Second Thoughts* (1967), New York: Jason Aronson, pp. 93–109.

Bishop, P. (1990) *The Greening of Psychology: The Vegetable World in Myth, Dream and Healing*, Dallas, TX: Spring.

Boa, F. (1988) *The Way of the Dream: Conversations on Jungian Dream Interpretation with Marie-Louise von Franz*, Boston, MA and London: Shambhala.

Bohm, D. (1980) *Wholeness and the Implicate Order*, London, Boston, MA, and Henley, UK: Routledge and Kegan Paul.

Bowlby, J. ([1969] 1981) *Attachment and Loss: Volume 1, Attachment*. Harmondsworth, UK: Penguin Books.

Bowlby, J. (1980) *Attachment and Loss*. Vol. 3. *Loss: Sadness and Depression*. International psycho-analytical library no.109. London: Hogarth Press.

Bowlby, J. (1988a) *A Secure Base: Clinical Applications of Attachment Theory*, London: Routledge.

Bowlby, J. (1988b) "Attachment, Communication, and the Therapeutic Process," in *A Secure Base: Parent-Child Attachment and Healthy Human Development*, London: Routledge, pp. 137–157.

Brennan, J.H. (1994) *A Guide to Megalithic Ireland*, London: The Aquarian Press.

Bromberg, P. (1996) "Standing in the Spaces: The Multiplicity of Self and The Psychoanalytic Relationship," *Journal of Contemporary Psychoanalysis*, 32: 509–535.

Bromberg, P. (2006) *Awakening the Dreamer: Clinical Journeys*, Mahwah, NJ: The Analytic Press.

Cannon, W.B. (1932) *The Wisdom of the Body: How the Human Body Reacts to Disturbance and Danger and Maintains the Stability Essential to Life*, New York: W.W. Norton & Co.

Capra, F. (1975) *The Tao of Physics: An Exploration of the Parallels Between Modern Physics and Eastern Mysticism*, Boston, MA: Shambhala Publications.

Capra, F. (1982) *The Turning Point: Science Society and the Rising Culture*, London: Flamingo.

Chodorow, J. (1986) "The Body as Symbol," in *The Body in Analysis*, Nathan Schwartz-Salant and Murray Stein (eds.), Wilmette, IL: Chiron Publications, pp. 87–91.

Chodorow, J. (1991) *Dance Therapy and Depth Psychology: The Moving Imagination*, London: Routledge.

Chodorow, J., ed. (1997) *Jung on Active Imagination: Encountering Jung*, Princeton, NJ: Princeton University Press.

Chodorow, J. (1999) "Joan Chodorow," in *Authentic Movement: Essays by Mary Starks Whitehouse, Janet Adler and Joan Chodorow*, Patrizia Pallaro (ed.), London and Philadelphia, PA: Jessica Kingsley Publishers, pp. 209–311.

Condren, M. (1989) *The Serpent and the Goddess: Women, Religion and Power in Celtic Ireland*, San Francisco, CA: Harper Collins.

Congram, S., Mayes, M. and Musselbrook, M. (2017) *Engendering Balance: A Fresh Approach to Leadership*, 2nd edition, Dolgarren, St. Weonards: Engendering Balance Ltd.

Cozolino, L. (2002) *The Neuroscience of Psychotherapy: Building and Rebuilding the Human Brain*, New York: W.W. Norton & Co.

Damasio, A. (2000) *The Feeling of What Happens: Body, Emotion and the Making of Consciousness*, London: Vintage.

Damasio, A. (2003) *Looking for Spinoza: Joy, Sorrow, and the Feeling Brain*, Orlando, FL: Harcourt Books.

Davies, J.M. and Frawley, M.G. (1992). "Dissociative Processes and Transference-Countertransference Paradigms in the Psychoanalytically Oriented Treatment of Adult Survivors of Childhood Sexual Abuse," *Psychoanalytic Dialogues*, 2, 5–36.

Dickinson, E. ([1863] 1999) "There is a pain – so utter –." No. 515. In *The Poems of Emily Dickinson, Reading Edition*, R.W. Franklin (ed.), Cambridge, MA; London: Harvard University Press.

Dowd, I. (1995) *Taking Root to Fly: Articles on Functional Anatomy*, New York: Irene Dowd.

Dubuc, B. "How Drugs Affect Neurotransmitters". The Brain from Top to Bottom. Accessed 22 August 2018 at: http://thebrain.mcgill.ca/flash/i/i_03/i_03_m/i_03_m_par/i_03_m_par_heroine.html.

Dykema, R. (2006). "How Your Nervous System Sabotages Your Ability to Relate: An Interview with Stephen Porges About His Polyvagal Theory." NexusPub. March/April 2006. Accessed 29 August 2018 at: https://acusticusneurinom.dk/wp-content/uploads/2015/10/polyvagal_interview_porges.pdf. Pp.1–11.

Edinger, E.F. (1994) *Anatomy of the Psyche: Alchemical Symbolism in Psychotherapy*, Chicago and La Salle, IL: Open Court.

Edinger, E.F. (1972) *Ego and Archetype: Individuation and the Religious Function of the Psyche*, Boston, MA: Shambhala.

Eliot, T.S. (1943) "Little Gidding," in *Four Quartets*, New York: Harcourt, Brace, and Company, pp. 241–242.

Fechner, G.T. (1873). *Einige Ideen zur Schöpfungs- und Entwickelungsgechichte der Organismen* [*Ideas in the History of Organism Creation and Development*], Leipzig: Breitkopf und Härtel.

Fonagy, P., Gergely, G., Jurist E. and Target, M. (2004) *Affect Regulation, Mentalization and the Development of the Self*, London: Karnac Books Ltd.

Fordham, M. and Heath, B. (1989) "The Infant's Reach: Reflections on Maturation in Early Life," *Psychological Perspectives: A Quarterly Journal of Jungian Thought*, 21(1): 59–76.

Fosha, D. (2009) "Emotion and Recognition at Work: Energy, Vitality, Pleasure, Truth, Desire, and the Emergent Phenomenology of Transformational Experience," in *The Healing Power of Emotion: Affective Neuroscience, Development and Clinical Practice*, D. Fosha, D.J. Siegel and M. Solomon (eds.), New York: W.W. Norton & Co., pp. 172–203.

Fosha, D., Siegel, D., Soloman, M., eds. (2009) *The Healing Power of Emotion: Affective Neuroscience, Development and Clinical Practice*, New York: W.W. Norton & Co.

Freud, S. ([1900] 1976) *The Interpretation of Dreams*, Harmondsworth, UK: Penguin.

Freud, S. ([1923] 1961) *The Standard Edition of the Complete Psychological Works of Sigmund Freud. Volume XIX, 1923–1925, The Ego and the Id and Other works*. London: The Hogarth Press and The Institute of Psycho-Analysis.

Freud, S. ([1930] 2001) *The Standard Edition of the Complete Psychological Works of Sigmund Freud. Vol. 21, 1927–1931, The Future of an Illusion; Civilisation and its*

Discontents; and Other Works. London: Hogarth Press and The Institute of Psycho-Analysis.

Gallese, V. (2006) "Mirror Neurons and Intentional Attunement: A Commentary on David Olds," *Journal of the American Psychoanalytic Association*, February 2006, 54(1): 47–57.

Gendlin, E. (1981) *Focusing*, New York: Bantam Books.

Gendlin, E. (1986) *Let Your Body Interpret Your Dreams*, Wilmette, IL: Chiron Publications.

Gendlin, E. (1992) "The Primacy of the Body not the Primacy of Perception: How the Body Knows the Situation and Philosophy," excerpt from *Man and World*, 25(3–4): 341–353. Accessed 29 August 2018 at: http://www.focusing.org/pdf/primacy_excerpt.pdf.

George, C., Kaplan, N. and Main, M. (1985) "The Adult Attachment Interview Protocol (AAI)." Unpublished manuscript held at the University of California, Berkeley.

Gerhardt, S. (2004) *Why Love Matters: How Affection Shapes a Baby's Brain*, East Sussex, UK: Routledge.

Gerhardt, S. (2011) "Why Love Matters: How Affection Shapes a Baby's Brain," *Improving the Quality of Childhood in the European Union – Volume II*, The European Council for Steiner Waldorf Education, pp. 80–97. This article is based on a verbal presentation given to the Quality of Childhood Group in the European Parliament in December 2009. Accessed 29 August 2018 at: http://www.ecswe.net/qoc-vol2/.

Gerson, Jacqueline (2005) "Wounded Instincts, Weeping Soul: Working with Embodied Countertransference," *Spring, A Journal of Archetype and Culture*, Body & Soul: Honouring Marion Woodman, 72: 205–217.

Gianino, A. and Tronick, E.Z. (1986) "Interactive Mismatch and Repair: Challenges to the Coping Infant," *ZERO TO THREE, Bulletin of the National Center for Clinical Infant Programs* 5: 1–6. Reprinted in: Tronick, E.Z., (2007) *The Neurobehavioural and Social–Emotional Development of Infants and Children*, New York: W.W. Norton, pp. 155–163.

Gimenez Ramos, D. (2004) *The Psyche of the Body: A Jungian Approach to Psychosomatics*, Hove, UK and New York: Brunner Routledge.

Green, N.P.O., Stout, G.W., Taylor, D.J. and Soper, R., eds. (1984) *Biological Science*, Cambridge: Cambridge University Press.

Greene, A.U. (2005) "Listening to the Body for the Sake of the Soul," *Spring, A Journal of Archetype and Culture*, Body & Soul: Honouring Marion Woodman, 72: 189–204.

Hamilton, M. (2009) *The Dragon Fly Principal: An Exploration of the Body's Function in Unfolding Spirituality*, London and Ontario: Colenso Island Press.

Hanlon Johnson, D. and Grand, I.J., eds. (1998) *The Body in Psychotherapy: Inquiries in Somatic Psychology*, Berkeley, CA: North Atlantic Books.

Hanlon Johnson, D., ed. (1995) *Bone, Breath, and Gesture: Practices of Embodiment*, Berkeley, CA: North Atlantic Books.

Harding, E. ([1947] 1973) *Psychic Energy: Its Source and Its Transformation*, Bollingen Series X, Princeton, NJ: Princeton University Press.

Harris, J. (2001) *Jung and the Body: The Psyche – Body Connection*, Toronto: Inner City Books.

Harris, J., ed. (2016) *The Quotable Jung*, Princeton, NJ: Princeton University Press.

Hartley, L. (2004) *Somatic Psychology: Body, Mind and Meaning*, Berkeley, CA: North Atlantic Books.

Heidelberger, M. (2004) *Nature from Within: Gustav Theodor Fechner and his Psychophysical Worldview*, trans. Cynthia Klohr, Pittsburgh, PA: University of Pittsburgh Press.

Heller, L. and LaPierre, A. (2012) *Healing Developmental Trauma: How Early Trauma Affects Self-Regulation, Self-Image, and the Capacity for Relationship*, Berkeley, CA: North Atlantic Books.

Hillman, J. (1962) *Emotion*, London: Routledge.

Hillman, J. (1975) *Revisioning Psychology*, New York: Harper & Row.

Hillman, J. (1979) *The Dream and the Underworld*, New York: William Morrow Paperbacks Harper Collins.

Jacoby, M. (1999) *Jungian Psychotherapy and Contemporary Infant Research: Basic Patterns of Emotional Exchange*, London: Routledge.

Johnson, S. (2009) "Extravagant Emotion: Understanding and Transforming Love Relationships in Emotional Focused Therapy," in *The Healing Power of Emotion: Affective Neuroscience, Development and Clinical Practice*, D. Fosha, D.J. Siegel and M. Solomon (eds.), New York: W.W. Norton and Co., pp. 257–299.

Jones, C. (2007) *Temples of Stone: Exploring the Megalithic Monuments of Ireland*, Cork: Collins Press.

Joyce, J. (2000) *A Portrait of the Artist as a Young Man*, Oxford; New York: Oxford World's Classics.

Jung, C.G. (1912) *Symbols of Transformation*, Collected Works 5, Princeton, NJ: Princeton University Press.

Jung, C.G. (1916) *General Aspects of Dream Psychology*, Collected Works 8, Princeton, NJ: Princeton University Press.

Jung, C.G. (1917) *On the Psychology of the Unconscious*, Collected Works 7, Princeton, NJ: Princeton University Press.

Jung, C.G. ([1916] 1958) *The Transcendent Function*, Collected Works 8, Princeton, NJ: Princeton University Press.

Jung, C.G. (1921a) *Schiller's Ideas on the Type Problem*, Collected Works 6, Princeton, NJ: Princeton University Press.

Jung, C.G. (1921b) *Psychological Types*, Collected Works 6, Princeton, NJ: Princeton University Press.

Jung, C.G. (1926) *Spirit and Life*, Collected Works 8, Princeton, NJ: Princeton University Press.

Jung, C.G. (1928a) *Analytical Psychology and 'Weltanschauung'*, Collected Works 8, Princeton, NJ: Princeton University Press.

Jung, C.G. (1928b) *On Psychic Energy*, Collected Works 8, Princeton, NJ: Princeton University Press.

Jung, C.G. (1928c) *The Therapeutic Value of Abreaction*, Collected Works 16, Princeton, NJ: Princeton University Press.

Jung, C.G. (1929/33) *The Aims of Psychotherapy*, Collected Works 16, Princeton, NJ: Princeton University Press.

Jung, C. G. (1931a) *A Psychological Theory of Types*, Collected Works 6, Princeton, NJ: Princeton University Press.

Jung, C.G. (1931b) *Archaic Man*, Collected Works 10, Princeton, NJ: Princeton University Press.

Jung, C.G. (1933) *The Meaning of Psychology for Modern Man*, Collected Works 10, Princeton, NJ: Princeton University Press.

Jung, C.G. (1934) *A Review of the Complex Theory*, Collected Works 8, Princeton, NJ: Princeton University Press.

Jung, C.G. (1935) *The Tavistock Lectures: On the Theory and Practice of Analytical Psychology*, Collected Works 18, Princeton, NJ: Princeton University Press.

Jung, C.G. (1936) *Individual Dream Symbolism in Relation to Alchemy*, Collected Works 12, Princeton, NJ: Princeton University Press.

Jung, C.G. (1937) *Psychological Factors Determining Human Behaviour*, Collected Works 8, Princeton, NJ: Princeton University Press.

Jung, C.G. (1938) *Psychology and Religion*, Collected Works 11, Princeton, NJ: Princeton University Press.

Jung, C.G. (1939) *Conscious, Unconscious, and Individuation*, Collected Works 9/1, Princeton, NJ: Princeton University Press.

Jung, C.G. (1942) *Paracelsus as a Spiritual Phenomenon*, Collected Works 13, Princeton, NJ: Princeton University Press.

Jung, C.G. (1943) *The Psychology of Eastern Meditation*, Collected Works 11, Princeton, NJ: Princeton University Press.

Jung, C.G. (1946) *The Psychology of the Transference*, Collected Works 16, Princeton, NJ: Princeton University Press.

Jung, C.G. (1947) *On the Nature of the Psyche*, Collected Works 8, Princeton, NJ: Princeton University Press.

Jung, C.G. (1949) *The Psychology of the Child Archetype*, Collected Works 9/1, Princeton, NJ: Princeton University Press.

Jung, C.G. (1952) "Combat Interview," in *C.G. Jung Speaking: Interviews and Encounters*, W. McGuire and R.F.C. Hull (eds.), Princeton, NJ: Princeton University Press (1977), p. 229.

Jung, C.G. (1955) *The Components of the Coniunctio*, Collected Works 14, Princeton, NJ: Princeton University Press.

Jung, C.G. ([1955–56] 1970) *Mysterium Coniunctionus: An Inquiry into the Separation and Synthesis of Psychic Opposites in Alchemy*, Collected Works 14, Princeton, NJ: Princeton University Press.

Jung, C.G. (1959) *Flying Saucers: A Modern Myth of Things Seen in the Skies*, Collected Works 10, Princeton, NJ: Princeton University Press.

Jung, C.G. (1961) *Symbols and the Interpretation of Dreams*, Bollingen Series XX, Collected Works 18, Princeton, NJ: Princeton University Press.

Jung, C.G. (1962) *Commentary on "The Secret of the Golden Flower"*, Collected Works 13, Princeton, NJ: Princeton University Press.

Jung, C.G. (1964) *Man and his Symbols*. Conceived and edited by Carl G. Jung. New York: Doubleday.

Jung, C.G. (1973) *Letters, Vol. 1, 1906–1950*, G. Adler (ed.), trans. R.F.C. Hull, Princeton, NJ: Princeton University Press.

Jung, C.G. (1988) *Nietzsche's Zarathustra: Notes of the Seminar Given in 1934–1939*, James L. Jarrett (ed.), in two volumes, Bollingen Series XCIX, Princeton, NJ: Princeton University Press (London & New York: Routledge: 1989).

Jung, C.G. (1995) *Memories, Dreams, Reflections*. A. Jaffé (ed.), trans. R. Winston and C. Winston, London: Fontana.

Jung, C.G. (1997) *Visions: Notes of the Seminar Given in 1930–1934*, Claire Douglas (ed.), in two volumes, Bollingen Series XCIX, Princeton, NJ: Princeton University Press (London & New York: Routledge, 1998).

Jung, C.G. (2000) *Collected Works of C.G. Jung*, Sir Herbert Read, Michael Fordham, Gerhard Adler (eds.) and William McGuire (executive editor), Bollingen Series XX, Princeton, NJ: Princeton University Press (London & New York: Routledge).

Jung, C.G. (2009) *The Red Book: Liber Novus*, S. Shamdasani (ed.), trans. M. Kyburz, J. Peck, and S. Shamdasani, New York: W.W. Norton.

Kalsched, D. (1996) *The Inner World of Trauma: Archetypal Defences of the Personal Spirit*, London: Routledge.

Kalsched, D. (2005a) "Dante's Dis: Archetypal image and Clinical Reality with Early Trauma Patients," *Quadrant* 35(1): 10–33.

Kalsched, D. (2005b) "Hope vs. Hopelessness in the Psychoanalytic Situation and in Dante's Divine Comedy," *Spring, A Journal of Archetype and Culture*, Body and Soul: Honouring Marion Woodman, 72: 167–188.

Kalsched, D. (2010) "Innocence, Benign or Malignant," in *Trust and Betrayal: Jungian Odyssey*, S. Wirth, I. Meier and J. Hill (eds.), New Orleans, LA: Spring Journal.

Kalsched, D. (2013) *Trauma and the Soul: A Psycho-Spiritual Approach to Human Development and its Interruption*, London: Routledge.

Kalsched, D. (2015) "Uncovering the Secrets of the Traumatised Psyche: The Life-Saving Inner Protector who is also a Persecutor," in *Understanding and Healing Emotional Trauma Conversations with Pioneering Clinicians and Researchers*, D. Sieff (ed.), London: Routledge, pp. 11–24.

Knox, J. (2003) *Archetypes, Attachment Analysis: Jungian Psychology and the Emergent Mind*, London: Routledge.

Knox, J. (2004) "Developmental Aspects of Analytical Psychology: New Perspectives from Cognitive Neuroscience and Attachment Theory," in *Analytical Psychology: Contemporary Perspectives in Jungian Analysis*, J. Cambray and L. Carter (eds.), Hove, UK: Brunner-Routledge, pp. 56–82.

Knox, J. (2011) *Self-Agency in Psychotherapy: Attachment, Autonomy and Intimacy*, London: W.W. Norton and Co.

Krieger, N. (2014) *Bridges to Consciousness: Complexes and Complexity*, London: Routledge.

Kugler, P. (2002) *The Alchemy of Discourse: Image, Sound and Psyche*. Einsiedeln, Switzerland: Daimon Verlag. This is a revised edition of the earlier, 1982 edition published by Associated University Presses, Inc.

Ladinsky, D. (2002) *Love Poems from God: Twelve Sacred Voices from the East and West*, New York: Penguin Compass.

Ladinsky, D. (2006) *I Heard God Laughing: Poems of Hope and Joy*, London: Penguin.

LeBaron M., MacLeod, C. and Floyer Acland, A., eds. (2013) *The Choreography of Resolution Conflict: Movement and Neuroscience*, Chicago, IL: American Bar Association Publishing.

Leri, D. (2014) "The Risk of Serious Inquiry – Part Three: Fechner Makes a Difference." SEMIOPHYSICS. Accessed 26 August 2018 at: http://semiophysics.com/SemioPhysics_Articles_risk_3.html.

Levine, P. (1997) *Waking the Tiger: Healing Trauma - The Innate Capacity to Transform Overwhelming Experiences*, Berkeley, CA: North Atlantic Books.

Levine, P. (2010) *In an Unspoken Voice: How the Body Releases Trauma and Restores Goodness*, Berkeley, CA: North Atlantic Books.

Levine, P. (2015) *Trauma and Memory: Brain and Body in a Search for the Living Past: A Practical Guide for Understanding and Living with Personal Trauma*, Berkeley, CA: North Atlantic Books.

Levinson-Castiel R., Merlob P., Linder N., Sirota L. and Klinger G. (2006), "Neonatal Abstinence Syndrome After In Utero Exposure to Selective Serotonin Reuptake Inhibitors in Term Infants," *Arch Pediatr Adolesc Med*, 160(2): 173–176. 10.1001/archpedi.160.2.173.

MacLean, P.D. (1990) *The Triune Brain in Evolution*, New York: Plenum Press.

Macnaughton, I., ed. (2004) *Body Breath and Consciousness: A Somatics Anthology*, Berkeley, CA: North Atlantic Books.

Macy, J. (2009) "The Greening of the Self," in *Ecotherapy: Healing with Nature in Mind*, L. Buzzell, and C. Chalquist (eds.), San Francisco, CA: Sierra Club Books, pp. 238–245.

Maguire, A. (2004) *Skin Disease: A Message from the Soul*, London: Free Association Books.

Main, M., and Soloman, J. (1990) "Procedures for Identifying Infants as Disorganized/ Disoriented During the Ainsworth Strange Situation," in M.T. Greenberg, D. Cicchetti and E.M. Cummings (eds.), *Attachment in the Preschool Years: Theory, Research, and Intervention*, Chicago, IL: Chicago University Press, pp. 95–124.

McDougall, J. (1989) *Theatres of the Body: A Psychoanalytic Approach to Psychosomatic Illness*. London: Free Association Books.

McFarlane, A.C., van der Kolk, B. and Weisaeth, L., eds. (1996) "Trauma and its Challenge to Society," in *Traumatic Stress: The Effects of Overwhelming Experience on Mind, Body, and Society*, New York, The Guilford Press, pp. 26–46.

McGilchrist, I. (2009) *The Master and his Emissary: The Divided Brain and the Making of the Western World*, New Haven and London: Yale University Press.

Merleau-Ponty, M. ([1945] 1962) *Phenomenology of Perception*, Paris: Gallimard; London: Routledge.

Miller, J.C. (2004) *The Transcendent Function. Jung's Model of Psychological Growth through Dialogue with the Unconscious*. New York: State University of New York Press.

Monte, C. (2015) *Corpus Anima: Reflections from the Unity of Body and Soul*, Ashville, NC: Chiron Publications.

Muller, R.T. (2014) "Fragmented Child: Disorganized Attachment and Dissociation." *Psychology Today*. 20 June 2014. Accessed 28 August 2018 at: https://www.psychologytoday. com/ca/blog/talking-about-trauma/201406/fragmented-child-disorganized-attachment-and-dissociation.

"Myelination," Your Dictionary. Accessed 26 August 2018 at: http://www.yourdictionary. com/myelination.

Neumann, E. (1973) *The Child: Structure and Dynamics of the Nascent Personality*, London and New York: Karnac.

Neumann, E. (1989) *Place of Creation*, Bollingen Series LX1 – 3, Princeton, NJ: Princeton University Press.

Ogden, P., Minton, K. and Pain, C. (2006) *Trauma and the Body: A Sensorimotor Approach to Psychotherapy*, London and New York: W.W. Norton & Co.

Oliver, M. (1992) *New and Selected Poems*, Boston, MA: Beacon Press.

Olsen, A. and McHose, C. (1999) *BodyStories: A Guide to Experiential Anatomy*, Barrytown, NY: Station Hill Press.

"Overview: Seasonal Affective Disorder (SAD)." NHS Choices. Accessed 28 August 2018 at: http://www.nhs.uk/conditions/seasonal-affective-disorder.

Pallaro, P., ed. (1999) *Authentic Movement: Essays by Mary Starks Whitehouse, Janet Adler and Joan Chodorow*. London and Philadelphia, PA: Jessica Kingsley Publishers.

Palmer, Linda. "Bonding Matters... The Chemistry of Attachment – Baby Reference." Baby Reference. September 10, 2016. Reprinted from the Attachment Parenting International News, 5(2), 2002. Accessed 26 August 2018 at: http://babyreference.com/ bonding-matters-the-chemistry-of-attachment/.

Payne, P., Levine, P.A., Crane-Godreau, M.A. (2015) "Somatic Experiencing: Using Interoception and Proprioception as Core Elements of Trauma Therapy," *Frontiers in Psychology*, 6: 1–18. DOI=10.3389/fpsyg.2015.00093. Accessed 30 August 2018 at: https://www.frontiersin.org/article/10.3389/fpsyg.2015.00093.

Pert, C. (1997) *Molecules of Emotion: The Science behind Mind-Body Medicine*, New York: Scribner.

Porges, S. "Dr. Stephen Porges: What Is the Polyvagal Theory". YouTube. Retrieved from: https://www.youtube.com/watch?v=ec3AUMDjtKQ. Last updated 23 April 2018.

Porges, S.W. (1997) "Emotion: An Evolutionary By-product of the Neural Regulation of the Autonomic Nervous System," *Annals of the New York Academy of Sciences*, 807: 62–77.

Porges, S.W. (2004) "Neuroception: A Subconscious System for Detecting Threats and Safety," *Zero to Three*, 24(5): 19–24. Accessed 27 August 2018 at: https://eric.ed.gov/?id=EJ938225.

Porges, S.W. (2009) "Reciprocol Influences Between Body and Brain in the Perception and Expression of Affect: A Polyvagal Perspective," in *The Healing Power of Emotion: Affective Neuroscience, Development and Clinical Practice*, D. Fosha, D. Siegel, and M. Soloman (eds.), London and New York: W.W. Norton & Co., pp. 27–54.

Porges, S.W. (2011a) "Somatic Perspectives" Series: Interview with Serge Prengel. USABP and EABP. Accessed 20 August 2018 at: www.SomaticPerspectives.com.

Porges, S.W. (2011b) *The Polyvagal Theory: Neurophysiological Foundations of Emotions, Attachments, Communications and Self-Regulation*, London and New York: W.W. Norton & Co.

Prengel, S. (2016) In conversation with Steven Hoskinson. Relational Implicit, https://relationalimplicit.com/somatic-perspectives/. Accessed 31 August 2018 at: https://relationalimplicit.com/zug/transcripts/Hoskinson-2016-05.pdf. Pp.1–10.

Prengel, S. (2014) In conversation with Raja Selvam. "Raja Selvam: Integral Somatic Psychotherapy". https://relationalimplicit.com/somatic-perspectives/. Accessed 31 August 2018 at: https://relationalimplicit.com/zug/transcripts/Selvam-2014-07.pdf. Pp.1–18.

Reeves, P. (2003) *Heart Sense: Unlocking your Highest Purpose and Deepest Desires*, Boston, MA: Conari Press.

Reeves, P. (2011) *Women's Intuition: Unlocking the Wisdom of the Body*, Boston, MA: Conari Press.

Reinau, M. (2016) *Love Matters for Psychic Transformation: A Study of Embodied Psychic Transformation in the Context of BodySoul Rhythms*, Wyoming, WY: Fisher King Press.

Rich, A. (1993) "Transcendental Etude," in *The Dream of a Common Language: Poems 1974–1977*, New York and London: W.W. Norton & Co.

Rilke, R.M. (2000) *Letters to a Young Poet*, trans. J. M. Burnham, Novato, CA: New World Library.

Ronnberg, A., Martin, K. and Archive for Research in Archetypal Symbolism (2010) *The Book of Symbols: Reflections on Archetypal Images*, Köln: Taschen.

Rossi, E.L., (1986) *The Psychobiology of Mind-Body Healing: New Concepts of Therapeutic Hypnosis*, New York: W.W. Norton & Co.

Russell, C. R. (2018) *The Feminine Path to Wholeness: Becoming a Conscious Queen*, CreateSpace Independent Publishing Platform.

Ryley, N. (1998) *The Forsaken Garden, Four Conversations on the Deep Meaning of Environmental Illness*, Wheaton, IL: Quest Books.

Sabini, M., ed. (2008) *The Earth has a Soul: C.G. Jung on Nature, Technology and Modern Life*, Berkeley, CA: North Atlantic Books.

Schiwy, M. (2018) *Gypsy Fugue: An Archetypal Memoir*, Halfmoon Bay, BC: Caitlin Press Inc.

Schore, A.N. (1994) *Affect Dysregulation and the Origin of the Self: The Neurobiology of Emotional Development*, Mahwah, NJ: Lawrence Erlbaum Associates.

Schore, A.N. (2001) "The Effects of Early Relational Trauma on Right Brain Development, Affect Regulation, and Infant Mental Health," *Infant Mental Health Journal*, 22(1–2): 201–269.

Schore, A.N. (2002) "Dysregulation of the Right Brain: A Fundamental Mechanism of Traumatic Attachment and the Psychopathogenesis of Postraumatic Stress Disorder," *Australian and New Zealand Journal of Psychiatry*, 36(1): 9–30.

Schore, A.N. (2003a) *Affect Regulation and the Repair of the Self*, London and New York: W.W. Norton & Co.

Schore, A.N. (2003b) *Affect Dysregulation and Disorders of the Self*, London and New York: W.W. Norton & Co.

Schore, A.N. (2009) "Right Brain Affect Regulation: An Essential Mechanism of Development, Trauma, Dissociation, and Psychotherapy," in *The Healing Power of Emotion: Affective Neuroscience, Development and Clinical Practice*, D. Fosha, D. Siegel and M. Soloman, (eds.), New York: W.W. Norton & Co., pp. 112–144.

Selye, H. ([1956] 1978) *The Stress of Life*, New York: The McGraw-Hill Companies, Inc.

Shewell, C. (2009) *Voice Work: Art and Science in Changing Voices*, Chichester, UK: Wiley-Blackwell.

Sieff, D. (2006) "Unlocking the Secrets of the Wounded Psyche," Jungian analyst Donald Kalsched is interviewed by Daniela Sieff, *Caduceus*, 69: 10–14 and 70: 16–20.

Sieff, D.F. (2008) "Unlocking the Secrets of the Wounded Psyche: Interview with Donald Kalsched," *Psychological Perspectives*, 51: 190–207.

Sieff, D.F. (2015) *Understanding and Healing Emotional Trauma: Conversations with Pioneering Clinicians and Researchers*, Hove, UK and New York: Routledge.

Siegel, D.J. (1999) *The Developing Mind*, New York: Guilford Press.

Siegel, D.J. (2010a) *The Mindful Therapist: A Clinician's Guide to Mindsight and Neural Integration*, New York: W.W. Norton & Co.

Siegel, D.J. (2010b) *Mindsight: Transform your Brain with the New Science of Kindness*, London: One World Publications.

Siegel D.J. (2012) *Pocket Guide to Interpersonal Neurobiology: An Integrative Handbook of the Mind*, New York: W.W Norton & Co.

Siegel, D.J. (2015) "Emotion as Integration": A Possible Answer to the Question, What is Emotion," in *The Healing Power of Emotion: Affective Neuroscience, Development and Clinical Practice*, D. Fosha, D.J. Siegel and M. Solomon (eds.), New York: W.W. Norton & Co., pp. 145–171.

Siegel, D.J. "Dr Daniel Siegel Presenting a Hand Model of the Brain". YouTube. Accessed 28 August 2018 at: https://www.youtube.com/watch?v=gm9CIJ74Oxw. Last updated 29 Feb. 2012.

Somatic Experience Trauma Institute (2007) *Somatic Experiencing Professional Training Course Manual*, Boulder, CO: Foundation for Human Enrichment (B1.27).

Steele, K. (2016) "Lean on Me—Dependency and Collaboration in the Psychotherapy of Relational Trauma," 33rd ISSTD Conference, San Francisco, CA, 31 March 2016.

Stein, M. (1998a) *Jung's Map of the Soul*, Chicago, IL: Open Court.

Stein, M. (1998b) *Transformation: Emergence of the Self*, Texas: A&M University Press.

Stern, D.N. (1985) *The Interpersonal World of the Infant: A View from Psychoanalysis and Developmental Psychology*, London: Karnac.

Stern, D.N. (2004) *The Present Moment in Psychotherapy and Everyday Life*, New York: W.W. Norton & Co.

Stern, D., Sander, L., Nahum, J.P., Harrison, A.M., Lyons-Ruth, K., Morgan, A.C., Bruschweiler-Stern, N. and Tronick, E.Z. (1998) "Non-Interpretive Mechanisms in Psychoanalytic Therapy: The 'Something More' than Interpretation," *International Journal of Psychoanalysis*, 79 (Pt 5): 903–921.

Stevens, A. ([1982] 2003) *Archetypes Revisited: An Updated Natural History of the Self*, Toronto: Inner City Books.

Stromstead, T. (2005) Interview with Marion Woodman, "Cellular Resonance and the Sacred Feminine: Marion Woodman's Story," *Spring, A Journal of Archetype and Culture*, Body and Soul: Honouring Marion Woodman, 72: 1–30.

Sunderland, M., (2007) *What Every Parent Needs to Know*, first published as *The Science of Parenting* (2006), London: Dorling Kindersley.

Tronick, E.Z. (2007) *The Neurobehavioural and Social–Emotional Development of Infants and Children*, New York: W.W. Norton.

van der Hart, O., Nijenhuis, E. and Steele, K. (2006) *The Haunted Self: Structural Dissociation and the Treatment of Chronic Traumatisation*, New York: W.W. Norton & Co.

van der Kolk, B. (2008) "The John Bowlby Memorial Lecture 2006. Developmental Trauma Disorder: A New, Relational Diagnosis for Children with Complex Histories," in *Trauma and Attachment*, S. Benamer and K. White (eds.), London: Routledge, 2008, pp. 45–60.

van der Kolk, B. (2014) *The Body Keeps the Score: Mind, Brain and Body in the Transformation of Trauma*, St Ives, UK: Penguin Random House.

van der Kolk, B., McFarlane, A. and Weisaeth, L., eds. (1996) *Traumatic Stress: The Effects of Overwhelming Experience on Mind, Body, and Society*, New York: Guilford Press.

van Loben Sels, R. (2003) *A Dream in the World: Poetics of Soul in Two Women, Modern and Medieval*, Hove, UK and New York: Brunner-Routledge.

Vanier, J. "Love and Belonging (50 Years at L'Arche with Jean Vanier)." Moses Znaimer and Richard Nielson (Producers). YouTube. Accessed 28 August 2018 at: www.youtube.com/watch?v=vDnfdHQu-rg. Last updated 4 Feb. 2015.

von Franz, M-L. (1988) *Psyche and Matter*, Boston, MA: Shambhala.

Von Franz, M-L. (1999) *The Cat: A Tale of Feminine Redemption*, Toronto: Inner City Books.

von Franz, M-L. (1980) *Alchemy: An Introduction to the Symbolism and the Psychology*, Toronto: Inner City Books.

Walcott, D. (2014) "Love after Love," in *The Poetry of Derek Walcott: 1948–1913*. Selected by Glyn Maxwell. New York: Farrar, Straus & Giroux; London: Faber & Faber.

West, M. (2011) *Understanding Dreams in Clinical Practice*, London: Karnac.

West, M. (2013) "Trauma and the Transference-Countertransference: Working with the Bad Object and the Wounded Self," *Journal of Analytical Psychology*, 58(1): 73–98.

West, M. (2016) *Into the Darkest Places: Early Relational Trauma and Borderline States of Mind*, London: Karnac.

Whitehouse, M. S. (1999) "C.G. Jung and Dance Therapy: Two Major Principles," in *Authentic Movement: Essays by Mary Starks Whitehouse, Janet Adler and Joan Chodorow*, Patrizia Pallaro (ed.), London and Philadelphia, PA: Jessica Kingsley Publishers, pp. 73–101.

Wilkinson, M. (2006) *Coming into Mind: The Mind-Brain Relationship: A Jungian Clinical Perspective*, London and New York: Routledge.

Wilkinson, M. (2010) *Changing Minds in Psychotherapy: Emotion, Attachment, Trauma and Neurobiology*, London and New York: W.W. Norton & Co.

Wilmer, H.A. (2013) *Practical Jung: Nuts and Bolts of Jungian Psychotherapy*, Wilmette, IL: Chiron Publications.

Winnicott D.W. ([1962] 1990) "Ego Integration in Child Development," in *The Maturational Process and the Facilitating Environment: Studies in the Theory of Emotional Development*, London: Karnac Books.

Winnicott, D.W. ([1971] 2005) *Playing and Reality*, London and New York: Routledge.

Wirtz, U. (2014) *Trauma and the Beyond, The Mystery of Transformation*, New Orleans, LA: Spring Journal.

Woodman, M. (1980) *The Owl was a Baker's Daughter: Obesity, Anorexia Nervosa and the Repressed Feminine*, Toronto: Inner City Books.

Woodman, M. (1982) *Addiction to Perfection: The Still Unravished Bride*, Toronto: Inner City Books.

Woodman, M. (1984) "Transference and Countertransference in Analysis with Eating Disorders," in *Transference and Countertransference*, N. Schwartz-Salant and M. Stein (eds.), Wilmette, IL: Chiron Clinical Series, pp.53–66.

Woodman, M. (1985) *The Pregnant Virgin: A Process of Psychological Transformation*, Toronto: Inner City Books.

Woodman, M. (1990) *The Ravaged Bridegroom: Masculinity in Women*, Toronto: Inner City Books.

Woodman, M. (1993) *Conscious Femininity: Interviews with Marion Woodman*, Toronto: Inner City Books.

Woodman, M. (1995) "An Interview with Marion Woodman," in *The Round Table Review*, 2(5).

Woodman, M. (2000) *Bone: Dying into Life*, New York: Viking Penguin Group.

Woodman, M. (2015) "Spiralling Through the Apocalypse: Facing the Death Mother to Claim our Lives," Interview with D.F. Sieff, *Understanding and Healing Emotional Trauma: Conversations with Pioneering Clinicians and Researchers*, Hove, UK: Routledge, pp. 64–87.

Woodman, M. and Dickson, E. (1996) *Dancing in the Flames: The Dark Goddess in the Transformation of Consciousness*, Dublin: Gill & MacMillan.

Yeoman, A. (1998) *Now or Neverland: Peter Pan and the Myth of Eternal Youth: A Psychological Perspective on a Cultural Icon*, Studies in Jungian Psychology, 82, Toronto: Inner City Books.

Zappacosta, J.D., ed. (2014) *Pearls: Defining Moments in Our Lives*, self published.

Index

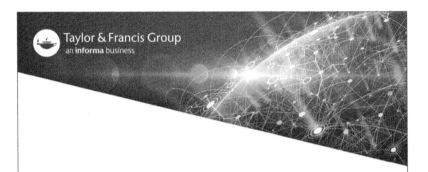

Made in the USA
Monee, IL
11 November 2021